The Experts Comment on
The Professional's Guide to Value Pricing

Ron Baker is arguably the profession's most original thinker. If you want to make money—and I mean significantly *more* money—from your practice, this book is a must-read. Ron understands this subject like the back of his hand and he's passionate about it. He could safely offer a hundred-fold money-back guarantee.

Chris Frederiksen, CPA
Frederiksen & Co.
Mill Valley, California, and Bristol, United Kingdom

I have long been frustrated to watch CPAs leave so much on the table because of their timidity about obtaining the full value of their services. This is particularly true for practitioners who have worked hard to increase the value of their services, but who have no idea how to increase their prices. Ron Baker's *Value Pricing* provides the long-needed guidance for matching price to value. I highly recommend this book to every CPA.

Jim Kurtz, CPA
California Society of Certified Public Accountants

Ron Baker is one of the master thinkers in the accounting profession. Few people have thought as long and hard about Total Quality Service and Value Pricing as he has. Every serious CPA who wants to add value and be compensated accordingly should own, read, and re-read this extraordinary book.

Troy Waugh, CPA, MBA
President, *Waugh & Co.*
Brentwood, Tennessee

Ron Baker is a true visionary for the CPA profession. He understands both the economic side and the human side of our business. He has taught me how to determine the services our clients most value. When true value has been provided, our clients have compensated us accordingly. This compensation has far surpassed any measurement of hourly rate or time involved. I encourage my fellow professionals to put Ron Baker's concepts into practice and discover for yourselves how richly your efforts will be rewarded.

Daryl B. Golemb, CPA
San Diego, California

I have been involved in moving the legal and CPA professions to alternative billing since 1981. I know the difficulties of changing a professional's paradigm from hourly billing to billing based on value added. This book provides excellent guidance and precedents for installing alternative billing. Professionals who use the help available in this book will be able to increase their own income while providing clients top quality service at lower costs—a win-win situation.

William Cobb, CPA
Consultant to the Legal and Accounting Professions

Ron Baker's book is a first in changing the accounting profession's compensation culture. Being paid for VALUE rather than by the HOUR is a radical concept that makes enormous sense. *Value Pricing* should be the operating bible not only for the CPA, but also for every professional service provider who charges money for time.

Len Pepe, CPA
BDO Seidman, LLP

Ron Baker is one of the few original thinkers in our profession. This book is a must-read for CPAs who are tired of being underpaid for what they do and are willing to change how they do business. His book is a guidepost for the ultimate success of the professional firm because it's customer focused—from service delivery and collection to service retention.

Allan S. Boress, CPA, CFE
Allan S. Boress and Associates

The Professional's Guide To

VALUE PRICING

JIM,

BEST WISHES,

To my father, Sam Baker,
who genetically encoded me to
challenge the conventional wisdom

ð. ð. ð.

I bargained with Life for a penny,
And Life would pay no more,
However I begged at evening
When I counted my scanty store.
For Life is a just employer,
He gives you what you ask,
But once you have set the wages,
Why, you must bear the task.
I worked for a menial's hire,
Only to learn, dismayed,
That any wage I had asked of Life,
Life would have willingly paid.

—Jessie B. Rittenhouse, "My Wage,"
The Door of Dreams (1918)

That is a good book which is opened with expectation,
and closed with profit.

—Amos Bronson Alcott
American teacher and philosopher, 1877

2000

The Professional's Guide To

VALUE PRICING

Ronald J. Baker

Harcourt
Professional Publishing

San Diego   New York   Chicago   London

The publisher has not sought nor obtained approval of this publication from any other organization, profit or nonprofit, and is solely responsible for its contents.

Portions of this work were published in a previous edition.

DILBERT cartoon, March 10, 1997, reprinted by permission of United Feature Syndicate, Inc.

Value Curve, from William C. Cobb, "The Value Curve and the Folly of the Billing-Rate Pricing," in *Beyond the Billable Hour: An Anthology of Alternative Billing Methods*, Richard C. Reed, ed., Chicago: American Bar Association, 1989, p. 18, reprinted by permission of the author and the American Bar Association.

Cover photo © 1998 PhotoDisc, Inc.

Printed in the United States of America

ISBN: 0-15-606993-8

99 00 01 02 EBA 5 4 3 2 1

CONTENTS

FOREWORD

Picture this scene.

I'm presenting a seminar in Australia. I'm talking about using Fixed Price Agreements as part of running a far better practice.

I mention Ron Baker's book (the one you're holding now). I describe it as "the best book that's been written on the accounting profession in the last 18 months."

One of the participants raises his hand and his voice. " I take serious issue with that comment," he says.

"Oh," I say, "and you've read the book?"

"Yes, and it's the best book that's *ever* been written on the profession."

My seminar participant is right. I cannot recall a book that gives so much—so much research, so much sound theory, and, at the same time, so much downright valuable, right-on-the-point, practical material—material you can use the moment you read about it. Yes, you're right, I like this book!

When I first spoke with Ron about the book, I asked him what his mission was in life. "To get rid of the Almighty hour," he said. He went on to talk about how the "professional" absolutely and categorically knows that billing based on time does not equate to value. In mathematical terms, we know that Time multiplied by Rate does not equal Value.

Yet we behave as if we did not understand that truth. We see the timesheet, we multiply the hours by the rate, and we know that the number we get does not value the job appropriately. So we add on some time units to "make up the value." As my partner Ric Payne observes, "We add a few units on for each walk past the photocopier." It's dishonest, isn't it? Yet it happens. Frequently.

Using the ideas in this book changes that for you.

Let me give you one more important perspective—that of the client.

At Results Accountants' Systems, we've been face-to-face with literally thousands of A-class clients of accounting firms. When you ask them about pricing they universally (and I do mean that literally) decry the Rate x Time method of pricing things. They hate it. In this book, Ron tells you about some major companies that won't have a bar of it either.

So when you move to the Value Pricing methodologies in this book, you're doing your clients a huge favor, too—you're responding to what they want.

I began by talking about a seminar. Just two weeks ago at a seminar in Detroit a man came up to me thinking (I don't know why) that I was Ron Baker. "Love your book," he said. And before I could explain who I was he said, "Just last week I used the book to move a $2,000 client to a $27,000 client. I could never have done it without using the ideas."

The real key to that is in the last three words—using the ideas. I urge you to do that. As great as Ron Baker has made this book, it needs *you* to implement the ideas. Follow the example of Accountants' Boot Camp firms around the world and take a tip from Nike—just do it. You'll never look back.

Paul Dunn
Founding Chairman—Results Accountants' Systems

NEW IN THIS EDITION

You will find new or expanded coverage on the following topics in the 2000 edition of *The Professional's Guide to Value Pricing*:

- Total Quality Service
  —The importance of customer service and loyalty
  —A discussion of why Total Quality Service is crucial to implementing Value Pricing

- The CPA as consultant

- Electronic commerce and pricing in a virtual world

- Financial services, commissions, and contingencies

- The CPA Vision Project

- Menu pricing, write-up work, and minimum and set-up pricing

- Advanced price theory

- Antitrust law and policy
  —Guidance on which businesses the laws apply to
  —How to advise customers on pricing decisions and strategies

PREFACE

*People of the same trade seldom meet together, even for merriments
and diversion, but the conversation ends in a conspiracy against
the public, or in some contrivance to raise prices.*

—Adam Smith, *The Wealth of Nations*

I have been conducting seminars around the United States on the shift from hourly billing to Value Pricing, and if an observer from outside the profession were to attend, Adam Smith's charge would certainly ring true. In a sense, this book is about how to raise your prices. But it is not a conspiracy against the public. In fact, the main message of this book is that the customer is the ultimate judge of the value that we, as professionals, provide. We should charge the customer only for the value received from our services. If we don't provide something of value to the customer, we have no business being in business.

This book has been a personal odyssey for me. In June 1989 I attended a three-and-one-half-day seminar titled "Increasing CPA Firm Profitability." In the tranquil setting of Lake Tahoe, Nevada, I learned three major lessons on how to increase my firm's profitability:

1. Raise my hourly billing rate by at least $10.
2. Grade my customers "A," "B," and "C," and fire all the "C's."
3. Offer my customers fixed fees on all services.

Inspired, I immediately shared all of these ideas, and more, with my new partner. We talked about becoming a "Winning Firm," the term the instructor used throughout the seminar, which meant, by today's standards, a world-class firm. The course provided me with the tools I needed to put some of these ideas into place immediately. In other words, it taught me *how* to do it.

What it didn't teach me is *why* I should do it. It was all case studies and examples, but had absolutely no theory. So when I returned to my firm I had a hammer—the tool I needed to implement some of these concepts— and I started hitting things. I raised my rates but didn't convince the customer that my value rose commensurate with that increase. I began grading my customers, and ridding my firm of the "C's," but it wasn't until I began researching the ideas behind Total Quality Service that I learned that *my customers weren't going to get better until I did.* Without the solid theoretical foundation of *why* I was doing these things, I failed miserably.

This is the single biggest weakness of most management ideas, CPE seminars, and business books: They're all practice with no theory. Pick up a business book today and one of the first things the author will say is how this book is not some "ivory tower" theory, but practical, real-world ideas that you can use Monday morning at the office.

All learning starts with theory. Therefore, the book you are about to read is more theoretical than you may be used to if you're an avid reader of business books or attend many practice management seminars. I make no apologies, for that is the best way to learn. I am skeptical of consultants and self-professed management "gurus" who have claimed to discover the next paradigm shift or even what the future will bring. While this book draws from many sources—some of them even the better known "gurus"—I have always tried to have the theory drive the ideas, and not the other way around. While I do claim that the hourly billing method will die out in the next decade or so, the observation is rooted in empirical evidence.

In their piercing book *The Witch Doctors: What Management Gurus Are Saying and Why It Matters*, John Micklethwait and Adrian Wooldridge, two staff editors for *The Economist*, level this charge against the immature discipline of management theory:

> Management theory, according to the case against it, has four defects: it is constitutionally incapable of self-criticism; its terminology usually confuses rather than educates; it rarely rises above basic common sense; and it is faddish and bedeviled by contradictions that would not be allowed in more rigorous disciplines. The implication of all four charges is that management gurus are con artists, the witch doctors of our age, playing on business people's anxieties in order to sell snake oil. The gurus, many of whom have sprung suspiciously from the "great university of life" rather than any orthodox academic discipline, exist largely because people let them get away with it. Modern management theory is no more reliable than tribal medicine. Witch doctors, after all, often got it right—by luck, by instinct, or by trial and error (Micklethwait and Wooldridge, 1996: 12).

I have tried to avoid these four defects, because I see them in almost every business book I have read that professes to offer you the surest way to stay ahead of the competition, or achieve superior financial results, or whatever the latest fad is.

My goal is not to have you think *like* me, but to have you think *with* me. I want you to be skeptical about the concepts in this book, to subject them to your own rigorous analysis and experience. Do not accept anything at face value. Be wary of anyone who considers himself an expert, for as Harry Truman said: "An expert is someone who doesn't want to learn anything new, because then he wouldn't be an expert."

Chapters 1 through 5 of the book cover a history of the accounting profession and move into why people buy what they buy, and how much they will pay. I have been working on this topic for nearly a decade, and I still consider myself a student of price theory. Price is an issue that all businesses grapple with every day, and it is one of the most complex components of marketing.

Price is a major marketing decision for any business. That is why it is one the four "P's" of marketing—Product, Place, Promotion, and Price. While professionals have become more sophisticated with respect to the other three "P's," Price has been largely ignored. As professionals and experts in law, auditing, taxes, and internal control systems, we know our Product like no one else. We have even become more sophisticated with respect to Promotion. While 20 years ago it was rare to find a professional firm that spent even 1 percent of its gross revenue on marketing and promotion, today it is not uncommon to find firms spending between 2 and 8 percent. Some firms even have their own in-house marketing consultants. This is a dramatic change from the attitude that "professionals don't advertise." We are doing better on Place too, by niching ourselves and specializing in various markets.

But we have ignored Price. Most of the literature within the legal and accouting professions—with the exception of the ABA books I have cited throughout—has little to say with respect to price, and unfortunately what is said is often wrong. Some literature treats billing as nothing more than an administrative task, with little discussion of how a pricing strategy communicates a marketing message. We have let Price be determined by the number of hours that we spend working on various projects.

Chapters 6 and 7 challenge the 40-year-old practice of hourly billing. If you apply the rigorous economic theory of price and value to this practice, you will understand the risk–reward trade-off you have made by using hourly billing: In exchange for a minimum floor, you have placed an artificial ceiling over your head.

Chapter 8 looks at price psychology and at why professionals suffer from write-downs.

In Chapters 9 through 13 you will find alternatives to the hourly billing method that are superior in obtaining the value for the services provided. Far too many professionals are so attached to the hourly rate that they end up working 16-hour days, charging for 8 hours, and getting paid for 4. There is a better way.

Chapter 14 reinforces the importance of customer service and loyalty. Chapter 15 is about making the transition from a compliance CPA to a consultant.

Chapter 16 discusses the morality of hourly billing vs. Value Pricing, along with some of the ethical quandaries that attorneys are struggling with as they shift away from hourly billing.

In Chapter 17 we will explore the critical link between a professional's level of self-esteem and the ability to Value Price.

Chapters 18 and 19 are for those who want to delve deeper into theory and law and cover anti-trust policy and price theory.

Chapter 20 concludes with some thoughts regarding the death of the Almighty Hour and whether or not Value Pricing is a fad that will disappear or a portentous "paradigm shift" that will permanently alter the way in which professionals price their services.

All business people live the ultimate contradiction: We spend our nights praying for the ability to charge monopoly prices, and we spend our days engaged in the very activity that drives those prices downward—that is, increasing the market supply of our services. We will examine why we price the way we do. For too long, our prices have been set by our competitors—those who gauge the value of what they do only by the time they spend.

The theories and concepts in this book are passed on to you in the hope that your transition from hourly billing to Value Pricing will be easier—and less prone to failure—than mine was. CPAs and attorneys add tremendous value to the lives of their customers, and an inordinate amount of empirical evidence backs this up. It is time we start to receive what our customers already believe we are worth.

Ronald J. Baker
Corte Madera, California

ABOUT THE AUTHOR

Ronald J. Baker started his accounting career in 1984 with KPMG Peat Marwick's Private Business Advisory Services in San Francisco. Today, in Corte Madera, California, he is a partner in Baker & Barnett, CPAs—the firm he co-founded in 1988. He is a Contributing Editor to *Partner-to-Partner Advisory*, published by Harcourt Professional Publishing. He travels across the United States as a frequent speaker at CPA events and conferences and as a consultant to CPA firms on implementing Total Quality Service and Value Pricing. He is an instructor with the California CPA Education Foundation and has authored four courses for them: *How to Build a Successful Practice with Total Quality Service*; *The Shift from Hourly Billing to Value Pricing*; *Value Pricing, Part II*; and *Alternatives to the Federal Income Tax*. He graduated in 1984 from San Francisco State University with a Bachelor of Science degree in accounting and a minor in economics. He is also a graduate of Disney University. Mr. Baker currently resides in Petaluma, California.

ACKNOWLEDGMENTS

No book is written in a vacuum. I have relied upon the wisdom and ideas of many seminal thinkers, and if I have been able to gain a better insight into pricing beyond some, it is because I have stood on the shoulders of these giants.

I had the great pleasure of meeting David Friedman in 1996 at a lecture he gave on his book *Hidden Order: The Economics of Everyday Life*. His ideas permeate this book and I thank him, again, for offering a vision of the world that is impossible to find anywhere else. He, like his mother and father (Rose and Milton Friedman), is truly thought-provoking.

I would also like to thank Allan Boress, Editor of *Partner-to-Partner Advisory* (published by Harcourt Professional Publishing), for giving me a forum to express my views on Total Quality Service and Value Pricing. Allan has had an enormous impact on my life, as an editor, colleague, author, instructor, and mentor. He took a chance on me, and I will never be able to repay him. I quote his thinking throughout this book, but his ideas have permeated me to the point that it's possible I have failed to give him credit for concepts that he has transmitted to me over the years; I hope he forgives me for the transgression.

Stella Ashen, also Contributing Editor of *Partner-to-Partner Advisory*, has always been supportive and encouraging with respect to my work and has put up with me missing every deadline.

Thank you to August J. Aquila, Editor of *Partner-to-Partner Advisory*, who has written his own pioneering book on this topic, *Breaking the Paradigm: New Approaches to Pricing Accounting Services*, published by the AICPA. I admire August greatly and believe his efforts at American Express will have a salutary effect on our profession.

Timothy J. Beauchemin, who passed away in February 1997, also contributed immensely to my thinking about our profession. Although I never had the good fortune to meet him, he was one of a few truly gifted consultants, able to focus on the right things, rather than just doing things right. Tim convinced me of the value of self-esteem, which became the genesis for Chapter 17, which may be the most important portion of the book.

Troy Waugh, another excellent consultant to CPAs, helped shape my thinking about the profession. He is keeping the spirit of Timothy Beauchemin alive by building on his seminal work.

I would like to thank Christian Frederiksen, who reviewed the book in manuscript form and offered many suggestions and improvements. While I am sure he will not agree with all of my opinions, I promise to think about the topics we disagree on in greater depth.

A very special debt of gratitude must go to George Gilder. I believe that he is truly the Adam Smith of the twentieth century. So much of his thinking and ideas have become part of my being that I am forever in his debt. I have just begun to catch up with his treatises, *Wealth and Poverty* and *Recapturing the Spirit of Enterprise*, two profound works written in the 1980s that permanently altered my vision of the way the world works. He, more than any other author, has clarified the role of profits in a free market economy and explained why they are moral.

Michael Novak, of the American Enterprise Institute, and Richard John Neuhaus, editor of *First Things: A Monthly Journal of Religion and Public Life*, introduced me to the encyclicals of the various popes, which aided me tremendously in formulating my views with respect to the morality of Value Pricing, as shared in Chapter 16. The idea of business as a moral calling—that is, serving others first before you receive anything in return—is finally gaining the attention it deserves from theologians, economists, politicians, and the general public, thanks in large measure to these two individuals.

My friend and customer, Mark Key, has allowed me to participate in his pricing decisions, and I have truly learned at the feet of a master. His intuitive grasp of the myriad of factors that go into setting a price continue to amaze me.

Thank you to all of my colleagues from seminars and with whom I have privately consulted, who have implemented these ideas and who have shared their triumphs—as well as their admonishments when they failed. They, too, have made me sharpen my thinking and have contributed substantially to my knowledge of price theory and how it works in the real world. There is no greater joy than to watch my "students" surpass their instructor.

I would also like to thank Daryl Golemb, Michael McCulloch, Mike Ringler, Arthur Jacob, and Shirley Nawkawatase, CPAs who constantly keep me engaged professionally and whose friendship I am grateful for.

Thank you to William Cobb for giving me permission to use his Value Curve, which is the best graphical depiction of the professions I have seen.

The accounting profession owes an enormous debt of gratitude to Paul Dunn, founder of Results Accountants' Systems, for his trailblazing work.

He has been an indefatigable supporter of this work, and I want to express my thanks to him for teaching the principles of Value Pricing in the United States, Australia, the United Kingdom, and Canada.

I am indebted to the California CPA Education Foundation's entire staff for taking a risk by letting me develop and teach my courses, which aided me in clarifying my thinking and the presentation of this material. I marvel at the efficiency of that group and would like to thank John Dunleavy, Fred Albe, Nicolette Martin, Kurtis Docken, Denise Strom, and Nancy Heubach for all of their support and encouragement.

My friend and partner of nearly ten years, Justin Barnett, successfully implemented many of these concepts, even though it took me a few years to convince him of their validity. Thanks, Justin, for holding down the fort and putting up with my schedule that takes me out of the office so much. I can't express it any better than Justice Cardozo, who once wrote, "There is no greater loyalty than a partner's to his fellow partner."

Thank you to Sidney Bernstein, Vice President and Publisher at Harcourt Professional Publishing, for taking the ultimate risk and publishing this work. While the substance of what we think is born in thought, it must live in ink. Sid has made my first foray into publishing a pleasure, not to mention relatively painless. Sharon Odegaard, Associate Editor at Harcourt, improved every single page of this book with skill and gentle professionalism. She is a pleasure to work with.

My brother, Ken Baker, put up with this material over many early morning lattes and late night dinners. His marketing insights helped me clarify my thinking and improved the application of these concepts to professional firms. One could not ask for a better coach.

My mother, Florence Baker, instilled in me the tenacity and perseverance to forge ahead in the face of the odds. Her mother, Angelina Zimmerman, provided me with a home to hibernate in while I put the finishing thoughts into this work.

I would not be where I am today without the inspiration of my father, Sam Baker. He has spent many hours with me recounting the days of the British invasion in the late 1960s and the impact it had on his chosen profession, barbering. His embrace of hairstyling, chemical services, retail, education, and the "unisex salon," long before they became commonplace in his profession, truly inspired me to push forward with this book. He accomplished back then what for me would be the equivalent of tripling my prices in a few years, while challenging the conventional wisdom of colleagues. His is a story I treasure, both for the lessons it teaches and the pride it gives me. Goethe wrote, "*Was du ererbt von deinen Vatern hast, erwich es, um es zu besitzen,*" which translated reads, "What you have inherited from your father, you must earn in order to possess." I hope I have earned his legacy.

ABOUT THE COMPUTER DISC

System Requirements

- IBM PC or compatible computer with CD-ROM drive
- WordPerfect® 6.0 for Windows™ or Microsoft Word® 6.0 for Windows™.
- 3 MB available on hard disk/drive

The CD-ROM provided with *The Professional's Guide to Value Pricing,* 2000 edition, contains word processing files of items in "Useful Checklists" as well as a sample Fixed Price Agreement and a sample Change Order.

The word processing forms are intended to be used in conjunction with your word processing software. The word processing forms have been formatted in Word 6.0 for Windows and WordPerfect 6.0 for Windows versions. If you do not own either of these programs, your word processing software may be able to convert the documents into a usable format. Check the user's manual that accompanies your word processing software for more information about the conversion of the documents.

Subject to the conditions in the license agreement and the limited warranty, which is displayed on screen when the disc is installed and is reproduced at the end of the book, you may duplicate the files on this disc, modify them as necessary, and create your own customized versions. Installing the disc contents and/or using the disc in any way indicates that you accept the terms of the license agreement.

If you experience any difficulties installing or using the files included on this disc and cannot resolve the problem using the information presented in this section, call our toll-free software support hotline at (888) 551-7127.

Installing the Templates

To install the files on the disc using Windows 95 or above, select the Control Panel from the Start menu. Then choose Add/Remove Programs and select Install. You will be asked a series of questions. Read each question carefully and answer as indicated. If you are using Windows 3.1, choose File, Run from the Windows Program Manager and type D:/ INSTALL in the command line or type D:/INSTALL at the DOS prompt.

First, the installation program will ask you to specify which drive you want to install to. You will then be instructed to specify the complete path where you would like the files installed. The installation program will suggest a directory for you, but you can name the directory anything you like. If the directory does not exist, the program will create it for you.

You can choose which word processing program to install (Word or WordPerfect). The program will automatically install the files in Word or WordPerfect subdirectories.

Opening the Files

Open your word processing program. If you are using Microsoft Word or WordPerfect 6.0, choose Open from the File menu. Select the subdirectory that contains the loaded files to list the names of the files. Highlight the name of the file you want to open and click OK or press ENTER. You can also open a document in Windows Explorer (in Windows 95 or above), or in Windows 3.1 from the File Manager, by highlighting the name of the file you want to use and double-clicking your left mouse button.

Refer to the Disc Contents section of the book to find the file name of the document you want to use. The Disc Contents are also available on your disc in a file called "CONTENTS." You can open this file and view it on your screen or print a hard copy to use for reference.

Word Processing Tips

Wherever possible, the text of the documents has been formatted as tables so that you can modify the text without altering the format of the documents. To maneuver within a table, press TAB to move to the next cell, and SHIFT + TAB to move backward one cell. If you want to move to a tab stop within a cell, press CTRL + TAB. For additional tips on working within tables, consult your word processor's manual. It might be helpful to turn on the invisible table lines in Microsoft Word while modifying the document by selecting Gridlines from the Table menu. In WordPerfect, select Reveal Codes from the View menu to reveal all formatting codes at the bottom of the screen; this will help you to determine the shape of the table.

Microsoft Word and WordPerfect are equipped with search capabilities to help you locate specific words or phrases within a document. The Find option listed under the Edit menu performs a search in both Microsoft Word and in WordPerfect 6.0.

Important: When you are finished using a file you will be asked to save it. If you have modified the file, you may want to save the modified file under a different name rather than the name of the original file. (Your word processing program will prompt you for a file name.) This will enable you to reuse the original file without your modifications. If you want to replace the original file with your modified file, save but do not change the name of the file.

Print Troubleshooting

If you are having difficulty printing your document, the following suggestions may correct the problem:

Microsoft Word

- Select Print from the Microsoft Word File menu. Then choose the Printer function.
- Ensure that the correct printer is selected.
- From this window, choose Options.
- In the media box, make sure that the paper size is correct and that the proper paper tray is selected.
- Check your network connections if applicable.
- If you still have trouble printing successfully, it may be because your printer does not recognize the font Times New Roman. At this point, you should change the font of the document to your default font by selecting the document (CTRL + A) and then choosing Font from the Format menu and highlighting the name of the font you normally use. Changing the font of the document may require additional adjustments to the document format, such as margins, tab stops, and table cell height and width. Select Page Layout from the View menu to view the appearance of the pages before you try to print again.

WordPerfect

- Select Print from the WordPerfect 6.0 File menu. Then choose Select.
- Make sure the correct printer is selected.

- From this menu, press Setup.
- Ensure the correct paper size and paper source are selected.
- You may be having difficulty because your printer does not recognize the selected font. You can correct this problem by changing the base font of the document to your default font. From the Edit menu choose Select All (or press CTRL+A). The entire text of the document should be highlighted. Then choose Font from the Layout menu and highlight the font you normally use. Changing the font of the document may require additional adjustments to the document format, such as margins, tab stops, and table cell height and width. Select Two Page from the View menu to view the appearance of the pages before you try to print again.

The Professional's Guide to Value Pricing

DISC CONTENTS

INTRODUCTION

Whoever desires constant success must
change his conduct with the times.

—Niccolo Machiavelli,
Florentine statesman and philosopher

My father is a barber. One night over dinner, he told me a fascinating story about his profession in the late 1960s. I repeat it here because what is happening today in the law and accounting professions is similar, and dramatic change usually takes us by surprise.

In the late 1960s, something was going on in this country that had a profound impact on barbers: The British Invasion. To this day, if you talk to old-time barbers, they still curse the Beatles. Men growing their hair long meant fewer trips to the local barber. The profession that had always done well, both in good economic times and bad, was taking it on the chin, and the barbers didn't know what to do about it.

In the fall of 1969, my father ran for president of the Santa Rosa, California, local barber union. At the election meeting my father and his opponent gave their "campaign" speeches. His opponent went first and ran on the following three platform items:

1. Haircut prices would be increased from $2.50 to at least $2.75, if not $3.00 (as the San Francisco barber union had just increased their prices to $3.00);

2. Hours of operation would be standardized for all members—9:00 a.m. to 6:00 p.m., Tuesday through Saturday; and

3. The local union would codify the above into a new union contract.

These three items were very serious to the barbers, and my father's opponent generated a lot of excitement by promising to work hard to achieve them.

Then it was my father's turn. He got to the platform and asked the assembled barbers what was happening to their incomes? They all grumbled, for incomes were dropping precipitously throughout the industry. Even during the Great Depression, barbers didn't experience the decline they were now suffering. My father began to exhort the crowd on what they had to do to meet the challenge that was being thrust upon them. And it had nothing to do with the three items that his opponent was clamoring for. He started talking to them about how barbers had to get into hairstyling, retail sales, chemical services, and even hiring cosmetologists and bringing them into the barber shop to form unisex salons. Understand that this was all very radical in those days—there was no such thing as a unisex salon, and the barbers protested against this change the loudest. Now my father is the first to admit that he was no sage; he didn't have a crystal ball that allowed him to peer further into the future than his colleagues. He gives the credit to his continual learning with Roffler and Redken Laboratories, two leaders in the industry that were helping the participants cope with the systemic changes taking place.

My father won the election, which teaches us that while people may not like change, they will elect leaders that they trust to lead them through it. A leader takes people where they would not go themselves. Under my dad's presidency, the barbers increased their prices to $2.75, they standardized the hours of operation, and they codified all of it in their new union contract. But my father was conducting a radical experiment in his shop. He partitioned off a chair in the back and started booking hairstyles in the evenings by appointment only, for $7.50. He knew that he could sell the men on this new style of haircut and teach them how to blow dry and care for it, because it would reduce the frequency with which they had to visit him (from every two to three weeks to every four to six), and as a result he could command more than two-and-a-half times the price of a clipper cut.

After a few months, my father was astonished to learn that approximately 80 percent of his revenue came from these new hairstyles, and that he was making more in four hours than his fellow barbers were making in eight. He decided he needed to pursue this full-time, so he closed up his traditional barbershop, moved across town, and opened the Hairistocrat. This was one of the first unisex salons in the area. My father started doing permanent waves and hair coloring and he became more actively involved with retail sales. In 1972, while most of the barbers in the union were still working at $3.00, my father had increased his haircut prices to $10.00, and by 1975 he was charging $15. It doesn't sound like momentous change now, but back then this was radical approach for a very staid profession. In fact, visit any town, and you will still find a few traditional barbershops—

the last few holdouts that resisted change and are still charging less than $10 for a haircut.

As I listened to my dad tell this story, I was astonished at how similar it was to the accounting profession. After all, I had been giving a *Total Quality Service* seminar for the California CPA Education Foundation and had encountered my share of CPAs who were resistant to change. A revolution is going on in the business world today, and it is one of customer service. If you look at the history of management movements, in the big picture, here are the stages of thought it has gone through:

1960s = Marketing

1970s = Manufacturing

1980s = Total Quality Management

1990s = Total Quality Service (Final Frontier)

In the 1960s, marketing was the model that businesses embraced. It was the Proctor & Gamble model: Manufacture a product and sell it to as many people as you can; capture market share through marketing. The 1960s was a seller's paradise, so this model worked well. In the 1970s, companies coming off of their successes in the 1960s became arrogant. They began to diversify and added manufacturing capacity, on the assumption they could sell everything they produced. This was the age of the big conglomerates. It did not matter what business you bought; business was business, so ITT could do communications *and* sell Wonder Bread.

This horizontal and vertical integration began to fall apart in the 1980s. Businesses discovered that it *did* matter what business you were in (core competencies, to use today's parlance), and with the adoption of the Total Quality Management movement, they began to divest themselves of divisions that they really did not know how to run effectively. Also, the Japanese, and other global competitors, had taken a large chunk of the automobile and electronics markets, and U.S. businesses finally heeded the message from management thinkers such as W. Edwards Demming and Joseph Juran and began to focus on quality.

Today, quality is not enough. It has become a table stake, the minimum you need to be in the game. For professionals, quality is no longer an effective competitive differentiation. In the eyes of the customer; our quality is all the same. Who would stay with an incompetent CPA? Thus, the only way we can differentiate ourselves in today's marketplace is through Total Quality Service, or what I call the Final Frontier. All CPAs have lost customers, even though they did outstanding technical work, because customers do not evaluate CPAs on the basis of technical work. They would not know a good audit or tax return from a bad one. But what they do know is how CPAs treat them—our bedside manner, so to speak.

Total Quality Service is not the topic of this book, but it is an essential prerequisite to Value Pricing. The only way to get full value for the services your firm offers is to provide your customers with Total Quality Service, and that means entering into monogamous partnerships with them. It means moving beyond *doing* business with them to *being in* business with them. This is a difficult concept for us as CPAs, because we are trained to be objective and independent and to look at our customers with a jaundiced eye. If all a CPA firm does is audits, this attitude may work, but not if you are interested in performing value-added services. The Roman statesman and philosopher Seneca once said: "The mind is slow in unlearning what it has been long in learning."

We have a lot of unlearning to do as a profession. We can no longer look back to the halcyon days of our predecessors and assume that what they did will work for us. Consider the predicament of Mikhail Gorbachev when he took over the Soviet Union. Here was a man whose entire world paradigm—communism—was swept onto the ash heap of history. He immediately blamed his predecessors for all his problems. In fact, the running joke in the Soviet Union at the time went something like this:

> A new manager of a collective farm finds two letters from his predecessor, with instructions to open the first when difficulties begin. When the farm fails to meet its quotas, the manager opens the first letter, which says, "Blame me." He does. It buys some time. But the farm fails again and he comes under fresh criticism, so he opens the second letter. It says: "Prepare two letters." (Will, 1992: 67)

It is time to stop emulating our predecessors blindly and instead to embrace the opportunities that the dramatic changes taking place in our profession present. Let us now turn to what some of those changes are.

The
Professional's
Guide To

VALUE
PRICING

1 A BRIEF HISTORY OF THE ACCOUNTING PROFESSION

Nothing stops an organization faster than people who believe that the way they worked yesterday is the best way to work tomorrow. To succeed, not only do your people have to change the way they act, they've got to change the way they think about the past.

—John Madonna, Chairman, KPMG International

Italian Fra Luca Pacioli published his *Summa de Arithmetica Geometria, Proportioni et Proportionalita* in 1494, representing the collected knowledge of mathematics at that time. In the portion of the work titled *Particularis de Computis et Scripturis*, he introduced double-entry bookkeeping, a creation for future accountants that was as big as the Arabs' invention of zero for mathematicians. Unfortunately, one could also make the argument that it was significant for being the last revolutionary idea to come from the accounting profession. In *Intellectual Capital*, David Wilson, CPA and partner at Ernst & Young, wrote: "It has been 500 years since Pacioli published his seminal work on accounting and we have seen virtually no innovation in the practice of accounting—just more rules—none of which has changed the framework of measurement" (Stewart, 1997: 58).

The balance sheet dates from 1868, the income statement from before World War II. Generally Accepted Accounting Principles (GAAP) fit an *industrial* enterprise, not an *intellectual* one. Currently, GAAP measure the cost of everything, and know the value of nothing. As Robert K. Elliott pointed out in an essay titled "The Third Wave Breaks on the Shores of Accounting":

> [GAAP] focuses on tangible assets, that is, the assets of the industrial revolution. These include inventory and fixed assets: for example, coal, iron, and steam engines. And these assets are stated at cost. Accordingly, we focus on *costs*, which is the *production* side, rather than the *value created*, which is the *customer* side (Stewart, 1997: 58).

Accounting Today

The profession of public accounting as it is known today came into existence in Great Britain in the 1850s with the introduction of the Companies Acts and the Bankruptcy Acts, legislation designed to protect shareholders and promote capital accumulation during the early stages of the Industrial Revolution. In the decades following the American Civil War, British chartered accountants came to the United States to monitor the capital investments of the Old World in the New World.

The city directories of New York, Chicago, and Philadelphia showed an increase in the number of public accountants, from 81 in 1884 to 322 in 1889. During the 1890s, the predecessors of at least three of the Big Eight were established, and on April 17, 1896, New York became the first state to pass legislation establishing the title of certified public accountant. By 1899, the New York Exchange had initiated steps to require financial statement reports on a regular basis from listed companies.

After the turn of the century, the Progressive Era ushered in another wave of growth for the public accounting profession. This was a natural fit for the public accountant, as the profession gained considerable visibility and recognition through its work in the governmental sector. As the "disinterested expert," the public accountant would command a central role for many of the Progressive reformer's policies: Increased efficiency in government and business, regulation of large businesses and trusts, and the passage of the income tax in order to redistribute and equalize wealth.

The United States' adoption of the income tax, along with the announcement of official accounting standards and guidelines by the Federal Trade Commission and the Federal Reserve Bank, led to an increased demand for accounting services. In the aftermath of the stock market crash of 1929, the most significant legislation was the Securities Act of 1933 and the Securities Exchange Act of 1934, which produced the largest growth in demand for public accounting. Subsequently, the rules promulgated by the American Institute for CPAs were known as ARBs (Accounting Research Bulletins).

During the 1930s and 1940s, CPAs experienced high growth and high incomes. In 1945, Milton Friedman and Simon Kuznets published a fascinating study of five different professions, titled *Income from Independent Professional Practice*. This study, which was the basis of Friedman's Ph.D. dissertation at Columbia University in 1946, was actually completed in 1941, but its publication was delayed because of the controversy it created. Friedman concluded in this study that the medical profession had monopolistic powers that enabled it to raise physicians' incomes above a competitive level. Since then, Friedman has been one of the most articulate spokesmen against all forms of occupational licensure, a position he has expanded upon in his later works, especially *Capitalism and Freedom* and *Free to Choose*. A majority of economists who have studied the topic find Friedman's position compelling.

The astonishing results of the study are as follows:

Arithmetic mean annual income (dollars)	Average 1929–34
CPAs	$5,311
Physicians	$4,081
Dentists	$3,081

(Friedman and Kuznets, 1945: 104)

How could this be? How did CPAs make more money than doctors and dentists? It's an interesting question, and while there may have been some supply-side effects, due to the licensure requirements for CPAs, the answer is found on the demand side. Between 1929 and 1934, the United States was in the throes of the Great Depression, so doctors and dentists were probably among the last to be paid (and were most likely receiving a lot of barter payments as well). This was before the introduction of employer-paid health insurance.

During World War II, businesses wanted to attract talented employees. The government had frozen wages and prices, while at the same time, the labor pool was limited, as most men were off fighting the war. Businesses came up with the idea of offering tax-free health insurance. The IRS ruled that this was, indeed, a tax-free benefit, and ever since, companies have provided health insurance for their employees. After health insurance was introduced, the economics of healthcare spending changed dramatically. Prior to health insurance, individuals paid their own healthcare expenses, and thus doctors and dentists had to satisfy one customer at a time. Now individuals were spending someone else's money—namely, that of the insurance companies—on themselves, which is not a motivation to be economical. One of the main reasons healthcare costs have been increasing faster than the rate of inflation in this country is that third-party payments account for some 76 percent of all healthcare spending. Almost half of that is from the government and the remaining portion is from insurance companies. Economists are fond of pointing out that if consumers spent only 25 cents on the dollar (of their own money) for food, clothing, and housing, costs would skyrocket in each of those markets. This is the economic rationale for the Medical Savings Accounts: have people spend their own money on themselves and competition will drive down prices. Chapter 4 will look more closely at the different ways that one can spend money.

Meanwhile, CPAs were mainly performing attest services during this period and were benefiting from the effects of the new SEC regulations. They weren't doing tax returns at this point, because only about 10 percent of the population filed returns during this time. The country didn't pull most citizens into tax return filing until the Current Tax Payment Act, which was signed into law by President Roosevelt in June 1943.

One more point on CPAs' income being higher than that of doctors and dentists: This was *before* the profession engaged in hourly billing. During this time, CPAs charged fixed fees for their services. They sometimes charged by the day. An article in Fortune magazine in 1932 states that the rate for Juniors was $20 a day; Semi-seniors earned "15 to $30 a day; Seniors earned $35 a day; Supervisors brought in $50 to $75 a day, and Partners earned $100 to $1,000 a day.

This is not to say that they made more because they did not use hourly billing, but only that not using hourly billing did not prevent them from being more profitable. The reasons outlined above are closer to the real explanation.

In 1954, all of the existing tax laws were codified into the Internal Revenue Code of 1954. Most Americans had been drawn inside the tax system through the Withholding Act of 1943. Since CPAs were well-versed in tax law, they naturally and enthusiastically entered the tax preparation market, much to the chagrin of the attorneys. Almost immediately, attorneys brought lawsuits against the CPAs for practicing law—meaning tax law—without a license. They lost in courts around the country that basically said they should have sued the CPAs back in 1913, with the passage of the 16th Amendment. It is an interesting analogy to the lawsuits involving American Express Tax and Business Services (AmEx), which the Florida and Texas State Boards of Accountancy have charged with violating professional standards by holding themselves out as CPAs. Because the free market will ultimately prevail against government regulation, AmEx will prevail in these suits.

In 1955, Henry Block borrowed $5,000 from his aunt and launched a one-man bookkeeping company for small businesses. He later took his brother, Richard, into the business at his mother's insistence. By 1995, H&R Block was preparing and filing more than 13 million tax returns, 12 percent of all individual tax returns filed that year. It has 9,000 offices worldwide, employs 90,000 people during tax season, and earns approximately 200 million dollars on nearly 2 billion dollars gross revenue, half of which is derived from tax preparation. CPAs scoffed at H&R Block when it entered the market, charging it with being incompetent and unprofessional. The marketplace prevailed, and most economists would argue that the biggest beneficiaries were the 13 million consumers who received economical tax services.

In 1960, the computer made its debut. This allowed CPAs to perform write-up work more efficiently and to begin consulting on computer hardware and software. The computer also allowed hourly billing to take hold in the profession. With the computer, billing became nothing more than a clerical task—input the hours spent, the computer grinds hours times the rates, and a bill is sent to the customer—all done with low-cost administrative staff and very little partner or manager time. It took all the *art* out of pricing and turned it into an *administrative task*.

Then the Tax Reform Act of 1969 (Pub.L. 91–172) was passed, allowing companies to claim Investment Tax Credits and, more important from the CPA's point of view, instituting one of the most complex provisions of the tax code that exists to this day: the Alternative Minimum Tax. This section was placed in the Code largely due to Joseph Barr, Secretary of the Treasury during the Johnson administration, who testified before Congress in January 1969 that 155 taxpayers with adjusted gross incomes over $200,000 paid zero tax in 1966. Congress heard the outrage from the citizenry and placed what many called at the time "the Accountant's and Lawyer's Retirement Act" into the Code. The tax laws became so complex that even small business owners needed a CPA.

Seven years later, Congress passed the Tax Reform Act of 1976 (Pub.L. 94–455), which created what soon replaced baseball as America's favorite pastime: tax shelters. Americans from across the political spectrum rushed to reduce their ever-increasing tax bills. These included Barry Goldwater, George McGovern, Norman Lear, Barbara Streisand, Lorne Greene, Eddie Murphy, Sydney Poitier, and many well-known athletes.

It was also during the 1970s that a large number of baby boomers entered the CPA profession. It was easier to enter than other professions, such as medical or legal, and it offered high status and a good living. In 1977 the Supreme Court ruled, in *Bates & O'Steen v State Board of Arizona*, 433 US 350 (1977), that attorneys could market their legal services. This had a profound effect on both the legal and accounting professions.

Prior to this landmark Supreme Court decision, the AICPA Code of Professional Conduct for CPAs explicitly proscribed advertising, stating:

> Solicitation to obtain clients is prohibited under the Rules of Conduct because it tends to lessen the professional indepen- dence towards clients which is essential to the best interests of the public. . . Advertising, which is a form of solicitation is prohibited. . . Promotional practices such as solicitation and advertising, tend to indicate a dominant interest in profit.

In 1978, the profession responded to the Bates decision by amending this rule to read:

> A member shall not seek to obtain clients by advertising or other forms of solicitation in a manner that is false, mislead- ing, or deceptive.

Despite the accounting profession's reluctance to advertise, due to the traditional belief that advertising accounting services was unprofessional, the consumer welcomed the change as both appropriate and helpful in disseminating information about the capabilities of the profession. In today's highly competitive environment, the idea that CPAs should not advertise seems preposterous, indicating the pace of change with which the profession has had to deal.

In the 1980s, the single biggest revolution since double-entry bookkeep- ing, the introduction of the personal computer, took place in the accounting profession. This machine changed the profession like nothing else up to this point. The PC liberated ordinary workers and businesses, putting more computing power in their hands, which lessened the leverage of the "ex- perts." Now many tasks that were once the private domain of professionals were taken over by the customer or were outsourced to others vying for a piece of the market once taken for granted by CPAs.

The Tax Reform act of 1986 (Pub.L. 99–514) simplified the Code for many taxpayers and eliminated the tax shelter industry, but it also added the passive loss provisions, which complicated the preparation of returns even beyond the capabilities of CPAs. Enter low-cost tax preparation software and accounting systems such as Quicken and Quickbooks, and a myriad of consultants and Certified Financial Planners, and CPAs discovered that work they used to get automatically was now being lost to this increasingly competitive field of players.

Summary and Conclusions

This brings us to today. How will the actions taken today by the profession affect the future? This chapter looked at where CPAs have been; the next chapter will look at where the profession is headed.

2 THE ACCOUNTING PROFESSION IN THE NEW MILLENNIUM

Whom the gods would destroy,
they first grant forty years of business success.

—Peter F. Drucker

Life is a series of collisions with the future.

—Jose Ortega y Gasset

An astute observer of the retail industry would be the first to notice that within the last decade or so, *inventory* has been replaced by *information*. When you study the success of Wal-Mart, you realize that this was the exact formula by which Sam Walton dealt a knockout blow to Sears, once America's preeminent retailer. Sears didn't even see it coming; it wasn't until the late 1980s that Sears' internal position papers even mentioned Wal-Mart as a competitor. The store that once sold the equivalent of one percent of America's Gross National Product and held a 50 percent market share of the household credit card market was suddenly brought to its knees by a man from Arkansas with a better idea. Some believe that Wal-Mart eliminated the Mom and Pop stores. Nonsense. Wal-Mart did not eliminate these stores; the American consumer did. Today, more than 40 million Americans shop at Wal-Mart stores throughout the country every week. And why shouldn't they, if that is where they receive the most value for their dollar?

The same trend is found in bookstores. Visit a Borders or a Barnes & Noble and you'll see over 100,000 titles. Log on to amazon.com and you can browse (by author, topic, keyword) through 2,500,000 titles. Amazon doesn't have expensive brick and mortar buildings, a big distribution system to warehouse and store inventory, or the ever-increasing costs of employees and employee benefits. It relies on databases and the Internet, whose costs are continuing to fall, and thus Amazon poses the biggest threat to the traditional bookstore. It has changed the playing field on selling books, and if the megastores do not start offering similar conveniences to their customers, they, like Sears, will watch their market shares continue to erode.

Because of the plummeting cost of information storage and retrieval, the artificial boundaries between professions will dissolve. In the past, professions held all of the trade secrets and specialized information, and the consumer was forced to seek out these experts and pay relatively high prices for their wisdom. Today this is no longer the case. Information that was once available only to lawyers, doctors, and accountants is now available to anyone with a computer and a modem. A patient suffering from a specific medical affliction can download from various medical databases the most recent studies and latest treatment regimes, and chances are the patient will know more about the condition than the doctor knows. The economic value of memorization as a skill is falling, and the importance of locating the right information is increasing. To be a professional, which means to "profess" something, was always considered to be several notches above a businessman. This thinking is obsolete. Now that information is available to anyone, what is professed is not as important as how information is synthesized and used in its most creative applications to add value to customers.

What is happening in the accounting industry is similar to the stage in which the retail industry currently finds itself—that is, a mature industry. This is a stage in the Product Life Cycle, which all products and services eventually pass through. The four stages of the Product Life Cycle are as follows:

1. Introduction
2. Growth
3. Maturity
4. Decline

The accounting profession has entered stage 3, and some would even argue that certain services in accounting, such as audits, are in stage 4. During the period between 1989 and 1995, Gross Domestic Product grew 28 percent, yet audit revenue has been flat since 1989 and has declined as a portion of GDP. This trend will continue. Consulting work will continue to increase as a percentage of firm revenues, as it is in the Introduction and Growth stages of the Product Life Cycle. As August J. Aquila, Ph.D., points out in his book *Breaking the Paradigm: New Approaches to Pricing*

Accounting Services, the signs that the accounting profession is in the Maturity stage are many:

- Consolidation
- Brand-Name Recognition
- Price Competition
- Increased Involvement in Marketing
- Competition From Outside the Profession
- Sophisticated Buyers

(Aquila, 1995: 33–34)

A more detailed look at each of these trends will show they are permanently changing the market conditions in the accounting profession.

Consolidation

Since 1987, the Big Eight has gone to the Big Five. Many CPAs say this has occurred because the big players want to reduce the level of competition among themselves. But every business wants to reduce competition. This is confusing cause and effect. Consolidation takes place in a mature industry in order to eliminate redundancies in overhead, and this very rarely happens in the Introduction or Growth stages of the Product Life Cycle. What is happening can be referred to as *dinosaurs mating*. As Tom Peters once humorously pointed out with respect to a particular bank merger: "Why anybody thinks that they will produce a gazelle by mating two dinosaurs is beyond me." This trend will continue not just with the big firms, but with regional and local firms as well. Someday the business world may be referring to the Big One.

In addition to the consolidation taking place in the profession, CPAs also seem destined to replace insurance agents and brokers as their customer's primary financial advisor. Further, a majority of states now allow commissions and contingency pricing as well as non-CPA ownership. These ideas were anathema a decade ago, but now even the AICPA has accepted the realities of the marketplace exerting its sovereignty, and it has become an agent for change, rather than defending the status quo.

Brand-Name Recognition

Obviously, the Big Five already possess brand-name recognition, and many other firms are forming alliances throughout the United States and the rest of the world to achieve the same recognition. Before the Coopers Price merger, H&R Block ranked Number 7 among the top 100 accounting firms. This is the firm that many CPAs said would not last and was unprofessional, reflecting a repeat of Sears' attitude with respect to Wal-Mart. More recently, AmEx has caused a major controversy in the accounting world by buying up practices throughout the country. Because competition is the lifeblood of the free enterprise system, this is a good thing. No industry should be allowed to control who enters. Although various state societies try to erect barriers against AmEx in the name of "protecting the consumer," economic evidence shows that occupational licensure does not protect the consumer but rather protects the profession from the consumer. AmEx is here to stay, as long as it adds value to the customer. Customers will be won by the firm that offers more value than the competition. CPAs who fail at this deserve to fail at business as well.

Price Competition

At the inception of accounting firms and for many years thereafter, the way to make money was to leverage *people*. This is no longer true. Today, accounting firms leverage *technology*. This has caused a flattening of the traditional pyramid structure, and the folks getting squeezed out tend to start their own firms, with low overhead, intensifying price competition. According to the AICPA membership database, in 1998, "of the 47,751 public practice units, 41,252, or 86%, have 10 or fewer professionals and thus are considered to be small firms. Just over 21,166, or about 44%, are sole practitioners."

For the past several years, the "virtual office" has provided an excellent advantage, since business opportunities exist in the customer's offices, not the CPA's. Here's a story about a CPA who wants to start a virtual office but doesn't know how to go about it, so he sets off to get advice at the feet of the Master.

> The [CPA] slowly climbed toward the summit of the mountain, hand over hand, pulling upwards toward the guru's cave. The [CPA] reached the top, fingers raw and clothing tattered. He beheld the master: long white hair, wearing a flowing robe, indeterminate age. The master sat in the lotus position and seemed completely detached from worldly concerns.

The pilgrim knew he could ask only one question. A question for which there were no answers in the books, the journals, or the consultancies. He approached the master and asked: "Master, what is the secret of virtual operations?"

The Master was still for a long time, considering this question. At last he spoke: "You could have sent e-mail." (Grenier and Metes, 1995: 99)

More and more CPAs are taking advantage of the "virtual office," something easy to achieve given a laptop computer, modem, Internet and e-mail access, cellular phone, pager, and FedEx. This doesn't involve much overhead, and CPAs who work in this manner tend to have very low "hourly rates," which is baffling since their low overhead does not translate into low value to the customer. As a result of start-ups and small firms, price competition is enormous and will continue to increase for all services, not just the so-called "commodities" (audits, reviews, compilations, and tax returns).

Increased Involvement in Marketing

CPAs have been forced into this arena, kicking and screaming all the way. In the past, especially after watching the experience of the attorneys, CPAs had the attitude that marketing and advertising were unprofessional. Good firms did not need to stoop that low; it was unbecoming of a true professional. This attitude today will bring nothing but early, involuntary retirement. Marketing is an essential ingredient, perhaps the most essential, to running a successful firm. According to Aquila, "Whereas ten years ago accounting firms spent very little on marketing, today it is not unusual for them to spend from 2 percent to 8 percent of their net fees on marketing" (Aquila, 1995: 34). It is not uncommon for a firm today to have in-house a non-CPA marketing professional, either full- or part-time. All professions have had to become more sophisticated in this area, as it's no longer a seller's market, but a buyer's market.

Competition from Outside the Profession

Some work that once automatically went to the professional firm can now be done by a myriad of outside consultants—financial planners, employee benefit consultants, paralegals, and computer specialists—not to mention inexpensive software products that can produce tax returns, wills and trusts, and legal contracts. It is no longer possible to make money selling paper. More and more the choice for the customer is not just which of various professional firms to employ. Instead, the choice is whether to hire a professional firm, hire a consulting firm, do it themselves, or not do it at all. Firms have seen their "share of customer" decrease. Because of outsourcing and increased competition, the typical firm's share of the entire accounting, tax, and consulting dollar of the average customer has declined. Part of this is due to CPAs having the wrong focus. Many pursue market share, which is selling one service to as many customers as possible, rather than pursuing share of customer, which is selling as many services as possible to one customer from cradle to grave. Since the only real monopoly CPAs have is in the attest service, and this market is in its mature phase (if not decline), it behooves the CPA to focus on each customer's need for value-added consulting services and not take for granted that work will be rewarded by virtue of being a company's auditors. The CPA must earn a customer's business, proving to be better than the alternatives. Competition is not going away; in fact, it will increase dramatically as AmEx, H&R Business Services, Century Business Services, and others enter the market, and competition will come from out-of-state and around the world, due to the Internet, which is rapidly shrinking geographical boundaries.

Sophisticated Buyers

Today's customer is more *value*-conscious (though not necessarily *price*-conscious) than ever before. It is not unusual for a customer to come into a firm knowing exactly what he wants with a good idea of the value of the service desired. Over time, customers become more sophisticated, especially when they have instant access to information that in the past would have taken a prodigious amount of time to gather and assimilate.

According to Kevin Davis, in his book *Getting into Your Customer's Head*, today's buyers are:

- More demanding
- More value-conscious
- More knowledgeable about buying

- Less loyal
- Deluged by choices
- More uncertain about the future
- More at risk if a mistake is made
- Much more cautious
  (Davis, 1996: 3)

Customers are becoming less tolerant of poor service. Many organizations provide outstanding service, from FedEx and Marriott to Disney and Lexus, and once customers experience this level of service, they want more, and they become less tolerant of bad service from their local restaurant, dry cleaner, or hairstylist. Their expectations are being raised constantly. The final frontier of business—Total Quality Service—will be explored in Chapter 14.

All of the aforementioned signs of a mature industry force firms to seek out services that are in the growth stage or to design innovative new services to launch into the introduction stage of the Product Life Cycle. The profession has moved away from merely manipulating financial information and attesting to it and has taken on a full-service financial advisory role, as customers gravitate to CPAs as the most trusted and respected of all business advisors. See Chapter 15 for more discussion of CPAs as consultants.)

The Value Curve

The Value Curve is a model for analyzing which services add relatively high value and thus command higher prices in the marketplace, compared with other services that add relatively little value and thus are more price-sensitive. This curve, which to the trained eye is really an indifference curve, was developed by William C. Cobb, CPA, who approaches pricing in the classical economics tradition. This curve was published in the seminal work by the American Bar Association Section of Economics of Law Practice, *Beyond the Billable Hour*, edited by Richard C. Reed. This is what Cobb had to say about value, as perceived by the customer:

> Sophisticated clients do not tie benefits to hours; they tie benefits to the impact on their business. Some services are

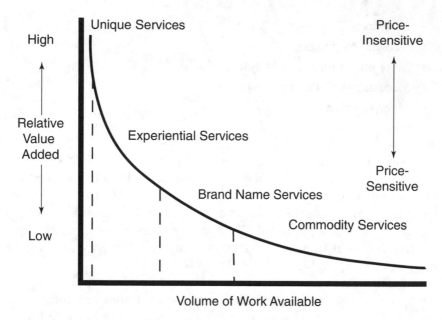

© William C. Cobb
SOURCE: Adapted from William C. Cobb, "The Value Curve and the Folly of the Billing-Rate Pricing," in *Beyond the Billable Hour: An Anthology of Alternative Billing Methods*. Richard C. Reed, ed. Chicago: American Bar Association, 1989, p. 18.

lifesaving. Other services are mundane, commodity services that must be performed in the course of getting the client's product produced and sold. In such situations, value has no real relationship to the hours involved. . . . Legal services do not escape the laws of economics (Reed, 1989: 17).

Let's examine each one of the categories on the graph.

1. **Unique Services**   These services are typically distinctive to a particular customer and add high value because either they avert a major catastrophe or they have a significant impact upon the customer's future. Examples would include succession planning, major tax litigation, a merger or acquisition, and bankruptcy. It is estimated that less than 4 percent of work in any given market is unique.

2. **Experiential Services**   This is work of high-risk or high-impact nature, and the customer will typically select the professional perceived as best able to handle the matter effectively. Such services

might include real estate services, litigation support, and divorce planning (as one CPA humorously advertises). Approximately 16 percent of work in any given market fits this category.

3. **Brand-Name Services** This work, while perhaps routine, is important to the customer and tends to go to firms that have well established reputations in a particular area. The Big Five, for example, get a share of their work simply based upon their reputation in the marketplace, and they are the major players in SEC and Initial Public Offering work. National, regional, and local firms who may have a reputation for a particular niche, such as healthcare, construction, or automobile dealerships, tend to earn brand-name recognition over time. About 20 percent of work is of this nature.

4. **Commodity Services** This includes write-up, tax return compliance (income, payroll, sales, etc.), compilations, and basically any other work that customers expect their CPA to be able to provide. This is the largest slice of work in any market, approximately 60 percent.

Implications of the Curve

Ample opportunities exist to engage in Value Pricing no matter where a firm is on the curve. A firm that does nothing other than provide "commodity" services is still able to engage in the Value Pricing techniques discussed in this book. Any firm that has a downward sloping demand curve—what economists call market power—can be, to some extent, a price *maker* and not merely a price *taker*. Engaging in Value Pricing is not predicated on where a firm is on this curve, so if a firm profile fits the low end, this is no cause for despair.

A firm's position on the Value Curve can change. Many professionals, when they examine the curve for the first time, tend to sell themselves short, seeing the majority of what they do as "commodity" or low-end types of service. The empirical evidence does not support these self-assessments. Practically all but the most low-end compliance-driven firms will perform some experiential services, such as IRS audits or divorce work, and at one time or another, some customers will demand a unique service, tailored to their particular situation. The secret to Value Pricing is recognizing these opportunities, at the margin, and pricing accordingly.

Despite the conventional wisdom, audits are not "commodities," though practically every CPA firm will say that audits are just a commodity at some time when discussing the curve. The customer/CPA relationship is a personal one, commanding an immense amount of trust and respect. In fact, CPAs are the number one trusted business advisor, as ranked by occupational standing polls on public respect. Only members of the clergy and doctors are ranked higher.

There is no such thing as a commodity in today's marketplace, only commodity thinking. Anything from a chocolate bar to a haircut to a taxi cab ride can be differentiated, as the following story from *The Tom Peters Seminar* illustrates:

> Transformation. Breaking the mold. Anything—ANY-THING—can be made special. Author Harvey Mackay tells about a cab ride from Manhattan out to La Guardia Airport: First, this driver gave me a paper that said, "Hi, my name is Walter. I'm your driver. I'm going to get you there safely, on time, in a courteous fashion." A mission statement from a cab driver! Then he holds up a *New York Times* and a *USA Today* and asks would I like them? So I took them. We haven't even moved yet. He then offers a nice little fruit basket with snack foods. Next he asks, "Would you prefer hard rock or classical music?" He has four channels (Peters, 1994: 235–36).

This cab driver makes between $12,000 and $14,000 extra per year in tips. If he can build a rapport with a passenger in the short period of time from downtown New York to the airport, what can a professional do with long-term customers over a lifetime? Peters further expands on this in his book *The Pursuit of Wow!*:

> The idea of professional-service delivery becoming "commoditized" is ludicrous. That's as true for the two-person firm as for the Big Six accountancy. Professional services are inherently personal. They are commodities only if you are a commodity—that is, if you don't have anything special to offer, if you're just another accountant, engineer, trainer, or professional whatever. . . . I always try to personalize: Can I imagine saying, "Opened a management book today. Couldn't be sure whether it was mine or Peter Drucker's"? (Peters, 1995: 102–103)

Traditional auditors do not provide a commodity service. First of all, many small CPA firms—the majority of the practice units, as cited above—do not even perform audits, and that limits competition from the start. Second, all of the ancillary services that surround an audit—the management letter, board meetings, and internal control analysis, to name just a few—are tremendously valuable services in the eyes of the customer. These need to be differentiated and priced according to their value, rather than the time spent to produce them. Finally, with the consolidation going on among the Big Five, which will intensify concentration on the very upper end of the market, the gap left—the middle market—is wide open for other large national, regional, and local firms. Do not discount the value of an audit; it is still of significant help in obtaining other Value Pricing opportunities.

To promote a firm's value, and move up the curve, the firm must develop partnerships with its customers. Without a partnership, the firm very well may sell a commodity. With a partnership, however, it will have the ultimate monopoly—itself. Even though many businesses today deal with more than one firm, they would probably rather deal with just one, as it would be easier, more profitable, and less risky, and it would provide more opportunity for a value-added relationship to develop. Witness the trend of outsourcing, especially in the automotive industry, where the Big Three—following the lead of the Japanese—have chosen to form long-term partnerships with their outside suppliers and get them involved in the engineering and designing process of building cars. This practice might appear to be more risky, as it means putting all your eggs in one basket, but its advantages clearly outweigh the risks, or many of these firms would not be cutting back their supplier networks.

One of the main reasons businesses switch CPA firms, not to mention hiring outside consultants, is that the CPAs have not done an adequate job convincing the customers that they can perform the work and that they are a better choice than the competition. In other words, cross-selling efforts have failed. This is why it is so important to focus on share of customer, rather than on market share, to ensure that a firm does not miss those opportunities to climb up the curve. Too many CPAs spend their time cranking out the work at the lower end of the Curve, which should be delegated to someone else in the firm. Thus they miss myriad opportunities to cross-sell other value-added services to their customers. When customers talk with their CPAs and ask how business is, CPAs tend to complain about the next impending deadline, planting the notion in the customer's head that they are too busy to take on additional work from them or from others, thus discouraging referral sources from them. Chris Frederiksen, an internationally known consultant to CPAs, has a wonderful slogan: "Business is great and I'm looking for more." That sends the right message.

Another point to be emphasized about the implications of the Value Curve is what economists call umbrella pricing. For example, in an oligopoly setting, such as the Big Three American automakers, it's a known fact that when General Motors raises its prices, it puts an "umbrella" over Ford and Chrysler and allows them enough shelter to increase their prices as well. Walt Disney World in Orlando, Florida, under the new leadership of Michael Eisner, engaged in a series of price increases at the theme parks, and the surrounding competition—Busch Gardens, Sea World, Universal Studios—followed with their own increases. Likewise, within a firm, when value-added consulting services are offered, this will serve to place an umbrella over the prices of the more traditional tax and attest services. If the focus is on the totality of the value that a firm provides the customer, commanding prices at the top of the Curve becomes easier.

The CPA Vision Project

It is worth taking a look at the implications and trends the CPA Vision Project sets forth for the future of the profession. Here is how the report begins:

> This unprecedented Vision Process was a profession-wide effort involving the contribution of approximately 3,400 CPAs from all states, Washington D.C., Puerto Rico, and the Virgin Islands to craft the CPA Vision. A series of 177 professionally facilitated, day-long "Future Forums" were conducted to gather input from CPAs working in public practice, business and industry, government, and education. Participants evaluated global forces and scenarios that could emerge from the interplay of those forces using a visioning framework known as PESTHR, an acronym for the following categories of global forces: Political, Economic, Social, Technological, Human Resources, and Regulation (AICPA, 1998: 8-9).

The Project identifies eight major forces impacting the profession:

1. **Non-CPA Competitors** The number of new, non-CPA competitors, not bound by the profession's code of standards and ethics, is increasing at an alarming rate.

2. **Decline of New CPAs** The number of students and young people electing to join the CPA profession has dramatically declined.

3. **Technology Displacement** Many of the traditional essential skills of CPAs are being replaced by new technologies that are being rapidly developed, often from unexpected sources.

4. **Borderless World** As the world becomes borderless, the marketplace is demanding more complex, real-time advice and services, presenting unlimited opportunities for CPAs to expand their skills, competencies, and services.

5. **Leadership Imperative** Corporations are conducting business in a world of commerce that is global, technological, instantaneous, and increasingly virtual. The leadership they require from both internal and external advisors requires new insights, new skills, and extraordinary agility.

6. **Technological Advances** Technology will continue to challenge and reshape our lifestyles, work patterns, educational experiences, and communication styles and techniques. Technology will rewrite the "rules of business," leaving those far behind who will not harness it and effectively integrate it.

7. **Market Value Shifts** The perceived value of some of the profession's cornerstone services—accounting, auditing, and tax preparation—is declining in the marketplace.

8. **Pressure to Transform Finance From Scorekeeper to Business Partner** The CPA in business is being challenged to deliver value to the organization and help create a sustainable competitive advantage. (ibid., 1998: 3)

The report also points out that CPAs must become market driven and not dependent upon regulations to keep them in business; the market demands less auditing and accounting and more value-adding consulting services. Specialization is critical for the future of the CPA profession. This is essentially a move away from the traditional number-crunching image toward interpretation and value-added services (ibid., 11).

The report also sets forth the Economic Platforms model, as follows:

Economic Platforms	Scope of Knowledge	Distribution of Knowledge and Effect	Time Span of Impact
Platform 7	Global	Ability to determine the rules of the game at an international level	50 years
Platform 6	National	Ability to influence the rules of the game at a national level	20 years
Platform 5	Industry	Ability to conceptualize the the multiple realities that exist within the environment and capitalize on them	10–15 years
Platform 4	Market	Ability to create and manage multiple, parallel outcomes based on market needs and internal competencies	3–5 years
Platform 3	Value Chain	Ability to identify and improve alternative systems to achieve predetermined goals	1–2 years
Platform 2	Process	Ability to conform and adhere to linear and technical processes	3 months
Platform 1	Product	Ability to perform given tasks and focus on immediate, tangible tasks	Immediate

According to the report, the path to success is moving from information services on Platforms 1 and 2 to services in the emerging knowledge industry of Platform 3 and beyond. Of course, it is emphasized that the services with higher value are built on the base of traditional CPA services (ibid., 22–23).

In effect, the Vision Project is confirming what many CPAs have already discovered in the trenches of the marketplace: The customer is demanding more and more value-added consulting services and is turning to the most trusted and respected of all business advisors to perform that role—the CPA. But making the transition from a traditional, conservative paradigm to one that is innovative, entrepreneurial, and risk-seeking does not happen overnight. The profession has built up an enormous amount of human capital in the role of financial historian, and it now finds itself in the position of being forced into the more ambiguous and less rule-bound atmosphere of the business advisor. How does one make that transition?

What the CPA Offers Today

According to Stuart Kessler, AICPA chairman, the new "CPA" designation might be defined as *certified professional advisor*, a "forward-looking assurer of the integrity of real-time, customized data." Customers tend to judge CPAs as members of a profession rather than individually. Making the transition to advisor is one way to differentiate your firm from the competition. (See Chapter 15.)

According to consultants, surveys conducted by the AICPA, and various state societies, as well as customers of CPA firms, the following services tend to be located at the top of the Value Curve and have significant growth potential. The list is not meant to be comprehensive but it is a way to get you to think differently about the future, which has already arrived:

- Benchmarking
- Business Valuations
- Mergers & Acquisitions
- International Services
- Buy-Sell Agreements
- Key Person Insurance
- Mission Statement Development
- Marketing Analysis and Planning
- Customer Retreats as Annual Events
- Business Planning
- Cash Flow Analysis
- Choice of Entity
- TQM/ISO 9000 Consulting
- Business Process Reengineering
- Information Technology
- Personal Financial Planning
- Estate and Succession Planning
- Consulting on Pricing (using the concepts discussed in this book)
- Continuing Professional Education (Drucker believes this is the growth industry of the future.)
- Economic Analysis

- Eldercare (Individuals age 65 and over control approximately 11 trillion dollars to 13 trillion dollars in wealth.)
- Negotiation
- Forensic Accounting
- Business Turnaround
- Dispute Resolution
- Regulatory Compliance
- Ethics Attestation and Implementation
- Internet and electronic commerce
- School Performance (As the country shifts more and more to private choice schools, CPAs can attest to their performance standards.)

One last point with respect to the future of the profession: The debate between the generalist and the specialist is over, and the specialist has won. The majority of successful firms all specialize in a few industries or niche markets. CPAs are one of the last businesses to specialize. Doctors, dentists, lawyers, auto mechanics, and even retail stores have all carved out a particular expertise. You can no longer be everything to everybody. The difference between a generalist and a specialist is the difference between an incandescent light and a laser beam. Each requires the same amount of energy to operate, but one can burn a hole through metal because of its intense focus. As Confucius said: "The man who chases two rabbits catches neither."

Summary and Conclusions

Members of the accounting profession no longer have the luxury of launching a practice and having an automatic ticket to prosperity. The seller's market is over, and the customer is sovereign, demanding more and more every day. Accounting is a profession rich in history and traditions. Some of those traditions have served CPAs well for the past century or so. Others, such as government regulations and psychological attachment to hourly billing, are beginning to hinder the ability to service customers adequately.

Recall that the accounting profession is in the maturity stage of the Product Life Cycle and that this alone will alter the marketplace. Combine this with the increasing expectations of the customers, who now demand that their CPA be a total financial advisor and business consultant, and the environment CPAs operate in has been permanently altered.

Study the Value Curve and commit it to memory. Its lessons are many and vital, rooted deep in economic theory. The lesson imbedded in the curve—and it is not obvious at first—is that no matter where a firm is on the curve, opportunities are available to Value Price its services.

This chapter was not written to predict the future, but because CPAs need to think differently about the future and the customer's ever-changing needs. Nobody can keep up with the market. The best anyone can do is to be on the lookout for changes in direction and trends and be among the early adopters of change in order to capitalize on emerging opportunities. Forecasts about the future of the profession are interesting, but leadership requires decisions in the present. Even if one knew exactly what the future held, that would only be half the battle. To take advantage of this knowledge, a firm would have to be formed, which leads to the question: Why are professionals in business?

3 WHY ARE PEOPLE IN BUSINESS?

If you aim to profit, learn to please.

—Winston Churchill

When participants in a course for the California CPA Education Foundation were asked why they are in business, more than 75 percent answered: "To make a profit." Even the father of double-entry accounting, Fra Luca Pacioli, began the second chapter of his book with the following proposition:

> Begin with the assumption that a businessman has a goal when he goes into business. That goal he pursues enthusiastically. That goal, the goal of every businessman who intends to be successful, is to make a lawful and reasonable profit (Pacioli, 1494: 4).

But is the answer really that simple?

Any business needs to earn a profit to survive; indeed, profit is the measurement of how much value an organization adds to the lives of others. However, to think that a business exists solely to make a profit is to confuse cause and effect, putting the cart before the horse. As Peter Drucker indefatigably points out, not only is the notion that businesses exist to make a profit false, it is irrelevant. Profit is a *result* of customer behavior. More accurately, profit is a *lagging indicator* of customer behavior. The real results of any organization take place in the hearts and minds of its customers. The central purpose of any business organization is to *create a customer*. This is a difficult concept to understand, especially for accountants and attorneys who have been trained to focus on the financial and transactional side of business life. Nonetheless, it is definitely true, which will be shown in this chapter.

The Economist's Definition of Profit

The economics profession has a different definition of profit from the typical GAAP financial statement. Economists consider both parties to a transaction, because both parties must receive more value than each is giving up; otherwise no transaction would take place in the first place (assuming no fraud or coercion). United States congressman Samuel Barrett Pettengill (1886–1974) gave an excellent definition of *profit* from an economist's perspective:

> The successful producer of an article sells it for more than it costs him to make, and that's his profit. But the customer buys it only because it's worth more to her than she pays for it, and that's her profit. No one can long make a profit producing anything unless the customer makes a profit using it.

That is a good definition of profit because it focuses the organization on the customer and ensures that the customer, too, earns a profit from using your services. A most articulate expression of the above definition came from Stanley Marcus, chairman emeritus of Neiman–Marcus, the ultimate authority on customer service:

> You're really not in business to make a profit, but you're in business to render a service that is so good people are willing to pay a profit in recognition of what you're doing for them.

That is the ultimate mission statement for any business. The focus is right where it belongs—on the customer. This was common practice in the dark days of the Great Depression when Stanley Marcus ran the store founded by his father, Herbert Marcus. Back then, business owners understood the value of a customer and how hard it was to find one. Sometime after World War II, when businesses enjoyed a seller's market, this attitude was forgotten. Businesses had the attitude that customers were easily replaced, and not much attention was given to customer service and customer loyalty economics. It wasn't until the mid-1980s that extensive research began to appear on the importance of customer service and how critical customer loyalty is to any organization.

Forgotten Lessons from the Past

They say that you can't turn back the clock and go back to the old days. Nonsense. This is exactly what is happening with the Total Quality Service movement, the customer loyalty movement, and other concepts that put the customer at the center of the business organization. Millions of dollars are being spent with consultants to relearn what was once common sense, practiced by the great entrepreneurs from the turn of the century to the mid-1950s—individuals such as Stanley Marcus, Walt Disney, J.W. Marriott, and Ray Kroc. The movie *Miracle on 34th Street* is a testament to the importance of customer service and the value of loyalty. When the Macy's Santa Claus sends the customers to the competition because it has the toy the child desires—and it's on sale—management gets upset, but the customers love it and do the rest of their Christmas shopping at Macy's. Somewhere along the line, this common sense practice was lost, and just recently professionals have begun to recognize what their ancestors knew so well. Wisdom is timeless, and sometimes turning back the clock is the wisest course of action. Two books by Stanley Marcus, *Minding the Store* and *Quest for the Best*, are recommended reading. The latter is out of print so you'll have to call a library or good used book store to find it, but both are worth tracking down due to the many lessons they contain.

Today's excellent customer service organizations have not only learned the value of customer service, they have put the concepts into practice, and are obtaining superior financial performance as a result. Organizations such as Disney, FedEx, Marriott, Lexus, Nordstrom, Cadillac, and Xerox all have corporate cultures that are driven by the customer. Even though a customer may have had a bad experience with any of these organizations, recovery systems are in place to make good on errors, retain the customer, and in the process actually increase customer loyalty and goodwill. They also all understand that profit is a lagging indicator of customer behavior.

FedEx has an internal mission statement that sums up the importance of focusing on the customer in order to earn a profit. It is: People. Service. Profits. If FedEx takes care of its internal associates, they in turn will provide excellent service to its external customers, who in turn will pay FedEx a profit in recognition of what they are doing for them. That exact order comports with the real world of business, and it is also the reason a business does not exist solely to make a profit. A lot of work is done long before the bottom line on the income statement is black.

Businesses talk about profit centers, but this term, as Peter Drucker points out, is a misnomer. In any organization, from a for-profit business to a not-for-profit charity to a governmental agency, *all* results exist externally. Inside any organization all you have is *costs* and *efforts*. The result of a hospital is a well patient. The result of a school is an educated student. And the results of a business organization is a satisfied customer. As Stanley Marcus pointed out: "You achieve customer satisfaction when you sell merchandise that doesn't come back to a customer that does." If the focus is on the internal "profit centers," the firm is misguided. The only profit center is a customer's check that doesn't bounce.

At the Disney Institute Professional Development Program (formerly the Disney University), a course is offered titled *The Disney Approach to Customer Loyalty: Creating Service That Keeps Your Customers Coming Back.* The course emphasized customer loyalty and what a business has to do to earn that loyalty. But better yet, the participants got to see firsthand how Walt Disney World puts these theories into practice and achieves the astonishing result of 75 percent of its guests (Disney parlance for customers) at the Walt Disney World Resort being repeat guests in 1996. This is impressive, considering that Walt Disney World's annual attendance is approximately 31.5 million.

The Walt Disney World Success Formula is as follows:

Quality Cast Member (employee) Experience

plus

Quality Guest Experience

plus

Quality Business Practices

equals

Future

Disney achieves this formula by focusing on its employees and their needs first. Employees are encouraged to set customer satisfaction as a priority. Out of this grows customer loyalty. The ultimate goals—profits and growth—follow naturally.

For Disney and other successful companies, profit follows an entire process of adding value both internally and externally. Focusing solely on profit is analogous to playing tennis by focusing on the scoreboard rather than keeping your eye on the ball.

When presented with these ideas, one CPA responded: "That's all well and good, but if I don't make a profit, first and foremost, I can't survive in order to serve." The obvious retort is that you must serve in order to survive. But CPAs are a tougher sell than that. So he was asked to perform this exercise: Figure out the lifetime value of each customer in your firm, multiply that amount by how many years you intend to practice, and compute the result. Then go to your balance sheet and make the following entry:

	Debit	Credit
Accounts Receivable	$XX	
Deferred Revenue		$XX

Then he was asked: "How do you intend to convert that to cash?" This focuses on the right area, i.e., the customer. Everything else is merely effort, and as they say, effort will be rewarded in Heaven—but customers want results.

Discovering the "P" in CPA

As a profession, CPAs find it much easier to focus on the "A" in the acronym rather than the "P." They focus on the "A" because they understand accounting and have been trained and certified in it; quite honestly, dealing with "A" is easier than dealing with the customer relationship. As Joan Baez once remarked: "The easiest kind of relationship for me is with 100,000 people. The hardest is with one." When CPAs give any thought at all to serving the public they think of processing tax returns, attesting to financial statements, or, worse yet, racking up billable hours.

It's certainly easy for a CPA to sit in an office, surrounded by a customers' files, and believe he or she is serving the customer well. This attitude will handicap efforts to climb up the Value Curve, however. The CPA needs to focus on the customer, or on *who* benefits, rather than on *what* to do. This places the customer relationship at the center and puts the emphasis on the *outcome* of effort, not on the *activity*. The old joke about how CPAs are easily suited to be morticians because of their disdain for customer contact may have some truth to it, but no longer can a CPA be successful based exclusively upon backroom technical competence. The best professionals, in any of the professions, are those who care deeply about their customers as fellow humans. As David H. Maister says in his book *True Professionalism*, "The opposite of the word *professional* is not *unprofessional*, but rather *technician*. Professionalism is predominantly an attitude, not a set of competencies. A real professional is a technician who cares" [Emphasis in original] (Maister, 1997: 16).

An inspiring story of excellent service comes from my father, who you met in the Introduction. While giving a haircut, my dad learned that his customer had recently, and unexpectedly, lost his job. During the course of the usual barber chair banter, the customer explained that he was financially strapped and having a difficult time. After the haircut, as the customer pulled out his wallet to pay, my father held up his hand, refused to take his money, and told him it was on the house, as all future haircuts would be, until the customer had a chance to get back on his feet.

That is compassion. That is empathy. That is actively listening to customers and hearing what they say. It is responding to the *person*, not just to the *need*. It was a small investment—a few 45-minute haircuts, and lost revenue of $50 to $100, for a customer who is so enamored with my father that he will stay with him for life. From the perspective of loyalty economics, it was a worthwhile investment, as it can cost *five* times more to obtain a new customer than it does to keep an existing one. (CPAs take note: the AICPA states that it costs *eleven* times more.) Imagine increasing advertising and marketing effectiveness by a factor of between five and eleven by investing in your existing customers.

This story is the embodiment of the Spirit of Service. In his trailblazing book, *The Only Thing That Matters: Bringing the Power of the Customer into the Center of Your Business*, Karl Albrecht defines the Spirit of Service as follows:

> *The Spirit of Service*: An attitude based on certain values and beliefs about people, life, and work, that leads a person to willingly serve others and take pride in his or her work.
>
> It's an element of giving—a spirit of generosity that makes people give something of themselves in addition to just doing the job. It's going beyond the bare minimum or the standard actions. It's being attentive to the *person* behind the need, and responding to the *person* more than just responding to the need. It's being there psychologically and emotionally as

well as being there physically [Emphasis in original] (Albrecht, 1992: 88).

Rewards follow service, and so does profit. Henry Ford said it this way: "The man who will use his skill and constructive imagination to see how much he can give for a dollar, instead of how little he can give for a dollar, is bound to succeed." George Gilder, author, economist, and technologist, defines the spirit of enterprise:

> It is a world where service of others—solving their problems and taking on new ones for yourself—is the prime source of leadership and wealth. . . . "Do unto others as you would have them do unto you" and "give and you will be given unto" are the central rules of the life of enterprise (Gilder, 1992: 298, 308).

Is All This Just So Much "Fluff"?

Business is about serving others and adding value to their lives in excess of payment in cash. If an organization doesn't succeed in that mission, the market should squeeze it out of existence unmercifully, as it is merely wasting society's resources by not deploying them to the advantage of others. Business is not about survival of the fittest (i.e., only the strong survive), as if Social Darwinism ruled the world of enterprise. This notion can be disproved simply by looking at where all of the growth and innovation come from in a free market economy—the small business sector. If Social Darwinism ruled business life, only the Fortune 500 would exist, since all the money is there.

Another preposterous notion found in almost any business book is that business is *war*. Popular novelists such as Michael Crichton and Tom Clancy have added to this myth. If business were war, everyone would be dead. In a 8 trillion dollar plus economy, literally billions of transactions are taking place every day. The only way to win in a war is to annihilate the enemy or overwhelm the enemy with such force that they surrender. In business, the only way to win against competition is to add more value to the customer. That's not *war*, it's *peace*. It puts all of the advantages into the hands of the customer, where they should be. Business is all about volitional acts under no threat of coercion, fraud, or duress. Certainly illegal acts take place, and that is why contract law and the court system exist, to enforce restitution and award damages to injured parties. But the majority of business transactions happen without dishonest intent, based upon mutual trust and respect. Economists focus their attention on the customer, not the business sector, because they, too, profit from each transaction.

So much of business terminology is borrowed from the battlefield that it has been ingrained into the average person since college. Even everyday business attire has its roots in the battlefield, as was pointed out by Adam M. Brandenburger and Barry J. Nalebuff in the book *Co-opetition*:

> Drawing on the work of Anne Hollander, Eric Nash points out that the clothing people wear to work also comes from war: the tie was long called a cravat, after the seventeenth-century Croatian mercenaries who wore them on French battlefields; the vestigial brass loops on trench coats are actually grenade hooks; the tailored suit can be traced back to the linen padding worn under a suit of armor; men's coats unbutton from the left so that a right-handed man might draw a sword or gun quickly (Brandenburger and Nalebuff, 1996: 267).

Despite this attitude, economists, sociologists, theologians, and even Pope John Paul II have spoken on the morality of capitalism and the vital role profits perform in its functioning, a topic explored in Chapter 16.

The theory of Total Quality Service is grounded in empirical evidence: It works. Organizations whose cultures are driven by the customer outperform those that are not. It is both that simple and that complex. Total Quality Service enables a business to charge premium prices, just like FedEx, Disney, and Nordstrom. Do people turn away at the gate at Disneyland or Walt Disney World when they discover that prices are higher than the local competition? Hardly. Disney practices Total Quality Service, or what they call Disney Quality Service (DQS)—because it's the right thing to do both morally and ethically, and it has the salutary effect of tremendously increasing profitability.

The purpose of this book is to help you make more money. The book focuses on the *top line* (i.e., pricing policies) with the sole purpose of increasing the *bottom line*. You will not be able to do that unless you provide your customers Total Quality Service, emanating from a firm possessing the Spirit of Service, which is cultural and attitudinal. Once

Total Quality Service and the Spirit of Service are the driving forces of a firm, Value Pricing can be implemented.

Customer vs. Client

Many organizations have tried to call their customers something other than a customer. Here is what Albrecht had to say with respect to the words professionals use:

> In an organization, the language that people use when referring to customers, or when describing service-quality programs, signals very clearly how they view their customers and how they see themselves as relating to them. Many organizations have evolved a special terminology that enables them to *avoid* referring to people as customers [Emphasis in original] (Albrecht, 1992: 9).

If you've read this far, you have already noticed the use of the word *customer* rather than *client* when referring to the people served by professionals. This is deliberate and is done for several reasons, which will be discussed.

Where Does the Word *Client* Come From?

Professionals tend to substitute the word "client" for "customer." However, the word *client*, when you look at its etymology, is an inappropriate word to describe the person the professional serves in today's marketplace. *Client* is derived from the Latin word *cliens*, which is a follower, retainer, one who hears his patron.

According to the dictionary, "among the ancient Romans a client was a citizen who placed himself under the protection of a patrician, who was called his patron; a dependent; one under the protection or patronage of another."

In the legal profession in the early Roman Empire, individuals learned in the law provided legal services without compensation. According to William G. Ross in his book, *The Honest Hour: The Ethics of Time-Based Billing by Attorneys*:

Early Roman lawyers were . . . obliged to advise and defend their clients, because these were duties which lawyers, as patrons, owed to those who were dependent upon them. Later, as clients ceased to be the dependents of their lawyers, persons who performed legal services often continued to work without pay because they were wealthy and hoped to achieve public recognition and political benefit from pleading the cases of their clients (Ross, 1996: 9).

The dictionary also describes a client as "a person or company for whom a lawyer, accountant, advertising agency, etc. is acting; loosely, a customer; a person served by a social agency." Visit any governmental agency that dispenses aid to individuals and you will soon discover that it uses the term client. The welfare state may have clients but the same term does not need to be used to describe the relationship professionals desire to have with those they serve.

Today the word "client" is used simply because that's what professionals have always called their customers. It is time to question the appropriateness of this word.

Use of the Word *Customer* Provides a Competitive Differentiation

Professionals have attempted to elevate themselves above the "crass commercialism of the marketplace," as if something is inherently wrong with professionals having to compete for customers, although auto companies, grocery stores, malls, airlines, and all other businesses in the free market do so.

What has happened to the word *customer*, and why do so many businesses attempt to describe the people they serve as something else? After all, *customer* is derived from the word *custom*, which is something done regularly. Therefore, a customer is a person who buys, especially one who buys regularly. Why businesses, and particularly the professions, have adopted other terms is an interesting question, and one worth thinking about. Doctors see "patients," which is a Latin word for "Suffering" or "endurance" (*patientia*). Thus a patient is by definition "long-suffering." Airlines carry "passengers." Taxi drivers transport "fares." Utility companies have "ratepayers." Insurance companies service "policyholders." News-letters solicit "subscribers." The IRS deals with "taxpayers."

Businesses have replaced the word *customer* with other terms. Albrecht offers an explanation:

> These labels signal that the company sees the customer as a passive figure, an object to be acted upon, or something to be processed through a system. The choice of these words makes the customer into a thing rather than a person. The words make it easier to obscure the fact that customers are *people*, entitled to judge the quality of the delivered experience and who make the ultimate decision about doing business with the organization.
>
> Apparently we don't like giving the customer that much power. We don't like the feeling of having to earn the customer's approval. We want to change customers into things we can manipulate, statistics we can analyze, or wild animals we have to capture to gain 'market share.'
>
> The loss of this focus on the customer as a human being is probably the single most important fact about the state of service and service management in the Western world today [Emphasis in original] (Albrecht, 1992: 10).

Walt Disney insisted that his customers be called "guests." His attitude, which still permeates the entire culture of all Disney theme parks, is that the role of employees ("Cast Members") is to entertain the guests and show them a good time. The words used to describe the people served by a business are a good indication of the attitude of the firm.

Customers will develop a deeper respect for professionals if they are treated like *people*, rather than viewed as *tasks* to be processed through the firm. Customers are much more sophisticated with respect to other services offered them by professionals, and they have access to more information than ever before. With the dramatically increased level of competition over the past decade, professionals must strive to serve and please the customer to win their continued patronage. *The customer is sovereign, period.* You may not like it; you may wax nostalgic for the old days, when customers lined up like sheep to be fleeced once every year, but those days are gone, forever. Professionals can no longer place themselves above the

"crass marketplace." They must participate in it and differentiate themselves from the competition if they are to succeed.

For professionals who do start referring to clients as customers, this will
have a salutary effect on the attitude, firm culture, customer loyalty and
respect, and ultimately, on the professional's bottom line.

Summary and Conclusions

The seller's market, which existed after World War II up until the end of the
1970s, is over. Today, the customer is sovereign, and businesses are
"turning back the clock" to learn the lessons their predecessors knew so
well from the turn of the century up until the 1950s—that each customer
wants quality service and wants to be treated individually. The Total
Quality Service leaders of today—companies such as Disney, FedEx,
Marriott, Lexus, Nordstrom, Cadillac, and Xerox—are studying the lessons from the entrepreneurs of a bygone age—Herbert and Stanley Marcus,
Ray Kroc, J.W. Marriott, and Walt Disney—who understood the importance of treating customers well.

Serving people is what being a professional is, or should be, all about.
Focus on your customers, and continually solve an ever-increasing share
of their problems and burdens. Give as much as you can for a dollar, rather
than as little as you can. The profits and rewards you seek will be yours.

4 WHAT AND HOW PEOPLE BUY

The secret of staying afloat in business is to create
something people will pay for.

—Thomas Edison

To engage in Value Pricing, a professional must understand exactly *what* customers are buying, and it helps to understand *how* they are buying as well. Ask any group of professionals what their customers are paying them for and the result is a wide range of answers that unfortunately focuses on what the professional thinks the customer needs, not what the customer actually buys. Here is a listing of the most frequent responses:

- Preparation of financial statements, tax returns, and tax planning
- Management advisory services
- Expertise, knowledge, and experience
- Time

All of these answers emphasize the technical aspect of what a CPA does, rather than the benefits perceived by the customer. With the exception of time, most of the answers are subjects emphasized in college and CPE courses, and any relationship to what customers pay for is truly coincidental. Other industries don't suffer from this dilemma; they have an excellent understanding of exactly what the customer is buying. Automobile salesmen know that they aren't selling utilitarian transportation; they are selling status, personality, performance, fun, and image. Booksellers don't sell books; they sell information and reading enjoyment. Insurance salesman aren't selling policies (who reads them?); they are selling peace of mind.

So, What Do People Really Buy?

It's the old marketing axiom that people aren't buying *drill bits*, which are small and easily misplaced; they are buying *holes*. One doesn't buy *golf clubs* but the *activity* they allow the customer to engage in. Gillette is selling *shaves*, not *razors*. 7-11 is selling *convenience*. McDonald's is selling *fast*, not *food*. An owner of a Roto Rooter business would quickly discover that a good percentage of business comes not from unplugging drains but from retrieving wedding rings, which is useful information to place in a Yellow Pages ad for the customer in a panic. The manufacturer of Rogaine is not selling hair but is really selling *hope*. Charles Revson, who created the cosmetic empire Revlon, said, "When it leaves the factory, it's *lipstick*. But when it crosses the counter in the department store, it's *hope*."

In his book *How to Win Customers and Keep Them for Life*, Michael LeBoeuf, Ph.D., states: "Despite all of the untold millions of products and services for sale in today's market place, customers will exchange their hard-earned money for only two things:

1. Good feelings
2. Solutions to problems
   (LeBoeuf, 1989: 39)

Professionals are excellent at solving problems. Sometimes they are even too good, because they tend to jump right into the solution without first discovering what the customer really wants and expects, almost completely ignoring the creation of the good feelings that are so essential to developing long-term relationships. Simply offering solutions to problems isn't enough. The customer automatically expects problems to be solved, which is why they seek out a professional, but more emphasis should fall on creating good feelings.

The Dynamics of Customer Expectations

Theodore Levitt, marketing professor from Harvard Business School, simplified LeBoeuf's two factors by observing that customers are really buying only one thing: Expectations. This view focuses on the utility that the customer is trying to maximize. All consumers are out to maximize their own utility, measured either by happiness, pleasure, or something similar. No two customers are alike; each one is trying to maximize something different.

Marketing brochures of CPA firms all claim to offer outstanding service and customer satisfaction. It is important to understand, however, just how customer satisfaction is measured, which is as follows:

$$\text{Customer Satisfaction} = \frac{\text{Perceived Performance}}{\text{Customer Expectations}}$$

The *customer's* perception of and expectations of CPA performance are what matter. This equation drives home the importance of ascertaining, prior to starting each engagement, exactly what the customer's expectations are, since that is how, ultimately, the firm will be judged. Meeting a customer's expectations is hard enough when they are known. To exceed those expectations is nearly impossible if they are unknown. Customer satisfaction is no longer enough. Customer *satisfaction* must move on to customer *delight*. According to the *Harvard Business Review*, 65 to 85 percent of customers who chose a new supplier said they were satisfied or very satisfied with their former supplier. That is an astonishing statistic, one that should strike fear into the hearts and minds of all of us.

Prior to every single engagement, it is essential to ask the customer: What are your expectations? Asking this gives a CPA the ability to manage and control the outcome. For instance, if a millionaire anticipates paying zero taxes, he has an unrealistic outlook. The options are to educate him, to lower his expectations, or to refuse the engagement altogether. The onus is on the CPA to discover what the customer is counting on, then to control and educate the customer. The CPA is then able to exceed the customer's expectations. (For more information on meeting with a customer, see Chapter 10.)

Customers arrive at a professional's office with preconceived ideas of what can be done for them. These ideas have been created by professionals through marketing, advertising, and promotional material. Some expectations have been created by others—referral sources and existing customers who rave about the service they received. Managing and controlling what the customers anticipate is critical. Southwest Airlines does this well. Many people see flying on this airline as a cattle call. The passengers are fed peanuts and it is strictly no frills. This is intentional. Expectations are lowered and it becomes much easier for Southwest to exceed those expectations when they arrive on time, with the passengers' luggage, crack jokes, and do other irreverent things that make the airline so much fun to fly on. Compare that to buying a first-class ticket on another airline, say, United Airlines. What are your expectations then? If any inconvenience were to occur on that flight, satisfaction would be less, since expectations started out higher. The higher the customer's expectations are from the start, the higher the probability of being dissatisfied.

By always asking the customers what they expect, you can discover Value Pricing opportunities. A CPA met for the first time with the CEO of two companies. Due to banking covenants, the CEO was required to prepare a full disclosure compiled financial statement. During the meeting, the CPA asked, "What do you expect from us?" The CEO sat back and replied: "Obviously I need the compilations, but what I really want from you is to for you to develop a relationship with my banker. You see, during the year I tend to fall out of compliance with my loan covenants, and if my banker were comfortable with you it would make my life much easier." When the CPA heard that, he knew exactly what the customer expected. Upon returning to his office he immediately called the banker to set up a lunch. He also priced the services at three times his "standard hourly rate," based upon what he knew the engagement, and the relationship with the banker, was worth to the CEO.

In order to discover what the customer really wants, the professional must treat each customer individually, with custom-designed services (and pricing) delivered on every engagement. In her book *Measuring and Managing Customer Satisfaction*, Sheila Kessler recounts this story:

> Motorola noticed a radical increase in its pager revenues in Korea. When investigating how people there were using them, Motorola found that young women sometimes carried as many as seven pagers tucked into their waistband. Each pager represented a different boyfriend who was paging the woman—an exclusive communication link. The numbers of pagers a young woman wore was a status symbol (Kessler, 1996: 179).

Customers should not be treated *equally*; they should be treated *individually*.

One characteristic of customer expectations is that they are *dynamic*, not *static*. Over time, customers get spoiled as competition progresses from *features* to *cost* to *quality* to *service*. Karl Albrecht describes this phenomenon with a hierarchy of customer value, similar to Maslow's hierarchy of needs (Albrecht, 1992: 113).

Because of the dynamic nature of a customer's expectations, it is imperative that a professional continually asks what is expected. Customers judge CPAs not only against other professionals in the same trade, but *against any organization that has the ability of raising customer expectations*.

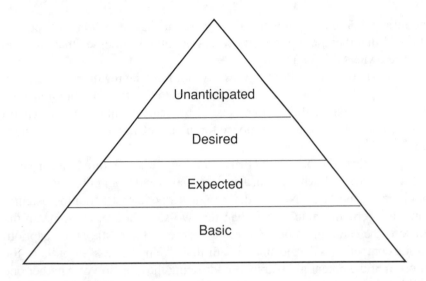

What does this mean? It means that CPAs compete against Disney, FedEx, L.L. Bean, Lexus, Marriott, and Xerox. While CPAs do not run amusement parks or overnight services, their customers frequent these businesses. Once customers receive good service, they want more.

The lesson is vital, and it is this: Either the professional raises the customer's expectations or these other organizations will. Instead of comparing a professional service firm's level of service with that of another professional firm, compare it to Disney, or Ritz–Carlton, or FedEx. If the firm's level of service isn't up to these other organizations, then the customer may legitimately ask: Why should I do business with you?

You will find a valuable checklist, "Discovering Customer Expectations," in "Useful Checklists" at the end of this book and on the disc.

Focus On What You Do, Not What You Are

Ask professionals what they do, and they almost always respond: "I'm an attorney," or "I'm a CPA." However, that is what they *are*, not what they *do*. Telling people what they are leaves the judgment open about what they do, and that probably means the questioner will conjure up the stereotype of the profession. At the Results Accountants' Systems Boot Camp, they teach you not to refer to yourself as a CPA, as this is too restricting. They

encourage their participants to say they are business development specialists, and that they help business owners develop businesses that work so
that the owners don't have to.

The customer cares about the *results*, not how the results are achieved.
Yet most professionals will tell customers not *what* they do, but *how* they
do it. Firm brochures boast about use of the latest technology, or explain
that they process tax returns in-house for greater efficiency. To a customer,
this is boring.

An effective ad is put out by Ernst & Young. It's a picture of a very nice
two-story house, all white, with a spacious lawn and front porch in a decent
looking neighborhood. Next to that is a picture of a castle, not too ostenta-
tious, but certainly much nicer than the two-story house. Underneath the
house is the caption: "Your house." Underneath the castle is the caption:
"Your competitor's." And underneath that: "Why?" This ad pulls at the
emotion of the potential customer, addressing the question of whether one
could be doing better, along with the fear that he is falling behind the
competition.

Customers want to hear the *benefits* available. By focusing on the value
to the customer, a professional will discover how to move up the Value
Curve.

How People Buy

I like best the wine drunk at the cost of others.

—Ascribed to Diogenes The Cynic, c. 380 B.C.

People buy *emotionally* and justify *intellectually*. A customer may walk
into a Porsche dealership, take a test drive, and sign on the dotted line. This
is an emotional purchase. When the customer goes home, and has to justify
the purchase to his wife, the intellectualizing begins. "Honey, we deserve
this. We had a good year. We didn't even take a vacation."

The best time for earthquake insurance sales is right after an earthquake.
This is curious, especially from an actuarial point of view. If customers are
willing to assume the risk prior to a quake, why would they not be willing
to assume the risk after one strikes? The probability of another earthquake
striking simply because one just did is no greater, as fault lines don't have

memories. The purchase is not made based upon the intellectual calculation of the statistical odds, but on the emotional desire for peace of mind. The customer is attempting to maximize serenity.

One application of this principle of emotions is that people don't like to be *sold* something, but they do like to *buy* (and own). People do not like to be sold something because that makes them feel like they are out of control. The best salesperson in the world actually empowers the customers to buy and helps customers envision the future with their product or service. Forget *selling*; focus on what the customer *buys*.

This leads to *how* people buy. In any economy, according to Milton and Rose Friedman in *Free to Choose*, people can spend money in four ways (Friedman and Friedman, 1990: 116–17):

Whose Money	**On Whom Spent**	
	You	Someone Else
Yours	I	II
Someone Else's	III	IV

Category I: When you spend your money on yourself, you will do everything in your power to maximize your utility. For example, if you are in the market for a car, you will shop around, talk to friends, visit dealerships, take test drives, and read consumer reports to get the best value for your dollar.

Category II: Perhaps you are buying a gift for a spouse, friend, or colleague. You still want to maximize your utility and theirs. You will still shop around to get the best value for your dollar.

Category III: The greatest luxury of all is to spend someone else's money on yourself. An expense account is a perfect example. Little incentive to economize exists. You might fly first class, upgrade your rental car, not eat all of your dinner, and remove items from the minibar. This is why airlines, hotels, and rental car agencies discriminate in their pricing against business travelers, since they know these people aren't paying their own bills. They are, by definition, less price sensitive. The airlines would be missing a wonderful opportunity if they did not charge these passengers higher prices.

When you encounter customers who are in Category III, you have an opportunity to Value Price, even if your firm is on the low end of the Value Curve.

Category IV: When you spend someone else's money on strangers there is virtually no incentive to economize. Government programs are a perfect example, and that is why government spending is out of control. This also explains the paradox explored in the Introduction of how CPAs once made more money than doctors and dentists. Healthcare spending has moved from Category I and II to III (health insurance) and IV (government spending on healthcare). Representative Dick Armey has this axiom: "Three groups spend other people's money: children, thieves, politicians. All three need parental supervision" (Armey, 1995: 316).

These categories hold many lessons about how other businesses Value Price their goods and services and will be referred to throughout this book.

Summary and Conclusions

Understanding exactly what a customer buys—expectations—will help a firm to exceed those expectations and thus be able to charge premium prices for services. Understanding the customers themselves—that they buy *emotionally* and justify *intellectually*, and that they don't like to be *sold* but they like to *buy*—helps the professional focus on the true needs of the customer and makes cross-selling the firm's services more effective.

5 WHY IS MOVIE THEATER POPCORN SO EXPENSIVE?

*The economist's greatest passion is not to change the world
but to understand it.*

—Steven E. Landsburg, *The Armchair Economist*

Why Study Economics?

Economists take the intellectual high ground when it comes to price theory, defined as how prices coordinate economic activity. If a business book supposedly dealing with pricing a product or service does not mention economic theory, or cite any economists, it is intellectually bankrupt. To understand how prices are set, what signals they send, how they distribute income, and a given society's resources, one *must* study economics. This is the starting point to understanding the theoretical underpinning of Value Pricing.

Economists are often seen as people who try to predict (and measure) macroeconomic activity—the stock market, inflation, unemployment, the budget deficit, monetary policy, etc. This is far too parochial a view of what economists do. The really fascinating economists are engaged in the study of *human behavior*. The most fertile minds in economics today, the likes of Gary S. Becker, Thomas Sowell, Walter Williams, Milton and Rose Friedman, David Friedman, and Steven E. Landsburg, to name just a few, deal with observing the world and trying to understand it, not with predicting it.

They all start with the basic assumption that human behavior is, overall, rational. This assumption has been challenged because it seems people do many irrational things. It is true that not all human behavior is rational, but that is not what the economists are saying. Here is how David Friedman (Milton Friedman's son) defined economics and how it may be used to observe human behavior, in his book *Hidden Order: The Economics of Everyday Life*:

Economics is based on the assumption that people have reasonably simple objectives and choose the correct means to achieve them. Both assumptions are false—but useful.

Suppose someone is rational only half the time. Since there is generally one right way of doing things and many wrong ways, the rational behavior can be predicted but the irrational cannot. If we assume he is rational, we predict his behavior correctly about half the time—far from perfect, but a lot better than nothing. If I could do that well at the racetrack I would be a very rich man (Friedman, 1996: 4).

The theory of rationality is a paradigm, a mental model of the way the world works. Economists are reluctant to part with this theory because it serves them well. Here is how the consummate economist Steven E. Landsburg explained it in his textbook *Price Theory and Applications*:

Economists insist on seeking explanations that are grounded in rational behavior. There are two reasons for this insistence. First, on the basis of his past experience, the economist is aware of the power and wide applicability of economic analysis, which presumes rationality. Second, by attempting to extend such analysis into realms where it first appears inapplicable, the economist tests the limits and the durability of his theories.

If physicists abandoned their theories so easily, physics could never progress. The first physicist to have observed a helium-filled balloon would have admitted that there was no gravity, and the true physics of the situation would not have been discovered. By attempting to fit unfamiliar phenomena into familiar patterns, we arrive at deeper understandings of both the patterns and the phenomena (Landsburg, 1996: 690–691).

Price theory is grounded in the theory of rationality. For example, take .99¢ pricing. Why do businesses price their products this way, making the consumer give and take those useless pennies? The common answer is, "It's a sales gimmick. The customer perceives $2.99 being cheaper than $3.00." From an economic approach, this contradicts the theory of rationality, because it implies that consumers, over the long run, are too ignorant to tell the difference between $2.99 and $3.00. Might there be a better explanation? How is .99¢ pricing serving the interests of someone?

Here is how Landsburg explained the phenomenon of .99¢ pricing, in his book *The Armchair Economist: Economics and Everyday Life*:

> The phenomenon of "99-cent pricing" seems to have first become common in the nineteenth century, shortly after the invention of the cash register. The cash register was a remarkable innovation; not only did it do simple arithmetic, it also kept a record of every sale. That's important if you think your employees might be stealing from you. You can examine the tape at the end of the day and know how much money should be in the drawer.
>
> There is one small problem with cash registers: They don't actually record *every* sale; they record only those sales that are rung up. If a customer buys an item for $1 and hands the clerk a dollar bill, the clerk can neglect to record the sale, slip the bill in his pocket, and leave no one the wiser.
>
> On the other hand, when a customer buys an item for 99 cents and hands the clerk a dollar bill, the clerk has to make change. This requires him to open the cash drawer, which he cannot do without ringing up the sale. Ninety-nine-cent pricing forces clerks to ring up sales and keeps them honest (Landsburg, 1993: 15–16).

Upon reflection, this appears a more adequate explanation than "sales gimmick," doesn't it? And that epitomizes the advantages of the economic way of viewing the world and assuming that behavior is rational.

Another interesting phenomenon is movie theater popcorn. To the outsider, a good question to ask might be, Wouldn't they sell more popcorn if they lowered the price? You never see any movie theater popcorn price wars, as you do with airlines or automobiles. Why is that? Why is movie theater popcorn so expensive? This question, asked in Value Pricing seminars, elicited these answers, ranked from most common to least common:

- Captive audience (represents 90 percent of the answers)
- Limited selling time
- Part of the experience

- High fixed cost of concession stand
- It's where the theater makes all of its profit
- Higher clean-up costs imposed on theater
- Tastes and smells better than you make at home
- You feel guilty if you sneak food in

These answers seem reasonable at first glance, but they are all wrong, if you view the world through the eyes of an economist. Indeed, theater owners have a captive audience and thus no other competition in the sale of popcorn. However, they also have a monopoly on bathrooms and don't have pay toilets. If they did, this would make the theater less attractive to customers and what the owner made from the pay toilets would be lost at the box office. The limited selling time seems to be a plausible explanation, but now with mega-theaters that are open practically 24 hours, popcorn prices still haven't dropped.

That popcorn is part of the experience is certainly true, as you are buying a set of opportunities when you purchase a theater ticket—one to watch a movie, and the other, if you desire, to eat popcorn. However, that doesn't explain the high price. The fixed cost of the concession stand is a plausible reason, but that cost is probably a small percentage of the premium charged for the popcorn, so that explanation, too, is inadequate. That it is where the theater makes all of its profits is certainly true, but that doesn't answer the riddle of why the theater owner doesn't just raise the price of admission tickets and make the profit there. The higher clean-up cost, again, cannot be anywhere near the premium charged. And the popcorn certainly tastes and smells better, and is more fattening, than what you could make at home, but that still doesn't explain the high price.

To the economist, all of the answers are inadequate. Something else must be happening to explain the phenomenon. What does the theater owner know that the above answers ignore? Landsburg explains:

> I believe he knows this: *some moviegoers like popcorn more than others*. Cheap popcorn attracts popcorn lovers and makes them willing to pay a high price at the door. But to take advantage of that willingness, the owner must raise ticket prices so high that he drives away those who come only to see the movie. If there are enough nonsnackers, the strategy of cheap popcorn can backfire.

The purpose of expensive popcorn is not to extract a lot of money from customers. *That* purpose would be better served by cheap popcorn and expensive movie tickets. Instead, the purpose of expensive popcorn is to extract *different* sums from *different* customers. Popcorn lovers, who have more fun at the movies, pay more for their additional pleasure (Landsburg, 1993: 159).

This is an excellent explanation, and many lessons can be learned from the practice of the theater owners. They know that some moviegoers like popcorn more than others, and they have no way to identify who these folks are when they purchase their admission tickets. They don't stand outside in the queue and ask people if they plan to purchase popcorn upon entering; if they did, how many people would tell the truth, especially if discounts were offered to popcorn lovers? Once in the theater, the popcorn lovers identify themselves by walking up to the concession stand, and that is where the owner extracts the "consumer surplus" from their pockets. By keeping the admission price low, and separate from the price of popcorn, the theater is not turning away starving students, parents with a large number of children, and other financially-challenged patrons.

Price Discrimination

Charging different prices to *different* customers is the definition of *price discrimination*. The term was coined in 1920 by Arthur Cecil Pigou in *The Economics of Welfare*. Other terms for the same concept are *revenue management* and *segmented pricing*. Price discrimination occurs when a good or service is sold at different prices that do not reflect differences in production costs. Firms engage in price discrimination to extract the consumer surplus from the customer. Consumer surplus is defined as the amount by which consumers value a product over and above what they pay for it. The traditional economic graph of supply and demand shows the customers that a firm is trying to identify in order to capture the consumer surplus.

To be included on a demand curve, customers must meet two require-ments: 1) They have to be *willing* to buy the product; and 2) They have to be *able* to buy the product. For instance, a customer may not be on the demand curve for a Rolls Royce because, although the customer is *willing*

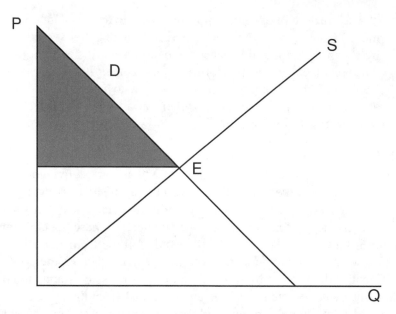

P = Price; D = Demand; S = Supply;
E = Equilibrium price; and Q = Quantity.

to buy the car, the customer is not *able* to buy it. The shaded area of the graph depicts the consumer surplus, and represents the individuals who are *willing* and *able* to pay more for the product than they are being charged at the equilibrium (i.e., market) price. On any downward sloping demand curve, certain customers will be willing and able to pay more for a product than they are being charged.

To measure the elasticity of demand for various professional services, use the following coefficient of elasticity:

$$E = \frac{\text{Percentage change in quantity demanded}}{\text{Percentage change in price}}$$

Elastic demand exists when E is greater than one. Conversely, an inelastic demand curve exists when E is less than one. The traditional example of an elastic demand curve, one that is more horizontal than that shown above, but downward sloping nevertheless, is a bale of hay. If the bale of hay is a true commodity, meaning farmer John's bale is no different from farmer Joe's, it wouldn't make sense for a customer to pay a higher price for one than the other (unless, of course, there was some other way to differentiate the two farmers—location, delivery, service, personality, etc.). In other words, if farmer John increased the price of his hay relative to farmer Joe, the quantity demanded would drop, thereby lowering his gross revenues overall. Elastic demand exists in markets with competitors and many substitutes, such as chewing gum or groceries.

Inelastic demand, on the other hand, exists when a firm can raise the price, and the quantity demanded, while it will decrease, will not fall enough to lower revenues overall. The classic example is gasoline. When oil companies increase prices, demand falls, but not enough to offset the price increase, because not many substitutes for gasoline can be found, and each consumer needs a certain amount for necessities (commuting, grocery shopping, etc.). Blood is an example of a perfectly inelastic demand curve—at least in an emergency situation—meaning that the customer would demand a fixed quantity at any price, represented by a perfectly vertical demand curve.

What is the elasticity of demand for professional services? There is ample evidence that the demand curve for the legal and accounting professions is relatively inelastic. Many firms that have increased their prices find that their top lines have increased concomitantly, even though they are selling to fewer customers. There is no doubt that the elasticity of demand differs not only for the type of service being offered, but also the value the particular customer places on a particular service. For instance, a customer who is 25 years old will have a much more elastic demand curve for estate planning than a customer who is 75 years old.

The goal of a firm owner is to try to place a customer on the firm's demand curve. This is a difficult process, but it can be achieved. Ample evidence comes from other industries that it is worth the effort to engage in price discrimination and thereby capture the consumer surplus.

Price discrimination is demand-motivated, not cost-motivated, as Kenna C. Taylor points out in *Puzzles and Paradoxes in Economics*:

> In a single-price market there is a great deal of consumer surplus because the price in the market for all units derives from the value attributed by consumers to the last unit consumed, thus making for consumer surplus on the earlier more valuable units consumed. This reflects the fact that the desire

for any good or service is subject to the law of diminishing marginal satisfaction, so that the more valuable first units are consumed earlier and less valuable ones are consumed later as the price declines (Skousen and Taylor, 1997: 57–58).

This is the answer to the famous diamond-water paradox, as pointed out by Adam Smith (1729–1790) in Chapter 4 of Book I of *The Wealth of Nations*: "Nothing is more useful than water: but it will purchase scarce anything. . . . A diamond, on the contrary, has scarce any value in use; but a very great quantity of other goods may frequently be had in exchange for it" (ibid., 27). Most people believe the answer to this paradox is scarcity—that is, diamonds are far less abundant than water. But that is not the answer. Imagine signing your name on a piece of paper in pink crayon. How much would a stranger be willing to pay for this autograph? Even though it may be the only signature of yours in pink crayon, it is not going to bring a high price. Scarcity does not automatically lend value. So what is the answer to diamond-water paradox?

Besides being abundant, water tends to be priced based upon the marginal satisfaction of the last quantities consumed. Therefore, while the first several gallons of water may be imperative for your survival, the water used to shower, flush the toilet, and wash the dishes is less valuable. And even less valuable is that quantity used to wash your dog, wash your car, and clean your driveway. The price of water reflects the last uses of the good for the aggregate of all consumers of water. On the other hand, the marginal satisfaction of one more diamond tends to be very high (except, perhaps, for Elizabeth Taylor).

If water companies knew that you were dehydrated in the desert, then they would be able to charge you a higher price for those gallons of water consumed, and then they would gradually adjust the price down the demand curve to coincide with exactly what you were using the water for. However, they don't possess that information, and thus, water is priced in the aggregate based upon its *marginal* value.

Think back to the Value Curve introduced in Chapter 2. Moving up the curve, the marginal value of the service is higher, and this certainly comports to the evidence in the market. The marginal value of one more audit is lower than the marginal value of a business valuation or of a merger and acquisition engagement. If professionals are to engage in Value Pricing, they must understand the marginal value of their services from the perspective of customers (and not from their own internal costs).

In a perfect market (from the seller's perspective), consumers would each pay their reservation price for each product or service. The reservation price is defined as the maximum amount a customer would be willing and able to pay for a product or service. This would be the ultimate expression of pure price discrimination. Unfortunately, the market is not perfect from a seller's perspective, and other methods must be devised to ascertain how much different buyers value their offerings, such as popcorn lovers valuing popcorn. Sellers who are successful in constructing price discrimination strategies that induce consumers to reveal their reservation prices will increase their profits.

To achieve price discrimination, four conditions must be present:

1. **The firm must have market power**—Not monopoly power, but a negative sloping demand curve.
2. **Buyers with different demand elasticities must be separable into submarkets**—Differences arise from income disparities, preferences, locations, etc.
3. **The transaction cost is less than the potential profit**—Costs associated with separating buyers with differential demands must be lower than the differential gain in profit expected from the multiple-price as compared with the one-price strategy.
4. **The seller must separate buyers to avoid arbitrage**—Products sold more cheaply in one location can be purchased there and transported to a higher-price location

   (Skousen and Taylor, 1997: 58–59).

How well do professional service firms meet these conditions?

First, firms must have market power, meaning a downward-sloping demand curve. Even if this requirement is met, the degree of elasticity of demand for professional services is a factor. However, no one would argue with the conclusion that the demand curve was other than downward sloping.

Number two, separating buyers with different demand elasticities, is easily achievable by attorneys and CPAs, who possess a great deal of information about their customers. They know exactly the motivations of their customers for each purchase of service, how it will be used, and how the customers will benefit by it; therefore, professionals are able to judge marginal value to the customer. Professionals also have the luxury of knowing the financial backgrounds and preferences of their customers, which aids in assessing demand elasticities. This second requirement is certainly easier for professionals to meet than it is, say, for car salesmen or manufacturers of appliances.

The third requirement, that the transaction costs associated with separating the buyers be less than the potential profit from doing so, is also met by the professional service provider. All customers are met with individually, and professionals can easily develop a psychological, as well as financial, profile of them. The marginal cost to the professional of doing this is negligible, and it is far less than the potential profit.

A case in which the third requirement was *not* met was Disneyland's A–E coupon system (E stood for *exciting*), used to price its attractions. From a pure economic perspective, this was the perfect price discrimination strategy, whereby the park charged the highest prices to those Guests who simply had to ride the most exciting rides many times. It was similar to theater owners extracting the consumer surplus from the popcorn lovers. Take it from a card-carrying member of American Coaster Enthusiasts (ACE): If amusement parks were to charge admission prices for their top roller coasters, over and above the basic admission price, no doubt they would maximize revenue. ACE members will ride a coaster 30 to 50 times in a row. If each ride cost, say, $3, ACE members may not ride that many times but they would probably still ride more than ten times. However, the problems with the A–E ticket system outweighed the benefits. Disney had to print the tickets, its guests had to wait in long lines to purchase them (thus diminishing the fun and experience of the park), and the Cast Members at each ride had to handle and police the coupons. The costs of engaging in this type of customer segregation exceeded the profits derived from it. In 1982 Disneyland changed to a fixed-price, all-day pass.

Another example in which requirement number three has forced a change is automobile pricing. Saturn's no-haggling price policy, and General Motors' Value Pricing campaign, are instances where the auto companies have discovered that customers prefer a hassle-free, non-adversarial relationship when purchasing their cars. The old method of the sticker price and the eventual negotiation was a tactic the dealers used because they knew some customers would pay the sticker price (maybe even a markup beyond it) with no questions asked. It was their way of getting at each customer's reservation price. It worked, and works to this day. However, Saturn and General Motors believe that the customer satisfaction generated with a no-hassle pricing policy outweighs the benefits of the more discriminatory (but adversarial) method.

The fourth, and final, requirement, avoiding arbitrage, is much easier for service providers to meet than product sellers. If a bakery were to sell pies in two towns, and price them $10 in one town and $5 in the other, eventually customers would buy in the lower price location. Some customers would even buy pies in the lower priced location and transport them back to the higher price location and sell them, thus keeping the consumer surplus for themselves. This is known as arbitrage. But one cannot engage in arbitrage with services. You can't send your butler, who may be charged on a sliding scale based on his income, to get your kidney transplant. And your customer can't sell his audit or tax return to someone else. Services consumed on the spot, such as movie theater popcorn or medical and dental services, are not susceptible to arbitrage.

It should be evident that attorneys and CPAs (and engineering, consulting, and medical companies) have the capability to engage in price discrimination.

Now that we've looked at the requirements necessary to price discriminate, let's examine the three degrees of price discrimination:

1. **First-degree price discrimination**—Charging each customer the most that he would be willing to pay for each item that he buys, thereby transferring all of the consumer surplus to the seller.

2. **Second-degree price discrimination**—Charging the same customer different prices for identical items.

3. **Third-degree price discrimination**—Charging different prices in different markets.

(Landsburg, 1996: 363–65)

Due to the high transaction cost of determining what each and every buyer is willing to pay, auctions and negotiable price markets are the closest approximations to first-degree price discrimination. Whether it's Princess Diana's dresses or articles from the Kennedy estate, buyers line up and identify the maximum amount they are willing to pay, and thus the item ends up being sold to that individual who *values* it the most. Some of the more famous examples from the Kennedy estate were JFK's golf irons and woods, which sold for $387,500 and $772,500, respectively, to Arnold Schwarzenegger. A $100 necklace of fake pearls went for $211,500. Even the Lunar Hod 2 vehicle, which sits on the moon's surface and can never be brought back to Earth, secured a bid of $68,000 (Lacey, 1998: 11, 301).

Auctions make interesting studies in human behavior, because no matter how much you pay for an item, you can console yourself that you only overpaid by one bid (see the discussion of bidding in Chapter 12). Auctions have been a popular method of selling estates due to today's litigious atmosphere. Since heirs can bring a suit against a trustee for failing to obtain the maximum value for the property in their charge, lawyers tend to consign estates to auction houses, rather than to dealers, to ensure they get the maximum market value for the property.

Other than in auction houses, perfect first-degree price discrimination rarely exists, because more knowledge is required than most producers can ever have. However, this knowledge can be approximated, as is pointed out by Landsburg:

> In the ancient days when people spoke with their computers through the medium of gigantic stacks of "computer cards," IBM required users of its computers to buy all of their cards from IBM. The cards were priced above marginal cost. This strategy was widely misinterpreted as an attempt to extend IBM's monopoly power from the market for computers to the market for cards. However, this explanation makes no sense. If buyers of computers are required to pay more for cards, their willingness to pay for computers is reduced and IBM loses on the computers what it makes on the cards. In actuality, *the card strategy enabled IBM to charge different prices to different customers*. In effect, those who used more cards were charged more for their computers [Emphasis in original].
>
> IBM's ideal strategy was to require each buyer of a computer to pay the amount that a computer was worth to him. This was well-approximated by charging a higher price to the heavier users. The card strategy accomplished this (ibid., 365).

Why not have the attitude that what you are doing in your firm is auctioning off a limited number of services, and you want them to go to the highest bidder? Obviously people will not line up and reveal the true value that you are worth to them, but many will reveal more than you may initially believe, a topic included in the discussion of a Fixed Price Agreement (Chapter 10). It is a splendid analogy, and one that is important to your firm's pricing culture.

Second-degree price discrimination exists when businesses charge the same customer different prices for identical items, such as Proctor and Gamble giving Wal-Mart a discount on Pampers for larger quantity orders. Another example is utility companies and cellular phone companies charging different rates for "peak" and off-peak" use. Some CPA firms use this tactic in their hourly rate pricing by having a rate of, say, $225 per hour between February and April 15, and beginning April 16 the rate changes to $175. This effort should be applauded since this is a form of price discrimination and proves that the firm is on the right track. However, the partners can be asked this: "What happens at midnight on April 15 that causes you to lose nearly 30 percent in value to your customers?" Again, this is CPAs being internally focused on *their* work flow and *their* time pressures, with no regard to the external value of what they are providing the customer. In addition, it is not good customer relations to discriminate based upon a government-imposed deadline and to imply that a professional's value is at all contingent upon the time of year he or she performs a service.

An example of third-degree price discrimination—charging different prices in different markets—is coupons. If Proctor and Gamble can make a profit selling a box of Tide soap with a .50¢ off coupon, what are they making when a customer buys a box without a coupon? Coupons are a way in which manufacturers attract those customers whose demand is more elastic. Not everyone redeems coupons and that is the point, for if everybody did, they would be superfluous. The manufacturer would simply discount the price of the product by the coupon amount and be done with it, saving the costs of printing, distributing, and redeeming the coupons.

Professional firms engage in third-degree price discrimination when they charge lower rates to not-for-profits, for instance, or when lawyers engage in pro-bono or sliding-scale work. Also, when firms are entering a new market or industry, they will sometimes reduce their prices simply to climb down the learning curve and gain a foothold in that particular area.

While second-degree and third-degree price discrimination are used by professional firms, first-degree discrimination is less common. This is likely because professionals spend far too little time building (and explaining) the value of what they are accomplishing for the customer, and they do not price in accordance with *external value*. Instead, they focus on *internal cost*, using the cost-plus pricing method of standard hourly rates.

In terms of degree, professionals, more than any other business, have the capability of implementing first-degree price discrimination, since they don't inhabit a single-price market, such as water or food. They have the potential to meet with every customer to determine each one's particular demand elasticity. It merely takes asking the right questions and educating the customer as to the value of what they do. Professionals inhabit a market that most sellers would die for, with the ability to negotiate each price for each service, at a non-prohibitive cost. The professions need to start taking advantage of this enormous opportunity to achieve first-degree price discrimination.

Make no mistake about it, no two customers are created equal. Consider these astonishing statistics:

- Lexus accounts for 3 percent of unit sales for Toyota, yet contributes approximately 30 percent of Toyota's total profits;
- The top third of credit card holders account for 66 percent of credit card charges;
- Only 21 percent of moviegoers account for 80 percent of the attendance;
- The top third of personal long-distance callers account for 68 percent of long distance billing;
- MCI derives nearly 40 percent of its revenues from the top 5 percent of its customers;
- Blockbuster Video earns half of its profits from late charges;
- A study of the revenues of 300 movies released over an 18-month period found that four (1.3 percent) accounted for 80 percent of box office receipts and the other 296 movies (98.7 percent earned 20 percent of box office receipts;
- The top third of diners at family restaurants account for almost 90 percent of the visits;
- The top third of shoppers account for 80 percent of the grocery spending in any particular supermarket;
- 5 percent of households buy 85 percent of Levi's blue jeans;
- 3 percent of households buy 82 percent of L'eggs pantyhose; and
- 60 percent of Delta Air Lines' profits comes from 6 percent of its customers.

Not only do economists understand the consumer surplus, so do marketers. They spend an inordinate amount of time "building fences" around these high value customers, trying to segregate them from the rest of the pack and extract the consumer surplus from them in very creative ways. As the above statistics prove, the profits of mass-market brands do not come from the mass market. The majority of the profits in your firms do not come from the majority of your customers, but, more likely, the top 5 percent generate 50 percent of your profit, or the top 20 percent generate 80 percent of your profit.

Professionals understand this, just as they understand that 5 percent of their customers account for more than 50 percent of their headaches or their liability risk. If that is the case, the Pareto Principle is at work in your firm. Named after the Italian economist and sociologist Vilfredo Pareto (1848–1923), the Pareto Principle is this: *In any phenomenon, only a few of the contributors account for the bulk of the effect.* He was referring to the distribution of income. If this rule applies to your firm, then why do all of your customers get charged the same standard rate regardless of the work you are performing for them? As Don Peppers and Martha Rogers point out in their book *The One to One Enterprise*:

> The truth is, it's actually *more fair* to treat different customers differently. A customer who invests more in your firm is certainly owed a greater level of service and attention, and by treating customers individually the enterprise can usually raise the general level of service for nearly *all* customers.
>
> Customers don't *want* to be treated equally. They want to be treated *individually*... Any company that treats a customer the same as "everybody" is treating that customer like nobody [Emphasis in original] (Peppers and Rogers, 1997: 127, 133, 321).

The mistake made by most firms is treating each customer like an "average customer." In reality, there's no such thing as an *average* customer. There are only *individual* customers, and therefore you should set an appropriate, customized price for each of them.

Here are some examples of price discrimination in various industries. Notice the creativity, ingenuity, and thought that has gone into these practices, and compare this to the level of thought you have given pricing in your firm. You may never look at pricing the same way again.

Hardcover vs. Paperback Books

A John Grisham or Tom Clancy novel is priced at nearly $25 in hardback, and around $10 in paperback. Would you be shocked to discover that the production cost to the publisher is approximately the same for both books? What the publisher is doing is having those fans of Grisham or Clancy who simply cannot wait for the paperback version, due out in six to twelve months, identify themselves and buy the hardcover. The publisher extracts the additional $15 of consumer surplus from them. The fact that serious book lovers prefer hardcover books to paperbacks (they last longer, look more impressive in one's library) is simply icing on the cake, and merely adds to the perceived value of the hardcover. The real goal is *charging different prices to different customers* based upon their individual demand elasticities.

Bookstore owners (or, if you have customers who own bookstores) take note. There is a lesson here, and amazon.com has already learned it. Owners should inform their best customers when certain books are due to be published, those written by the customer's favorite author, and perhaps ship the books to them automatically upon arrival (in hardcover, of course).

Senior Discounts

The one demographic group in the United States least in need of discounts is seniors. As a group, they are the wealthiest people in society. They have worked all their lives, have had longer to save, and thus have more to show for their accumulated efforts. So why do businesses offer these wealthy individuals discounts? Seniors have one thing on their hands that a lot of other consumers lack: Time. They tend to seek out establishments that offer them discounts, even if they must arrive at certain times or clip coupons. If a restaurant can make a profit serving a senior citizen a prime rib dinner at $7.95, what are they making off a customer who will pay $12.95? Restaurants engage in the same practice with "early bird" dinners and by charging much higher prices on the dinner menu than on the lunch menu for the same food.

Children's Prices

At the fair, Disneyland, and the movies, and on trains, planes, and buses, kids take up one seat, yet they are charged a lower price than an adult. This is done to prevent discouraging parents from bringing their families, and because of the fact that children have a more elastic demand curve than their parents. But from a cost standpoint, is it any cheaper for the airline to fly a child?

Kodak Film at Disneyland

Part of the opportunity of visiting Disneyland is taking pictures, and if you're unlucky enough to run out of film, you will pay a premium to get some inside the park. This is Kodak's way of charging the heavy users of film—and thus those customers who place a higher value on pictures—a premium, and extracting the consumer surplus from the photo bugs. (Note the "Kodak Picture Spots" throughout the park.)

Nightclubs

Arrive early and admission is free and happy hour drink prices are less—tactics used by the owner to attract crowds early so that by nighttime it is a happening place, when the owner will be able to extract a cover price from the nightclub crowd. The concept of a cover charge will be discussed later in the chapters on the Fixed Price Agreement. An economist calls it a two-part tariff—that is, charging a customer a fee in exchange for the right to purchase more of your product.

Newspapers

This one is obvious, in that subscribers pay a cheaper, subsidized rate, covered by the advertisers. The cheaper subscription rate helps boost circulation, thereby increasing the advertising rates that can be charged. *Different customers, different prices.*

General Motors

Many cars from the six divisions of GM—Chevrolet, Pontiac, Buick, Oldsmobile, Cadillac, and GMC—are produced in the same plant, with little variance in cost (albeit some in material). Yet when those cars arrive at the showroom, the sticker price of a Cadillac is far higher than that of an Oldsmobile, and no doubt higher, as a percentage, than the variance in the cost of production. This is GM's way of having a car for each location on the demand curve, the theory being you'll be loyal to GM from your first car (a Chevy) to your last (a Cadillac).

Intel 386 and Other High Technology Products

The 386 was introduced in two versions: with and without a math coprocessor. Both contain the math coprocessor, but the less expensive chip merely disables the coprocessor. What's the cost difference? Whenever a new generation computer, printer, or chip is put on the market, the manufacturers know that a certain segment of the population—known as early adopters—will rush to buy the latest and greatest. These individuals are price-insensitive when it comes to technology. Thus, the product is put on the market and a high price is set, allowing the technology mandarins to identify themselves, and shortly thereafter, the price makes its way down the demand curve until everyone else can afford it. This happens with computers, and it happened with car phones, CDs, laser discs, VCRs, and camcorders. The early adopters transfer the consumer surplus to the manufacturer.

Trade-In Discounts

Apple Computer, and others, sometimes offer trade-in allowances for your old printer if you purchase a new one. Jewelers do the same with watches. They will discard the item as soon as they get it. Why do they do this? Because if you already own what they are trying to sell you, chances are good that your demand curve is more elastic than someone who doesn't own the product. Thus, people who already have printers are charged less than those who do not.

Cosmetics

My brother, Ken Baker, was formerly in marketing for a large cosmetics firm. He spent most of his time trying to price products just right for each particular market. He recently decided to demonstrate to me a particular example of price discrimination.

He sent me down to a drugstore to buy L'Oreal eye shadow. For $5 I got four colors and one brush (no compact, no mirror), a net weight of 0.17 oz. of eye shadow. My brother then instructed me to go to Macy's and buy Lancome eye shadow. This eye shadow comes in an attractive gold leaf box, has a compact with a mirror, and has two brushes. It has only three colors, with a net weight of 0.15 oz. The price is $35.

I called my brother back, perturbed about being out $40 for eye shadow that I have no use for, and asked him what the point was. He told me to check the ingredients on the back of each box, and they were identical. The only difference, according to my brother, is less than one dollar in chemicals and about $3.50 in packaging; the contents are 95 percent the same. I protested that my secretary, who uses Lancome, says it lasts longer, doesn't smear. She swears it's a better product. My brother replied, "Of course she does; how do you think we get the extra $30 out of her purse?"

The two eye shadows are made in the same vat, with virtually the same ingredients, and at almost identical cost. Yet one sells for $5 and the other for $35. It's the "P's" of marketing coming together creatively to segregate the customers and extract the consumer surplus. The first P, product, is segregated into two different quality markets, the low-price drug store line and the upscale department store line. Marginal quality improvements to Lancome and different color pallets are combined to enhance the perceived quality. The second P, place, is how the manufacturer, Cosmair, is able to segregate the two different buyers, the one in drug store distribution and the other in fine department stores such as Macy's and Nordstrom—excellent distribution segmentation. The third P, promotion, is actually quite curious because L'Oreal does most of the advertising and has many expensive models who represent the product line. Lancome, on the other hand, has very limited advertising (mostly print, hardly ever television) and has only one official spokesmodel to represent the entire line.

Based on true cost-plus pricing, perhaps CPAs would price Lancome at $10 (because of the compact and the mirror and one extra brush). Perhaps some would suggest $15. Few would be bold enough to price it at a $30 differential.

Airlines—Leaders in the Art of Price Discrimination

Once the airlines were placed into open competition by the Airline Deregulation Act in the late 1970s, pricing decisions were no longer set by government fiat. Southwest Airlines perfected a two-tier pricing system—peak and off-peak—that basically applied the economics of price elasticity to passenger flight, and charged passengers based upon their price sensitivity to a given fare. Other airlines soon followed, and the pricing of tickets became very sophisticated, not to mention complicated as the United States airline industry changes its prices 12 million times a day.

A fascinating book by Robert G. Cross, *Revenue Management*, candidly reveals the secrets of airline pricing. Cross, a lawyer, accepted a position in the legal department of Delta Air Lines at the time of airline deregulation. In the mid 1980s, he found himself in the marketing division in a "free-formed position designed to identify problems and new opportunities on the marketing side."

He explains that airline performance is measured by two basic standards:

1. Yield—the amount of money the airline gets per passenger mile

2. Load—the percentage of seats filled by paying passengers

Cross estimated that if Delta were simply discounting one seat unnecessarily on every flight, it would cost the company *52 million dollars in annual revenue*. Delta operates approximately 1,500 daily flights for a total of 86 million seats on an annual basis. Here is the dilemma Cross faced in looking into Delta's pricing policies:

> Some flights that had been loaded with discount seats sold out well in advance of the departure. But on these flights, Delta would also turn away significant last-minute, full-fare traffic. This added up to a lot of lost revenue. Also, on numerous occasions we had severely limited discount fares and ended up sending flights out with empty seats that could have been filled with discount passengers . . . . I estimated that Delta was leaving as much as 200 million dollars a year on the table, just from misallocating discount seat availability on its flights. This number was so mind-boggling, I didn't dare tell anyone. No one would have believed it!
>
> In one year's time, Delta realized an incremental revenue gain of *$300 million* solely from the new seat inventory control process. This 300 million dollars accounted for half the 600 million dollar turnaround Delta reported in fiscal 1984 (Cross, 1997: 42, 45).

Have you ever noticed that you can sit next to someone on an airplane who paid five times more than what you did? Does it cost the airline any more (or less) to fly that passenger than to fly you? Does it cost the airline four to eight times more to fly a first-class passenger? Oh, sure, they give you edible food, Starbucks coffee, miniature drinks, and a Mrs. Fields cookie, but could that possibly justify the price differential between first class and coach fare? One passenger made the observation that he recently had flown to Europe first-class, and all of the passengers were reading hardcover books. Coincidence?

How do the airlines identify the business traveler and the leisure traveler? They do it by determining when you are booking your ticket—the closer you get to the flight, the less price- sensitive you are because you need to go, no matter what—and if you are laying over Saturday night. If you are not, statistically, you are a businessperson and chances are you are not paying for your ticket anyway (remember Category III from Chapter 4, spending someone else's money on yourself), and thus you will be charged a premium. This is precisely how Delta derives 60 percent of its profits from 6 percent of its [business] passengers.

The lessons here are many, but perhaps the biggest one is the declining importance of the demographics and psychographics of your customers. In the 1960s, marketing managers paid a lot of attention to segregating their customers based on demographics—income, race, neighborhood, gender, etc. This is well and good for narrowing target markets. Then in the early 1970s, an article was written asking if you would treat Tricia Nixon Cox the same as Grace Slick (former lead singer with Jefferson Starship). Demographically, these two ladies (at the time) were indistinguishable— both were 25–34 years old, family size of three, urban residents, and college educated. Psychographics opened up a whole new way of thinking about consumer behavior, and many firms started to pay attention to it.

Demographics and psychographics play an important role in pricing professional services. Think of the former as shedding light on the customer's *ability* to pay, and the latter as indicating the customer's *willingness* to pay. But pricing is more complicated than that. For instance, a customer who is buying a ticket for a business trip may not be at all price-sensitive about airfare. He may wait until close to the trip to call for fares and will put very little effort into trying to find a bargain rate. But when this customer flies on vacation, he will stay up until 3:00 a.m. trying to get one of the $99 special rates on Southwest Airlines. Demographically and psychographically, the customer is the same person but his approach to buying tickets is not consistent.

The final lesson with respect to the examples presented and how they relate to pricing your firm's professional services is this: *Price on the margin.*

The margin is what happens next. Everyone lives on the margin. Life itself is a marginal adventure. It really doesn't much matter what you did yesterday, what counts is what you do next, i.e., on the margin. When you price on the margin, what you charged in the past for the same service to another customer, or even, perhaps what you charged in the past to this customer, does not matter. *Measure that customer's demand elasticity at that time, for that particular service, one service at a time, every time.* Don't let the past guide your marginal pricing decisions, and don't let your cost influence your price (except as a minimum). If you begin to price in this manner, you will be surprised how many opportunities arise for you to climb up the Value Curve, even with a so-called commodity service.

How Much Money Is Your Firm Leaving on the Table?

You can think of your firm as an airplane—you have first-class customers, business-fare customers, and coach customers. How do you identify them? If you cannot identify what your customers are willing and able to pay for a given service (and hourly billing will not help you), you are leaving between **20 and 50 percent** of your *gross* revenue on the table.

Last year, I received a referral from an attorney who was working on the estate of one of his deceased customers. The decedent hadn't filed his last three year's income tax returns. To get duplicate 1099s and other records meant tracking down the third parties. I proceeded to file the returns, get the penalties waived, etc. The time came for the U.S. Income Tax Return for Estates and Trusts (Form 1041) to be filed (no Form 706 was required as the estate was less than $600,000). I was not going to be in town very much over the following two months, as I would be away teaching seminars and consulting. A CPA friend referred me to someone who would do this work for me. I sent her the information and a letter asking her to get back to me with a fixed price.

A week later she called and said she got the material, and the return would be no problem to prepare. She also said she had received a flyer listing the three courses I would be teaching, and she thought the Value Pricing course looked interesting. She quoted her fixed price for the job as $500 (the tax return was relatively simple and no longer than a four-hour project). When she said this, I knew I had just made $1,500, because I charged my customer $2,000 for the return. Had she asked more questions, she would have quickly discovered that I was not very price-sensitive. In fact, she possessed the one piece of information that should have tipped her off: My schedule of classes for the next several months (18 in all).

Had she priced on the margin, rather than simply multiplying her rate times hours, she would have asked herself why I came to her in the first place (either I do not have the expertise or the time to do the work). Second, she knew that I made my money filing the prior three year's tax returns, and this return was more of a nuisance to me than anything. Third, she could have asked what I was willing to pay, which was up to $2,000.

This sad story is an example of how CPAs underprice their services. In my seminars, I pick one person, give him or her the facts as outlined above (including the flyer showing all the dates I would be away from my office), and send that person out of the room with instructions to return in five minutes, ask me anything, and quote me a price. While the CPA is out of the room, I bet the class that he or she won't even consider the fact that I'm out of the office so many days, and that the CPA won't quote me a price higher than $1,000. I have yet to lose. The participants come back and ask questions such as: "When does this need to be completed?" "Who is signing the return?" "Will you refer them other work?" When the participants are asked what was learned from the flyer, the response is usually, "Nothing, except that you teach three courses." Other savvy businesspeople would consider other factors, but CPAs are so focused on hours spent, rather than on value delivered, that they miss many opportunities to capture the consumer surplus.

The Use of Knowledge in Society

Friedrich A. Hayek, a Nobel Prize winner and perhaps one of the best economists of the twentieth century, addressed the American Economic Association in 1945 on the occasion of his retirement as its president. The title of his address was "The Use of Knowledge in Society," wherein he called attention to the important social role of prices as carriers of information and contrasted this knowledge with so-called scientific knowledge. In this address he articulated the theoretical justification for price discrimination, whereby firms can take advantage of "special knowledge of circumstances of the fleeting moment not known" to their competitors:

> Today it is almost heresy to suggest that scientific knowledge
> is not the sum of all knowledge. But a little reflection will

show that there is beyond question a body of very important but unorganized knowledge which cannot possibly be called scientific in the sense of knowledge of general rules: the knowledge of the particular circumstances of time and place. It is with respect to this that practically every individual has some advantage over all others in that he possesses unique information of which beneficial use might be made, but of which use can be made only if the decisions depending on it are left to him or are made with his active cooperation. To know of and put to use a machine not fully employed, or somebody's skill which could be better utilized, or to be aware of a surplus stock which can be drawn upon during an interruption of supplies, is socially quite as useful as the knowledge of better alternative techniques. And the shipper who earns his living from using otherwise empty or half-filled journeys of tramp-steamers, or the estate agent whose whole knowledge is almost exclusively one of temporary opportunities, or the *arbitrageur* who gains from local differences of commodity prices, are all performing eminently useful functions based on special knowledge of circumstances of the fleeting moment not known to others [Emphasis in original].

It is a curious fact that this sort of knowledge should today be generally regarded with a kind of contempt, and that anyone who by such knowledge gains an advantage over somebody better equipped with theoretical or technical knowledge is thought to have acted almost disreputably. To gain an advantage from better knowledge of facilities of communication or transport is sometimes regarded as almost dishonest, although it is quite as important that society make use of the best opportunities in this respect as in using the latest scientific discoveries (Hayek, 1945: 521–22).

This observation has far-reaching implications for the pricing policies of for-profit entities. What Hayek is basically saying is that it is perfectly normal—and beneficial—for firms to take into account special circumstances in order to provide the most value, and hence receive the highest price, in the delivery of its services.

A lot of the knowledge that exists in the economy today is so-called tacit knowledge—that is, knowledge that is specific to time, place, and circumstance. Travelers in unfamiliar cities will befriend a local in order to discover good restaurants, sight-seeing locations, etc. Think of the advantage a golfer has who has played on the course many times and is said to have "local knowledge."

Summary and Conclusions

The economic way of explaining human behavior has many lessons to teach the willing student. The fact that management gurus, consultants, and members of the professions ignore economics as some sort of ivory tower babbling is negligence at best, malpractice at worst. There is simply no better profession to look to for explaining how and why prices are set the way they are, and that is the reason for this theoretical exploration of the world through the economist's paradigm.

Now that you possess the paradigm of the economist, observe how the consumer surplus is being captured by using price discrimination. Once you start looking for the many creative ways in which other businesses engage in price discrimination, you soon discover it is a ubiquitous practice.

How do professional firms use this theory? How do they identify and segregate different customers to obtain a portion of the consumer surplus? What pricing methods help them achieve this goal? The short answer is that professionals have not paid conscious attention to these theories, and their pricing method—hourly billing—offers absolutely no guidance in capturing the consumer surplus. An understanding of the genesis of hourly billing, discussed in the next chapter, will help you to understand how professionals were led to price in this manner.

6 THE GENESIS OF HOURLY BILLING

Custom is the whole of equity for the sole reason that it is accepted.
That is the mystical basis of its authority. Whoever tries to trace this
authority back to its origin, destroys it.

—Blaise Pascal, *Pensées*

You can tell a lot about a culture by the way it views time. Anthropologist Edward Hall labeled rules of social time the "silent language." The pace of our lives determines our views about the passage of time. J. T. Fraser, the founder of the International Society for the Study of Time summed it up well: "Tell me what to think of time, and I shall know what to think of you" (Levine, 1997: XV, XIX).

Robert Levine points out in his fascinating book, *A Geography of Time*, that before the first mechanical clocks had been invented, the idea of coordinating people's activities was almost impossible. Appointments usually took place at dawn. "It is no coincidence that, historically, so many important events occurred at sunrise—duels, battles, meetings" (ibid., 60).

The first known mechanical timepieces appeared in Europe in the fourteenth century. These clocks had a specific purpose: "to inform pious monks when it was time to pray" (ibid., 56). Throughout history, clocks have come progressively closer to the person. We have progressed from the public clocks of the Middle Ages to clocks inside the home to pocket watches to those attached to our bodies. The wristwatch appeared around 1850 (referred to by some as "the handcuff of our time"). In fact, some would argue that it is the clock, not the steam engine, which is the key machine of the industrial age. Active economies all over the world place great emphasis on time, and economics certainly drives the pace and tempo of modern life.

> As proof of this, it was the railroads that exerted pressure to coordinate time zones because as late as the 1860s, the United States alone had approximately 70 different time zones. In 1883, the railroads established the four time zones used in the country today. In 1918, the federal government codified these

time zones into law. It's also interesting to note that IBM initially sold time clocks in order to "save money, enforce discipline and add to the productive time" (ibid., 68).

The Labor Theory of Value

Ideas have consequences. As John Maynard Keynes wrote in the final passage of the *General Theory*:

> The ideas of economists and political philosophers, both when they are right and when they are wrong, are more powerful than is commonly understood. Indeed, the world is ruled by little else. Practical men, who believe themselves to be quite exempt from any intellectual influences, are usually the slaves of some defunct economist. Madmen in authority, who hear voices in the air, are distilling their frenzy from some academic scribbler of a few years back. . . . Soon or late, it is ideas, not vested interests, which are dangerous for good or evil (Buchholz, 1989: 219).

1998 was the 150th anniversary of an idea that changed the history of civilization and has affected the lives of billions of people. For over a century, it was the leading intellectual paradigm on several continents and commanded an enormous amount of influence on the destiny of nations.

The Communist Manifesto, the famous revolutionary treatise published in 1848 by Karl Marx and Friedrich Engels, still wields considerable power over the world's political systems and even over the professional's pricing strategies.

Marx is far from dead. Even though Marxist ideology and theory has been thoroughly repudiated by empirical evidence, we still pay him the ultimate compliment: His ideas are so deeply ingrained into our value paradigm that we don't even notice them, let alone analyze their validity. In the nineteenth century, Marx posited a definition of value that has been subsequently called the "labor theory of value." In its simplest form it says that the price of an item is determined by the amount of labor used in its production. This theory is so deeply ingrained that it is essential to explore it somewhat at length, in order to prove its speciousness. Here is how Marx explained his labor theory of value in *Value, Price and Profit*, published in 1865:

A commodity has a *value*, because it is a *crystallization of social labour*. The *greatness* of its value, or its *relative* value, depends upon the greater or less amount of that social substance contained in it; that is to say, on the relative mass of labour necessary for its production. The *relative values of commodities* are, therefore, determined by the *respective quantities or amounts of labour, worked up, realized, fixed in them.* The *correlative* quantities of commodities which can be produced in the *same time of labour* are *equal* [Emphasis in original] (Marx, 1995: 31).

This sounds reasonable, and in fact this misconception deceived many great economists, such as Adam Smith and David Ricardo. It is not uncommon throughout history to measure the value of a product or service as a function of labor time. The word *acre* in medieval English meant the amount of land that could be ploughed in one day.

The problem with the labor theory of value is that it does not comport with human behavior. It fails to explain how land or raw materials have value, since they contain no labor input. The Army, for instance, can order soldiers to dig trenches and refill them, day after day, which is precisely why there is no such thing as unemployment in the Army (or in former Marxist countries, for that matter). But certainly, in the private marketplace, there must be a demand for a good (or service) in order for it to possess any value whatsoever.

Taken to its extreme, the labor theory of value would mean that countries that work longer and harder should have higher standards of living. This is demonstrably false, since China should have the highest standard of living—given its large amount of labor hours available. In fact, what we see throughout the world is that countries with less labor input and more entrepreneurship have vastly higher standards of living, including shorter hours for workers.

If the labor theory of value was correct, a diamond found in a mine would be of no greater value than a rock found right next to it, since each took an equal amount of "billable hours" to locate. Yet how many rocks do you see in your local mall's jewelry store display cases?

Look around your office. Do you have any pictures of your spouse, family, or friends? Under the labor theory of value, someone should, theoretically, be able to replace each one of those pictures with a picture of a perfect stranger. The value of the strangers' pictures should be the same as your original pictures, because the new pictures most likely took the same amount of "billable hours" to produce.

When you go to lunch today, perhaps you'll have pizza. Under the labor theory of value, you must necessarily value the fifteenth slice just as much as you valued the first, since each took the same amount of "billable hours" to produce. The labor theory of value doesn't take into account the well-established law of diminishing marginal utility, which states that the value to the customer declines with additional consumption of the good in question.

Marx tried to circumvent these dilemmas by proclaiming that only "socially necessary labor" creates value:

> It might seem that if the value of a commodity is determined by the *quantity of labour bestowed upon its production*, the lazier a man, or the clumsier a man, the more valuable his commodity, because the greater the time of labour required for finishing the commodity. This, however, would be a sad mistake. You will recollect that I used the word "social labour," and many points are involved in this qualification of "social." In saying that the value of a commodity is determined by the *quantity of labour* worked up or crystallized in it, we mean *the quantity of labour necessary* for its production in a given state of society, under certain social average conditions of production, with a given social average intensity, and average skill of the labour employed.
>
> If then the quantity of socially necessary labour realized in commodities regulates their exchangeable values, every increase in the quantity of labour wanted for the production of a commodity must augment its value, as every diminution must lower it [Emphasis in original] (ibid., 33–34).

How does one determine what is "socially necessary"? That is where the consumer enters the theory, and in a competitive market it is ultimately the consumer who determines value—bringing Marx right back to the values of the free market which he so vehemently abhorred. Marx derived his definition of value from the assumption that there must be an equality in two goods which are exchanged—namely, labor hours. But the nature of exchange is the exact opposite—it is based on an inequality in the subjective value of the good received and the good exchanged. In order for any transaction to take place, both the buyer and the seller must profit from the exchange, and receive more value—in their perception—than what they are giving up. Were this not so, we could simply exchange five dollar bills with each other and achieve a Marxian Utopia.

Marx claimed that the number of hours of "socially necessary working time" that goes into the production of a commodity determines its comparative value in the marketplace, and any profit that goes to an employer above his payroll is in effect stolen from his "exploited" workers. One is left to the conclusion that the true Marxian exploitation is the exploitation of people's misunderstanding of economics. Perhaps this is why President Ronald Reagan made this statement in September 25, 1987: "How do you tell a Communist? Well, it's someone who reads Marx and Lenin. And how do you tell an anti-Communist? It's someone who understands Marx and Lenin."

In all fairness, it must be stated that even Adam Smith posited his own false theory of value, and it too has held sway over a large majority of business people. Smith's "cost of production" theory basically said that all of the costs of production—including depreciation of equipment, interest, and Marx's dreaded profit—determined the value of a commodity in the marketplace. The flaw in this theory is that "costs of production" are also prices, and reflect their own calculus of value. This cost-plus pricing mentality can lead to serious errors in Value Pricing goods and services because it ignores the external value to the customer.

The Correct Theory of Value

The alternative to an incorrect theory is not to do away with the theory and simply rely on "common sense." The alternative to an *incorrect* theory is a *correct* theory. All learning starts with theory. The alternative to the labor theory of value is the theory that value is subjective—goods and services have no inherent value but are valuable only to the extent that there is a valuer desiring them.

The subjective theory of value was well understood by both the Spanish Scholastics and the French laissez-faire school of economic thought. The theory was widely advanced, and became accepted as the way the world works, by the Austrian school of economics, in the tradition of Eugene von Bohm-Bawerk, Carl Menger, Ludwig von Mises, and F. A. Hayek.

Ever since Ben Franklin wrote, "Time is money," professionals have taken this statement literally, believing that time is value. However, effort—that is, hours spent—emphatically does not equate with value. Results are what counts to the customer. Value is in the eye of the beholder, not the labor time of the seller. There is no doubt that time is a nonrenewable, precious resource. But even resources are useless until a purpose is found for them that people will value. Oil, for example, was worthless until man invented the combustion engine.

Why the Professions Adopted Hourly Billing

Why did the professions adopt pricing based upon the hour? What is the historical context in which the practice arose? Old habits die hard, but understanding how the habit started in the first place is imperative before it can be replaced with a better practice. Replacement is easier if the original circumstances for adopting the habit no longer exist.

Hourly billing is a practice that dates back to the 1940s, when large Wall Street law firms adopted time sheets. The practice was advocated by business school graduates who entered the professions conversant in cost-accounting techniques used by the railroads, textile, chemical, and auto industries.

The most comprehensive history of the billable hour is William G. Ross' *The Honest Hour: The Ethics of Time-Based Billing by Attorneys*. Here is what Ross says with respect to the antecedents of time-based billing:

> During the 1950s and early 1960s, various studies indicated that attorney compensation was failing to keep pace with inflation and was lagging behind that of other professionals, particularly physicians. Starting as early as the 1940s, management experts concluded from various studies that lawyers who kept time records earned more than attorneys who did not. Management experts advised lawyers to raise their compensation by selecting a target annual salary and dividing that figure by the number of hours that they could bill to a client during a year and factoring in overhead costs in order to arrive at an hourly billing rate.

Although many commentators have suggested that time-based billing dates from 1960s, it was actually being used by many attorneys during the previous decade. While even so large a firm as New York's Shearman and Sterling did not keep time records until 1945, timekeeping had become much more common by the 1950s than is now usually supposed.

Between the 1950s and the middle 1970s, management experts extolled the benefits of timekeeping and exhorted law firms to institute time-based billings. As one commentator exclaimed in 1960, "lawyers who *do* keep personal time records have a *net* income which is almost equal to the *gross* income of lawyers who *do not* keep time records. Need more be said!" [Emphasis in original] (Ross, 1996: 16–17)

Indeed, what better motivation existed than the opportunity to make more money with the hourly billing method?

Prior to billing by the hour, attorneys (and CPAs) charged fixed rates for everything they did. According to Ross:

During the late 1930s and 1940s, more and more state and local bar associations adopted fee schedules because they provided a more objective means for attorneys to justify their fees to clients. Left to their own devices, many attorneys were uncertain about how to charge clients or were embarrassed to charge for minor work or to request a reasonable compensation for their services. Fee schedules gave lawyers the courage to charge higher fees. . . . By the 1950s, fee schedules existed in virtually every state.

Fee schedules were not obligatory, since bar associations recognized that mandatory fees might run afoul of the antitrust laws and that such fees would fail to take account of the special expertise of individual attorneys (ibid., 14–15).

With fixed fees, billing was an *art*—not the administrative task hourly billing ultimately turned it into. The professional always asked, "What results have we achieved?" and "What is the value to the customer?" That is a much more daunting task than merely multiplying hours spent by an arbitrary rate and cranking out a bill. During the 1950s and 1960s, when the management experts were extolling the virtues of hourly billing, studies put out by the American Bar Association also documented other discoveries besides the one that lawyers who tracked their time made more than those who didn't that seemed to lend even more support to hourly billing. For example, the studies claimed that customers valued *efforts* over *results*. What better way to document every minute of effort than the time sheet?

In fact, this effort vs. results debate continues to this day. One of the primary reasons that lawyers will bill for every single fax, copy, phone call, and quarter hour is to convince the customer of all the effort expended on his behalf. In his book *How to Draft Bills Clients Rush to Pay*, J. Harris Morgan advocates that lawyers follow this practice, and he cites a 1960 Prentice–Hall Missouri Motivational Study: ". . . 47 percent of the respondents listed effort as the most important single element in setting a fee and creating a bill." Morgan added: "The clients said that effort is the most important element in a lawyer's bill! No subsequent research has disproved this conclusion" (Morgan, 1995: 2).

Hourly billing also converted major overhead costs into "profit centers" allowing firms to leverage their capital and human investments. For instance, paralegal salaries, fax machines, word processing, and copies could all be charged out at a multiple of their cost, adding to the firm's bottom line. This was one reason beginning salaries for Ivy League law school graduates increased so much in the late 1980s, up to around $80,000. The firms could simply pass the cost through to the customer in terms of marking up the hourly rate of the new associate, usually by a factor of three to five times their cost.

Another factor that accelerated the adoption of hourly billing by the professions was the computer. It became very easy to input time sheets and have the computer crunch out the invoice, freeing up the professional's time to bill even more hours.

The final nail in the coffin of fixed fee pricing was the Supreme Court's decision in 1975 that the fee schedules published by the ABA and local courts violated the Sherman Antitrust Act, in *Goldfarb v. Virginia State Bar*, 421 U.S. 773 (1975), *rehearing denied*, 423 U.S. 886 (1975). But by then, both the legal and the accounting professions billed predominantly by the hour.

What buried the coffin was the *Bates* decision, as explained in *Win-Win Billing Strategies: Alternatives That Satisfy Your Clients and You*, the second book published by the ABA Section of Law Practice Management:

Until the late 1970s, most lawyers gave little thought to the pricing of their services. This lack of concern stemmed in part from the prosperity that many lawyers enjoyed and the lack of competition.

To understand why the concept of pricing is new and sometimes difficult for lawyers to understand, it is helpful to review the nature of the legal profession before the landmark United States Supreme Court decision in *Bates & O'Steen v. State Bar of Arizona*, 433 U.S. 350 (1977), which enabled lawyers to market legal services. [In the past], the fees lawyers charged their clients were determined by minimum-fee schedules authorized by state and local bar associations and some courts. Because marketing was restricted before the *Bates* decision, most clients were unaware of the scope, availability, and cost of legal services (Reed, 1992: 31).

The Customer's Role in the Adoption of Hourly Billing

What was the customer's role in the shift from fixed-fee to hourly billing? Did customers ask for hourly billing or was it imposed on them because the professions enjoyed a seller's market? The opinions on this point vary.

Ross quotes Professor Herbert M. Kritzer of the University of Wisconsin Law School, who contends:

> The current form of hourly billing was not "foisted off onto an unsuspecting business community by a bunch of sharp-eyed lawyers" but rather "probably results largely from the accounting culture, produced by elite business schools, that came to dominate the senior management circles of the American corporations." Kritzer explains that "as the offices of corporate general counsel became professionalized (in a business sense, not a legal sense), there was a need to apply business principles to their operation, including the purchase of outside services. Hours and rates could be easily measured and compared, and general counsel began to demand that

their outside law firms provide detailed bills with this information" (Ross, 1996: 21).

Perhaps since all lawyers started to bill by the hour, the customer began to use hours as a basis for comparing one firm to another, and historical revisionists assume that the customer demanded it be done this way. Another plausible explanation for the shift to hourly billing is that customers were complaining about the high price of legal services, under the minimum fee schedules and prior to the 1975 Supreme Court decision ruling them unconstitutional, and embraced hourly billing as a consumer-protection measure, thinking they would be better off. The flaw in this argument is that hourly billing started in the 1950s, well before the Supreme Court ruling.

Is Hourly Billing a Cost-Accounting Tool?

What was ignored by all of the attorneys was that tracking one's time was originally intended to be a *cost-accounting* tool, not a *pricing* method. Timekeeping was viewed as a guideline that would allow a firm to measure the *profitability* of an engagement, not as the means of *pricing* that engagement. The time sheet was originally developed to control the "inventory" of the professional, but since hourly billing became endemic, it *became* the inventory. The focus changed from how much value a professional added to how many hours were spent. It was the ultimate quantification of Abraham Lincoln's utterance: "Time is an attorney's stock in trade." Mary Ann Altman, a lawyer and principal in the consulting firm of Altman & Weil, discusses this in *Beyond the Billable Hour: An Anthology of Alternative Billing Methods*, published by the ABA, Section of Economics of Law Practice (one of three seminal books published by the ABA on the death of the billable hour):

> Because I was involved personally in the introduction of time records to the legal profession approximately thirty years ago, I can attest to the fact that one of the reasons that time records were instituted originally was to determine the cost of providing legal services. At that time, lawyers had, for many decades, produced bills to clients that were based on the value of the services rather than on the time involved,

although time certainly was a mental factor in determining value. Once time records became available to lawyers, lawyers quickly began to use these time records as billing, rather than as a cost-accounting tool. It was much easier to ask the bookkeeping department to multiply the time record by a dollar factor and prepare a bill than it was for the lawyer to exercise judgment in a determination of the value of the case (Reed, 1989: 11).

When professionals today are asked to consider eliminating time sheets from their firms, most of them protest that they wouldn't know whether or not they were making money on any one engagement. This is a valid point, but not as valid as you may, at first, think. The problem with the current "standard rates" is that the "desired net income" is loaded on top of the overhead amount, then divided by expected billable hours. That is not *cost accounting*, but *profit forecasting*, and it is an especially egregious error for CPAs who, for all their fastidiousness when it comes to GAAP and attesting to financial statements, should know better. This subject will be explored in greater depth in Chapter 7.

Summary and Conclusions

In the years since hourly billing was adopted, the Berlin Wall has fallen, the Soviet Union has imploded, China has embraced free markets and taken back Hong Kong, and the personal computer and the Internet have changed the world. Amidst all of this tumultuous change, CPAs (and to a lesser extent, attorneys) still price by the hour.

The market has changed. Customers are demanding fixed prices, set up front, from their attorneys and accountants. The inside legal counsel in a number of American corporations will no longer accept hourly billing from their outside attorneys. Ford Motor Company, for example, demands fixed price agreements with all of their outside counsel. Wal-Mart is at 60 percent and is moving towards 100 percent as well. As Jay D. Logel, In-House Counsel for Ford Motor Company, said at an ABA seminar titled *Alternative Billing: The Sequel*, "Billable hours don't win lawsuits." That basically sums up the attitude of today's customer with respect to the Almighty Hour and is the reason that the method, in the law profession, for all practical purposes, is already dead. And just as CPAs followed attorneys into the method, lagging by about five years or so, it is their destiny to follow the attorneys right back out of it.

7 THE DELETERIOUS EFFECTS OF HOURLY BILLING

Custom doth make dotards of us all.

—Thomas Carlyle, *Sartor Resartus, III,* 1836

A foolish consistency is the hobgoblin of little minds.

—Ralph Waldo Emerson

The last chapter explored the fallacy of Karl Marx's labor theory of value and how it fails to explain human behavior in the real world. The reader is justified in asking the following questions: If people are supposedly rational—the assumption of rationality as discussed in Chapter 5 is the bedrock assumption of economists—why is it that intelligent members of various professions have continued to apply the wrong theory to the value of their services? Doesn't this disprove the economist's assumption of rationality? If Marxism is an incorrect theory at the macroeconomic level, what are the ramifications of implementing the incorrect theory at the microeconomic level—that is, in the professional service firm?

The fact that hourly billing is so deeply entrenched and has been widely used for decades proves that it has some advantages. This is a case of cognitive dissonance—two completely contradictory ideas exist at the same time in one's mind. The only way to eradicate this paradox is to prove that hourly billing is a rational policy. Therefore, before showing that the disadvantages exceed the advantages, this chapter will explore what is right about hourly billing and why it is a rational pricing policy for the professional.

The Advantages of Hourly Billing

Hourly Billing Is a Relatively Easy and Efficient Pricing Method

Hourly billing is easy and efficient and can be handled simply with an appropriate software program that will prepare bills, generate reports, and calculate work-in-progress and realization rates, all with minimal partner and manager time. Administrative staff usually is responsible for this task and that allows the professional staff to take care of what is more important—customer relations. This was one of the major reasons firms began using the method, especially once the computer was introduced. What is proposed in this book—customized pricing—is more complex and requires more thought, creativity, and interaction with the customer. More attention is paid to value created rather than to hours spent, and this attention must come from those who have the relationship with the customer—the professional staff, not the administrative staff.

Richard C. Reed, in *Billing Innovations*, discusses what may become a new career in the law firm: "the position of estimator, a specialist who will have expertise in cost accounting and in determining the price to be charged." (Reed, 1996: 140) This would be, however, a grave mistake. The person best equipped to set a price is the one who is in charge of the relationship. From the customer's perspective, an estimator has no perceived value. However, customers see enormous value in the relationship with their attorney or CPA.

Sometimes the Customer Demands Hourly Billing

No doubt, some customers demand to be billed by the hour, or at the least demand to know how many hours a given task will take the firm, especially alumni of accounting and law firms who now work in private industry. It is also true that sometimes a customer just wants to buy your time (perhaps to ask a multitude of questions) and the only benchmark of value in that instance is the time spent. This is not the type of customer you want to do business with, since the customer really has no idea of the value you are providing. Nevertheless, sometimes it may be necessary to price according to time spent.

Hourly Billing Documents Effort in Case of Litigation

In a lawsuit, the attorneys are undoubtedly going to want to see time reports to support the tasks performed, and if you believe this is a serious concern, then by all means document the hours for the file. However, this does *not* preclude your firm from pricing its services on an alternative basis, and as long as you have an explicit agreement with the customer (preferably in writing) of the price being charged and the services being performed, then the only place hours might be logged is in the file.

Further, one could produce the three seminal books published by the ABA which encourage attorneys to use alternative pricing methods (a.k.a. Value Pricing or Value Billing) in a court of law to justify why hours were not the criteria for pricing. If firms were run under the constant assumption that they were going to be sued, they would not get anything accomplished. Slowly, but surely, the rules of the game are changing, and hours are becoming superfluous in the pricing of professional services. Eventually Value Pricing will be common practice in the professions, and the threat of litigation as justification for tracking every minute will wane.

Hourly Billing Is a Cost-Accounting Tool

This is probably the single biggest advantage of hourly billing. People wonder, "If you did not keep time reports, how would you know if you are making money on a particular job? How would you measure the productivity of your staff?" These are valid questions that go right to the heart of why lawyers began tracking time back in the 1950s—to measure *efficiency* and *profitability*. However, as mentioned earlier, what started as a method to control and measure the inventory (i.e., the professional's time) *became* the inventory. The other problem with the cost-accounting defense is that hourly billing isn't really about cost-accounting, but rather *profit-forecasting*, as it includes the "desired net income" of the owners of the firm in the cost-plus formula. Other businesses, except for regulated utilities and the post office, do not use the cost-plus formula to set their prices. Examine your manufacturing customer's books, and ask the CEO or CFO how costs are allocated, or how they price their products. It is probably not based solely on cost-plus accounting.

Does this mean the elimination of time sheets from your firm? Yes. And no. I have benchmarked with firms anywhere in size from five to 30 who do not keep time sheets at all. The partners couldn't tell you how many hours they billed, nor could the staff, nor does anyone care. These firms are the models to emulate since they are making more money by pricing smarter than firms with time sheets.

However, the cause and effect should not be confused. It is not true that if you eliminate your time sheets you will become more profitable. In fact, the causation runs in the opposite direction. These firms eliminated their time sheets *because* they became profitable as a result of Value Pricing. When partners in these firms are asked how they know if they are making money, they all respond with the same answer, "We look at our income statement." Managing from the income statement by looking at cost of labor as a percentage of gross revenue is a different mindset from poring over hourly time reports.

I have also benchmarked with firms that retain their time and billing program, but they have converted it into a true *cost-accounting system*, rather than a *pricing* method. The attorneys who began tracking their time made more money in net income than those who didn't, but they were using the tracking solely for cost-accounting purposes, *not* as a pricing method.

This topic will be discussed in more detail in the section later in this chapter on the deleterious effects of hourly billing. Suffice it to say that tracking hours can be a useful cost-accounting tool.

Hourly Billing Transfers Risk to the Customer

This advantage is truly a double-edge sword, for while the professional prefers that the risk be with the customer, which is what happens with hourly billing, the customer prefers the exact opposite. For the professional, however, this advantage is the answer to the question of why hourly billing is rational.

With hourly billing, generally the customer must bear the entire risk of the job going over budget, or of unforeseen circumstances arising. This comforts CPAs, because at least they are assured of receiving the "standard rate." CPAs have paid a reverse risk premium to the customer, the customer assumes the risk, and CPAs will only ask for their hourly rate; no more, no less.

This is quite rational, if you are risk adverse, and many professionals are. It puts a nice, comfortable floor beneath professionals, because a decent net income is inserted into the cost-plus formula. But in exchange for the comfort of this floor, professionals have created an artificial ceiling, and they cannot seem to rise above it. This is demonstrated by the fact that average realization rates in CPA firms across the country are between 70 and 95 percent of the standard rate.

Another example of removal of risk is the practice of labor unions. Talk with union members, and you quickly discover that they credit the union for their standard of living. Certainly, they are paid an above-market wage (Milton Friedman, again, has proved this point) and receive good benefits, a healthy pension, and generous time off. But have you ever met a wealthy rank-and-file union member? The trade-off they made for this union compensation package is an artificial ceiling that they can never rise above, at least not while employed in a union job. Seniority and other restrictions limit their potential.

Profits come from *risk*. No risk, no reward. The entrepreneur (a French word meaning "undertaker") is society's perennial risk taker. Bill Gates, Larry Ellison, and other members of Forbes 400 did not become wealthy by charging hourly rates. Some entrepreneurs win, some lose, but any profits are the result of giving to others, filling their needs first. A professional puts his fate into the hands of others—customers—and provides them with service that is so good they willingly pay a profit in recognition of what is being done for them.

A business organization that doesn't take risks is doomed to mediocrity, and perhaps extinction. When risk is transferred to customers, they will implicitly limit the professionals' rewards, for that is how a free market works. The bigger the risk, the greater the reward (and potential failure). By adopting Value Pricing, you assume more risk. However, it's an intelligent and calculated risk, and one that is worth assuming because the gains exceed the losses. In fact, the risk is quite small compared with the rewards. As Peter Drucker pointed out:

> A business always saws off the limb on which it sits; it makes existing risks riskier or creates new ones... Risk is of the essence, and risk making and risk taking constitute the basic function of enterprise... This risk is something quite different from risk in the statistician's probability; it is risk of the unique event, the irreversible qualitative breaking of the pattern (Quoted in Kehrer, 1989: 53).

Drucker is expressing the basic economic theory known as Boehm–Bawerk's Law, which states: "Existing means of production can yield greater economic performance only through greater uncertainty; through taking greater risks" (ibid., 298). Businesses, and CPAs in particular, have very sophisticated means of measuring the costs and benefits of risks, *once they have been taken*. But the risk occurs only *before* the event, and cannot be accurately measured until *after* it has occurred. There is no theory—either in economics or finance—that measures the costs of *not* taking a risk. Yet, it is precisely these losses that cost the business the most.

Risk and uncertainty are the twin banes of human existence. Consider what people will sacrifice to avoid them. Risk avoidance has created a 1.5 trillion dollar worldwide insurance industry. Risk is the reason rental car companies make more from the "collision damage waiver" insurance they sell than from renting cars and why buyers of appliances (e.g., microwaves and stereos) will spend large sums on extended warranties for products that could be replaced more cheaply. Risk causes criminals and prosecutors to plea bargain, each being uncertain as to what a jury is going to do. It even explains why some Americans will eat at McDonald's in France—they are fearful of making a bad choice on a local restaurant, and thus they will settle for the certainty of a known commodity.

Economists estimate that risk and uncertainty cost Americans roughly 575 billion dollars each year. Such costs estimate the amount of money people would give up in order to reduce the following uncertainties: Macroeconomic fluctuations (recessions); job insecurity; retirement uncertainty; and fear of future supply-demand shifts. Economists distinguish between uncertainty and risk in the following manner: An economic decision is "risky" if you can assign a numerical probability to each possible outcome (e.g., 50 percent chance that a coin will come up heads). By contrast, a decision has "uncertain" consequences when you do not know enough even to assign probabilities to the different outcomes (Mandel, 1996: 147).

By linking your fate to your customer's, and sharing in the risk, you will also avail yourself of the opportunity to share in the rewards. That is what free enterprise is all about. As Walter Wriston, former CEO of Citibank, makes clear in his book *Risk and Other Four-Letter Words*:

> It is almost impossible to exaggerate the importance to the general welfare of the willingness of individuals to take a personal risk. The worst thing that can happen to a society, as

to an individual, is to become terrified of uncertainty. Uncertainty is an invitation to innovate, to create; uncertainty is the blank page in the author's typewriter, the granite block before a sculptor, the capital in the hands of an investor, or the problem challenging the inventive mind of a scientist or an engineer. In short, uncertainty is the opportunity to make the world a better place (Wriston, 1987: 230).

The more professionals understand about risk taking, and the better they become at risk analysis, the more it can be minimized. In his exhaustive study of risk, *Against the Gods: The Remarkable Story of Risk*, Peter L. Bernstein explains why risk management plays a vital role in a society's progress:

The ability to define what may happen in the future and to choose among alternatives lies at the heart of contemporary societies. Risk management guides us over a vast range of decision-making, from allocating wealth to safeguarding public health, from waging war to planning a family, from paying insurance premiums to wearing a seatbelt, from planting corn to marketing corn flakes.

Without a command of probability theory and other instruments of risk management, engineers could never have designed the great bridges that span our widest rivers, homes would still be heated by fireplaces or parlor stoves, electric power utilities would not exist, polio would still be maiming children, no airplanes would fly, and space travel would be just a dream (Bernstein, 1996: 2).

Professionals should take greater risks in pursuit of gain. Though hourly billing carries the advantage of placing the risk with the customer, that advantage is really small in comparison with the potential profit made possible when a professional shoulders more of the risk and prices based on value.

This Book Summed Up in Two Words

One day I entered my office and found my partner agitated. He had just finished a telephone conversation with a customer he had been auditing for several months. He had a Fixed Price Agreement with this customer, including the audit, but the customer's books were not in the best of shape, adjustments were mounting, and the Prepared By Customer (PBC) schedules were not tying to the general ledger, all contributing to the audit taking longer than he originally estimated.

He called one of the owners to discuss the situation and was trying to extract a few extra thousand dollars for the cost overruns. He explained to the customer that he had already spent the hours, and the customer replied, "**Hours schmours**." This did not make my partner happy.

The customer was right not to equate hours spent with value. The firm had given him a fixed price and should stick to it. The fact that my partner underestimated the job is really not any of the customer's concern. The moral of the story, and the reason it sums up this book, is that when you and your customer see things differently, *you change*. (Better ways of dealing with cost overruns will be discussed in Chapter 11.) A professional who clings to hourly billing and ignores the psychology of it from the customer's perspective may cause irreparable injury to the health of a firm.

The Disadvantages of Hourly Billing

Here, in no particular order, is a list of the deleterious effects of hourly billing for you to consider.

Hourly Billing Misaligns the Interests of Professional and Customer

Even ardent supporters of hourly billing, such as William G. Ross, will admit that there exists, right from the start, a conflict between the professional's interest and the customer's. In *The Honest Hour*, Ross writes:

> The first step toward more ethical billing practices is for both attorneys and clients to frankly admit the harsh truth that hourly billing creates an inherent conflict of interest between the client's needs for expeditious work and the attorney's desire to bill time. Only by recognizing that this tension tends to create abuses can attorneys begin to cultivate ethical standards for billing (Ross, 1996: 6).

When you make hours important, then the customer is bound to focus on hours. Those professionals caught "padding" time sheets because they believe the value of what they did exceeded the price measured in hours will lose the respect of their customers.

This conflict of interest also exists because in a cost-plus pricing system one way to increase a firm's revenue is to increase its costs. This explains the willingness of law firms to raise beginning associate's salaries in the late 1980s. The cost was passed right through to the customer. Hospitals and defense contractors used to have this perverse incentive as well. The market has changed. Cost-plus pricing is rarely used by hospitals, building contractors, and defense contractors (except for Strategic Defense Initiative work). In fact, cost-plus pricing is really thriving in only three industries: regulated utilities, government-owned operations (Amtrak and the post office), and professional service firms. Probably no one will benchmark the post office to learn world-class customer service. The professions need to turn away from using the same pricing method as the post office and associate with more practical and forward-looking industries.

In an age of corporate downsizing, reengineering, and businesses (and government) trying to do *more with less*, cost-plus pricing is the antithesis of efficiency. Customers are beginning to recognize this, which explains why the Fortune 500 companies, such as Ford Motor Company and Wal-Mart, will not even discuss "billable hours" with their outside counsel, as they no longer want to be the sole risk bearer, but they want their law firms to participate in their uncertainty. The whole objective of the Total Quality Service movement is to become partners with your customers and to link your fate to theirs. This goal is difficult enough to achieve without the added burden of an inherent conflict of interest in how you price your services.

Hourly Billing Focuses on Hours, Not Value

Today's sophisticated customers understand the subjective theory of value; they do not automatically correlate value with billable hours. Remember when online services priced according to the amount of time the customer was connected to the system? Is it any wonder customers devised methods to get the information in the least time possible? Pricing by the time they were connected had no value to the customer because what they were really purchasing—and hence what they valued—was the information.

This would be the equivalent of shoppers trying to minimize the amount of time shopping for a product or trying to maximize the number of products they purchase within a given period of time, neither of which would affect the value of the purchases.

Whenever professionals have to justify price to a customer, they inevitably resort to discussing hours spent. Marketers would never do this, as they always try to create value in the minds of the customer first, and talk price last. By having a billing rate that is anywhere from four to ten times what customers make per hour, you are putting them in a psychological frame of mind to focus on how long it will take you.

Imagine learning from a doctor that you have a condition that is difficult to diagnose, possibly a rare disease, and saying, "Well, doctor, please don't think about my case *too* long and don't consult with your colleagues, since I want to keep the billable hours down."

Richard C. Reed points out in *Billing Innovations:* "If you are buying an automobile, do you really care how much time it took to install the hood of the car?" (Reed, 1996: 103)

If the customers focus on hours, they are constantly trying to calculate whether or not they can afford what you are doing for them and they ignore the value you are providing. The multidimensional value that professionals provide is turned into a one-dimensional, commoditized billing rate. You have to wonder how much of what is referred to as customers being fee resistant is actually the customers simply doubting the value they are asked to pay for, because the professionals have not discussed this aspect of their service.

A few years back, a customer leased me a car as part of my compensation. He reasoned that he wasn't hiring me for my ability to do his tax return, but for my brain power and perspective on his business. He said, "Whose business will you think about every time you get into that car?" He was right—I thought about his problems and opportunities everywhere I drove.

Ultimately, in a free market economy, "all prices and quantities are determined by just two things: the technology available to firms and the tastes of individuals" (Landsburg, 1996: 549). If that is the case, then professionals need to educate the customer regarding the value they provide, including factors such as the resources of their firm, the experience and judgment of their staff, the risk they are assuming, and the convenience they are providing.

Hourly Billing Places the Risk on the Customer

As discussed earlier in this chapter, if you offer your customers fixed prices you will be able to charge a premium because you are reducing their risk. If this sounds counterintuitive, look at the mortgage market. Which commands a higher interest rate, a fixed rate or an adjustable rate mortgage? Surveys conducted by the American Bar Association Section of Litigation's Committee on Corporate Counsel "indicate that most clients are willing to pay a premium in exchange for a predictable fee" (Reed, 1996: 89).

Hourly Billing Fosters a Production Mentality, Not an Entrepreneurial Spirit

Over the years, the professions have lost sight of the all-important question: What did you accomplish? It has been replaced with: How many hours did you bill? Firms have rewarded production, measured in hours, and have been slow to recognize customer service, retention, loyalty, and other yardsticks of long-term profitability. As Ross states in *The Honest Hour*:

> Although associate compensation has increased tenfold during the past thirty years, the billing rates of associates have increased only about fourfold. Since law firm profitability has generally increased rather than fallen, law firms have paid for the higher salaries by increasing billable hours rather than charging higher rates (Ross, 1996: 2).

Hourly billing has the pernicious effect of de-emphasizing marketing, especially at the lower levels of the firm, because the professional doesn't want to forego billable hours, since most compensation plans are based on them. Over time, the professional becomes production oriented, becoming adept at solving problems but lethargic at pursuing opportunities. This is a costly mediocrity, as the professional is simply living off existing skills and not taking any risks in order to become more valuable to customers. Again, Ross sums up this attitude:

> During my nine years of practice in law firms in New York City, I rarely heard a fellow lawyer boast of resolving a

problem, settling a dispute, or developing an elegant legal theory. Instead, I found that all too many attorneys seemed to evaluate their accomplishments solely in terms of the sheer number of hours that they had billed (ibid., 3).

Developing an entrepreneurial culture is the responsibility of the firm's leadership, as staff members do not automatically become outstanding producers simply because they get promoted to the partnership. On the contrary, an entrepreneurial attitude has to be developed in associates from day one, rather than just training for technical competence. As Allan S. Boress points out in his book *Building Entrepreneurial People*:

> Although most colleges today claim to be producing more well-rounded accounting school graduates, I have yet to meet a single person who has taken a course in a School of Accountancy on managing and improving client relationships, managing a CPA firm, or building a practice. This largely one-sided, technically oriented education has prepared accounting graduates for entry-level positions at most CPA firms, but has not prepared them for the real world. It is up to accounting firms to shift new graduates away from total concentration on technical competence (Boress, 1995: 4).

The Almighty Hour is nothing but a hindrance to cultivating this environment.

Hourly Billing Creates a Subsidy System

If all customers are charged the same hourly rate, it is a safe bet that some will be overcharged and others will be undercharged in order to meet hourly quotas. This is true for individual professionals and thus must be true for firms as a whole.

An example of this effect is a tax research project that is billed to one customer for, say, $5,000. If a different customer then has the exact same issue, how much would be billed? Attorneys are still trying to resolve the question. Is a firm justified in charging the second customer $5,000, even if the time spent was only 20 percent of what was billed to the first customer?

If the hours logged were equal to the first customer's billing, one could certainly argue that the first customer underwrote the R&D costs, and the majority of the second customer's bill was pure profit to the firm. If the second customer was charged less than the first, perhaps due to ethical considerations, or a feeling of guilt, then certainly the first customer subsidized the second.

These are the kinds of issues that arise in any pricing method, as good customers will always, to some extent, subsidize poorer (or, more accurately, less valuable) ones. But the subsidy is especially pronounced with hourly billing because it is an internal cost method. If all customers were charged what they perceived as the value of the service, an argument could be made that no one customer is being subsidized. This is not one of hourly billing's more severe consequences, but it certainly has generated its share of ethical arguments within the legal profession. (See the discussion of this issue in Chapter 16.)

Hourly Billing Transmits No Useful Information

One of the most useless pieces of information is everybody's billable hours. It transmits little information of value, except perhaps to separate the "finders" (rainmakers), the "minders" (managers), and the "grinders" (technicians). Far more significance is found in a person's customer service attitude, customer retention (and defection) rates, customer loyalty, profitability and collection, ingenuity, imagination, experience, productivity, efficiency, ability to delegate, mentoring skills, risk taking, and practice development activities—in short, all the virtues necessary to build a successful practice. Billable hours, in and of themselves, shed no light in any of these areas. Consider this scenario:

> Assuming two lawyers within the same firm with identical year-end statistics, how often do firms then go on to measure the relative profitability of those two fee producers? One lawyer's practice may have required a high level of staff support, high-level advance of costs, and delayed collection of fees. The other lawyer, with the same total statistics, may have had substantially lower cost production and hence greater profitability. For the most part, law firms using hourly billing tended to charge an established hourly rate (or possibly more

than one rate) pretty much across the board without regard to differences in cost of production of certain services, including benefits conferred or the exposure to malpractice risks (Reed, 1996: 137).

This is a valid point, and proves that hourly billing rates are not truly a cost-accounting tool. If an outside consultant can enter a firm and make an assessment of its performance without considering billable hours, then the question becomes, What kinds of decisions are being made internally by collecting hourly information? In other words, if it is not the right question to ask from an outside perspective, why is it so important on the inside?

Is it possible that internal measurements are being assembled simply because that's the way it has always been done? Most of the decisions that are made in a professional firm regarding staffing, hiring, firing, productivity, and raises, are based on information that is discovered long before it is seen on an hourly billing report. How many major, profit-enhancing decisions have you made as a result of hourly information? It is considered sacrosanct simply because it is so closely correlated to how professionals price their services. If you begin to price based upon external value, you will soon discover that hours are superfluous. You may come to agree that counting hours is, as Fra Luca Pacioli said in his treatise on double-entry accounting, *De minimis no curat Praetor* "one of the little items that don't contribute knowledge of the business to its owner" (Pacioli, 1494: 47).

Hourly Billing Encourages Hoarding of Hours

Due to compensation, bonuses, and performance reviews being based on billable hours, professionals have a tendency to hoard work to fulfill their hourly quotas. This results in low level work being performed by high level associates, which is terribly inefficient. Just as surgeons should not pierce ears, managers and partners should not spend their time on compliance work that could be more efficiently completed by lower level associates. Effective delegation not only provides lower level associates with the experience and on-the-job training they require, it frees the upper echelon of the firm to focus on offering value-added consulting services, thus moving up the Value Curve.

Hoarding hours also lessens the advantages of a diversified firm by not delegating the work to the person(s) who can most efficaciously complete it. This results in a constant reinventing of the wheel, instead of using systems and procedures based on work that has been done before. The goal of every business is to increase productivity, which means to produce more output with less input. Hoarding hours is the antithesis of this.

Another negative effect of hoarding hours deals with write-offs. Who decides when time should be written off? And whose time is usually discounted? Partners and managers usually decide that write-offs are due to staff inefficiency, and concomitantly compensation and bonuses are reduced, lowering the morale of the staff.

Hourly Billing Focuses on Effort, Not Results

Who buys efforts in the marketplace? One brilliant epiphany that occurs while driving may be worth more to the customer than 1,000 plodding, inefficient hours spent researching and pondering an issue. You may come up with an idea that saves a customer thousands of dollars, and yet you spend only one hour developing the solution. What do you do when it comes to completing the time sheet? Hourly billing simply doesn't reward creativity and ingenuity. On the contrary, it rewards inexperience, inefficiency, and even incompetence.

This is precisely why professionals pad their time sheets. Not only is it the perfect crime, it is the logical and rational course to take if you believe that what you did is worth more than the time you spent. By focusing on the hourly rate, you are forced into a Hobson's choice: Either be honest and undervalue your services, or lie on your time sheet to collect your just compensation. Is it any wonder that many professionals choose the latter option?

In his book *Start Consulting*, William L. Reeb made some interesting observations with respect to tracking time. Reeb's book is all about consulting, the new growth area for the accounting profession, and one would expect new ideas and approaches in marketing and pricing that type of service. Unfortunately, the Almighty Hour is firmly embedded in his thinking. Notwithstanding the fact that he discusses pricing—one of the essentials of marketing—in a section of the book that deals with administrative and organizational issues, here is what he has to say regarding tracking time:

> Accounting for hours and minutes has to be the most tedious and boring task associated with our profession. . . . So mak-

ing an effort to record *all of your time* is essential if you want consulting to be profitable [Emphasis in original].

Consulting is different. Because the client is usually very comfortable with the objectives and implementation plan of most management projects, he or she is more likely to scrutinize the manner in which the time was spent. By providing an itemized bill, you give your client an easy way to review your efforts and progress.

When there is price sensitivity, an itemized bill gives the client an opportunity to satisfy his or her concerns by reviewing the detailed time.

> Detailed billing is especially helpful in the worst-case sce-
> nario, in which the client challenges the value of some spe-
> cific portion of your work. It's advantageous because, at this
> point, instead of arguing about the overall fee, you are now
> only discussing a few line items on the bill. This helps
> resolve issues expeditiously and, if concessions are made,
> they are based on smaller numbers.
>
> Immediately after our "we bill for our time" explanation, we
> would likely continue with, "Would you like for us to remove
> that line item from the bill?" (Reeb, 1998: 285-87)

This approach leads to all of the deleterious effects listed in this
chapter. It is as if the professional is setting herself up for write-downs
right from the start, and she is trying to convince the customer that efforts
and value are equated. Rather than taking on these issues at the beginning
of the engagement and discussing value, the professional should simply
capitulate when the customer expresses "price sensitivity" (or is it value-
doubting?) and write-down the price. The profession makes the same
mistake over and over, and professionals wonder why they are not even
receiving the "standard rate." This issue will be discussed in more detail
in Chapter 8.

Professionals have done a poor job at ascertaining exactly what it is that
its customers are buying. While customers are focusing on the results
provided (not to mention service, that is, *how* professionals provide those
results), professionals are counting hours. Other businesses don't make
this fatal mistake when it comes to their customers and their pricing.

After the Gulf War, when the oil wells in Kuwait were on fire, the
pundits agreed that it would take at least six months, if not longer, to
extinguish the fires. Red Adair (and others) went over to the Middle East
and performed the job in about three months. Do you think Red Adair
charged by the hour? What would have been the result if he had?

If efforts–and thus, hours–were the sole determinant of value, then
perhaps CPA firms should scrap their computers and complete tax returns
with manual typewriters and carbon paper. This would certainly require
more effort, but who in his right mind would pay for it?

This is not such an obsolete and Luddite attitude. In *A History of
Accountancy in the United States*, Gary John Previts and Barbara Dubis
Merino point out the following:

> Accounting reports rendered during this period [the 1880s] were prepared and submitted in longhand, since the popular acceptance of the typewriter did not occur until the mid-1890s. One of the requisite skills of the accountant was to have "an accomplished hand" in penmanship and a modicum of patience: when multiple copies were required they had to be produced in the same tedious and exacting longhand.
>
> Some accountants, then as now, were skeptical as to the advantages of new office technologies, such as the typewriter when it first appeared. "Why should I pay $125 for a machine when I can buy a pen for two cents?" some asked (Previts and Merino, 1998: 134).

Only two things determine prices in today's market: preferences and technologies. A customer will be reluctant to pay for anything that doesn't utilize the latest technologies. Even a handmade Rolls Royce is subject to this reality.

David Friedman humorously (but profoundly) illustrates the point in *Hidden Order*: *The Economics of Everyday Life*:

> When I was very young, I used to amuse myself by shooting stalks of grass with a BB gun. That is an expensive way of mowing the lawn, even at a nine-year-old's wage. I think it unlikely that anyone would pay a correspondingly high price to have his lawn mowed in that fashion (Friedman, 1996: 23).

Many professionals object that if you do not focus on efforts, corners may be cut in quality to meet the fixed price of the service and not lose money. However, due to the perverse incentives inherent in hourly billing, many argue that corners should be cut. Second, quality is a table stake—the minimum you need to play the game. Cut corners on quality long enough, and you will not survive in a free marketplace. What customer is going to stay with an incompetent professional?

By focusing (and pricing) on efforts, professionals are fulfilling the prophetic vision of C. Northcote Parkinson, who developed Parkinson's Law: Work expands so as to fill the time available for its completion. Any professional who has performed work according to a predetermined budget can attest to this law and that it is not a prescription for success.

Hourly Billing Penalizes Technological Advances

This is perhaps the most egregious effect of the hourly billing method. Every year, professional firms make substantial investments in technology (computer hardware, software, printers, modems, etc.) that allow any given task to be performed in less time. Technology investments are being made, yet professional firm revenue is not declining. How can this be? Economists refer to this as the *productivity paradox*.

When businesses invest in technology, usually the result is higher profits—either due to increased internal efficiencies (thus lowering costs) or by price reductions to the customer resulting in increased sales (as in the high-tech industry). You do not need to reduce the price of your services when you invest in technology, although that is certainly a strategy if your firm is on the lower end of the Value Curve. Firms should reap some of the cost savings that result from investments in technology. Does a doctor's revenue *decrease* after the purchase of an MRI machine? Hardly. That is because the price for using that machine is determined by its value to the patient, not by the time it takes (or saves) the doctor in diagnosing the medical problem.

Under hourly billing, however, revenues drop as a result of technological advances. Professionals who use hourly billing have a tendency to reinvent the wheel rather than develop systems, procedures, and methods to perform routine tasks. They have little incentive to implement more efficient methods to complete work, because by doing so they would forego billable hours. The exception, perhaps, to the productivity paradox is professionals who are trying to meet billable hour quotas.

Hourly Rates Are Set by Reverse Competition

Hourly rates are often set by *reverse competition*. This means that you look at the rates of your fellow professionals operating in your geographical market, made a decision on where you want to fit in on the competitive spectrum, and set your rates accordingly. Unfortunately, most pick a rate that is somewhere in the middle. What kind of message does this send to your customers? "We are not the most expensive, but we are not the cheapest either; we are right in the middle." In other words, you have chosen to compete with everybody. It is little wonder some professionals think of themselves as commodities—they act like it. Professionals should not let competitors dictate price. Me-too pricing leads to serious pricing errors for any one customer in your firm. Professionals are not *price takers*. Professionals need to learn the art of becoming *price makers*.

Be honest. Did you set your hourly billing rate by crunching the numbers? You know, the rate equals overhead plus desired profit divided by expected billable hours. Only 10 percent of the CPAs I've asked admitted they did it in this manner. The rest confessed that they never performed any numerical analysis. This is an astonishing confession from a profession of proverbial number crunchers. Ardent defenders of the hourly billing method claim that it is an excellent cost-accounting tool. Yet, the majority concede that they have not even run the numbers.

This makes the notion of a "standard" hourly rate a pure fiction. Professionals have varied hourly rates since they've been adopted, charging a lower hourly rate for more volume or charging different rates for different types of work. Since professionals haven't taken the rate seriously, neither have their customers. Pricing policies need to be more sophisticated than this, based upon an assessment of value to the customer rather than on conjured-up standard rates set by competitors.

Pricing policy needs to be reevaluated continuously; it is not simply a one-time event whereby you set an hourly rate and increase it every few years by an inflation factor. When a professional changes jobs from one firm to another, why is it possible for his or her hourly rate to increase anywhere from $25 to $100 per hour? Has the professional become more valuable merely by changing work locations? Worse yet, the hourly rate selected at the beginning is not necessarily the right one once you become adequately profitable. After you are comfortable that you can meet your overhead and payroll and provide yourself with an adequate living, your prices should be adjusted upward. Low prices at the beginning of a business may make sense in order to attract customers, though this is doubtful, but that same policy could prevent you from succeeding in the long term. As business conditions change and as you enter new markets, offer new services, become more proficient, develop larger networks, and gain more experience, your pricing policies need to be changed. This is an ongoing process, as any marketing person will tell you. Yet professionals sometimes set a rate and stick to it for years, paying inadequate attention to price, one of the most fundamental elements of marketing.

Hourly Billing and Net Income

Customers do not believe that it is their job to provide the professional with a decent profit. They see it as the professional's job to provide them with a service that is so good that they willingly pay the professional a decent profit. Professionals must learn to accept the cause and effect that these different attitudes generate. The move towards activity-based costing offers a solution to this dilemma. While cost-accounting measures the cost to do something, activity-based costing captures the cost of not doing something, such as down time, inventory shortages, or rework.

Usually, the cost of not doing something far exceeds the cost of doing something, and cost accounting does not capture the former. Activity-based costing always asks, Does this process have to be done? If so, what is the most efficient way of doing it? This costing method has provided manufacturers with the information they need to cut costs substantially, but the real promise of activity-based costing may rest with service industries. Peter Drucker makes this observation in his book *Managing in a Time of Great Change*:

> Activity-based costing shows us why traditional cost accounting has not worked for service companies. It is not because the techniques are wrong.
>
> It is because traditional cost accounting makes the wrong assumptions. Service companies cannot start with the cost of individual operations, as manufacturing companies have done with traditional cost accounting. They must start with the assumption that there is only *one* cost: that of the total system. And it is a fixed cost over any given time period. The famous distinction between fixed and variable costs, on which traditional cost accounting is based, does not make much sense in services.
>
> But that all costs are fixed over a given time period and that resources cannot be substituted for one another, so that the *total* operation has to be costed—those are precisely the assumptions with which activity-based costing starts. By applying them to services, we are beginning for the first time to get cost information and yield control.
>
> Banks, for instance, have been trying for several decades to apply conventional cost-accounting techniques to their business—that is, to figure the costs of individual operations and services—with almost negligible results. Now they are beginning to ask, Which one *activity* is at the center of costs and of results? The answer: Serving the customer. The cost per customer in any major area of banking is a fixed cost.

> Thus it is the *yield* per customer—both the volume of services a customer uses and the mix of those services—that determines costs and profitability. Retail discounters, especially those in Western Europe, have known that for some time. They assume that once a unit of shelf space is installed, the cost is fixed and management consists of maximizing the yield thereon over a given time span. Their focus on yield control has enabled them to increase profitability despite their low prices and low margins [Emphasis in original] (Drucker, 1995: 124–25).

This is precisely the method that airlines began to use after deregulation. Recall from Chapter 5 how Delta Air Lines began focusing on yield (the amount of money the airline gets per passenger mile) and load (the percentage of seats filled by paying passengers) in order to price its tickets and balance supply and demand (and capture the consumer surplus). It should be no different with a professional service firm. Yet, professional firms spend an inordinate amount of time trying to allocate fixed costs to *one* particular customer, and even more absurd, to *one* particular job for that one customer. Activity-based costing, on the other hand, would look at the total revenue yield from that one customer and compare it to an allocation of the total fixed cost to that customer.

This raises an interesting question: How should a firm allocate its fixed costs to any one customer? Labor hours certainly seem a logical way to achieve this. But if labor hours are used as the designated allocation, then the cost per labor hour should be a true cost and should *not* include a desired profit for the firm's owners. This is based on the logic that a professional firm's fixed costs, over a given period of time, cannot be changed. In fact, they are sunk costs. And here is the advice David Friedman received from his father Milton with regards to such costs:

> When, as a very small child, I quarreled with my sister and then locked myself in my room, my father would come to the door and say, "Making a mistake and not admitting it is only hurting yourself twice." When I got a little older, he changed it to "Sunk costs are sunk costs" (Friedman, 1996: 181).

CPA firms know their fixed costs, to the penny. It would be logical to manage the firm from the income statement, analyzing the ratio of labor and overhead costs to gross revenue, spotting trends, and making adjustments accordingly. This is precisely how the firm's manufacturing customers manage their businesses, but it seems a foreign concept to CPAs. This is strange; they assist their customers in managing their businesses this way, and yet they do not follow these same procedures when running their firms.

You may try changing your firm's time and billing program standard hourly rates to a true cost- accounting number. If you continue to keep time sheets (and you probably will, at least for a time), then by all means plug in the correct cost per labor hour. Take out the desired net income from the cost-plus formula and measure the cost and profitability based on true cost-accounting principles. This one simple change will have a dramatic impact on your attitude regarding pricing, because no longer will you assume that the price charged is calculated by your time and billing program. That alone is enough reason to make the change.

The question always arises of what to do about the firm's partner draws. Should salaries (or guaranteed draws) be included in this formula? An economist would say this is a legitimate cost to the firm. After all, if the partner were not there, the firm would have to go into the labor market and hire a replacement; thus the replacement cost of the partner should be used. Another method would be to include the partner's opportunity cost, that is, the minimum the partner has to make to keep him or her employed at the firm.

I prefer not to include any partner draw or opportunity cost, on the theory that if an amount is put in for that cost, the partners will be less aggressive in pricing the firm's services, because they will feel that a cushion is built in to the cost. Remember that the focus is cost accounting, not profit forecasting. Some firms use both methods (many time and billing software programs will accommodate multiple rates to be used), but it is simply too early to tell which method produces better pricing decisions. If you do use the partner draw in the formula, make sure that it is understood to be the absolute minimum price that should be charged, with a good justification for doing so (such as entering a new market or attracting a high profile customer). The hourly billing method, to the extent it is used at all (if your time and billing program allows multiple rates), should always be the floor below which the firm will *never* price.

Talk it over with your partners, agree on a method, and then monitor it to see if you are making better pricing, costing, and profitability decisions as a result. Let the income statement play a pivotal role in your firm's hiring, budgeting, and profitability decisions. The attitudinal effects of the costing method are more important than trying to allocate your sunk costs to any one customer. Firms that do not use time sheets at all analyze their income statements to monitor overall results. Asked how they know if they are making money on any one given customer, their response is, "Well, in reality, we do not." Intuitively they do know they are making money, because they serve only customers that they can charge a high price to, and therefore they know there is very little subsidizing of low-priced customers taking place. Remember, these firms are not profitable because they have eliminated time sheets; they have eliminated time sheets because they are profitable.

Hourly billing is an *inward-looking* pricing mechanism, focusing on competition and cost. Professional firms need to change to an *outward-looking* pricing mechanism, one that focuses on customer value. By changing your standard hourly rate to a true cost-based amount per labor hour, you will be forced to look to the customer for determining the value of any given service. This is how it should be. The ultimate arbiter of value is the customer, not internal costs.

Hourly Billing Creates Bureaucracy

A CPA firm recently calculated that it could save approximately $30,000 per year by eliminating time sheets, and that was only the direct cost of inputting, producing, and generating the reports. It did not include the countless hours spent by professional staff tracking every quarter hour, the morale problems of having to account for every single hour, the negative effect of hourly quotas on marketing and practice development, and the other myriad effects that have been discussed.

The next logical question is this: Does the time and billing program generate at least $30,000 worth of useful information? Nobody could answer this with any certainty, because it is very hard to quantify whether or not better decisions are being made with time reports than would be made in their absence. One point all the partners agreed upon was that the majority of important decisions that are made—hiring, firing, staffing jobs, and raises—are determined long before they even see the results of the time reports. If, for instance, a particular staff person is not performing up to minimum standards, time reports are not going to indicate that as much as grumbling from other staff, missed deadlines, or customer complaints. If the firm is understaffed, the managers and partners will usually hire an additional person, not as a result of analyzing time reports but because the staff people who report to them can justify the extra need.

CPAs often ask how they will be able to monitor and control their staff people if they do not make them account for their time. If they do not trust their staff people, why did they hire them in the first place? Firms that do not use time sheets have very effective communication between the staff, managers, and partners. Methods such as weekly meetings, whereby the staff talk about the work-in-progress and if they are overused or under-used, take place, and adjustments are made. Revenue is tracked per staff person, which is then compared to fixed cost. Sometimes this can be difficult, as with a project that has several staff assigned. But these firms have not brought back time sheets. They seem to manage well enough without them. You may want to attempt this method on one particular job and see what type of decisions are made in the absence of time sheets. If the results are unfavorable, then by all means bring back the time sheets. But you may be surprised.

Hourly Billing Does Not Set the Price Up Front

Few products or services in the marketplace are purchased without the customer knowing the price up front. The more common ones are cab rides, medical services, legal services, and accounting services. In most cases, though, before you purchase any item, you know the price. Think how frustrating it must be for a customer to be told, "We cannot give you a price up front because we just do not know how long this will take." When the customer complains, the professional tends to launch into an explanation of how complex the project at hand is and how many unforeseen variables there are. The professional may think to themselves, and sometimes even have the temerity to inform the customer, that the customer obviously does not understand the complexity of the business.

In *Billing Innovations*, Reed quotes this scenario written by Kevin B. Pratt, a lawyer in Colorado Springs, Colorado:

AIRLINES GOING TO BILLABLE HOURS?

The Denver lawyer stepped up to the airline ticket counter and asked to buy a ticket for a flight to Chicago.

"No problem," said the clerk, "but before I issue the ticket, I should remind you of the new way we charge for tickets.

This year we have adopted a 'basic rate' of three dollars a minute for our flights. The clock starts when you check in at the gate and stops when you pick up your luggage. We mail you a bill about two months after the flight."

"Well, I guess that's okay," commented the lawyer.

The clerk continued, "Remember, we call it a 'basic rate' because we sometimes adjust that rate up or down if the flight is very empty or very full. Too, we may multiply that rate if our expert pilot finds a tail wind. We also adjust the rate according to what you will be doing in Chicago. You look like a lawyer, so I'll assume it's very important that you get there by plane, so we quadruple the basic rate. [They actually do this, sort of—see Chapter 5.] Another thing, how much is your annual income? You see, if you earn a great deal and it turns out the plane crashes, we will have to pay more on your spouse's damage claim, and we have, of course, to consider that increased risk of the airline."

The astounded lawyer choked, "But how much will this trip cost me? How do I know you do not slow down on purpose? How do I know your bill will be correct?"

The clerk stared down over the end of his nose. "I can see you're not familiar with the complexities of airline work. There are so many things we just cannot know in advance— the winds, traffic delays, the weather, the routing. Airlines are a business, and we have to make a profit to stay in business. Now do not worry, we're very honest and sensitive about all this billing business and I am sure you'll be pleased with our fully itemized bill when you get it. If there's any question just call." Then the clerk whispered, "But just so we understand each other, if you do not pay the bill in full and promptly, you'll never fly on this airline again."

"Oh," grunted the Denver lawyer, "is there anything else I should know?"

The clerk smiled thoughtfully and murmured, "On your flight there is a new copilot in training, and we charge an additional 50 cents a mile. Copilots are really very important, you know, to carry the pilot's charts, to fly on clear calm days, even to land the plane if the pilot is busy with other matters. Too, if you fly with us again, your copilot may have become your pilot. Wouldn't that be great? One other thing, if the copilot uses computerized flight routing there will be an additional $75 charge. But of course computerized flight routing is almost standard charge with technologically advanced airlines."

"But I just wanted to get to my meeting in Chicago and come home. Now I do not even know if I should fly at all," groaned the lawyer.

The clerk smiled again. "Mature passengers come to understand that flying is just a cost of doing business. They never know how much it costs 'til we bill them. But then, there's really no choice, is there?"

"No," conceded the lawyer, "I guess not."

And then the lawyer tried again. "Why can't you just give me a fixed price and I'll decide if I'll go or not?"

The clerk frowned. "But we can't do that. That wouldn't be fair to you. We might overcharge you and then you'd be unhappy. Or we might underestimate and then the airline would lose money and couldn't maintain the planes, and we certainly do not want that."

And so the Denver lawyer came to hate airlines and took his revenge by regaling acquaintances at cocktail parties about the new pitfalls of airline travel (Reed, 1996: 3–4).

This story illustrates the absurdity of hourly billing from the customer's viewpoint. By not setting a price up front, the customer has no control over the situation, which is not a good position to put your customer in. People like to feel they are in control, especially when they are spending their money. With hourly billing, the only involvement the customers have is paying the bill, and that means they have to make the value judgment after the service is rendered, which is not a good time to discover they do not agree with the price.

Lawyers used to be taught that it was unprofessional to discuss fees with the customer during the first meeting, fearing they might get the wrong impression. Today, an overwhelming majority of customers want their professional to discuss price up front, as it relieves them of the burden. The Mobar-Pren-Hall Survey, which was published by Prentice-Hall and the Missouri State Bar Association, found the following results:

- 80 percent of customers want lawyers to discuss their fees up front.
- 88 percent said not to wait until the end of the case.
- 92 percent said to discuss the fee at the start of each matter.
- 78 percent want to know the basis for the fee.
  (Reed, 1992: 74)

The study also found that nearly 36 percent of the lawyers studied did not perform in accordance with the customer's desires. If the only price customers are aware of at the initial meeting is the hourly rate, then they will be forced to consider whether or not they can afford to pay that fee. They will not be considering the value of the service rendered. Mary Ann Altman sums up this predicament:

> The process of discussing the way in which the fee will be charged at the initial meeting with the client again is a prime factor. If "time billing at hourly rates" is the only explanation of the fee-calculation method, the client is making a decision based on the ability of his or her pocketbook to pay a given hourly rate but not on the value of the services in the short or long run. The lawyer should raise the question of the value of services and allow the client to make a determination as to whether or not he or she wishes to receive those services. A great deal of future grief may be avoided by such an initial discussion (Reed, 1989: 13–14).

Whether you discuss price up front or not, rest assured that customers have some price in mind, whether it is what they paid in the past, a quote from a competitor, or a completely unreasonable estimate that they have pulled from thin air. The time to find out what they think is *before* your firm has performed any services, rather than after, when you will be on your knees trying to collect a bill from the customer whose value assessment is radically different from yours.

Hourly Billing Does Not Differentiate Your Firm

The vast majority of CPA firms (and to a lesser extent, law firms) charge by the hour, thus converting their crown jewels of experience, expertise, culture, and relationships, into a commodity, codified in an hourly rate. Pricing is not an effective competitive differentiation, unless you enjoy price wars, since someone, somewhere, is always willing to do what you do for less money. Yet price is one of the most important signals that a firm can transmit to the marketplace regarding its services.

Since competition really means conformity, why not get out of the pack and offer fixed prices? This is especially effective with new customers, as they will welcome receiving an up-front quote and it will project confidence and experience on your part, characteristics valued highly by customers, even if subjectively. This strategy is very effective with Yellow Pages customers. If people call your firm from the Yellow Pages they will usually ask what your hourly rate is. If you say you do not charge by the hour, they will be intrigued, probably enough to come in and see you for an initial consultation, during which you can review their needs and offer them a fixed price. The logic is that once they are in your office you will have a better chance of success in making the sale than if you are one of a dozen they are considering from the Yellow Pages herd.

The typical professional firm will put more creativity, mind power, and time into a brochure or an advertisement than in thinking about pricing policies. This is a serious mistake. Pricing is how the firm captures the value it provides to the marketplace. Analyze other industry advertising, and notice that much of it contains the price. Professional advertising, on the other hand, does not. This is a large advantage. Customers don't expect professionals to advertise based upon price; they might even perceive a firm that did as possessing lesser professionalism and dignity. Yet, firms engage in me-too pricing, simply following the herd and using cost-plus pricing or fictional "standard" rates. This is not an effective strategy to differentiate your firm from the competition. Remember, accountants are not commodities. Imagine thinking that coffee beans and water are nothing more than commodities, and the effect that thinking might have had on Starbucks?

Hourly Billing Diminishes the Quality of Life

There's no doubt that morale in the professions is suffering, and one major cause is the relentless pursuit of the billable hour. In *The Honest Hour*, Ross quotes an associate attorney at a Chicago law firm who billed more than 2,000 hours per year during the prior four years:

> One negative effect of hourly billing is the stressful impact
> on attorneys—particularly associates who in big firms have

target hours of 2000 or more per year. It's not so much the fact that we must work hard but that we're slaves to the clock—almost like piecemeal workers. Perhaps that's why "sweatshop" well describes many firms. A young associate feels that an hour not billed is an hour wasted—an incredibly stressful state of mind. In short, hourly billing is a barrier to the quality of one's professional life (Ross, 1996: 232).

Not only is one's professional life diminished, but also one's overall sense of well being. According to the American Bar Association:

From the lawyers perspective, total dependency from revenues on hours billed means that compensation also is totally dependent on hours billed, which in turn means long hours, burnout, increased family problems and personal stress, and decreased morale.

Simply put, if billable hour goals prevent a lawyer from having time for things other than work, that person cannot be a truly good lawyer without time to pursue whatever outside interests a lawyer has, be it family or a personal hobby. The lawyer lives to work, rather than works to live. At a certain point, the demand for billable hours on lawyers became so great that initiatives like better training and communication, or part-time work options that only a handful lawyers in fact can actually utilize, no longer make enough of a difference. At a certain point, lawyers may simply have no life outside the office, with a resulting negative impact on the lawyer, the family, and the firm (deKieffer, 1995: 91).

This lessening in the quality of life results in a high cost to firms, measured in associate turnover, low morale, absenteeism, inefficiencies, and neglect of practice development. These costs should be included in any cost/benefit analysis of maintaining hourly billing; these costs are likely to outweigh any benefits derived.

In reality, the whole notion that professionals don't have enough time may be false, if you follow Pareto's 80/20 principle, as discussed in Chapter 5. Richard Koch, in *80/20 Principle: The Secret of Achieving More With Less*, explains his unconventional—but compelling—argument this way:

We have more than enough time. We demean ourselves, both by lack of ambition and by assuming that ambition is served by bustle and busyness. Achievement is driven by insight and selective action. The still, small voice of calm has a bigger place in our lives than we acknowledge. Insight comes when we are feeling relaxed and good about ourselves. Insight requires time—and time, despite conventional wisdom, is there in abundance.

There is no shortage of time. In fact, we are positively awash with it. We only make good use of 20 percent of our time. And for the most talented individuals, it is often tiny amounts of time that make all the difference. The 80/20 Principle says that if we doubled our time on the top 20 percent of activities, we could work a two-day week and achieve 60 percent more than now. This is light years away from the frenetic world of time management. . . . It is our use of time, and not time itself, that is the enemy.

The 80/20 Principle says that we should act less. Action drives out thought. It is because we have so much time that we squander it. The most productive time on a project is usually the last 20 percent, simply because the work has to be completed before a deadline. Productivity on most projects could be doubled simply by halving the amount of time for their completion. This is not evidence that time is in short supply.

It is not shortage of time that should worry us, but the tendency for the majority of time to be spent in low-quality ways (Koch, 1998: 141, 149).

Hourly Billing Limits Your Income Potential

There are only so many hours in a year. During the early 1990s, net earnings of most professional firms were flat, and costs were increasing at a faster rate than revenue; yet, firms refuse to consider their pricing and tend to spend a high percentage of their resources obtaining new customers. Or, they raise their hourly rates, much to the chagrin of their existing customers. Or they may simply try to bill more hours, perhaps by working inefficiently, all of which David H. Maister refers to as the *donkey strategy*—achieving more by pulling a heavier load.

Consider circus elephants. When young, the elephant is chained to a stake, and the elephant learns that its movement is restricted. Once the elephant gets older, the chain around the leg is effective at restraining the elephant, even though the elephant has enough power to rip the stake out of the ground. The barrier is not *physical*, it is *mental*. It is the same with hourly billing. The only way to make more money is to *work harder*. With Value Pricing, however, you will make more money by *pricing smarter*.

The Tyranny of Time

Ever since Abraham Lincoln muttered those infamous words, "Time is an attorney's stock in trade," professionals have been taught that that is all they sell. It has become part of their paradigms—their mental models of the way the world works. But *time is not money*, it is simply a *precious, nonrenewable resource*. And a resource, by itself, is not valuable until one finds a use for it and it produces results that are valuable to others.

The "time is money" attitude is endemic to the professions and is summed up nicely in the following letter to the Winter 1996 *Outlook* magazine, published by the California Society of CPAs, from an "I only sell my time" CPA:

> I am writing to comment on the tactics of Quickbooks, whose latest ad appears in the fall issue of *Outlook*. Quickbooks and Turbotax, both owned by Intuit, market their products to both consumers and the CPA profession. My concern is the attempt by Intuit to be both the vendor *and* competitor to our profession.
>
> The ad suggests that we counsel our clients to use Quickbooks for their businesses. However, some time after the client purchases Quickbooks, they will receive a direct mailing from Intuit essentially suggesting that they can now also handle their income taxes using Turbotax for business. The mailing uses terms such as 'quickly,' 'easily,' 'accurately,' 'fast,' etc. For the timid, they propose having a professional tax preparer review and sign the completed return. There's a

> tempting proposition: taking responsibility for a return in which I did none of the input, and for which the client expects to pay for about 30 minutes of my time!
>
> I realize that write-up and tax-preparation services are becoming more and more a commodity. We should not be helping it along with the Quickbooks/Turbotax package.

Notwithstanding his attack on the First Amendment right of a business to advertise, the point is the *mental attitude* that all he has to offer his customer is 30 minutes of his time. If this CPA cannot become more creative in selling value-added services to a Turbotax user—maybe through tax planning, projections, or financing packages—then perhaps he deserves being treated like a commodity and forced to compete with a $49 tax-preparation program. Another way to look at this scenario is that the customer has freed up your time to focus on the high end of the Value Curve. If the customer is interested in only 30 minutes of your time, and you cannot sell any additional services, then this is a customer you should not have in the first place.

Summary and Conclusions

> *Workers of the world . . . forgive me.*
>
> —Karl Marx, Graffiti on a statue, Moscow, 1991

Time is precious; it is what professionals are giving up when they are at work, and thus professionals have started to think their lives are divided into *billable* and *nonbillable* hours. But this focus is far too narrow, and professionals need to broaden their view of the value they add to customers' lives. That value is not measured by time but by results. Albert Einstein once wrote, "Our theories determine what we measure." Hourly billing measures the wrong things.

Even the AICPA Vision Project, which is an attempt to map the future for the profession into the year 2050, paid homage to the Almighty Hour on the first page of its report with this sentence: "Approximately 3,400 members of the CPA profession devoted a combined total of 21,456 hours … to identify both challenges and opportunities for the profession in

2011." They report this statistic proudly and prominently, as if the people reading it will value it more simply because of how much effort was put into it, and not because of the quality of its predictions and prescriptions for the future. It is as if a surgeon paid more attention to how long the surgery took than to whether the patient got well.

Professionals are subject to the same laws of supply and demand and customer psychology that all businesses are. Hourly billing tries to defy those laws by placing the risk on the customer and misaligning the interest of the firm and the customer. Professionals continue to thrust this method of pricing onto their customers, and then they wonder why they get beat up on price. It is an idea for which the French coined the perfect expression: *fausse idee claire*—a terrific idea that doesn't work.

Professionals need to forge a new paradigm of pricing based upon the objective value of services and stop ritualistically accepting the false labor theory of value proffered by Karl Marx 150 years ago. The billable hour should be relegated to the ash heap of history—along with carbon paper, the manual typewriter, and the slide rule—right next to *The Communist Manifesto*, as an idea whose time has past.

8 WRITE-DOWNS AND PRICE PSYCHOLOGY

Billing is like golf—
It is a game played on a six-inch course between your ears.

—Charles and Joseph Larson,
Innovative Billing and
Collection Methods That Work

Why do professionals suffer from write-downs and write-offs? Statistical surveys of CPAs, such as those conducted by the Missouri Management of an Accounting Practice (MAP) Conference and by the state of Texas clearly prove that write-downs are far more prevalent than write-ups. Studying the many theories for the underlying cause of this phenomenon perhaps gives a better understanding of the actions required to prevent write-downs and write-offs in the future. The role of Value Pricing is also important and will be included in the discussion.

One reason for write-downs is that professionals, by nature, are *loss adverse*. They tend to avoid conflict and anything that they believe may anger the customer and cause him or her to select another service provider. Not only does this translate into a lack of confidence, it also provides an opportunity for customers to beat up the professional on price, since business people are used to negotiating.

Another reason for write-downs is the low self-esteem that is prevalent among professionals. This will be examined in Chapter 17.

One other factor in the prevalence of write-downs is apparent after a look at how other industries price their products and services. Professionals have not given enough attention to the psychological aspects of pricing.

In their book *Innovative Billing and Collection Methods That Work*, Charles Larson and Joseph Larson discuss the results of asking CPAs at MAP conferences to list the reasons they take significant write-downs and write-offs. Here are the major reasons given:

1. Poor time and billing system
2. Changes not anticipated resulting from:
   - Client deficiencies
   - Staff
   - Poor budgeting (or no budgeting)
3. First-time work/one-time work on new engagements
4. Poor engagement management
5. On-the-job training that partners do not feel can be billed
6. Client is surprised by the fee and doesn't think the job is "worth it"
7. Poor results in situations regarding financing, IRS reviews, or similar matters—areas that should be premium billings
8. Delays in billing
9. Bad client—unable to pay
   (Larson and Larson, 1994: 6–7)

Most of the conditions listed above can be eliminated with better methods of determining client expectations up front, by setting a fixed price at the beginning of an engagement, and by issuing Change Orders if the customer is deficient in providing the necessary information or the engagement changes in an unanticipated way. As Larson and Larson point out: "***Most* fee problems occur because of violated client expectations**" (ibid., 31). This is true and is perhaps the main cause of most write-downs. Worse yet, write-downs create a lack of trust and foster disputes between you and the customer, leading to a vicious downward spiral.

Why Customers Don't Pay

Recall the demand curve from Chapter 5. To be included on a demand curve, one must be *willing and able* to pay for the product or service. The experiences of many practicing CPAs, confirmed by Larson and Larson in their research, show only two reasons customers will not pay their professional's bill:

1. They are not *able* (no money); or
2. They are not *willing*.

All write-downs can be traced to these two issues, so it is worth taking some time to explore each in more detail.

Unable to Pay

A customer that cannot pay you is a sign of a bad qualification process on your part. This is one of the biggest hurdles to overcome for any salesperson—properly qualifying a buyer. According to Tom Hopkins, in his book *How to Master the Art of Selling*, you will close one of every two properly pre-qualified leads, whereas unqualified leads require ten in order to close just one (Hopkins, 1980: 180).

All professionals need to do a thorough job pre-screening customers. Check references with bankers, attorneys, CPAs, and other businesses to determine their reputation, character, and financial ability. This is easier for CPAs and attorneys than, say, salesmen, simply because the former have a wealth of information on their potential customers, and are privy to information that most salesmen would kill for. Can they afford it? What do they pay for the service now? Who are the decision makers?

As the Greeks used to say, character is destiny. Character is the only thing that matters, especially in a professional relationship where trust is the foundation for a value-added partnership. It is a wise idea to pull a credit report on a prospective customer and check as many references as you can—in other words, do your homework. The time to discover potential problems with a customer is *before* your firm commits any resources to the engagement, not *after*. This requires an investment of up-front time, but this can save countless dollars in unpaid work, not to mention the stress, risk, and dissatisfaction of working with people who do not value your firm.

The lesson is this: **Do not take all comers**. In the insurance industry, this is known as *Adverse Selection,* "the problem that arises when people know more about their own risk characteristics than others do" (Landsburg, 1996: 329). Insurance companies are very cognizant of the fact that the customer in the market for insurance, statistically and actuarially, is most likely to be the worst risk, since they may not be insurable. Therefore, they subject potential policyholders to medical exams or fire inspections. Insurance companies do not take all comers, as they are in the business of managing risk and will avoid taking any unnecessary ones. Professional firms, especially in today's litigious society, should adopt the same attitude and implement methods and procedures that ensure that all new customers have gone through a rigorous pre-qualification process.

Starting a professional practice entails risk, and turning away business is especially difficult in the early years of building a practice. However, when your intuition tells you a customer is not right, follow it, even though it means sacrificing income. Most people choose a spouse, friends, partners, and acquaintances with an enormous amount of care and attention, and that same level of screening should be part of the customer acquisition process as well. Seriously flawed customer relationships have a pernicious effect, a sort of Gresham's Law: Bad customers drive out good. By holding on to customers who constantly doubt the value your firm is providing, or are unable to pay for it, you will adversely affect the morale within the entire firm. Life is too short to work with people you do not enjoy. Investing the time required to pre-qualify all comers makes for better quality customer relationships. Once you use better pre-qualifying techniques, the customers who are not *able* to pay will virtually disappear from your write-off headaches.

Unwilling to Pay

A customer's unwillingness to pay is much harder to deal with. Essentially, you are colliding with the customer's expectations. If those are violated, the customer is not going to be willing to pay your price, regardless of your technical quality. Therefore, it is critical to find out, *before* any firm resources are committed to the engagement, what the customer's expectations are. Sometimes those expectations are impossible to meet and the customer needs to be educated so that his or her expectations are lowered to a more realistic level. If you are unable to do that, withdraw from the engagement.

The lesson is vital, and it is this: By asking, probing, and listening to customers, you not only will determine their expectations, you will also be able to shape and manage them. Recall how Southwest Airlines manages its customer's expectations by offering no frills, then exceeds the customer's already low expectations by being irreverent, arriving on time, and not losing the customer's luggage. In order to exceed customer expectations in a professional firm, it is vital to invest time ascertaining what exactly the customer thinks he is purchasing and what they expect after the service is delivered. Rest assured that every customer you work for has expectations. Your job is to discover them and then exceed them. Exceeding those expectations is crucial if your goal is to provide Total Quality Service. By ascertaining and managing your customer's expectations at the beginning of each engagement, reason number two for write-offs and write-downs should diminish.

Please refer to "Considerations Before Accepting a New Customer," found in "Useful Checklists" at the end of this book and also on the disc.

So far, the negatives involved in write-downs have been discussed. Even more beneficial will be a study of some successful methods firms employ to prevent write-downs.

Do You Learn More from Success or from Failure?

In Peter F. Drucker's autobiography, *Adventures of a Bystander*, he states: "I suddenly realized that the right method, at least for me, was to look for the thing that worked and for the people who perform. I realized that I, at least, do not learn from mistakes. I have to learn from successes" (Drucker, 1994: 75). When participants in my courses were asked whether they learned more from success or failure, 90 percent said failure. When you start really pondering this, however, you realize that success is a far more valuable teacher than failure. Yet people are far more proficient in their rationalizations for failure than in planning for success.

Most people would agree with the statement that there are more wrong ways to do something than there are right ways. If that is true, then certainly it follows that learning the right way to do a particular thing is the best path to success. After all, incompetence is one thing found in abundant and never-ending supply. If you had to study all of life's failures, you would never have enough time to achieve success.

In a business context, studying success is becoming vital to remaining competitive. Witness the process known as benchmarking, which all major world-class firms conduct to improve their operations. Benchmarking is a continuous search for and application of significantly better practices that lead to superior competitive performance. It is a major criteria for the Malcolm Baldrige National Quality Award, and will likely be one of the largest growth areas for consultants in the coming century.

No business benchmarks the post office. If the management of the post office were smart, it would benchmark FedEx, but the government is not a learning institution. It does not learn from its mistakes, it simply perpetuates them.

Both success and failure are largely the result of habit. Failure breeds failure and success breeds success. When you program yourself to believe that you learn more from failure than success, you begin to make excuses for your failures. You will make statements such as, "Yes, I really messed that up, but look at the education I got from my mistake." Yet probably not that many people really improve from their mistakes. Examine the list of reasons for write-downs and write-offs; CPAs across the country are experiencing the same failures, over and over. Recounting them here is not going to assist you in preventing them. Being aware of why failures occur can be, no doubt, helpful. But not until you learn the correct way to achieve your goal will you gain the confidence needed to improve.

For instance, social reformers have been constantly preoccupied with the problem of poverty. However, poverty is the usual condition of man, and in reality, it needs no explanation. What needs an explanation is not poverty, but wealth. Adam Smith took this approach in his *Wealth of Nations*, which enabled countries to make real progress in ameliorating poverty by understanding what attributes create wealth.

Successful sports stars take the same approach. Earl Woods believes that success breeds success and used this principle to teach his son Tiger, at a young age, to shoot below par golf. He took the approach of rewarding success. He would assign Tiger a par higher than regulation par, making it possible for the child to come in often under par. Earl Woods explains the effect of this technique in *Training a Tiger*:

> It was the beginning of a competitive desire that knows no comfort zone. By that I mean when Tiger is five under par, he wants to be six under par. When he's six under par, he wants to be seven. He does not say, "Wow, I'm five under. I'm not supposed to be shooting like this." The truth is Tiger has been shooting like that since he was two years old. He's been shooting five, six, seven under par with those assigned pars (Woods, 1997: 26).

Here is the major point regarding success vs. failure, and it comes, once again, from Drucker: *"Do not solve problems; pursue opportunities."* The difference is critical. A firm should spend at least as much time pursuing opportunities as it does solving problems, if not more. It is imperative to adopt the procedures necessary to avoid the two causes of write-downs and write-offs, but that is not enough. That is merely solving problems. You also want to pursue opportunities and discover how to provide Total Quality Service. You want to gain the ability to charge a premium price for your services. You can achieve these things by studying the success of others.

Studying Success

Why are some CPAs successful, making anywhere between $200,000 and $600,000 per year, per partner? CPAs earning this level of income are not that much different from other CPAs. However, they do tend to work *smarter*, not *harder*. Most of them have capitalized on Value Pricing and command premium prices for their services. According to Larson and Larson in *Innovative Billing and Collection Methods That Work,* factors that result in favorable CPA profit include:

- Good clients
- Effective engagement planning
- Superior communication
- Adequate performance
- Appropriate administrative support
  (Larson and Larson, 1994: 8)

I would add to this list Total Quality Service, high self-esteem, confidence, and continuous learning and development of skills. Nevertheless, if you study the top achievers in this profession, the preceding five factors are almost always present.

One of the best definitions of *high-quality professional services* was developed by Peter Giuliana, a consultant in Westport, Connecticut, written for attorneys but also relevant to CPAs:

- The ability to perceive client needs or commercial objectives quickly and correctly.
- The expertise and diligence needed to facilitate the satisfaction of client needs or commercial objectives.
- The professionalism, training, and skill to ensure that client needs are satisfied in a manner that conforms to and is in compliance with applicable law and ethical standards.
- The delivery of cost-effective, timely, and responsive service that adds value or achieves a result whose value exceeds the fee charged.
  (Reed, 1996: 168)

This is an excellent mission statement for any professional service firm, as it puts the focus on providing value to the customer, meeting expectations in the most efficacious manner possible, all the while providing Total Quality Service. Analyze your firm's Value Proposition and how it differs from that of your competition. Focus on the service aspect and you will discover that price and quality will both increase as a result.

What About Marketing Success?

Another characteristic of successful firms is the way they measure their success in the marketing realm. Most professionals will look at revenues, and if they increased, they feel their marketing efforts have succeeded—or at least paid off on their investment. The top rainmakers, by contrast, will look at the profitability of the new business generated. As David H. Maister points out in his excellent book, *True Professionalism*:

> Revenues are an insufficient (and potentially misleading) indicator of marketing success. Marketing in a professional firm is (or should be) about getting *better* business, not just *more* business.
>
> *Of course* low-profit work is better than no work—*this year*. But again, this can hardly be called marketing success: Taking any work you can get is no way to build a business. To be successful, a firm must win more than its fair share of the profitable work, and marketing-success measures must be established to track this [Emphasis in original] (Maister, 1997: 185, 187).

Maister also offers a two-prong test to measure marketing success: The Income Statement Test and the Balance-Sheet Test. The Income Statement Test, obviously, is the impact of the marketing efforts on the firm's top and bottom line. The Balance-Sheet Test, a more challenging test, is the impact of the new work on the firm's asset-building efforts—developing new skills, strengthening customer relationships that will pay dividends in the future, creating a reputation in new markets or segments, etc.

This Balance-Sheet Test is failed by most professional firms, and that is dangerous in the long run. Maister points out: "Too much asset-milking work will leave the firm exposed strategically. Skills and reputation depreciate over time, and only by building new skills, relationships, and reputations can a firm thrive over time" (ibid., 188).

Price Psychology

It is worth reiterating that pricing is a major marketing decision. And since people tend to buy *emotionally*, and justify *intellectually*, the study of pricing psychology is a worthwhile task. Two sources of wise counsel are Timothy Beauchemin, with his audio cassette program titled *Five-Star Client Service System*, and Troy Waugh, a nationally-known CPA consultant.

In his *Five-Star Client Service System*, Beauchemin teaches that CPAs should run their practices like five-star restaurants, pointing out the many similarities between the two businesses. Each relies on word-of-mouth advertising, each values repeat business, each sells a product that is available elsewhere, and each makes money on "dessert" (value-added services). He also identifies the two characteristics of price psychology:

1. Price Leverage
2. Pricing Emotions

Price Leverage

Price leverage is not so much an advantage possessed by one party over the other as a question of who has the most (or least) price sensitivity at a given time. Before an engagement has begun, the professional possesses the price leverage. This is because the customer is able and willing to do business with you (otherwise you would not have made it this far in the process) and desires (or badly needs) the service. Consider the psychological factors when the customer is confronted with an IRS audit. The fear and anxiety of the customer is very serious. The time to negotiate and set the price for your representation is not *after* you have completed the audit, but *before*.

By setting the price up front, you can command a premium because you have assumed some of the risk involved in not knowing exactly how much time and resources it is going to require. You will also provide the customer with control over the decision of whether or not to engage your services, and this sense of control is very important to customers. Once you complete an engagement (or particular project), the price leverage shifts to the customer and you are left trying to recoup any portion of your price the customer is willing to pay. This puts you at a severe disadvantage and is one of the reasons professionals experience write-offs.

Price leverage also works with Change Orders, a topic dealt with in Chapter 11. Contractors are notorious for using Change Orders. If the project is changed in the middle of the job, the contractor will notify the customer and a Change Order will be issued. At the time of a Change Order, the pricing leverage is on the side of the contractor, who has already started the job and is familiar with it. The switching costs are usually prohibitive at this stage. Change orders are an extremely effective mechanism for keeping in contact with the customer and retaining your price leverage when projects do not turn out as originally planned. In fact, many contractors will low-ball their bids and sit in their offices praying for a Change Order to occur, as this is where most of their profit comes from.

Beauchemin offers a wonderful analogy in his program, that of the dessert tray in the five-star restaurant. The restaurant makes a deliberate attempt to sell dessert while the customers are still hungry. This maintains the price leverage to the restaurant's advantage and allows the restaurant to earn more profit from the customer. You always want to establish your price when you possess the leverage, which is *before* the engagement begins.

Pricing Emotions

Customers will experience three primary pricing emotions at various times through the purchasing cycle:

1. Price Resistance
2. Payment Resistance
3. Price Anxiety

Price Resistance ("Sticker Shock")

As long as you are dealing with people, you will encounter price resistance, usually at the beginning of the negotiating process and thus it is easy to identify. The best way to overcome it is by educating customers as to the value you provide. The purpose of the FPA meeting with customers (see Chapter 10) is solely to discuss the value you add. This meeting is an excellent opportunity to educate them with respect to this value. By discussing value, rather than price, you will lower a customer's price resistance. One major reason for this is that you have changed the customer's focus from each service your firm provides to the totality of what your firm has to offer. When you codify a group of services into an Fixed Price Agreement (FPA) (see Chapter 11), you have, in a way, "tangibilized" the intangible. Whenever you can turn the intangible into the tangible, you have an advantage. The FPA serves this purpose.

Witness the success McDonald's has had with its Value Meals. Items most frequently purchased are combined, leading customers to consider the value of the total meal, not just its component parts. This has been an unquestionable success for McDonald's, so much so that all of its competitors have emulated the strategy. This same strategy can be used in professional firms through offering, for example, an "entrepreneurial business program" whereby a firm will help a business incorporate, select an entity type, draft the minutes of meetings, perform tax planning, and prepare the tax return, all for one standard price (negotiated with each customer, of course). This is highly successful, as it offers the customer an entire service package and changes their focus from the cost of each service to the value of the total offering.

To overcome "sticker shock," the professional must prove to the customer that the value they will derive from the service exceeds the cash price being paid. Value, from a customer's perspective, is computed by dividing the benefits received by the price of the service. If you cannot convince the customer that this ratio is greater than 1.0, you will not effectively overcome "sticker shock." If price resistance cannot be conquered through educating the customer, then you should probably not take the engagement. You do not want to work for people who do not understand, or refuse to pay for, the value you provide.

Never lower your price to acquire a customer who is suffering from price resistance, as this cheats your firm's best customers—those who value what you provide—and subsidizes your worst customers—those drawn to you by price considerations alone. These will be the first customers to defect once they find a service provider willing to do the work for less.

Many people automatically equate high price with high quality. In his fascinating book, *Influence: The New Psychology of Modern Persuasion*,

Robert B. Cialdini tells of a friend who had opened an Indian jewelry store in Arizona. She had an allotment of turquoise jewelry that she had not been able to sell, even during the peak tourist season. Before leaving town, she wrote a note to her head saleswoman, "Everything in this display case, price x 1/2," hoping just to be rid of the offending pieces, even if at a loss. When she returned, she was surprised to learn that all of the jewelry had been sold. But the employee had read the "1/2" in the scrawled message as a "2." The entire allotment had sold out at twice the original price (Cialdini, 1993: 1–2).

No doubt some customers will equate high price with high value, especially when there is very little else to judge your value on. Wise consultants know that if they price their services on the low end of the market, the customers do not have the incentive to take their advice seriously. On the other hand, if rates are at the upper end of the spectrum (say, $10,000 per day), the customers will hang on every word you say and the probability of implementing your suggestions is higher. If they do this, and what you are selling is good advice, they will be more successful and thus will value you that much more. This cycle spirals upward; the more you charge, the more people follow your suggestions, the more profitable they become, and the more valuable you are to them.

Payment Resistance

Payment resistance is simply the customer's unwillingness to cut the check. Who likes to pay their bills? Payment resistance is overcome by involving the customer in the design, price, and payment terms of your service. Because subjective terms such as "fair price" and "prompt payment" can have different meanings to a professional and a customer, these terms should be defined when you meet with the customer to draw up the FPA. An important part of any sale is the payment terms. In this area, professionals have been lackadaisical in realizing exactly how much value they offer their customers by giving them payment terms. Accounts receivable, a major headache in any firm, is largely the result of payment resistance. Customers of professionals do not have problems with the quality of the work, but they do know that there's not much downside to paying the professional last. Once people are committed to a written agreement, they are much less likely not to cut the check.

One effective method to overcome payment resistance, besides using the FPA that details the payment terms, is to deliver all services in person.

This provides the customer with a factor with which to judge your value, other than the bill you present. The personal relationship has a very salutary effect on lowering a customer's payment resistance and should be used as frequently as possible to speed up accounts-receivable collections.

Sometimes the problem is that the firm failed to get the customer to commit to payment terms. The all-important "ego investment" is missing, whereby the customer will strive to act in accordance with that commitment. The customer may have signed the Engagement Letter, wherein your firm spells out its price, payment terms, and what happens in the event the customer does not pay. But how many of your customers read that letter? How much customer involvement is there when the firm *imposes* payment terms on the customer?

In any other business, when terms are offered, a profit is made. Witness General Motors Acceptance Corporation and General Electric Credit, among others. These organizations are taking a risk, and thereby making a profit, by offering credit to customers. Yet professional organizations take a great risk by granting terms and they reap no profit as a result. They have all the downside of write-offs and write-downs but share none of the up side. Most other businesses have converted to cash terms (doctors, dentists). Converting your firm to a COD basis would be difficult, though some CPA firms do it, for instance, with tax returns. However, payment terms are a major bargaining chip when it comes to negotiating a price, as your customers will attest to in running their own businesses.

Make the payment terms an instrumental part of the price negotiation. The old axiom of business valuators is: "I'll let you set the price if you let me set the terms." Put terms on the table as part of the price negotiation. This gets that all important ego investment from the customer. For example, if you are dealing with a retailer who is cash poor in the spring (when most CPA firms are cash rich), they may prefer to make a smaller payment during that time of the year and gradually raise the payment through the last quarter, when they are flush with cash. This flexibility allows the customer to budget accounting or legal fees with the cyclical nature of the specific business, an enormously valuable offering from your firm, and one that should never be discounted. Customers may prefer to pay quarterly, monthly, semiannually, or even a third down at the beginning of the year with the rest paid evenly the following 11 months. As long as they pay the entire agreed-upon price in 12 months (this can be calendar or fiscal), leave them free to choose when they want to pay. For new customers, get a retainer, or a 25 to 50 percent downpayment. Always require a deposit from all new customers to gauge their seriousness and commitment to your firm. If customers are not willing to pay a portion *before* the service, they may be reluctant to pay *after* the service is performed.

Once the customer decides how to pay you, this is codified in the FPA and authorized by the customer. Once you get this commitment, the customer will usually behave in the manner agreed to. FPA customers simply load the payment terms as set forth in the agreement into their accounting system and a check is cut, like clockwork, at the designated due date. It reduces the administrative burden, as no invoice is required, and it removes the negative moment of truth that a bill creates each month in the mind of the customer. What more could you ask for? You may also want to consider accepting credit cards. Try to make paying your firm as easy as possible for the customer.

Price Anxiety

The FPA can help with price anxiety, or buyer's remorse. It is a well known fact that luxury automobile advertisements are targeted at existing owners, rather than potential owners. This is because after such a large purchase, first-time customers may regret the purchase or at least want reassurance that they made a good decision; price anxiety will be less likely to affect repeat customers. Price anxiety is a significant psychological emotion that customers will go through, especially after entering into an FPA with your firm. Overcome price anxiety by staying in touch with your customers, assuring them that they made the right decision in hiring you, and exceeding their expectations. You can also offer a service guarantee, which dramatically lowers price anxiety. (This will be discussed in Chapter 9.)

Summary and Conclusions

This chapter looked at the reasons professionals, as a group, tend to have write-downs and write-offs. Customers do not pay their bills for two reasons: They are *unable* or they are *unwilling*. Professionals can negate the former by becoming more adept at pre-qualifying all new customers. To lessen the latter, work to ascertain customer expectations at the beginning of each job, exceeding those expectations, setting prices at the beginning of each engagement, and emphasizing the service component. Firms that concentrate on these problems should be able to cut drastically the occurrence of write-downs.

9 THE ADVANTAGES OF VALUE PRICING

*A cynic is one who knows the price of
everything and the value of nothing.*

—Oscar Wilde

The successful professional firms of today will price their services according to external value, as perceived and determined by the customer, rather than by internal costs. By so doing, they will restore pricing to the strategic marketing tool that it is. One of the first tasks is to define exactly what is meant by "Value Pricing."

Just as businesses have gone out of their way to replace the word *customer*, they have done the same thing with the word *price*. People pay a postage *rate* to the United States Postal Service; *fees* to professionals; *premiums* to insurance companies; *rent* for apartments; *tuition* for education; *fares* for taxis, airlines, and buses; *tolls* to cross bridges; *admissions* for concerts, movies, and sporting events; *finance charges* for credit cards; and *tariffs* and *duties* for importing goods to another country. All of these euphemisms deal with the strategic marketing decision of price.

The term *Value Pricing* has a very positive connotation, and this terminology should become part of your firm's culture. Use the term *pricing* with your customers, as it is a more friendly term than *billing*. (Who likes to receive bills?) Consider the word *pricing* in contrast to the word *fee*. Webster's Dictionary describes the word *fee* as "payment, service, or homage due a superior; payment asked or given for professional services, admissions, licenses, tuition, etc.; charge."

The word *value* has an even more specific meaning, especially to an economist. It means: *"The maximum amount that a consumer would be willing to pay for an item."* (Landsburg, 1996: 784) This is the auction market concept again, wherein each bidder offers the maximum price he is willing to pay for a particular item.

Therefore, *Value Pricing* can be defined as *the maximum amount a given customer is willing to pay for a particular service, before the time of delivery.*

Value Pricing does not mean a percentage markup on your standard rate, or a contingency arrangement based upon a certain result, or a bonus added to the agreed upon price, though any price negotiation may include any of these factors. Value Pricing requires that you price on the margin, for each customer, for each service, disregarding the following:

- What you charge other customers for the "same service"
- What you have charged the customer in the past
- What your competition is willing to charge the customer
- What the competition used to charge the customer

Robert G. Cross in *Revenue Management* defines Value Pricing (he calls it Revenue Management) in this manner:

> Revenue Management is the application of disciplined tactics that predict consumer behavior at the micromarket level and optimize product availability and price to maximize revenue growth. In even simpler terms, Revenue Management ensures that companies will sell the right product to the right customer at the right time for the right price (Cross, 1997: 51–52).

Here is an examples of pricing on the margin. A customer's tax return is paid for by his wife's employer, up to a maximum amount of $1,000 each year. He is paid this amount in full, and if he can negotiate a price of less than $1,000, he pockets the difference. At standard rates, his tax return would cost $400. The CPA negotiates a price of $800. The customer is pleased because he pockets $200, and the CPA is happy because he earns twice the "standard rate." That price was determined irrespective of what the CPA had charged the customer in the past (when the wife's employer did not pay for it), and it was set without discussing time involvement, because that entire issue was removed from the consideration. The CPA discovered that the wife's employer paid the bill by asking questions, and the customer volunteered the information. Had the CPA simply focused on hours spent, he would leave approximately $400 on the table. That $400 represents part of the consumer surplus, as discussed Chapter 5, for this particular customer.

Another example of pricing on the margin is the stylist who does the hair and makeup for a bride on her wedding day, and maybe even for the entire wedding party. Do you think that the bride values this particular service, on this particular day, more than any other day? The cosmetologist does not require any more time to do their hair, but she charges more for accommodating the bride on a particular day. And, as proof that even more consumer surplus exists, the customer usually provides a very generous tip for the service.

Some argue that this is immoral, or that it's tantamount to taking advantage of someone based upon special circumstances. Nonsense. No transaction would occur if both parties did not derive a benefit from it (in the absence of coercion, duress, or fraud, naturally) and thus what this really represents is *consenting adults engaging in capitalist acts*. It is exactly what Friedrich A. Hayek discussed when he spoke of "special knowledge of circumstances of the fleeting moment." Superbowl tickets command a high price, as do apartments during the Olympics or vacation homes during ski season. Different time, different place, different circumstances, *different price*. The only reason professionals have such an ethical and moral problem with this type of pricing is that they treat all of their customers the same, regardless of what they are doing for them or how much the customer may value their service. Customers do not want to be treated *equally*, they want to be treated *individually*. The post office and your local cable company treat you *equally*, and they are not good models to emulate.

Many factors influence the prices of products and services in this 7 trillion dollar plus economy, and the only reason professionals run into ethical issues is that they live in a one-dimensional world of hours spent multiplied by a "standard rate," where any deviation from that formula is considered immoral. The ethical and moral issues of Value Pricing and hourly billing will also be discussed in Chapter 16.

We Live in a Barter Economy

It may be helpful, for the time being, to suspend talking about absolute price in terms of dollars and cents. **Absolute price** is defined as: "The number of dollars that can be exchanged for a specified quantity of a given good." Instead, let's think of price in relative terms. **Relative price** is: "The quantity of some other good that can be exchanged for a specified quantity of a given good." (Landsburg, 1996: 34) When you get to the heart of the matter, you really live in a barter economy. By purchasing this book you have traded some of your services as a professional for some of my services as an author. Money is simply a way to eliminate the necessity of a coincidence of wants. Since I did not need your particular service at this time, you were able to exchange money, earned serving others who did require your services, for this book. Money has no value, per se; value is based on what people are willing to give up. Individual demand can be no greater than the ability to supply others with the goods and services they want. Money simply facilitates the myriad of transactions that take place in the economy; its use is more efficient than bartering.

In the final analysis, any time you make a purchase, you are simply exchanging some of your labor for the labor of others. In microeconomics, when the word *price* is used, it always refers to a *relative price*. When you view the world through this paradigm, it is obvious that each individual has a very different relative price for any given product or service.

An interesting example of the effects of relative pricing is oranges that are grown in Florida and shipped to New York. Even though New Yorkers do not grow oranges, they tend, on average, to eat better oranges than the residents of Florida. To understand why, consider relative price. Suppose "good oranges" cost $1 in Florida and "bad oranges" cost 50¢ (not bad per se, but "bad" relative to the "good" oranges). Therefore, the relative price of a good orange in Florida is two bad ones. But for the New Yorker, because of 50¢ in transportation costs, a good orange costs $1.50 and a bad orange costs $1. Therefore, the relative price of a good orange is only 1.5 bad oranges. Since New Yorkers face a lower relative price, they eat, on average, more good oranges.

This explains why high quality goods tend to get exported and why luxuries are disproportionately represented in international trade. Examples are British Rolls Royces, grapes from California, leather goods from Italy, French wines, Texas steaks, Colombian coffee, Idaho potatoes, Hawaiian pineapples, and Washington apples. Whenever a tax, transportation expense, or other fixed cost is added to a variable price of a product, what is known as the Alchian–Allen effect takes place: *Consumers tend to shift their tastes in favor of higher quality products.*

For example, when the government began taxing packages of cigarettes, king-size and super-king-size were introduced to provide more smoking minutes per pack. The same logic applies to phone calls. Until recently, many phones on airplanes charged a flat rate of $15 per domestic call, no matter how long you talked. Charge a flat price for a phone call, and people will talk longer. Put a fixed charge on any product, and it will migrate to where it's relative cost is the lowest.

The point is this: The price of anything is influenced by a multitude of factors, and the more you understand about your customer's circumstances, the better able you will be to capture the consumer surplus that may exist. One residential contractor who builds spec homes raises the price if a home does not sell within a month of being listed. The contractor discovered that when he raised the price by $50,000, a different type of customer would show interest in the home—perhaps a customer who was trying to roll over a capital gain from the sale of a previous home and had to spend a minimum amount. The contractor operated in an area where people moved in from states with relatively high real estate prices. The contractor understood some of the factors that influenced people's willingness to pay. He was successful selling at the higher price between 80 and 90 percent of the time. This is price discrimination at its finest.

Relative price also has ramifications for pricing based upon opportunity costs. For example, airlines will frequently charge a penalty (or fee) to change a travel date. I recently was on a trip and had to move up my departure date by two days. The airline charged me $150 for accommodating this request. Did it cost them anything to do this? No, but they knew I would compare that $150 charge to two nights in a hotel room, two more days of my rental car, and two more days of airport parking. Had the airlines priced that change on a pure cost-plus basis, they would miss those marginal opportunities to tap into the consumer surplus.

The Fixed Price Agreement

Value Pricing can effectively be put in writing by meeting with the customer and drawing up a Fixed Price Agreement (FPA). Here is a sample draft of an FPA, offered here so that you can see what is being referred to. This Agreement will be presented again and discussed in detail in Chapter 11.

Sample Fixed Price Agreement

December 1, 1999

Dear Customer:

In order to document the understanding between us as to the scope of the work that ABC, CPAs will perform, we are entering into this **Fixed Price Agreement** with XYZ, Inc. To avoid any misunderstandings, this Agreement defines the services we will perform for you as well as your responsibilities under this Agreement.

2000 PROFESSIONAL SERVICES

ABC will perform the following services for XYZ during 2000:

• 1999 W-2s/1099s and 4th Quarter Payroll Tax Reports and Workers' Comp Report	$ XX
• 1st, 2nd, & 3rd Quarter Payroll 2000 Reports and Workers' Comp Reports and Fiscal Year Sales Tax Return	XX
• 1999 Year-End Accounting Adjustments and Closing of 1999 Books	XX
• 1999 XYZ S Corporation Tax Returns	XX
• 1999 Audited Financial Statements with PBCs to be provided by XYZ by March 15, 2000	XX
• Annual Consulting Service 2000*	XX
TOTAL 2000 PROFESSIONAL SERVICES	$XXX

* Included in the Annual Consulting Service are the following services to be provided by ABC to XYZ:

  • Unlimited meetings to discuss operations of XYZ, business matters, tax matters, and any other topic at the discretion of XYZ or its employees and/or agents.

  • Unlimited phone support for XYZ personnel and/or independent contractors and agents regarding accounting assistance, recording of transactions, etc.

Because our Fixed Price Agreement provides ongoing access to the accounting, tax, and business advice you need on a fixed-price basis, you are not inhibited from seeking timely advice by the fear of a clock running endlessly. Our services are designed around fixed prices, as opposed to hourly rates, and offer you access to the accumulated wisdom of the firm through CPAs with substantial experience who can help enhance your company's future and achieve its business goals.

While the fixed price entitles your company to unlimited consultation with us, if your question or issue requires additional research and analysis beyond the consultation, that work will be subject to an additional price negotiation before the service is to be performed, and a Change Order will be issued before delivery of the additional service, with payment terms agreed to in advance.

Unanticipated Services

Furthermore, the parties agree that if an unanticipated need arises (such as, but not limited to, an audit by a taxing agency, or any other exogenous service not anticipated in this agreement by the parties), ABC hereby agrees to perform this additional work at a mutually agreed upon price *before the service is provided.* This service will be billed separately to XYZ, as part of a Change Order, and will be payable upon presentation [or payable upon terms mutually agreed upon].

Service Guarantee

Our work is guaranteed to the complete satisfaction of the customer. If XYZ is not completely satisfied with the services performed by ABC, we will, at the option of XYZ, either refund the price, or accept a portion of said price that reflects XYZ's level of satisfaction. We will assume you are satisfied upon final payment received under the terms of this Agreement.

Quality Review

XYZ agrees to, and hereby consents to participate in, ABC's policy of in-house Quality Review. ABC subscribes to a policy of quality review to maintain the highest quality of product produced by our firm. As part of this program, all of the major services performed under this Agreement will be reviewed by another CPA within ABC under strict rules of confidentiality. The price for this review is included in the above professional services.

The following payment plan is hereby agreed to by XYZ and ABC:

- January 31, 2000   XX
- February 28, 1999   XX
- March 31, 2000   XX
- April 30, 2000   XX
- May 31, 2000   XX

- June 30, 2000   XX
- July 31, 2000   XX
- August 31, 2000   XX
- September 30, 2000   XX
- October 31, 2000   XX
- November 30, 2000   XX
- December 31, 2000   XX

TOTAL 2000 PAYMENTS $ XXX

To assure that our arrangement remains responsive to your needs, as well as fair to both parties, we will meet throughout 2000 and, if necessary, revise or adjust the scope of the services to be provided and the prices to be charged in light of mutual experience.

Furthermore, it is understood that either party may terminate this Agreement at any time, for any reason, within 10 days of written notice to the other party. It is understood that any unpaid services that are outstanding at the date of termination are to be paid in full within 10 days from the date of termination.

If you agree that the above adequately sets forth XYZ's understanding of our mutual responsibilities, please authorize this Agreement and return it to our office. A copy is provided for your records.

We would like to take this opportunity to express our appreciation for the opportunity to serve you.

Very truly yours,

BY: _____

Allan Somnolent, Partner
ABC, CPAs

Agreed to and authorized:

By: _____Date: _____

Customer, President
XYZ, Inc.

The Advantages of the Fixed Price Agreement and Value Pricing

Consider the following advantages of Value Pricing and an FPA, presented in no particular order, and contrast them to the disadvantages of the hourly billing method discussed in the prior chapter.

Value Pricing Clarifies the Customer's Expectations

We know how important it is, in today's environment, to exceed the customer's expectations. This goal is difficult enough without the added burden of not knowing exactly what those expectations are. One of the first questions to ask any customer, new or veteran, is, "What do you expect from us?" Simply by asking this question, you will be able to manage and control, to some degree, those expectations, and if you believe the expectations are unreasonable, withdraw from the engagement. No matter how unreasonable those expectations may be, the time to discover them is *before* you commit any of your firm's resources to the customer. If you do not ascertain the expectations up front, no matter how technically brilliant your work may be, your customer will not be satisfied, and you will encounter severe payment resistance, and most likely you will suffer write-downs and write-offs.

The other aspect of customer expectations that needs to be understood is that *each* member of the firm who works with a customer needs to be cognizant of the those expectations. It does no good for a partner to know exactly what the customer expects if he hoards that information and does not share it with the staff working on the engagement. Every staff person should understand the expectations of the customer and strive to exceed them. This separates the Total Quality Service firms from the mediocre firms. The entire firm, from receptionist to managing partner, should be involved in delivering excellent service to every customer.

Value Pricing Pre-Qualifies the Customer

Discovering a customer's expectations reduces the danger of the customer being *unwilling* to pay you; pre-qualifying the customer ensures that the customer is *able* to pay you. To pre-qualify a customer, check references (bankers, attorneys, CPAs, etc.) and examine credit reports from Dunn and

Bradstreet, as well as personal credit reports. This method is critical for all new customers. Pre-qualifying a customer before performing any work takes time but in the long run saves countless hours spent in pricing disputes, write-offs, and other problems that could have been avoided had there been better communication at the beginning of the engagement. Those firms which complain about bad customers are usually the same firms that don't adequately pre-qualify their customers, and they also rarely turn down work.

Value Pricing Provides the Opportunity to Cross-Sell

By brainstorming with the customer regarding future goals and aspirations, you will inevitably learn of many opportunities to cross-sell your firm's services. During meetings with customers, you may discover plans to sell the business, buy a business, expand a business, or start a new division, just to name a few, and all of these are rich with opportunities for additional services. David H. Maister offers the following reason why cross-selling among professional firms has been less than successful:

> Every professional service firm I have ever encountered has had, and still has, the goal of cross-selling—expanding relationships with existing clients in order to increase the range of services delivered. Yet success in this area has been limited. Few firms, if any, have made cross-selling work on a systematic basis. And there is a simple explanation for this apparent failure: Firms have been going about it in the wrong way.
>
> Cross-selling does little, if anything, for the *client*. . . . If it does not do anything extra for the clients and just benefits you, then it is almost certainly unsustainable, and will fail [Emphasis in original] (Maister, 1997: 178–179).

Your firm cannot automatically expect to receive additional work from the customer—you have to earn it. After all, if your firm is so adept at the additional service, you should be able to compete in the market against your competitors. By focusing on what the customers want, not on what you want, you have a much better forum for effective cross-selling. This is because you are not *selling* as much as the customers are *buying*; you are helping the customers achieve their vision of the future. A saying from

Cicero reads: *Cui bono?* (Who stands to gain?). If you want to be effective at cross-selling your firm's services, you must always make sure the *customer* stands to gain. Stanley Marcus' father, Herbert Marcus, gave his son this advice upon hiring him to work at Neiman–Marcus in 1926: "There is never a good *sale* for Neiman–Marcus unless it's a good *buy* for the customer." Convey the message that you want to help in making the customer's vision come true, and as a result you will be able to cross-sell your services effectively. Empirical evidence shows that you will be more successful in cross-selling services to an FPA customer. You will also command a higher percentage of the customer's "share of wallet," that is, the total amount spent on their tax, accounting, legal services, and consulting services, with less going to your competitors.

Value Pricing Allows You to Gain "Ego Investment" from the Customer

My biggest failure when implementing Value Pricing was a basic one: Failure to get the customer's ego investment. Having the customers involved in the design, delivery, and pricing of your firm's services is a powerful emotional investment on their part. Once an ego investment is made, the customer will tend to behave in a manner that is consistent with the commitment. This aspect of human psychology is documented in *Influence: The Psychology of Persuasion,* by Robert B. Cialdini. One example he gives relates to gamblers at a racetrack.

> A study done by a pair of Canadian psychologists uncovered something fascinating about people at the racetrack: Just after placing a bet, they are much more confident of their horse's chances of winning than they are immediately before laying down that bet. Of course, nothing about the horse's chances actually shifts; it's the same horse, on the same track, in the same field; but in the minds of those bettors, its prospects improve significantly once that ticket is purchased. Although a bit puzzling at first glance, the reason for the dramatic change has to do with a common weapon of social influence.... It is, quite simply, our nearly obsessive desire to be (and to appear) consistent with what we have already done. Once we have made a choice or taken a stand, we will encounter personal and interpersonal pressures to behave

consistently with that commitment. Those pressures will cause us to respond in ways that justify our earlier decision (Cialdini, 1993: 57).

A second story from Cialdini is illuminating from a human behavioral perspective and as a price discrimination strategy. He starts by saying he was in a toy store purchasing a big, electric road-race set for his son, in January. He ran into a neighbor making the same purchase for his son. They recalled that they had run into each other the previous January, too, making rather expensive post-Christmas gift purchases for their sons, and chalked this up to coincidence. Cialdini later recounted this story to a friend who had worked in the toy business, and the following conversation ensued:

> "No coincidence," the friend said knowingly.
> "What do you mean, 'No coincidence'?"
> "Look," he said, "let me ask you a couple of questions about the road-race set you bought this year. First, did you promise your son that he'd get one for Christmas?"
> "Well, yes, I did. Christopher had seen a bunch of ads for them on the Saturday morning cartoon shows and said that was what he wanted for Christmas. I saw a couple of the ads myself and it looked like fun, so I said okay."
> "Strike one," he announced. "Now for my second question. When you went to buy one, did you find all the stores sold out?"
> "That is right, I did! The stores said they'd ordered some but did not know when they'd get any more in. So I had to buy Christopher some other toys to make up for the road-race set. But how did you know?"
> "Strike two," he said. "Just let me ask one more question. Did not this same sort of thing happen the year before with the robot toy?"
> "Wait a minute. . . you are right. That is just what happened. This is incredible. How did you know?"
> "No psychic powers; I just happen to know how several of the big toy companies jack up their January and February sales. They start prior to Christmas with attractive TV ads for certain special toys. The kids, naturally, want what they see

and extract Christmas promises for these items from their parents. Now here's where the genius of the companies' plan comes in: They undersupply the stores with the toys they've gotten the parents to promise. Most parents find those things sold out and are forced to substitute other toys of equal value. The toy manufacturers, of course, make a point of supplying the stores with plenty of these substitutes. Then, after Christmas, the companies start running the ads again for the other special toys. That juices up the kids to want those toys more than ever. They go running to their parents whining, 'You promised, you promised," and the adults go trudging off to the store to live up dutifully to their words."

"Where," I said, beginning to see now, "they meet other parents they haven't see for a year, falling for the same trick, right?"

"Right. Uh, where are you going?"

"I'm going to take that road-race set right back to the store." I was so angry I was nearly shouting.

"Wait. Think for a moment first. Why did you buy it this morning?"

"Because I did not want to let Christopher down and because I wanted to teach him that promises are to be lived up to."

"Well, has any of that changed? Look, if you take his toy away now, he won't understand why. He'll just know that his father broke a promise to him. Is that what you want?"

"No," I said, sighing, "I guess not. So, you are telling me that they doubled their profit on me for the past two years, and I never even knew it; and now that I do, I'm still trapped— by my own words. So, what you are telling me is, 'Strike Three.'"

He nodded, "And you are out." (ibid., 65–66)

Everyone wants to be in control; this is basic human nature. Think of how you feel in an airport when your plane is delayed, and the gate attendants do not provide you with any information. You feel helpless, out of control. This is precisely why the pilot of an airplane will make an announcement during the flight of where you are, your estimated time of arrival, and how high you are flying. As a passenger, are you going to argue that he's flying too low? The announcement is designed to give you a sense of control in a situation in which you are virtually helpless.

Give customers a sense of ownership over your firm's services by providing them with information, offering them choices, and customizing your delivery to meet their needs. FedEx and UPS, for example, have spent billions of dollars providing customers with computers and software that allow them to track their own shipments. While this has not increased the efficiency or decreased the time of delivery, it has gone a long way toward giving the customers a sense of ownership over their shipping needs. The customer also has been given the power to access the internal workings of these two organizations, making for an "excuseless" culture. Some professionals would be uncomfortable giving their customers complete access to their work-in-progress, yet this is exactly what is beginning to happen among law firms. Customers are demanding instantaneous access to work as it is done on their case, through Internet and intranet links, a trend that will increase.

Value Pricing Improves Communication

Effective communication is one of the characteristics of the successful firms when it comes to Value Pricing. Better communication with the customer leads to fewer write-downs and write-offs, and also lowers the probability of litigation. Keeping the lines of communication open between your firm and the customer is critical in making your climb up the Value Curve. Offer the customer unlimited phone calls and meetings any time during the year to tear down the time-clock mentality. Nobody likes to be nickled and dimed for every phone call or meeting.

If customers have a "Consulting Service" in the FPA offering unlimited phone calls and meetings, they will seek your advice *before* engaging in a significant transaction. Many professionals look at their customers after the fact and say, "Why didn't you contact me before you did this? If we had structured it this way, we could have saved $X?" Customers do not contact you because they want to avoid paying for every call. By removing that negative feeling, you will learn what the customer is planning and have an opportunity to add value *before* a major event, thereby advancing up the Value Curve.

Furthermore, the process of drafting the FPA, with the customer's input, will dramatically improve the communication between the parties. The

FPA isn't so much a legal contract as it is a method of communication. Similar to the practice of companies having employees sign a mission (or value) statement, getting the customer's signature on the FPA is an effective way of cementing the relationship. Most people place great emphasis on their signature and take seriously the obligations signed. This is what makes the FPA so valuable, even though it contains a relatively easy exit clause.

Quoting Fixed Prices Projects Confidence and Experience

A most frequent question regarding offering fixed prices is: "How do you know how to set the price before you know how long it will to take to perform the service?" The response to this question is that the price of the service has absolutely nothing to do with how long it takes you.

If you are not yet comfortable with this thinking consider that you can set a price after a service has been performed, either by writing it up or, more likely, down, so why are you unable to determine the value before you start? Most of the work professionals perform (probably more than 90 percent) is routine, which means professionals have enough experience to quote a fixed price.

Sometimes when you quote a price, the nature of the engagement changes so much that a higher price is warranted. But that does not mean you should not quote a price up front. What it means is that you issue a Change Order when unexpected events arise that require more resources to be devoted by your firm. Change Orders require you to stop working and communicate with the customer that the nature of the engagement has changed, why it has changed, and how much additional it is going to cost them. Change Orders will be discussed more extensively later in this chapter and in Chapter 11. They are a wonderful device for communicating with the customer and extracting a higher price when the original job quoted has changed in scope.

Two other points need to be raised regarding quoting fixed prices up front. First, your competition is probably not doing this, except perhaps for audits and tax returns. Quoting fixed prices gives a significant competitive advantage; but as customers continue to revolt against hourly billing, this advantage will wane.

Second, never quote a range of price. When you are too timid to quote a single price and say something to the effect of: "It will cost between

$15,000 and $20,000," the customer heard $15,000 and you heard $20,000. When you submit a bill for $18,000, thinking you saved the customer $2,000, the customer is going to ask why it cost $3,000 more than you said. Never quote ranges. Straighten your back, push up your shoulders, get up your nerve, and quote the high end of your mental range, every time. This will avoid many disputes at the end of the engagements.

Value Pricing Increases a Customer's Switching Costs

When you enter into an FPA with your customers, you are increasing their switching costs over time. The higher the price of the agreement, the more services you are performing, and the more you know about a customer, the more expensive it will be for the customer to defect. This binds the two of you in "golden handcuffs" and is a prerequisite for creating a long-term partnership.

Think about the airline's frequent flyer programs. Because they impose a switching cost on travelers who might otherwise divide their flying budgets among several airlines, they encourage customers to use only one airline. These programs, which were introduced in 1981, are extremely effective in engendering loyalty among customers.

Creating a partnership with your customers interlinks your destiny and prosperity. When you have a partnership, you are no longer worried about your competition, but you are focused on your customer's competition. Your goal is to climb up the Value Curve by offering more consultative services.

Also, by bundling a package of services into an FPA, you are making it more difficult for a competitor to enter into the customer relationship, because they won't be able to single out one part of the bundled services in order to offer a lower price (this is one reason you may not want to price each service in the FPA separately, but rather as a whole package). Price bundling will also reduce the customer's propensity to haggle over each item and instead focus on the value of all the services being provided.

Value Pricing Forces Your Firm to Be Efficient

Needless to say, if your firm offers fixed prices, you must delegate the work to the level best equipped to handle it, and this will prevent surgeons from piercing ears. This will free up manager and partner time to cross-sell the firm's services as the firm makes its way up the customer's Value Curve. By developing efficient internal methods, procedures, and processes to complete routine work, you will also lower your internal costs and achieve higher profitability.

Start with a blank page and analyze each procedure, process, and method your firm performs, asking yourself the following questions:

- Why do we do this?
- Do we need to do it at all?
- Does it add value for our customers?
- If so, how can we do it better?

If it does not add value to the customer, there's no need to do it. There is no right way to do the wrong thing. Professional firms will charge for everything they can. Focus on those things that the customer values, not on faxes, copies, phone calls, technology fees, or computer processing fees, none of which the customer values. At Milliken & Company, a Malcolm Baldridge National Quality Award winner, a sign reads: "Quality is not the absence of defects as defined by management, but the presence of value as defined by customers." Also, if work is delegated to the most efficient person, the customer is assured that the person with the most experience is handling the work, a tremendous selling point if your firm is large.

Value Pricing Overcomes Buyer's Emotions

Value Pricing works to overcome price resistance, payment resistance, and price anxiety, common emotions experienced by buyers. These emotions are discussed in detail in Chapter 8.

Value Pricing Gives the Customer a Chance to Complain

A "100% Unconditional Money Back Service Guarantee" clause included in the FPA is a covenant with customers that if, for any reason whatsoever, they are not satisfied with your firm's value proposition (quality, service, or price), you agree to give them a complete refund, or let them pay what they believe is the worth of the service(s). Notice this is not based on any type of result or contingency (which may be in violation of various ethical and government laws), but is based upon the customer's level of satisfaction.

This involves taking a risk, but that is, after all, where profits come from. Here is what Maister says about the service guarantee:

> Consider the alternative. Without a guarantee, what is a firm saying to its clients? "We're committed to complete satisfaction, but if we fail to please you, we expect to be paid anyway!" (Maister, 1997: 196)

Consider the advantages of this strategy, then decide for yourself if you think the risk is worth the reward.

The service guarantee communicates a commitment to excellence and Total Quality Service on the part of your firm by *showing* your customers—not just *telling* them—how much better you are than your competition. Your entire firm will be driven to exceed the customer's expectations, as everyone, from the receptionist on up, will be cognizant of how important this is because your money is where your mouth is. A guarantee sends the message that there is no profit center in your firm that people can automatically count on, other than a customer's check that does not bounce. Your inferior competition cannot (and will not) offer a guarantee like this, and that gives you an advantage in the marketplace, which is especially effective with new customers. It may be the one element in your Request For Proposal (RFP) that sways the customer to go with your firm, by eliminating their risk. It also generates word-of-mouth advertising, the most effective advertising known.

A guarantee forces your firm to pre-qualify new customers more effectively. Because you realize you are liable to give back the money, you want to have a high level of trust with the customer. You must develop a mutually advantageous relationship, understand each other's expectations, and make sure that each party is receiving value from entering into the transaction.

All things being equal, a service that is guaranteed is worth more than one that is not. You will be able to command a higher price for offering this level of commitment to the customer. Why should the customer bet on you if you will not bet on yourself?

An additional benefit of offering the service guarantee, more important than those listed above is this: It gives the customer an incentive to complain. Customer complaints, when handled correctly, are actually opportunities in disguise to impress the customer with your great service and increase their loyalty, goodwill, and, ultimately, retention.

Only 4 percent of dissatisfied customers complain. The other 96 percent quietly go away and 91 percent of those will never come back. Further, a typical dissatisfied customer will tell eight to 10 people about his or her problem. One in five will tell 20. This is why it takes 12 positive service incidents to make up for one negative incident. If word of mouth advertising can build businesses, think how negative word-of-mouth advertising can destroy them. Generally speaking, customers will not complain for three reasons:

1. They think it will do no good;
2. Complaining is difficult; and
3. Most customers do not want to feel awkward and pushy. Competition is intense and customers find fleeing easier than fighting.

In 1988, more than 450 million people traveled by airplane. Yet, only 21,000 complained. In one month alone, 20,000 passengers had their baggage mishandled (lost, delayed, damaged) and only 156 passengers bothered to file complaints. These results are quite consistent with human behavior.

In Total Quality Service organizations, a complaint represents an opportunity to correct a problem and a second chance to preserve the customer relationship. When a customer complains, firms gain valuable knowledge of areas of service delivery that need improvement. A firm that is unaware of how or where it needs to improve is no better than one that is unable to improve. A complaint is a second chance to gain the customer's business. If corrected to the customer's satisfaction, a complaint can actually increase customer loyalty.

When it comes to defects, the customer will remember the *satisfying outcome*, not the original error. When customers bring errors to your attention, the customers need to be rewarded with fast, positive action. A customer problem represents a gap between what the customer wanted to have happen and what actually happened. When customers are upset enough to complain, their stress level is very high but their expectations are very low (they may even be expecting an argument). If you handle the error correctly, you have a wonderful opportunity to exceed those expectations and quite literally turn customers into raving fans who will tell their spouses, friends, and colleagues what a satisfactory service experience they had with your firm.

The golden rule with respect to customer recovery systems is simple: It is not *who is right;* it is *what is right.* Rather than abdicating personal responsibility for an error, take ownership of it. Hal Rosenbluth, CEO of Rosenbluth Travel, returns the commissions earned on any travel arrangements his company makes incorrectly, in effect, working for free whenever a mistake is made in the customer's travel itinerary. Now that is a service guarantee. According to Rosenbluth in his book *The Customer Comes Second and Other Secrets:*

> It's better to spend money refunding clients when they are not satisfied than to forfeit money in lost accounts for the same reason.
>
> Many of our service-guarantee refunds have been because of supplier error [airlines, hotels, rental car agencies, etc.], but we returned our commissions to our clients because we hold ourselves responsible for the entire process (Rosenbluth, 1992: 135, 204).

That is a practice that is virtually nonexistent in the travel agency industry. It is a commitment to Total Quality Service. No amount of marketing can purchase the loyalty that will result from that type of treatment. *If you wouldn't charge your best friend for the service, do not charge your customer.* It is a very high standard to live by, but that is what Total Quality Service is all about—constantly raising the bar of customer expectations.

Will customers take advantage of you? Perhaps. But at least they will identify themselves as problem customers, and you will refund their money *once,* then drop them from your customer base. The customers who try to take advantage of you are not the type of customers you want. Of the many CPAs I've met who offer service guarantees, not one has ever given a full refund. They have given partial refunds, but they will admit that the customer was entitled to them because the CPA was at fault. Most customers are not out to take advantage of you, but if you believe they are and this attitude prevents you from implementing a policy that has such tremendous advantages, then you are too involved in trying to solve problems. You are foregoing wonderful opportunities.

Studies done by Marriott on guest return rates found the following astonishing results: If the guest had no problems during their stay, the return rate was 89 percent. If the guest encountered a problem during the stay and it was not corrected to their satisfaction, the return rate dropped to 69 percent. However, if guests had problems that were solved to their satisfaction, the return rate jumped to 94 percent. This explains Marriott's zealousness to make sure that no guest leaves any of its properties unsatisfied. So even when you have defects—and you will never achieve zero defects in a professional firm, since to err is human—you can turn them into zero *defections* by correcting the problem to the customer's delight.

Consider Nordstrom, world-renowned for taking any item back, anytime, for any reason. Does the company get burned? Sometimes, but as they say, only by 2 to 3 percent of their customers. It's the other 97 to 98 percent that they are concerned with. And those customers appreciate and pay a premium for Nordstrom's no-hassle return policy. Wal-mart, Embassy Suites, and Hampton Inns all offer the same guarantee and have nothing but praise for the policy.

Another point with respect to client complaints is to be wary if you are not receiving any. Nobody is ever completely satisfied with the level of service you are performing; there is always room for improvement. Either your customers are not being candid, or, more likely, they are not being asked for feedback. In fact, according to the United States Office of Consumer Affairs, 37 to 45 percent of all service customers are dissatisfied but do not complain. This is an astonishing statistic that should alert you to encourage complaints and view each one as an opportunity to build customer loyalty and goodwill.

A last consideration is this: **You already offer a service guarantee.** If customers complain loudly enough, you write down or write off their bills. But you are doing this after the fact, when you receive no benefit from it. You already have the policy in place but it is *covert*, not *overt*. By placing the guarantee in your marketing literature, firm brochure, on your letterhead, fax coversheet, and in your FPAs, you will derive a tangible benefit. Not only will you be valued more highly and command a greater level of respect in the eyes of the customer, but this also will assist you in Value Pricing by removing more risk from the customer.

Value Pricing Prices Can Be Increased Each Year

When was the last time you raised your hourly rate? What did your customers think? (Did you even ask them?) Most customers do not like it because they do not equate your hourly rate with any tangible value. But with an FPA, on the other hand, the totality of your firm's value proposition is right in front of them, and they had a hand in designing it. Therefore, every year, even if no services are added to the FPA, you will be able to increase the price by a cost-of-living factor. How much should a no-change FPA be raised? Consider that your customers are used to most of their business costs increasing every year. Look at a customer's income statement, talk about major vendors, and try to ascertain how much the customer's costs went up. If you learn that a customer's major supplier, which makes up 20 percent of the cost of goods sold, increased prices by 8 percent, you will use that as a benchmark. You may increase your price by 5 percent. Other factors to consider are your relationship with the customer, whether you are getting a larger share of the customer's wallet, whether you are able to cross-sell them additional services in the upcoming year, and the payment terms.

It is a fact that you will be able to increase your prices every year with a customer who has entered into an FPA with less resistance than with one who did not. Also this will be easier than trying to raise your hourly billing rate.

Value Pricing Provides a Competitive Differentiation

Since each FPA is *customized* to the customer, the perceived value of your firm increases. In contrast, by using hourly billing, you are simply treating all customers the same, which is not a prescription for success in today's marketplace. Innovation is important in the business world today. Customers want their professionals to be creative and innovative in helping them solve their problems and pursue opportunities. Being innovative with respect to designing and pricing your firm's services, and customizing them to each customer, is a truly effective competitive differentiation in the marketplace.

Your close rate will increase when you offer fixed prices combined with a service guarantee to new customers. Customers love this type of pricing, and that alone will ensure increases in the years ahead. The competitive window of advantage will slowly begin to close, as customers will come to *expect* fixed prices, so the time to adopt the practice is before the rest of the crowd does. The early adopters always benefit the most by taking a new risk. Once the method is fully proven, and the rest of a population adopts it, the profit opportunities will diminish.

Value Pricing Specifies Conditions for Change Orders

Auto mechanics are sued principally over the quality of their work. You take your rough-running car to a mechanic, get it back, and it still runs rough. The issue is never how long it took the mechanic to perform the job, despite standard shop rates and estimated times to perform each job, which are used as a benchmark to provide estimates. Then consider why professionals have pricing and collection problems. The reason rarely concerns the quality of the work, but rather how much time it took, the most popular question from the customer being, "How could it have taken that long?" This is an interesting contrast and leads to the question, "What are the mechanics doing that professionals are not? The answer is that they are issuing Change Orders. Various state laws force mechanics to give the customer an estimate before each job is done, and this imposes on them the legal requirement to contact the customer and explain how the scope of the job has changed and provide an estimate of the cost. But why should you wait for a law to be passed to engage in a practice that is obviously highly effective? Part of being "professional" means that you are self-regulating and do not look to government licensing bodies to promulgate business practices that make sense for your customers (not to mention for you).

Value Pricing Lowers Asymmetrical Information

Customers will always try to conceal from you how much they are willing to pay for your services. Economists refer to *asymmetrical information* as information concerning a transaction which is unequally shared between the two parties to the transaction.

The FPA provides a venue for a meeting of the minds to take place between customer and professional when it comes to designing and valuing a firm's services. This is a tremendous opportunity to discover exactly what a customer values. The next chapter will discuss various questions you can ask the customer to lower the level of asymmetrical information that naturally exists between any buyer and seller.

Value Pricing Provides an Opportunity for a Two-Part Tariff

Steven E. Landsburg, in his textbook *Price Theory and Applications*, describes the two-part tariff:

It occurs when a firm charges an initial fee in exchange for the right to purchase its services. For example, an amusement park might charge an entrance fee, followed by a price for each ride. Private dining clubs require yearly membership fees that entitle the member to buy meals. Polaroid pictures provide a less obvious example. No consumer wants a camera for its own sake; the good that you actually purchase from the Polaroid company is Polaroid pictures. You pay for these pictures in two steps: First you pay for the camera, which then makes it possible for you to buy film and take pictures (Landsburg, 1996: 376).

How can you apply this pricing strategy to your professional firm? One way is to start charging new customers a setup fee for setting up the customer file, doing due diligence research, contacting the predecessor CPA (or attorney), and generally everything else that is entailed in taking on a new customer. This is a very effective strategy for tapping into the consumer surplus.

Second, your firm can establish a minimum price that you will never go below to serve a customer. Setting this price requires some creative thought on your part. One percent of gross revenue is sometimes used, and this appears to be a reasonable benchmark. For instance, if your book of business is $300,000, you should not spend your time on any one customer with less than $3,000 in revenue opportunity. One advantage of the percentage method is that it grows with your firm. As you grow, your customer base changes, you gain more experience, and you want to move up the Value Curve. By establishing a minimum price, you are ensuring that your firm will not devote its precious resources (and fixed costs) to customers who do not value them highly enough.

Value Pricing Opens Lines of Communications

The Annual Consulting Service provides all FPA customers with unlimited phone calls and meetings for an annual charge. This is similar to attorneys being paid a retainer whether they earn it or not and is very effective. Customers are guaranteed that you are always on call for them, willing to meet to discuss important issues affecting their businesses and personal lives. This breaks down that Berlin Wall of communication between you and the customer, you discover events *before* they happen, which is precisely the time that you can add the most value, and you can cross-sell additional services and Value Price them accordingly by issuing Change Orders.

This service will obviously be priced at different levels depending on the size of the customer, what is happening in their lives, how involved you are with them, and, of course, what they are willing to pay for it. And recall from the discussion of absolute vs. relative price, any time you put a fixed cost on a product or service, customers will gravitate to the higher quality goods.

By paying for an Annual Consulting Service, the customer is more likely to climb up the Value Curve of your firm and purchase the more expensive services you offer.

Summary and Conclusions

Overwhelming empirical evidence from inside and outside the professions proves that the advantages of Value Pricing outweigh the disadvantages. However, if you are still skeptical of Value Pricing, it is a hypothesis that can be tested in the marketplace. Begin to implement Value Pricing in incremental steps, allowing your firm to take the calculated risk of offering customers fixed prices. Once you begin to experience success, this will bolster your confidence enough that you will want to implement it on a wider range of services and engagements. It may take two to three years to get 80 percent of your firm's revenue under the aegis of Value Pricing. Move at a pace that is comfortable for your firm and for your customers. Creativity and intelligence will enable you to put these concepts into practice and to be successful in making the transition from hourly billing to Value Pricing, one customer at a time.

10 PREPARING FOR THE FIXED PRICE AGREEMENT MEETING

When I am getting ready to reason with a man I spend one-third of my time thinking about myself and what I am going to say, and two-thirds thinking about him and what he is going to say.

—Abraham Lincoln

Now that you have a good theoretical understanding of the advantages of a Fixed Price Agreement (FPA), this chapter will discuss how to negotiate a Fixed Price Agreement as you meet with your customer. Ideally, the resulting FPA will be tailored to a customer's needs as well as to the personality and culture of your firm.

My Early Failures with Value Pricing

In 1989, I began implementing fixed-fee engagement letters (what I called them at the time). I selected a few good customers (based on my relationship with them, not necessarily the size of their billings), and offered to enter into a fixed-fee arrangement with them. They were receptive to the idea, as it allowed them to budget exactly their accounting and tax costs. I had no idea why I was doing this (e.g., to remove the risk), so I did not engage in any price discrimination or charge a premium for the risk I was assuming.

Worse yet, I drafted these agreements in a vacuum, without any customer involvement. This was my biggest mistake, and it caused most of my early attempts at Value Pricing to fail. I would meet with the customer, explain the concept, and say something to the effect of, "I'll go back to my office and draft the agreement with what your accounting and tax needs will be in the forthcoming year, price it out, and send to you for your approval." For every five agreements drafted in this manner, four were rejected. I did so many things wrong that recounting my errors would be of little benefit. I want to share what I have since learned is a more effective way to negotiate and prepare the Fixed Price Agreement (FPA), namely *with* the customer's involvement.

The FPA Meeting

The sole purpose of this meeting is to discuss with the customers the value that you add to their business and their lives. Naturally price will come up, but you should build your value first—the many services that you can offer the customer that both of you believe are needed— and price should be the last topic on the agenda. I did not involve the customer in the design and nature of the services I was offering, and this was my biggest failure. Customer involvement is crucial to any sale.

Would you buy an automobile without test driving it? Would you purchase a stereo without listening to it? The more involved the customer is, the more positive emotions you will arouse, and positive emotions lead directly to more sales. Recall that nobody likes to be *sold* anything. When was the last time you purchased a big ticket item (car, house, appliance, etc.) and told your spouse or friends, "Guess what I was just *sold*?" The true sales professional involves the customers to the extent that they convince themselves on the sale; the sales professional merely helps rationalize what the customers want.

The major benefit of an FPA meeting is that the focus is on giving the customers exactly what they want and expect. This is an opportunity for you and a customer to create a shared vision of the future, to analyze where the customer is at this point, and to develop the necessary action plan to move them to where they want to be. The best salesmen in the world— from Tom Hopkins to Zig Ziglar—understand the power of getting the customer to envision a preferred future, and if you can assist the customer in attaining that vision, then you have made a tremendous move up the Value Curve.

Hold the meeting away from your office or the customer's, if possible. By getting out of your respective environments, you are less susceptible to distractions and interference. Avoid holding the meeting in the customer's office, where the customer will feel in control. Another disadvantage of meeting in the customer's office is that the customer may be less candid— the walls have ears—than in neutral territory.

Before the FPA meeting, refer to "Items to Consider Before Conducting a Fixed Price Agreement (FPA) Meeting with a Customer," found in the

"Useful Checklists" at the end of this book and on the disc, to make sure you have researched and analyzed your customer adequately.

Listen to the Customer

When you meet with a customer, let the customer talk. Try to maintain a ratio of the customer talking twice as much as you. This is difficult and requires self-restraint. Hardly anyone can achieve this ratio, even after several attempts, although it is desirable if you are to build value into your services. Listening is difficult because you think much faster than people talk. While someone is talking, you are usually listening with one-half of your brain and formulating your answer with the other. Active listening is a skill that needs to be developed. Professionals are fairly good at this, at least better than most salespeople. But you need to be even better.

Talkers may *dominate* a conversation but the listener *controls* it. In *The "I Hate Selling" Book*, Allan S. Boress says the best salesmen are good listeners:

> The best business producers listen much more than they talk. They know that by being quiet they'll learn more about other individuals and their needs. Also, clients and others greatly appreciate being listened to, which helps establish a good relationship and leads to more business. If you do more than 20 percent of the talking in a selling situation, you are doing something wrong. You must do whatever it takes to keep yourself from dominating the conversation. Instead of blab- bering away, ask relevant questions, and then sit back and take notes while the client gives you the information you need to make the sale (Boress, 1994: 16).

One of the best ways to get somebody to talk in more detail is to take notes. Taking notes conveys to the customer that what he is saying is important and that you care enough to record it. It also helps you remember exactly what was said. But most important, and this is precisely why psychiatrists and psychologists take notes, the person will provide much more detail. The more you know, the more value you will be able to add, and the higher the prices you will command.

Avoid the ever-present temptation to provide solutions to the customer's problems. That is not the purpose of the FPA meeting, at least in the initial stages. Your role at this point is to ask questions and have the customer formulate—or at least articulate—a vision of the future. Resist what William Reeb in *Start Consulting* has called "premature speculation" (Reeb, 1998: 92). Before doctors can prescribe, they must diagnose, which is the role you assume at this stage in the meeting.

Focus on Wants, Not Needs

Think of listening with having no preconceived notions of what the customer really wants. Karl Albrecht, in his book *The Northbound Train,* has this axiom that is true of professionals: "The longer you've been in business, the greater the probability you do not really understand what's going on in the minds of your customers" (Albrecht, 1994: 138). Professionals are so skilled at solving problems that they begin to believe they know what the customer needs better than the customer. And this may be true with respect to needs. A lawyer certainly knows how to draft a contract to avoid future problems, and a CPA knows how to structure a tax-free exchange in order to defer paying any tax. However, the focus is on *needs.* Customers want to know if you have a solution to a need and, if so what will be the cost? What is the risk of using your service vs. not using it? This is a rather straightforward process when dealing with a tax return, audit, or routine legal service. In contrast, when you are holding the FPA meeting, with the goal of building value, focus on the customer's *wants.* Moving up the Value Curve is easier when people get what they want rather than what they need.

As Werner Erhard used to say: "The access to people is through their concerns." Be confident in your professional abilities to solve people's problems, but focus on their wants, desires, goals, and visions for the future. When Martin Luther King, Jr. delivered his inspiring speech from the steps of the Lincoln Memorial on August 28, 1963, he did not proclaim: "I have quarterly objectives." Professionals need to devote more time learning as much about the customer as they know about accounting, tax, and law.

The FPA meeting is the venue for exploring these areas, and sometimes more than one meeting will be needed to determine exactly what the customer wants and desires from your firm. What better reason exists to meet with a customer than to discuss the value you are adding to the relationship?

In the old days when professionals enjoyed a seller's market, it was relatively easy to get the respect and trust of customers. In today's market, with more sophisticated customers, this is no longer true. The FPA meeting is a means of earning the respect of the customers because it aligns your interest to theirs and sends the signal that your firm is interested in their welfare and prosperity, not just billing hours. This type of face-to-face encounter is one of the most underused marketing tools of the professional, and yet it is one of the most effective ways to build perceived value in the mind of the customer. And since no seller imposes a price on a customer—after all, the customer is the one with the money—you must build up your value in the minds of your customers before you are able to prove your value with the results of your work.

You have to understand the importance of your existing customers, and how much more profitable they are than new ones. You also have to invest in those relationships—give something back, in effect—to *earn* people's loyalty. People want to be loyal, but only if you give them a reason. Long-term relationships are not static, they are dynamic. Either they are growing stronger or they are getting weaker. Far too many firms spend all of their marketing and advertising budgets chasing after new customers while ignoring their existing customers. You have no business getting new customers if you are not pleasing your existing ones. At least one-half of your marketing budget should be devoted to retention marketing—investing in current customer relationships, geared towards the top 20 to 30 percent of your customer base, which most likely represents 80 percent of your gross revenue.

Questions to Ask Yourself Before You Set a Price

The premise is that the more you know about your customers, the better able you will be to approximate their position on your firm's demand curve (not necessarily the Value Curve). For example, even if you are setting a price for a "commodity" service such as an audit, or tax return, you know that because you have a downward-sloping demand curve, customers exist who are willing and able to pay more than you would have charged them if you used a market price as a benchmark. Some businesses are fortunate in that the customers identify themselves. First-class passengers on an airline and hardcover book buyers come to mind. But how does a professional firm go about discovering which customers are at the top of its demand curve? For starters, by merely agreeing to enter into an FPA with your firm, such customers are, most likely, your least price sensitive, because they tend to recognize the value of the services being performed. The most effective method to discover your "first-class passengers" is by lessening the amount of asymmetrical information that exists between the buyer and seller, and that is done through extensive questioning and listening to the customer to find out their true wants (and needs). The following are questions and issues you should consider, either on your own or with your associates who serve the customer, prior to establishing a price.

The first group of issues to consider comes from the American Bar Association's Model Rules of Professional Conduct, which sets forth the basic ground rules governing all fees. Rule 1.5, dealing with lawyers' fees, states, "A lawyer's fee shall be reasonable." That is a highly subjective definition and is certainly subject to debate between the lawyer and the customer. The rule has eight factors to be considered in determining the reasonableness of a fee:

1. The time and labor required, novelty and difficulty involved, and the skill needed to perform the services
2. The likelihood, if apparent to the client, that acceptance of the assignment will preclude other employment
3. The customary fee charged for similar services in the locality
4. The amount involved and results obtained
5. Time limits imposed by the client or circumstances
6. The nature and length of the professional relationship with the client
7. The experience, reputation, and ability of the lawyers performing the services
8. Whether the fee is fixed or contingent

"Rule 1.5 recommends that the fee agreement be in writing unless the lawyer regularly represents the client. If the fee is contingent, then the agreement *must* be in writing" (Reed, 1992:15).

You can certainly advance the argument that this is a self-serving list of factors drawn up by a special interest group representing attorneys. But the point is not that these factors are self-serving as much as that these factors are considered *at all* in determining a price. In other words, more is being considered than just the time spent. The ABA showed creativity and sagacity in discussing factors other than time that add value to the customer. CPAs have no such rule and have for too long considered time as the main benchmark for their prices. However, attorneys consider several other factors, and CPAs should do the same.

A look at the eight factors will show how they contribute to the value professionals provide their customers.

Number one is obvious but number two is interesting. For CPAs, this is not as common an occurrence as for attorneys, but it certainly can happen. If it does, a premium price should be charged since you are foregoing other opportunities, especially if a particular customer does not want you to work with a competitor and you have built up substantial industry experience.

Number three is just a way to gauge what the local market charges for similar services and is not a reliable indicator of how much any one customer values your services.

Number four is important in a contingency or results-based price, which is only allowed for certain services and only in states that allow this type of pricing.

Number five is charging for convenience, which is not done enough by CPAs.

Number six proclaims an important law of customer loyalty economics: The longer you have a relationship with customers, the more highly they value your services. This is due in part to their switching costs being higher, but also because they are familiar with your firm, understand your capabilities, and are less likely to be lured away simply to save a few dollars. Also, your cost of serving veteran customers is much less than the cost of serving a new customer, as the latter tend to demand a lot of hand-holding from partners and managers and are less receptive to various staff members working on their engagement. Veterans, by contrast, are more familiar with your firm and its personnel and may even demand to have a particular staff work on their engagement. All these factors mean that a veteran customer will pay higher prices than a new one, on average.

Number seven is particularly important if your firm offers experiential and unique services, as indicated on the Value Curve, such as litigation support, real estate, business valuations, divorce planning, succession planning, major tax litigation, and mergers and acquisitions. This type of work will be performed by professionals seen by the customer as having extensive experience and skill in these areas; and by their nature, these services are valued more highly than services located lower on the Value Curve.

Number eight deals with contingent fees, and this is becoming a major issue for CPAs, especially since more than one-half of the states now allow this type of pricing.

Charles and Joseph Larson, in their book *Innovative Billing and Collection Methods That Work,* list the following factors that influence the value of your services, which should be premium priced accordingly:

- Special expertise or knowledge
- Special resources, such as software, or access to similar engagements completed for other clients
- Special contacts that facilitate a transaction
- Opportunity to achieve unique results
- Risk assumption, credit liability, or otherwise
- Extra effort based on deadlines or any form of accommodation for the client
- Potential profit or loss to the client
- "No one else can do it" factor
- Convenience
- Comfort level

   (Larson and Larson, 1994: 140)

Keep this checklist handy to see if any of these factors are present on a particular engagement. If so, you should be able to command a higher price. For instance, in our firm we have developed a good working relationship with various agents who work on the IRS Practitioner Problem Hotline. Usually we are able to get special accommodations for our customers, such as stays on collection activities, with a simple phone call. These relationships took years to develop and they are worth a great deal to the customers, especially to one who is about to have a bank account levied. We would be leaving substantial sums of money on the table by pricing according to the time involved. The same is true for networks you may refer customers to for various business deals—bankers, insurance agents, and attorneys. All of these relationships are part of your firm's unique human capital and should command a price in accordance with the value the customer receives, not the time it takes to place a phone call.

Before determining a price for any customer, it is a good idea to brainstorm with the team that serves the customer and at least one individual who does not even know the customer (if you have a large enough firm), just to have an outsider who is not familiar with the personalities and can be more objective. Here are some questions that are useful in establishing a price:

- Who on the organizational chart am I dealing with?
- Who referred the customer to me?
- What is the nature of the relationship with the referral source?
- What is the time line on the decision to select a CPA?
- What are the impending deadlines driving the decision to engage a CPA?
- Who is paying for the service?
- Are any competitors in the arena with me? Who?
- Do I have any price information from those competitors (bids, RFPs, etc.)?
- How profitable is the organization? How long has it been in business?
- Who was the prior CPA and what is the reason for the change?
- If the business is new, who is the banker, the attorney, etc.?
- How sophisticated is the customer with respect to my services?
- What is the relative price the customer would pay for the service?
- Is the service I am providing a want or a need?
- Does this customer add to the firm's skills, or am I simply using existing skills?
- Does this customer open up a new niche or market segment for the firm?
- Do I like this customer? Is it a business I am interested in?

A couple of years ago I got a call from a bookkeeper who works with one of my FPA customers and has been a good referral source over the years. She had recently picked up a new customer, a Limited Liability Corporation (LLC), that was in its first half-year of operations, had a fiscal year-end, and had a tax return due in approximately six weeks. The LLC was owned 25 percent by a company located in France and 75 percent by a local woman. The company needed a tax return, and the French company's CPA firm—one of the Big Five—had quoted a price that the bookkeeper was asked to see if she could improve upon.

When the bookkeeper called, my mind raced to the above questions. First, this was a warm referral source, who knows me quite well, and therefore I am probably pre-sold to the owner, as my abilities had already been testified to by the bookkeeper. Also, I would be dealing with the CEO of the company, and the higher on the organizational chart you are, the less price sensitive the employee will be. A CEO does not have time to interview multiple CPAs, so if you are at that level, your chances are fairly good of landing the customer. A CEO also has other concerns, such as productivity, profitability, and value that a CFO, or accounting manager, might not consider as important.

Also, the company had an impending deadline. In six weeks the company had to file its first tax return. The owner would be traveling to France in two weeks to stay for another three weeks. Therefore, she was ready to make a decision immediately. The French company had infused some working capital into the company, which was a consideration because when spending someone else's money you are less price sensitive.

The bookkeeper told me that the Big Six firm quoted $5,400 and the owner thought that was a little steep. This was a new business and not very profitable, so I had to come in at less than $5,400. In this case, the prior CPA was not an issue (there was no prior CPA), but that is always a consideration in your pre-qualifying routine. Checking references is also important, but since this came from a person I knew and trusted, I did not check any other references.

The owner was a first-time business owner, so she was not a sophisticated buyer of CPA services. Part of my job would consist of educating her as to what a CPA can offer and the value of these services. This particular customer would add to my firm's skills because LLC's are relatively new, and this was a customer with some interesting issues that needed to be explored. I did not do a personality grading, because I did not get a chance to meet the customer before I priced the service. I relied solely on what the bookkeeper told me, and did not learn anything that would prevent me from wanting to work with the people involved.

The bookkeeper faxed me the financial statements, which consisted of a one-page balance sheet and a one-page income statement (this was a new business, only in operation for six months out of the year). Looking at the financials, I knew the tax return would take me no longer than four hours. At a theoretical "standard hourly rate" of $200, I would quote this job at $800.

A partner once told me that, in a situation that was numerically similar to mine, he felt that the customer was being ripped off at $5,400, and he quoted the job at $1,000. He did not get it. He told me he learned a valuable lesson from that: Low prices command low respect. In the mind of the customer, his service could not be of equal quality at less than one-fifth the price. If all customers have is price to judge a service on, they will naturally assume that high price equals quality service.

Based on my answers to the above questions, I put together an FPA priced at $3,500, and the owner signed it and faxed it back immediately. And I left money on the table. Realistically, I could have bid $4,000 and perhaps as high as $4,500. With hourly billing I would have left $2,700 on the table—more than three times standard. This is what is meant by pricing on the margin and turning pricing into the art that it is, rather than an administrative task involving hours times rate.

You may ask: "What would happen if she goes to another CPA next year and discovers that the job is worth $1,000?" The answer is: "You do not let her go to another CPA next year." You meet with her, educate her, and sell her more services, thereby increasing her switching cost and creating a partnership with her so that she will not go out looking for another provider. The value of any product or service is what someone is willing to pay for it. A CPA can command $3,500 for a tax return some competitors may be willing to perform for $1,000, if the CPA provides $2,500 more value through Total Quality Service and developing a partnership with the customer.

Questions You Should Ask the Customer

There are questions you should ask the customer in order to lower the level of asymmetrical information and assist you in determining just where on the demand curve your customer is. The more information you seek from customers the better equipped you will be to assess their price sensitivity. Always ask open-ended questions to engage the customer in discussing goals, aspirations, fears, and desires. This has a tremendous psychological impact, as most people's favorite topic is themselves. Once you have determined the customer's needs, focus on *wants* because that is where the Value Pricing opportunities are. Start with the following questions (I am indebted to Troy Waugh for some of these questions):

- What do you expect from us?
- What is your current pain?

- What keeps you awake at night?
- How do you see us helping you address these challenges and opportunities?
- What growth plans do you have?
- Do you expect capital needs? New financing?
- Do you anticipate any mergers, purchases, divestitures, recapitalizations, or reorganizations in the near future?
- We know you are investing in Total Quality Service. What are the service standards you would like for us to provide you?
- How important is our service guarantee to you?
- How important is rapid response on accounting and tax questions? What do you consider rapid response?
- Why are you changing professionals? What did you not like about your former firm that you do not want us to repeat?*
- How did you enjoy working with your former firm?**
- Do you envision any other changes in your needs?
- Are you particularly concerned about any of your asset, liability, or income statement accounts?
- What are the best ways to learn about your business so we can relate your operations to the financial information and so we can be more proactive in helping you maximize your business success?
- Would you be comfortable if we were to attend certain of your internal management meetings as observers?
- May our associates tour your facilities?
- What trade journals do you read? What seminars and trade shows do you regularly attend? Would it be possible for us to attend these with you?
- What is your budget for this type of service?

---

* Do not denigrate the predecessor CPA (or attorney). First, this insults customers and reminds the customer of a poor decision. Second, this diminishes respect and confidence in the profession as a whole.

** Even though the customer is changing firms, almost certainly the customer liked some characteristics of the predecessor. Find out what these were and exceed them. For instance, if the prior CPA always returned phone calls within one day, return them within 4 hours.

Here is one of the most effective questions that you can ask during the FPA meeting, as suggested by Allan Boress in *The "I Hate Selling" Book:*

> If price was not an issue, what role would you want your CPA
> to play in your business? (Boress, 1994: 68)

These questions will lower the level of asymmetrical information. The importance of this can be illustrated by my experience a couple of years ago while I was wandering around in a used book store and came across an out-of-print book. I had been searching for this book for a few years and was shocked to discover, upon opening it, that it was signed by the author. I would have gladly paid the owner $100 for that book and I was delighted to turn to the next page and learn that it was priced at $10. I did not say to the owner: "I was willing to pay $100 for this, but you have priced it at $10, so I'll split the $90 difference with you." Hardly. From an economist's viewpoint I walked out of that store $90 wealthier, as I kept the entire consumer surplus in my pocket. Bookstore owners do not have the luxury of knowing all of their individual customer's wants, and perhaps the transaction costs of discovering what those wants are would be prohibitive. But would this owner have been better off had he known that I was searching for this particular book? Had he simply talked with me, he could have learned that I very much *wanted* this book, and he could have captured a portion of *my* consumer surplus. Professionals have the ability to ascertain their customers wants and goals. Simply by engaging your customer in a dialogue, you will learn all sorts of useful information that will assist you in setting a Value Price for your services.

In my seminar *The Shift from Hourly Billing to Value Pricing*, with a group of between 50 and 60 colleagues, I use the following experiment. I ask them to pretend that I have come to them as a customer who has spent his off-hours researching, writing, and developing a seminar. I have a business that provides me with a good living, but this is a serious avocation for me and the topic is in great demand. I have worked for years on my material and may someday write a book. The question is: "How should I price my seminar?"

These CPAs usually ask how much was spent in R&D for the course. The answer is approximately $20,000, including books, seminars, travel costs to benchmark with firms, etc. This does not include the opportunity cost of my time, which is what I could have made in my business had I spent the time working on it. But is this question even relevant? Sunk costs are sunk. Obviously I want to recover my costs and I hope to make a profit, but what I really want to know is how to price my seminar when someone from a professional firm calls me on the phone asking how much it would cost to bring me in for a day. What factors should I consider before quoting a price?

Here is a list of questions that my colleagues have advised me to ask before pricing the seminar (assume that all travel costs will be paid for by the customer):

- How many will be attending?
- How is the total number of attendees divided among partners, managers, professionals, and clerical staff?
- What is the location of the firm?
- What type of firm is it (CPA, PA, EA, or attorneys)?
- How long has the firm been in business? How profitable is it?
- What is the firm willing to pay?
- What is the firm's opportunity cost of coming to you?

This is a good group of questions. Notice how none of the questions has to do with time. These questions are designed to ascertain what the seminar is worth to this particular firm, at this particular time. The last question is especially good, because if a firm wanted to attend the one-day California CPA Education Foundation course, employees would incur travel costs, hotel and lodging, meals, and other incidentals. The costs naturally would be compared to the cost of bringing the instructor to them. Should I not compute what that opportunity cost is for them before setting my price?

The questions from my colleagues prove that they intuitively understand Value Pricing. Yet many of them will go back to their offices and multiply time spent by an hourly rate. How much money will they leave on the table by not pricing in accordance with these questions? In some cases, a firm would have to pay more than $10,000 to send personnel to the course. This is why there are no "standard prices" for my services. As Napoleon Hill said: "There is no standard price on ideas. The creator of ideas makes his own price, and, if he is smart, gets it" (Hill, 1937: 99). These are words to live (and price) by.

Ascertaining Customer Loyalty

While the FPA meeting is a venue to determine what the customer's expectations are, and how they have changed, it is just as important to continue to meet with the customer-face-to-face to ascertain satisfaction with your firm's service. This is an integral part of providing Total Quality Service and exceeding your customer's expectations, and these two components are essential to Value Pricing. What you want is a loyal, repeat customer. The goal should be zero defections.

In today's business world, the conventional wisdom is that only those things that are measured are managed. This may be true when you are producing widgets, but it is an absurd view when you are dealing with human beings, and all of their flaws, foibles, and emotions. When it comes to customer loyalty, the most important things cannot be measured; they are simply what is in the hearts and minds of your customer. After all, the most important things in life—love, beauty, friendship—cannot be precisely defined, let alone measured. Attempts to ascertain customer satisfaction may be common, but because of the intangibles involved, these efforts may spring hidden traps you should be aware of.

Many businesses have started conducting customer satisfaction surveys, either by mail, over the phone, or with on-site questionnaires. However, customer surveys are an abused tool, especially in professional firms, where the relationship with the customer should be a partnership. Imagine placing a customer satisfaction survey, a #2 pencil, and a self-addressed, stamped envelope next to your spouse's coffee in the morning, with a note reading, "Honey, here is a survey on the state of our marriage. Please fill it out at send it back to me in the enclosed SASE, and then we'll talk (maybe)." You would not behave this way towards a spouse; why would you want to do this with your best customer?

Written surveys to gauge customer satisfaction have many design and implementation problems. The questions will naturally be biased by how you formulate them and may not measure accurately how a customer truly feels about a particular service. You may leave out an issue (or questions) that the customer is particularly affected by, and therefore you may have a service defect that goes undetected through this type of feedback. Also, most people do not like to write, and they certainly do not spend the waking hours of their lives cogitating on the nuances of your firm's service delivery.

Another problem with a written survey is that you are not going to get a representative sample of your firm's customers, because most likely your response rate will not be anywhere near 100 percent. How many people get excited about filling out a customer satisfaction survey? Customers may actually become annoyed with a long, 4–6 page survey, or a 15–30 minute telephone interview. You are most likely to get complete surveys from customers who either love you or who have just had a very rotten experience with your firm. Written surveys *will not* generate a representative sample of your customers.

The biggest problem with customer satisfaction surveys concerns what economists call *revealed preference*: what people *do* counts, not what they *say*. The entire point of customer satisfaction surveys is to determine whether or not your customers will continue to patronize your firm. What you want is customer loyalty, revealed by the customer returning, over and over, to your firm, rather than increases in your customer satisfaction scores. You could earn very high customer satisfaction scores and still lose the customer. According to *Harvard Business Review*, 65 to 85 percent of customers who chose a new supplier said they were satisfied or very satisfied with their former supplier. Satisfaction is not enough—you must delight the customer.

In fact, this is exactly what happened to General Motors and other automobile companies in the 1980s. While GM was earning very high marks on dealer customer satisfaction surveys, the company was losing market share, and profits were anemic. Associates rewarded for high customer satisfaction surveys will get those scores up by using methods such as bribing the customer with a free detail or oil change. Some associates will even change the answers. Thus the written surveys did not reflect reality.

You see this same phenomenon with Saturn, a company that receives very high customer satisfaction scores and is ranked very high in the J.D. Powers surveys. However, Saturn is not getting many repeat customers. The problem is that a Saturn is usually sold to first-time car buyers, and once they own one for several years, they trade up to a more expensive line. So while Saturn has done a terrific job with customer satisfaction scores, it is not getting enough repeat business. The company has figured this out and is beginning to manufacture an upscale model line.

What is a better way than written surveys to measure customer satisfaction? Try informal feedback, which includes face-to-face meetings when you ask the customer open-ended questions, such as: How are we doing?

How could we service you better? How do you feel? Another tool is customer focus groups. Assemble your best customers and solicit their advice on serving them even better. These techniques may be informal, and not as quantitative as written surveys, but they are absolutely more effective.

Marriott, a Total Quality Service organization whose entire culture is driven by the customer, discovered that its in-room satisfaction surveys were often being done by children (who usually checked off "poor" in every category). So now Marriott has several other "listening posts" where they solicit customer feedback. One of the most effective has been its cocktail parties on the concierge floor. Managers mingle and informally interview the customers, and they claim to have learned more vital information from this technique than almost any other.

CPAs meet with all of their customers at least once a year anyway; they should be meeting with the large ones quarterly, at least. Ask your customers at each meeting, "How are we doing?" and "How could we serve you better?" and "How do you feel about our service?" You will be amazed with the amount of information your customers will willingly give you in an informal encounter. By asking the customers how they *feel*, you will elicit their true perceptions of your firm's service. This is better than asking them what they *think* because that is a question of intellect and can be challenged. They may be unwilling to express their true thoughts because they feel intimidated; thinking can be challenged, feelings cannot. Asking how they feel gets to the truth of what the customer is thinking.

Professionals often object to this approach for two reasons, both of which have false basis. First, they claim it is prohibitively expensive to meet this way with *every* customer and take the time to ask these questions. The answer to the objection is this: if you can't do it, have your staff do it. Focus on the top 20 to 30 percent of your customers, who generate 80 percent of your business, and let the staff informally interview the others. Actually, it is prohibitively expensive *not* to do this, as only 4 percent of customers complain, 96 percent just walk away, and 91 percent of those who walk away never come back.

The second objection to informal meetings is that, by asking the customer for feedback you are "raising the bar" of their expectations. If you do not provide a higher level of service as a result you have put the customer at risk. This is certainly possible, but research shows that just by asking your customers these questions, their satisfaction with you as a service provider actually increases.

Summary and Conclusions

It's important to understand that customers are not necessarily trying to minimize their legal and accounting bills; what they are trying to accomplish is maximizing the net value they receive from those costs. And net value is measured by taking the gross value of the service less its cash price. By engaging the customer, and getting an ego investment, you are offering a form of "participatory pricing" that in today's market customers expect. They can decide to fly first class or coach, shop at a department store or a discount store, and even place bids for airline travel at the price they desire through an online service such as priceline.com. Customers make these and a myriad of other decisions in which they have total control over the price/value equation.

Value Pricing provides you with competitive differentiation that will allow you to stand out from the crowd. Competition means *seeking together*. It means conformity, and the biggest gains are to be made not from playing the game differently, but from changing the game itself. The shift from hourly billing to Value Pricing changes the game completely, and the firms that adopt Value Pricing first, before it becomes adopted by the majority, stand to gain the most.

11 THE FIXED PRICE AGREEMENT AND CHANGE ORDERS

The goal of meeting with the customer is the Fixed Price Agreement (FPA). This chapter will focus on the agreement itself and the elements that can be included. A sample agreement is given and then discussed in detail to assist you in writing your own. Please take all of the numerical examples with a grain of salt, since professional practices differ in size, type of customer served, experience, market, and length of time in business. Prices for any given service are only stated to illustrate the relative percentage of value that is being left on the table if you do not engage in Value Pricing.

A Sample Agreement

An FPA that is drafted between your firm and a customer is the result of a negotiating process. This is your chance to provide the customer with a customized list of services to meet specific needs and wants, to offer a fixed price for those services, and to specify the payment terms. No two FPAs should look alike—they should be as unique and individual as your customers. One of the biggest advantages of the FPA is that it allows you to treat customers *individually*. The more customized the FPA is, the higher will be its perceived value.

Some of the firms that engage in Value Pricing do not use written FPAs but rely instead on verbal agreements. These firms are also self-insured when it comes to malpractice, so this procedure cannot be used by everyone. They also have long-term customers and a very high level of trust exists between the parties. These firms are admirable, and from a financial standpoint, they are among the top 5 percent in terms of annual partner income. However, use of written FPAs is still recommended. Also, if you have liability insurance, you must have written agreements, which leads to one final caveat regarding the sample FPA.

The FPA does not replace your firm's standard engagement letter. You still must use engagement letters for each major service you provide, in accordance with your professional liability carrier's guidelines. (For CPAs, this means an engagement letter for each audit, review, compilation, tax return, and management advisory service.)

The only modification you need to make to your standard engagement letter is in the discussion of price (or, more likely, fees). In that section, simply refer to the Fixed Price Agreement, dated xx/xx/xx, and that seems to satisfy the insurance carrier's requirements. The engagement letter is where you maintain all of the legal language (such as mediation and arbitration clauses in the event of a dispute, interest charged on past due amounts, the right to stop work for non-payment of services). Nothing in your firm's present engagement letter should change as a result of using an FPA, with the exception of the fee clause.

In the FPA you can discuss the value of your services that the customer will receive. You can tailor the FPA to build value in the eyes of the customer, without resorting to all of the legal language that must be contained in the engagement letter. The standard engagement letter has to comply with your liability carrier's requirements; it is not the vehicle for a discussion of value. The FPA, however, provides a venue to be as creative and imaginative as you'd like with respect to your services.

The following sample FPA is for use by CPAs; if you are an attorney, refer to the American Bar Association books edited and authored by Richard C. Reed that are listed in the Suggested Reading section, as they contain many sample engagement agreements used by law firms.

Sample Fixed Price Agreement

December 1, 1999

Dear Customer:

In order to document the understanding between us as to the scope of the work that ABC, CPAs will perform, we are entering into this **Fixed Price Agreement** with XYZ, Inc. To avoid any misunderstandings, this Agreement defines the services we will perform for you as well as your responsibilities under this Agreement.

2000 PROFESSIONAL SERVICES

ABC will perform the following services for XYZ during 2000:

- 1999 W-2s/1099s and 4th Quarter Payroll Tax Reports
  and Workers' Comp Report $ XX

- 1st, 2nd, & 3rd Quarter Payroll 2000 Reports and Workers'
  Comp Reports and Fiscal Year Sales Tax Return   XX

- 1998 Year-End Accounting Adjustments and Closing of 1998 Books   XX

- 1999 XYZ S Corporation Tax Returns   XX

- 1999 Audited Financial Statements with PBCs to be provided by XYZ by March 15, 2000   XX

- Annual Consulting Service 2000*   <u>XX</u>

TOTAL 2000 PROFESSIONAL SERVICES   <u>$XXX</u>

---

* Included in the Annual Consulting Service are the following services to be provided by ABC to XYZ:
  - Unlimited meetings to discuss operations of XYZ, business matters, tax matters, and any other topic at the discretion of XYZ or its employees and/or agents.
  - Unlimited phone support for XYZ personnel and/or independent contractors and agents regarding accounting assistance, recording of transactions, etc.

Because our Fixed Price Agreement provides ongoing access to the accounting, tax, and business advice you need on a fixed-price basis, you are not inhibited from seeking timely advice by the fear of a clock running endlessly. Our services are designed around fixed prices, as opposed to hourly rates, and offer you access to the accumulated wisdom of the firm through CPAs with substantial experience who can help enhance your company's future and achieve its business goals.

While the fixed price entitles your company to unlimited consultation with us, if your question or issue requires additional research and analysis beyond the consultation, that work will be subject to an additional price negotiation before the service is to be performed, and a Change Order will be issued before delivery of the additional service, with payment terms agreed to in advance.

Unanticipated Services

Furthermore, the parties agree that if an unanticipated need arises (such as, but not limited to, an audit by a taxing agency, or any other exogenous service not anticipated in this agreement by the parties), ABC hereby agrees to perform this additional work at a mutually agreed upon price *before the service is provided*. This service will be billed separately to XYZ, as part of a Change Order, and will be payable upon presentation [or payable upon terms mutually agreed upon].

Service Guarantee

Our work is guaranteed to the complete satisfaction of the customer. If XYZ is not completely satisfied with the services performed by ABC, we will, at the option of XYZ, either refund the price, or accept a portion of said price that reflects XYZ's level of satisfaction. We will assume you are satisfied upon final payment received under the terms of this Agreement.

Quality Review

XYZ agrees to, and hereby consents to participate in, ABC's policy of in-house Quality Review. ABC subscribes to a policy of quality review to maintain the highest quality of product produced by our firm. As part of this program, all of the major services performed under this Agreement will be reviewed by another CPA within ABC under strict rules of confidentiality. The price for this review is included in the above professional services.

The following payment plan is hereby agreed to by XYZ and ABC:

- January 31, 2000   XX
- February 28, 2000   XX
- March 31, 2000   XX
- April 30, 2000   XX
- May 31, 2000   XX
- June 30, 2000   XX
- July 31, 2000   XX
- August 31, 1999   XX
- September 30, 2000   XX
- October 31, 2000   XX
- November 30, 2000   XX
- December 31, 2000   XX

TOTAL 2000 PAYMENTS $ XXX

To assure that our arrangement remains responsive to your needs, as well as fair to both parties, we will meet throughout 2000 and, if necessary, revise or adjust the scope of the services to be provided and the prices to be charged in light of mutual experience.

Furthermore, it is understood that either party may terminate this Agreement at any time, for any reason, within 10 days of written notice to the other party. It is understood that any unpaid services that are outstanding at the date of termination are to be paid in full within 10 days from the date of termination.

If you agree that the above adequately sets forth XYZ's understanding of our mutual responsibilities, please authorize this Agreement and return it to our office. A copy is provided for your records.

We would like to take this opportunity to express our appreciation for the opportunity to serve you.

Very truly yours,

By: _____

Allan Somnolent, Partner
ABC, CPAs

Agreed to and authorized:

By: _____ Date: _____

Customer, President
XYZ, Inc.

Explaining the Sample FPA

A close look at each clause in the Agreement will give further clarification of the reason for its design.

Date of the FPA

The date of the agreement is, for me, usually in the last quarter of the year, as all my FPAs are on a calendar year basis. It is advantageous to meet to draft the FPA in the last quarter of the prior fiscal (or calendar) year, to clarify the customer's expectations before the new year begins, as well as to learn of opportunities that may be present to offer the customer additional services. Do not feel the need to rush this process. If it takes multiple meetings with the customer, as sometimes it does to overcome price resistance and anxiety, do not panic and feel the need to draft something. *The FPA is not a Request for Proposal (RFP).* There are no surprises in an FPA, as there are in an RFP, because the customer is instrumental in the design and is involved every step of the way. The more customer involvement you obtain, the higher the level of commitment you will get, and the more likely the customers will act consistent with their commitment.

Professional Services Provided

Obviously, you will describe each service to be provided by your firm, and you may provide additional detail to the degree necessary to have no misunderstandings between you and the customer. For example, with the audit service you are specifying that the customer is responsible for providing you with PBC (Prepared By Customer) schedules by March 15, 2000. If the customer does not deliver by this date, and the scope of the audit changes, then a Change Order should be issued. The customer will understand that the scope has changed, and that is the time to issue a Change Order—*before* the work is performed.

You will have to exercise your professional discretion as to the level of detail necessary to avoid misunderstandings regarding the level of responsibility being assumed by both parties. If you are entering into an FPA with a new customer, and one that may not be as sophisticated with respect to your services as a veteran customer, then a higher level of detail will be required. Always adapt the FPA to the customer's level of sophistication and experience with your services. This level will become apparent as you meet with them and begin to design (and price) the services. The old rule still applies to the FPA: The greater the written detail the less chance for misunderstanding between the parties.

Annual Consulting Service

This is your firm's two-part tariff as discussed in Chapter 9—charging the customer a price for the privilege of purchasing more services from you. Notice that this annual service offers the customer unlimited phone calls and meetings for the customer and the customer's support personnel. This is done on the theory that since you are on call for the customer at any time during the year, you should be compensated accordingly. Also, this breaks down the communication barrier that may come into existence if you charge for each meeting and phone call. The more you talk with the customer throughout the year, the better able you will be to provide the customer with additional, value-added services that will facilitate your climb up the Value Curve.

I am always asked if customers abuse this service. The answer is no. Any customer who enters into an FPA with your firm, first of all, is usually an "A" customer, and a high level of mutual trust, respect, and understanding already exists. Second, because they are such good customers, if they do need to call you at home on Saturday evening at 11:00 p.m. it is usually for a very good reason (a death in the family, an accident, etc.), and you *want* to talk to them. Third, unlimited phone calls and meetings does not imply that any additional work you have to perform as a result is free. A Change Order should be issued before you take on an additional project as a result of a phone call or meeting with the customer. Fourth, if after a period of time you find that the customer is putting inordinate (or unreasonable) demands on your time, increase the price of the Consulting Service. If the customer is using you that much, you are obviously adding value to them, and they should be willing to pay a higher price for this service.

Finally, if the customer becomes abusive and disrespectful of your time, you always have the option of withdrawing from the engagement. In fact, with FPA customers the opposite usually occurs—the customer is reluctant to contact you. Be sure to stay in touch whether you think the customer needs you or not. One of the dangers of the FPA is that you are increasing the customer's expectations, and when you do that you are also increasing the probability of defection if your performance fails to live up to those increased expectations. Constant communication with good customers is something you should strive for, with or without an annual Consulting Service. By charging for it, you will capture a portion of the consumer surplus, sell more services to customers, and have a higher perceived value in their eyes.

Unanticipated Services

This is the Change Order clause, and it basically says that if a service arises that is not specified in the FPA, then your firm agrees to provide that service at a mutually agreed upon price, in advance of performing the service. You do this by issuing a Change Order, a sample of which is found later in this chapter. This clause offers many advantages. By specifying the services that you are aware of at the time of drafting the FPA, you are leaving many opportunities for providing additional services, and because customers are paying you the Annual Consulting Service price, they are more likely to select you to provide those additional services, thereby effectively locking out your competition. Another advantage is that Change Orders are priced before the service is delivered, when you have the leverage, a critical advantage to have when negotiating a price. Also, whenever a Change Order arises, Value Pricing opportunities exist because by their nature Change Orders deal with marginal services that the customer *wants*, rather than what the customer *needs* (because the FPA has taken care of their basic needs). Lastly, the Change Order can also be used in conjunction with a loyalty program—similar to the airlines frequent flyer programs—that will be discussed in greater detail as well.

Service Guarantee

You may want to highlight this clause, or place it at the beginning (or end) of the FPA to build up its value to the customer. If you are reluctant to include this in your FPAs, you can always implement it gradually, perhaps providing it to new customers at first, and then, once you are convinced of its advantages, offering it to all customers.

This strategy has been used by many firms that are reluctant to adopt the guarantee for all customers, but there is one caveat. That strategy is backwards. Your existing customers are far more valuable to your firm than any new ones you may acquire (recall the AICPA statistic that it costs a firm 11 times more to attract a customer than to retain one). Customer *retention* is far more important than customer *acquisition;* therefore, if you are going to discriminate with the service guarantee, you should discriminate in favor of existing customers. However, either way you implement it, you will discover that its advantages outweigh its disadvantages and, eventually, you will offer it to *all* of your customers.

Quality Review

Most CPA firms have an in-house review policy. Some firms charge for this service. However, a customer made a good point against this practice. He said, "Why should I pay to have the work reviewed? I'm paying you to do it right the first time." Including the service in the price removes one more point of contention between you and the customer, and it focuses the customer on what is really important. Too many CPA firms over-review their work and needless waste occurs that does not add one ounce of value to the customer.

Payment Terms

The sample FPA shows 12 payments, but this clause can be designed for quarterly payments or biannual payments, or with a deposit (or retainer) made upon signing the FPA. The important point is to get customers to design the payment terms, usually in accordance with the cyclical nature of their business, in order to remove payment resistance (the unwillingness on the part of the customer to cut the check.) Again, if customers design and commit to the payment terms, they will act consistently with that commitment. Get a deposit (or retainer) for all new customers, as this demonstrates commitment on their part. Lawyers are excellent at demanding this; CPAs need to be just as insistent on receiving retainers *before* work is performed for a new customer.

Revisions to the FPA

This is a good clause to add, especially for new customers, or if you do not feel totally comfortable with your established price, because it reduces the risk the customer is taking. It also ensures that you will remain in communication with the customers and continuously solicit feedback on their level of satisfaction. Constant customer feedback is a critical component of offering Total Quality Service and enables you to exceed customer expectations as well as become aware of when those expectations change. Of course, this clause is optional and its use will depend upon the nature of the relationship your firm has with the customer.

Termination Clause

This clause removes risk from the customers. If they know, in advance, that they can always cancel the agreement for any reason, they will suffer less from price anxiety. This is an additional way, combined with the service guarantee, to overcome this pricing emotion. If the FPA is terminated before the term expires, then both parties will have to compute the value of the services delivered by the firm, less the amount already paid by the customer, and someone will owe someone a refund.

After a few years of drafting FPAs, you may discover that, rather than pricing each individual service, you offer one total price. If the customer should cancel the FPA in that scenario, then you will have to agree on the allocated value of the services already performed. However, FPA customers are the least likely to defect from your firm, so you probably will not encounter this problem. The potential disadvantages are not great enough to stop you from offering one total price. Again, pursue opportunities rather than attempting to solve every problem that may arise in the course of dealing with customers.

The Words You Should Use

Just as the word *price* is better than the word *fee*, you should make it a habit to say, "The services are valued at $X," not "the services cost $X." Your goal is to build up the gross value of your firm's services, not to have the customer focus solely on cost. Also, if you have broken down the FPA into a monthly or quarterly payment, the terminology should be, "Your monthly investment is $X," not "your monthly cost is $X."

The word *agreement* is preferable to the word *contract*. *Contract* conjures up images of disputes, lack of trust, courts, and lawsuits, but *agreement* has a much more positive connotation to the customer. Also, when the agreement is ready to be signed, ask the customer to authorize the Agreement rather than sign the contract. Again, the word *authorize* is far more positive than *sign*, because it puts the control with the customer.

Package Pricing Clause

The more you focus the customer's attention on the totality of your firm's service offering, the higher the price you can command. For new customers, for instance, the following clause could be used in the first-year FPA:

> ### The Entrepreneurial Business Program
>
> ABC created its Entrepreneurial Business Program in 1990 to assist customers in establishing their new ventures on an optimal foundation, based upon the owner's goals and objectives, tax considerations, and future direction of the business. For a fixed price of $X,XXX, ABC will incorporate a new venture and provide basic corporate legal [or accounting] services (tax preparation, planning, accounting setup) for 12 months. Under the Program, our customer can get the right start in structuring his or her corporation, have available the resources of a full-service CPA firm, and be able to predict basic accounting prices and budget for these.

The point of this clause is not to market one specific price for this bundle of services, but to get the customer to sign up for all of the services offered. You should still price each customer *on the margin*.

Handling Price Objections

One of the first questions professionals always ask about quoting a Value Price is what happens when the customer objects that it is simply too high. First, realize that price is always a consideration, and naturally every businessperson is going to attempt to get the best price possible. Consequently, if you are to succeed in getting full value for your services, you must learn how to handle price objections. As Tom Hopkins says in *How to Master the Art of Selling*:

> I think I'm safe in saying that money is an objection you are going to encounter frequently as long as you are in sales. That being so, can you reach your full potential without learning how to cope with it? (Hopkins, 1980: 232)

It helps to keep in mind the following equation when dealing with price:

$$\text{Value} = \frac{\text{Benefits Received}}{\text{Price}}$$

If the customer is objecting to your price, perhaps you have not done an adequate job in educating the customer as to the benefits of your services. The customer may not be objecting to the price as much as doubting the value of the services. This is a critical distinction because the majority of a professional's customers are not price sensitive. This is precisely why it is so important to discuss value first and set price last. The more you can build up the benefits offered, the higher will be the perceived value of your firm, and thus the higher the price you will command.

With new customers, most price objections are due to inadequate pre-qualifying. When meeting with new customers, the following may occur:

- **The customer's only consideration is price**—This is, most likely, a customer you should not deal with at all. These customers are attracted to you solely because of price and they will be the first to defect when they can locate a cheaper service provider. Be wary of these customers, and do not waste your precious marketing resources on them. You are better off spending those resources on existing customers, who are more loyal and more valuable to your firm.
- **The customer never asks about your price**—Although this may sound ideal, the reality is quite different. Price is always a consider-

ation, especially with business people. The person who never asks about your price is also the person who probably does not intend to pay your price. Always ask these customers for a large retainer up front to test level of commitment.

- **The customer says price is no object**—Again, this is probably because the customer has no intention of paying you anyway. Price is *always* important.

- **The customer asks a lot of questions, seeking your advice**—If customers are unwilling to commit to an FPA, they are merely using you as an unpaid consultant. Avoid them.

- **The customer complains about the predecessor professional**—In another year, you will be the subject of this customer's wrath. Employ Adverse Selection. If this is such a great customer, why doesn't one of your competitors have this customer already?

Allan Boress has an effective question to use to save time when meeting with potential customers: "We are not the cheapest CPA firm in town. Should we continue talking?" This projects confidence and lets the customer know that you think highly of yourself (you are what you charge for), as well as giving you the ability, early on, to judge the customer's price sensitivity and whether or not the customer is a good fit for your firm.

Price objections with existing customers require a different approach. Most likely, these customers will require a good deal of educating on the value of the FPA. Always remember that the FPA lowers the customer's risk and uncertainty, and that is one of its major value-added benefits that should be emphasized. If you are still encountering many price objections utilizing this approach, this is not a good sign. The popular view is that price objections are a good sign (who would object to your price if they were not serious about doing business with your firm?). Neil Rackham points out in his classic sales book, *SPIN Selling*, a different viewpoint:

> No, make no mistake about it, the more objections you get in a call, the less likely you are to be successful. It's a comforting myth for trainers to tell inexperienced salespeople that professionals welcome objections as a sign of customer interest, but in reality an objection is a barrier between you and your customer. However skillfully you dismantle this barrier through objection handling, it would be smarter not to have created it in the first place.

> When I was new to selling I thought that, next to closing, objection-handling skills were the ones most crucial to sales success. Looking back, I can now see that my concern was motivated by the large number of objections I was facing from my customers. I didn't ask myself what caused the objections—but just knew that there were lots of them, so I'd better improve my objection handling. I now understand that the majority of objections I faced were only a symptom caused by poor selling. By improving my probing skills, I've become more successful at objection prevention (Rackham, 1988: 133).

Despite the best probing questions, development of a future vision, and a focus on the customer's wants, it is inevitable that you will receive at least some price objections. While getting many may be a sign of a deficient sales approach, a few can usually be handled using some of the more common objection-handling techniques. Troy Waugh offers this Seven-Step Strategic Method for Handling Objections:

1. **Listen carefully; hear the customer out**—Avoid the temptation to talk or try to solve the objection right then and there.

2. **Confirm your understanding of the objection**—Repeat it back to the customer to ensure that you understand exactly what the objection is.

3. **Acknowledge the customer's point of view**—Practice empathy; do not try to impose your view on the customer, but help the customer become convinced of your view. As Benjamin Franklin said: "Men are best convinced by reasons that they themselves discover." You will only succeed when you see things from your customer's point of view, not the other way around.

4. **Select a specific technique**—No one technique works best for all customers, and you must select one that fits your personality as well as the customer's.

5. **Answer the objection**—Ultimately, you must answer the customer's objection if the FPA is to be authorized. You may postpone the price objection to the end of the meeting if you are still trying to build your firm's value, but in the end, price must be dealt with.

6. **Confirm that your answer satisfied the concern.**

7. Attempt to get authorization for the FPA—If the customer still objects, continue with the meeting until you reach an agreement as to your value.

If price objections occur late in the sales process, find out what underlying interest is causing the concern. Two typical causes trigger a concern over price late in the sales cycle: (1) fear and (2) the desire to get a better deal.

Once you know the underlying reason for the price objection, you have two choices:

1. If the underlying concern is fear, adopt the role of a therapist and draw the fear out into the open. Remember, traditional objection-handling techniques [such as those discussed below] are not effective with fear. They move too quickly to a logical conclusion and do not get to the heart of the problem. Fear is emotional, not logical.
2. If your prospect's price objection is caused by the desire to get a better deal, adopt the role of a negotiator and create a win-win agreement. (Davis, 1996: 200)

Here are some specific methods for overcoming objections to price, from Troy Waugh:

1. Postpone the price objection.
2. Use the lowest denominations.
3. Use comparison.
4. To get volume up, sell down.

Postpone the Price Objection

You cannot intelligently discuss price until you know exactly what the customer needs and wants. A car salesman would never walk you over to a car and say, "This one is $40,000." Before price is mentioned, the salesman will discuss your needs, features preferred, and desires. He will also be attempting to gauge your price sensitivity and the value your place on dealing with this particular dealership by asking you questions about your occupation, what the car will be used for, where you live, and whether you currently own a car. Here are two responses that postpone the price objection until you have had a chance to build your firm's value:

- I can appreciate that you would be interested in the price, and I assure you we will discuss it completely, but before we even consider the price, I want to be sure that our service can satisfy your needs. Will that be all right?

- Mr. Smith, your concern for price is quite understandable. The actual amount paid for the service, however, will depend upon the nature of the services you ultimately select. Let's consider the price for the services after we establish the specific services you will require. Is that fair?

If you discuss price at the beginning, the customer may think you have nothing else to talk about. Sometimes, a customer is insistent in knowing a ballpark amount, and in these cases you will not be able to postpone the objection. If you try, the customer may stay so focused on your reluctance to talk price that everything else you say regarding value will be mentally blocked out. If you have to mention price, err on the high side, for reasons that will become apparent.

Use the Lowest Denominations

One of the advantages of setting the payment terms in accordance with the customer's desires is that this will break down the price into the lowest denominations, usually monthly. A monthly price is a much more manageable number to deal with than the total FPA price. Also, this is the time to reiterate your service guarantee and the fact that you will be available any time to respond to the customer's needs, if you include an Annual Consulting Service in the FPA.

Use Comparison

An effective comparison to make is that of your customer's pricing policies, with a statement such as the following:

> Mr. Becker, your own company makes a high-grade product that commands an exceptionally high price, and deservedly

so. Your tool-and-die products warrant their outstanding reputation because of the top-quality materials used to make
them. Our high level of service and attention to helping you
create more value in your business are naturally suited for
you. Sure, you can buy less expensive financial help than
ours, but you would not be satisfied with the performance.

This approach achieves a level of parity between your firm and your
customer's business, which makes considerable sense, as all business
owners are convinced of *their* product's superiority. Testimonials from
other customers can also help prove your case.

To Get Volume Up, Sell Down

All customers have a price they are *able* to pay and a price they are *willing*
to pay. Do not project your own apprehensions about price resistance onto
the behavior of your customer. Never assume that a customer is only
willing to spend, for example, what you would spend in similar circumstances. A fascinating study done by Macy's of New York illustrates this
lesson:

> Macy's gave ten professional shoppers $1,000 each with
> instructions to enter one of Macy's departments to buy mer-
> chandise without mentioning price. The shopper was to buy
> whatever was offered by the salesperson up to $1,000. Not
> one of the shoppers was able to get rid of more than $350. For
> example, when one shopper asked about ladies' hats, the
> sales person brought out a hat within her own price range—
> $75; the buyer could have bought a $200 hat.

You should always present your most expensive price first, and then
move down. Men's clothing is sold in such a manner. The salesman will
first show you a $1,000 suit, make you try it on, and when you choke, he'll
then move down, gradually, to your price level. Once he has sold you the
suit, he will then move down to sweaters, shoes, shirts, ties, and socks. It is
easier to buy a $99 sweater after you have decided to purchase a $375 suit.
Psychologically, this is a very effective method.

Hopkins offers another effective technique called the "Bracket-up for
money" strategy. Here's how it works. You say, "Most customers who

desire this level of service are prepared to invest $12,000. A fortunate few can invest between $15,000 and $20,000. Then there are those on a limited or fixed budget who cannot go higher than $10,000. Which of these categories does your company fit into most comfortably?" (Hopkins, 1980: 184)

Most likely, the customer will not want to be in the bottom category, and will opt for the middle amount. Make sure you begin your pricing at a level that is approximately 20 percent above your price ($12,000). Then, continue by quoting a price 50 percent to 100 percent above your price ($15,000–$20,000). Finally, give your actual price ($10,000). Psychologically, you are tapping into the instinct of the customer that says: **Expensive = Good**. This is the good, better, and best strategy, and it works.

If price is still an objection, focus on the difference. Perhaps you are trying to price the FPA at $20,000, but the customer wants to pay $15,000. Do not focus on the $20,000; focus instead on the $5,000 difference. That is the real problem, and that puts the focus on the smaller, more manageable amount.

If price is still an objection, be slow to cut it, as you will lose credibility with the customer if you do not get a concession in return. Instead, work on the other terms of the FPA first. Perhaps you can change the payment terms; perhaps you can cut some services or add additional services. Remember the Pareto analysis: 20 percent of the issues will account for 80 percent of the value. Customers will want to win some points, even trivial ones. Concede on those 80 percent of the points that make up 20 percent of the value and chances are you will reach a more satisfactory negotiation for both parties.

Most people think that the final decision in the buying process is one of risk—either the risk of not buying or of not making the right decision on a service provider. However, the very last buying decision is ensuring that you get the best deal. This is a separate issue from the value of the service; the customer is already convinced of the value or you would not be this far along in the buying process.

When customers are trying to ascertain if they've gotten the best price, they will test you. As Michael Bosworth says in his excellent book, *Solution Selling*:

> At negotiation time, in the buyer's mind, the seller is a washcloth. . . . And if that buyer has an IQ over 80, he's going to take at least one wrenching squeeze to see what happens.

Am I right? And the squeezing will continue until the seller stops dripping. As long as the seller drips, the buyer squeezes.

How does a seller stop the squeezing? By resolving to stop dripping, by resolving to walk out if the business is not right, and by resolving to walk away from the business. The seller must take his stand with conviction—enough conviction to convince the buyer he is getting the best possible deal (Bosworth, 1995: 147).

If the buyer sees you panic—as most CPAs do—this reinforces their fear that they have not yet negotiated the best price. This is an emotional process, not a logical one; standing your ground is very important. Think of purchasing a car. When you have finally come to the decision to buy, you will attempt to get the best price from the salesman. Once he is willing to let you walk off the lot without the car, you know you made the best deal. That is exactly what you need to do— be willing to let customers walk out the door. Only then will they realize they have made the best deal possible.

Bosworth also suggests using the word "fair," such as "Is this a fair price to you?" People have an innate desire to be fair and it is a very powerful word. In fact, it is so powerful that you should use it sparingly.

Learn to accept price objections for what they are—opportunities in disguise. They can be a sign of an interested customer, and with practice and skill, you will be able to overcome them without cutting your price. Reading the books mentioned in this chapter will help you develop the skills you need to work with price objections and become an effective Value Pricer.

Change Orders

Change Orders should be used whenever the scope of a service changes, or when a service need arises that was not anticipated in the FPA. This is a very effective tool for keeping in constant communication with the customer, giving the customer control over any and all changes in your services, and allowing you to set a price when you possess the leverage. The cardinal rule with respect to Value Pricing is *no surprises*; the Change Order is a tested method of adhering to that rule.

In a typical CPA firm when problems are encountered (with for instance, the state of the customer's records), the lowest level staff person keeps right on working, spending time, without anyone's knowledge or consent. Managers and partners are guilty of this pattern as well, and this creates nothing but collection problems once the job is completed. Think of taking your car to an auto mechanic to get a bid for a tune-up. You return to the shop only to find that he performed additional services, without your prior consent, and he is now attempting to charge you. Not a very pleasant or effective way to cross-sell additional services, is it?

It is critical that all staff assigned to a particular engagement understand the parameters that have been set forth in the FPA, the responsibilities of the customer, and the price of the service. When a problem is spotted, staff should communicate to the supervisor, manager, or partner that a Change Order should be issued. Otherwise, they will unilaterally commit firm resources to complete the work with no commensurate increase in the customer's price.

Change Orders also present opportunities for Value Pricing and innovative pricing methods. Since the FPA has covered the basic services (i.e., those services on the lower end of the Value Curve), Change Orders usually represent opportunities to climb up the Curve and should be priced accordingly. By issuing Change Orders at the earliest possible time, and *before* the work is performed, your firm possesses the leverage—precisely when you want to set a price. You are also involving the customer and keeping the customer in control of the decision either to help solve the problem (if the Change Order is being issued due to their internal problems) or to partake in the design of the service. As Larson and Larson point out in *Innovative Billing and Collection Methods That Work*:

> Clients are more likely to respond favorably to an additional charge if they still have the opportunity to be part of the decision-making process in resolving the unanticipated problem (Larson and Larson, 1994: 91).

Think of the example of the mechanic. If he's got your car on the rack to perform a tune-up and discovers another problem and calls you to inform you of what it will cost to fix, at least you feel empowered to make the decision to proceed. In the majority of cases, you will simply agree to the additional charge because the mechanic possesses the leverage. You are not likely to pick up the car and take it to another shop. State laws require mechanics to do this; but why should professionals have to be compelled by law to do something that is clearly in the best interest of both the professional and the customer?

The following pages contain sample Change Orders. As with the FPA, this is nothing but an outline that should help your firm develop its own Change Order based upon your culture, personality, and the type of customer you serve. If you service auto mechanics or contractors, you may even want to obtain one of their Change Orders to help you design your own. They are well written, and your customer will be impressed that you are implementing this technique.

SAMPLE CHANGE ORDER

Customer:

Date:

Project Description {and estimated completion date, customer responsibilities, if appropriate, and any other level of detail needed}:

_____

_____

_____

_____

_____

_____

Price: $_____

Terms: _____

We believe it is our responsibility to exceed your expectations. This Change Order is being prepared because the above Project was not anticipated in our original Fixed Price Agreement, dated xx/xx/xx. The price for the above project has been mutually agreed upon by Customer XYZ and ABC, CPAs. It is our goal to ensure that XYZ is never surprised by the price for any ABC service, and therefore we have adopted the Change Order Policy. The price above is due and payable upon completion of the project described {or, payable up front, if agreed upon, or in installments, etc., whatever you and the customer agree to}.

If you agree with the above Project Description and the price, please authorize and date the Change Order below. A copy is enclosed for your records. Thank you for letting us serve you.

Sincerely,

Allan Somnolent, Partner
ABC, CPAs

Agreed to and authorized:

By: _____

Customer, President
XYZ

Date: _____

SAMPLE CHANGE ORDER—SERVICE NOT SPECIFIED IN THE FPA

Customer: XYZ, Inc.

Date: November 10, 1998

Project Description: ABC, CPAs will hereby represent XYZ, Inc. before the Internal Revenue Service for the audit of their 1996 Corporate Tax Return, for the issues as described in the IRS letter dated November 1, 1998.

XYZ, Inc. hereby agrees that its accounting department will provide all records, documentation, and schedules as deemed necessary by ABC, CPAs.

Based upon ABC, CPAs knowledge of the IRS' concerns and issues to be examined, we hereby agree to represent XYZ, Inc. for the fixed price stated below.

If, in the course of the audit, other issues are raised that are outside the scope of the IRS letter mentioned above, ABC, CPAs and XYZ, Inc. hereby agree to enter into another Change Order at that time, at a mutually agreed upon price.

Price: $X

Terms: 50% payable upon commencement of the IRS audit.

50% payable upon completion of the audit.

We believe it is our responsibility to exceed your expectations. This Change Order is being prepared because the above Project was not anticipated in our original Fixed Price Agreement, dated 01/05/98. The price for the above project has been mutually agreed upon by XYZ, Inc. and ABC, CPAs. It is our goal to ensure that XYZ, Inc. is never surprised by the price for any ABC, CPAs service, and therefore we have adopted the Change Order Policy.

If you agree with the above Project Description and the price, please authorize and date the Change Order below. A copy is enclosed for your records. Thank you for letting us serve you.

Sincerely,

Allan Somnolent, Partner
ABC, CPAs

Agreed to and authorized:

By: _____

Customer, President
XYZ, Inc.

Date: _____

SAMPLE CHANGE ORDER—SERVICE SPECIFIED IN THE FPA; SCOPE CHANGE DUE TO CUSTOMER NOT FULFILLING AN OBLIGATION

Customer: XYZ, Inc.

Date: August 20, 1998

Project Description: During fieldwork of the audit for the year ended June 30, 1998 ABC, CPAs discovered that the Prepared By Customer (PBC) Schedules were not accurately completed, in a timely manner, by the accounting staff of XYZ, Inc.

In order to complete the audit in a timely manner, both parties agree that ABC, CPAs will hereby complete the PBC Schedules.

Since this service was not originally anticipated by ABC, CPAs in its fixed price for the audit, both parties agree to the mutually acceptable price for this service as stated below.

Price: $X

Terms: Payable upon authorization of this Change Order.

We believe it is our responsibility to exceed your expectations. This Change Order is being prepared because the above Project was not anticipated in our original fixed price for the audit, as outlined in our Fixed Price Agreement, dated 05/01/98. The price for the above project has been mutually agreed upon by XYZ, Inc. and ABC, CPAs. It is our goal to ensure that XYZ, Inc. is never surprised by the price for any ABC, CPAs service, and therefore we have adopted the Change Order Policy.

If you agree with the above Project Description and the price, please authorize and date the Change Order below. A copy is enclosed for your records. Thank you for letting us serve you.

Sincerely,

Allan Somnolent, Partner
ABC, CPAs

Agreed to and authorized:

By: _____

Customer, President
XYZ, Inc.

Date: _____

Innovative Price Methods You Can Use with the Customer

Outside-In Pricing

One of the most innovative ways to capture the consumer surplus is simply to ask the customers what they think the service is worth. This method, which can be referred to as Outside-In Pricing, starts with the theory that, ultimately, a service is worth only what someone is willing to pay for it. Therefore, why not ask directly what it is worth? It sounds radical, but remember that *radical* is Latin for *getting back to the root*.

Consider this story from *People* magazine (February 15, 1999) titled "Priceless," with the tag line reading "London Restaurateur Michael Vasos lets diners pay what they choose—but woe unto those who choose cheap":

> Here's one worry that patrons of the London restaurant Just Around the Corner will never have—being stuck with a bill too big for their budget. That's because it's the customers themselves who decide how much to pay. "When I came up with the idea," says owner Michael Vasos, "everyone thought I was crazy."
>
> Turns out, Vasos's little marketing concept, begun in 1986, has been insanely successful. Most regulars who pack the pink-tableclothed, 85-seat eatery fork over about 25 pounds

(around $41), fairly standard in pricey London, for three-course meals featuring such pre-nouvelle noshes as lemon sole with hollandaise sauce. "If the food wasn't any good," says diner Mandip Phlora, "the novelty would wear off pretty quickly."

Cheapskates are rare, says Vasos, 42, but the worst get their just desserts. "One guy put down a fiver," recalls waitress Liz Noonan, "and Michael went over to the table and gave him back the five pounds. Then everyone in the restaurant stood up and applauded." In fact, patrons tend to overpay rather than underpay. One night, four American government officials handed over nearly $1,000 for a meal worth less than $200. "They asked me if they had left enough," recalls Vasos, who was too diplomatic, he says, to set them straight. "You can't tell people they've left too much—it's like putting them down."

Vasos, who left his native Cyprus at 18, credits Londoners' generosity for his success. Some diners beg to differ. "It's fear of embarrassment. If you don't pay enough, there might be a scene, and the English hate that more than anything," says Rob Gillies, 26. "This kind of place would never work in Scotland," chimes in native Scotsman Danny Easton, 30. "We'd feel no guilt at all about paying you just a pound."

This is a wonderful story, and perhaps the most poignant point made by Vasos, was this: "Trust people and they will trust you." That is a perfect attitude for professionals to have towards the people they serve. After all, if you don't trust your customers, why are they customers in the first place?

Outside-in pricing method has many advantages. First, it has the potential to identify your "first-class" passengers, because your firm has some customers who are *willing* and *able* to pay more than you are charging them. Second, it involves the customer in your pricing and gets that all important "ego investment." Third, it lowers price and payment resistance; what customer will dispute a price he set? Fourth, if the customer quotes a ridiculously low price you do not have to accept it. At least you have a chance to educate the customer with respect to the service's value and you still have the opportunity to decline the engagement if you believe the customer does not value you highly enough. When do you want to learn what the customer's value perception is—*before* or *after* you do the work?

Lastly, Outside-In Pricing allows you to build customer loyalty and goodwill. You need not always capture 100 percent of the consumer surplus. Invest in the relationship by letting the customer retain a portion of it. A customer once quoted a price of $3,000 as what he expected to pay for a certain project that he demanded on very short notice (over the weekend). At "standard rates," the job would have been priced at $1,200. The CPA told him what a valuable customer he was, and expressed a willingness to help him with this particular project. The CPA said he would do it for $2,500. The customer was happy; the CPA was happy. No amount of marketing or advertising can build that type of loyalty and goodwill. That is what Total Quality Service, customer loyalty, and developing partnerships with your customers is all about. A substantial amount of consumer surplus is still available for you to tap into, and you should at least get a portion of it when you can identify its existence.

Retrospective Price

The Retrospective Price is an innovative way to get at an approximation of what the customer thinks the full value of the service is worth. Others have called it the "To Insure Performance (TIP)" clause. A sample of this clause, which can be used in an FPA or a Change Order, is the following:

Sample Fixed Price Agreement Clause
Retrospective Price (Non-Attest Customer)

In the event that we are able to satisfy your needs in a timely and professional manner, you have agreed to review the situation and decide whether, in the sole discretion of XYZ, some additional payment to ABC is appropriate in view of the overall value of the service(s) rendered {and the financial results, if allowed by your state and professional society} by ABC during 2000.

For CPAs, this will apply only for a non-audit customer, and your particular state may not allow contingency fees. If so, simply remove the "financial results" portion, and base the price on the customer's satisfaction alone. By predicating the price on the customer's level of satisfaction with your service, you are not charging a contingency.

Value Pricing Opportunities

Recall the "hours, schmours" story in Chapter 7. Two years after the audit, the owners sold their business. The acquiring company's auditors (a Big Five firm) started looking over the books. As the financials had not been audited for two years, and the controller was less than competent, the auditors became skittish about the reliability of the numbers on which they were basing the business valuation. The price of the business dropped from 10 million dollars to 7 million dollars as a result. My partner got actively involved in this process, met with the auditors and the attorneys for the buyers and sellers, and worked almost exclusively for this company for approximately a week-and-a-half. Through his efforts he was able to save the sale and maintain the price at 7 million dollars. Everyone acknowledged that he did a great job, from the auditors to the attorneys. My partner was the hero who saved the day.

Unfortunately, my partner had an FPA with the customer that had a "frequent flyer" clause which said that "any service that is not anticipated in the FPA will be performed at 80 percent of the *standard hourly rate*." The firm has since removed any reference to an hourly rate and replaced it with the following: "We will perform the service at a discount of 10 percent [or sometimes 20 percent] of the *agreed-upon price*." Sadly, my partner was still enamored with the hourly billing method and was not ready to let go of it entirely.

The work he did was billed at $10,000 at standard rates, and he was under obligation to discount it to $8,000 based on the frequent flyer clause included in the FPA. When he met with the customer to go over the final sale documents, he learned that the attorney was paid $108,000 and the controller (whose incompetence caused the sale price to drop from 10 million dollars to 7 million dollars) received a bonus of $35,000. My partner was devastated. The customer even asked him: "Did we not pay you enough?" My partner is a moral person with impeccable character, and he stayed true to his commitment of 80 percent of the standard hourly rate, and thus he got paid $8,000.

It is precisely opportunities such as this that professionals let slip by, at the margin, at a significant loss in profits with the use of hourly billing. While my partner would not have been compensated as much as the attorney, he certainly would have been paid more than the controller. If he had had a Retrospective Price clause in a Change Order prepared before he performed the work, in all likelihood the customer would have paid him $75,000 for his efforts.

According to an illustration in Larson and Larson, my partner had made the ultimate accounting entry:

	Debit	Credit
Experience	$67,000	
Cash		$67,000

Another example comes from a CPA who assisted his customer in selling a business and was able to make a 15 million dollar difference in the purchase price, which directly accrued to his customer. He billed $38,000 for his services. When he was later asked what he thought the customer would have paid had he used a Change Order with a Retrospective Price clause, he said—to his chagrin—$500,000. In other words, he left $462,000 on the table.

These stories are the exception, rather than the rule, in terms of the opportunities that arise daily in your practices. However, opportunities such as these *do* present themselves. By using the Change Order you should become more cognizant of them. The Retrospective Price clause is obviously going to be used only with a customer with whom you have developed a high level of trust and respect. But this is precisely the customer who is going to value your services the most. Had my partner and the other CPA mentioned above simply issued a Change Order, with perhaps a minimum price to cover their efforts, and left it up to the customer to decide what the value of the service (or result) was worth, they would have been much better off, and the customer would have been just as happy with them. Good customers are not out to take advantage of their professionals, especially when a professional has helped them achieve a major goal.

A CPA from Southern California accompanied his customer to Las Vegas to negotiate the purchase of some real estate. They worked for about six hours, gambled a bit, played a round of golf, and then returned home. When he got back to his office to prepare the bill, he had no idea how much to charge the customer for his time. So he came up with a variation of Retrospective Price. He sent out a bill that read: "Professional Services Provided in Las Vegas, $X,XXX." He felt he couldn't possibly get $10,000 or more for the day, but the CPA decided to leave it to the sole discretion of his customer. The customer sent him a check the following week for $8,000, far more than he would have billed even for 24 hours at his standard rate. It would have been better to discuss the price before leaving for Las Vegas because the customer may have valued the service even more highly at that time. However, this appears to be an effective strategy to use when you find yourself in a position where you did not adequately discuss price up front.

These stories also illustrate that firms skilled at Value Pricing do not have to maintain time records. How many hours is $462,000 worth at standard rates? Again, these firms are not profitable because they do not use time sheets; they do not use time sheets *because* they are so profitable. It takes only one or two opportunities such as these each year to add tremendously to your bottom line.

Summary and Conclusions

Value Pricing offers tremendous rewards to enhance your bottom line. By entering into a Fixed Price Agreement with your customers, you will be able to communicate the value your firm is providing, command premium prices, and reduce price resistance, anxiety, and payment resistance.

Change Orders are another excellent device for communicating the value of your firm's services and receiving premium prices for them. By using Change Orders effectively, you will empower customers in the decision to continue an engagement or begin a new one, all the while gaining their ego investment and commitment to the process. Change Orders usually represent services at the top of the Value Curve, since most of the essential compliance services have already been covered in the Fixed Price Agreement. Change Orders help ensure that your firm is not committing resources without the customer's agreement as to the value and terms of those additional services. Widely used by contractors and auto mechanics, the Change Order should become standard operating procedure within your firm's pricing culture. With creativity and ingenuity, Change Orders can be combined with innovative pricing methods, such as Outside-In Pricing and Retrospective Pricing, that will allow your firm to capture a portion of the consumer surplus for any given customer.

12 VALUE PRICING ENGAGEMENTS AND METHODS

The following is a discussion on pricing various services. It will also address issues that are emerging in the professional services area, such as electronic commerce, financial services, contingency pricing, and menu pricing.

Audits

The financial statement audit is the flagship of the accounting profession. It is the reason CPAs have been granted their monopoly status, as they are the only professionals who can provide this service. The audit also serves as the main justification for the rules of objectivity and independence that are the hallmarks of the CPA designation.

The word *audit* in Latin is *audire*, which means "to hear," or more accurately "that which is heard." There has been a lot of discussion these days about the obsolescence of the audit, and the AICPA's Special Committee on Assurance Services recently proposed that the financial statement audit would be replaced by an information audit. With the advent of bar code scanners, it has even been suggested that financial statements could be updated in real-time.

Given the gap that exists between the investor's need for accurate and timely financial information and how accountants see the role of the audit, the profession can either educate the public on what the audit means (and what it doesn't) or develop an entirely new product which better serves the investor's needs. One of the problems with the way the current audit is designed is that the average investor—who the audit is designed to serve and protect—can't understand it. This causes the investor to place a "blind faith" dependence on the auditing firm, which of course leads to the litigation problems that have been plaguing the profession in recent decades.

One of the issues that must be confronted when pricing an audit is the actuarial risk that is being assumed in performing the service. Unfortunately, this risk has been ignored by the profession for too long. As one member of the profession observed, "Society is asking the CPA profession to do a $500 paint job for $300 and then to indemnify the job!" (Previts and Merino, 1998: 399)

In a free market economy a correlation exists between risk and reward. In a typical IPO, however, an *inverse* relationship exists between the risk assumed by the various service providers and price they receive. The investment bankers make the most, and they assume practically no risk. The attorneys earn the second highest income, and they assume relatively little risk. Next, the printers are paid, and they have virtually no risk at all. And then there's the CPAs—the lowest income earners in the group, yet the most exposed, liability wise, if something goes wrong. While CPAs suffer in all of the downside risk if a particular IPO does not go through, as do the investment bankers and attorneys, they share none of the upside reward in a successful IPO. Audits are considered "commodities" by a lot of CPAs and this is unfortunate, because it contributes to the low price they command. Following the logic of the Value Curve and marginal pricing, an audit for purposes of an IPO is worth more than a regular annual audit, say, for the bankers. Yet the price does not reflect the added risk.

In his book, *The Circle of Innovation*, Tom Peters makes this point:

> I've had Big Six accountants tell me that the audit is "becoming commoditized." I've had engineering-services professionals tell me that their business is being determined "entirely by price." I've had trainers lament that "leadership training" is now a commodity.
>
> Is the person you see when you look in the mirror at 6:00 a.m. a "commodity?" No! It's Tom Peters. It's Mary Jones. It's Jeff Smith. It's Jane Doe. It is a person. Singular. With character. Unique skills. The delivery of professional services is the delivery of . . . Jane Doe, Tom Peters, and so on.
>
> If professional services become "commoditized," it means that you and I have become commoditized. I say again: The delivery of a professional service is the delivery of who you are, who I am (Peters, 1997: 324).

From a marketer's perspective, the notion of a commodity is anathema. Brand names are one method marketing departments deploy in order to overcome the "commodity mentality" that afflicts so many in the professional service world. This is explained by former Harvard Business

School professor Theodore Levitt, in his article in the *Harvard Business Review*, "Marketing Success through Differentiation—of Anything:"

> There is no such thing as a commodity. . . On the commodities exchange, for example, dealers in metals, grains, and pork bellies trade in totally undifferentiated products. But what they "sell" is the claimed distinction of their execution—the efficiency of their transactions in their clients' behalf, their responsiveness to inquires, the clarity and speed of their confirmations and the like. In short, the *offered* product is differentiated, though the *generic* product is identical [Emphasis in original] (Shapiro, 1995: 164).

The audit is no doubt in the decline stage of the Service Life Cycle. (See Chapter 2) Today, fewer than 10 public firms account for more than 90 percent of the auditing services offered to publicly traded companies. According to classical marketing price theory, there are three strategies a firm can take when it finds its service in the decline phase:

- Retrenchment
- Harvesting
- Consolidation

A retrenchment strategy involves partial or complete capitulation of some market segments, and refocusing resources on where the firm's strengths and core competencies lay. This requires the firm to relinquish market share, but the tradeoff is better concentration in a segment in which the firm has a competitive advantage. Many CPA firms in the last decade, for instance, have focused their audit services on those industries they selected as their niche—banking, healthcare, etc. The increased efficiencies generated by this strategy allow the firm to compete against low-priced providers who attempt to invade their niche without the same competitive and cost advantages.

The harvesting strategy is a planned withdrawal from the market entirely. It may start out like the retrenchment strategy, whereby the firm devolves itself of its weakest links. The harvesting firm does not price to defend its existing market share but rather to maximize its revenues until it completes its withdrawal. Many CPA firms have adopted this strategy, as it relates to audits, deciding to forego offering the service altogether and outsourcing the work to other firms.

In consolidation strategy, the firm attempts to strengthen its position in the declining market. This strategy is effective when the firm has adequate resources to weather the storm that forces its competitors from the market. After the shakeout, the firm is well positioned with a larger market share and less competition.

One recurring pricing error is that of pricing the audit low in the hopes of securing the more lucrative tax—and, better yet, consulting—work. The customer has learned how to hold out the carrot of more work once you get past this audit proposal. For the customer, it has been a very successful negotiation tactic. Unfortunately for the firm, it is rarely a successful practice.

The problem with the low introductory price is that it serves as a reference price for evaluating all other services. And because customers tend to be more sensitive to perceived price increases, this strategy locks the firm into low-balling the other supposedly more lucrative services, if they are lucky enough to get them, that is.

Caution is called for when pricing an audit. Do not discount all of the other services which surround the service—the management letter, internal control reviews, etc.—that provide value to the customer. In December 1991, Arthur Andersen developed its Global Best Practices knowledge base because it noticed it was spending a lot of time inside of customer's businesses performing audits. The company determined that if it could compare one company's performance to its competitors, it would add significant value to the audit service. This proved to be a very successful differentiation strategy that separated Arthur Andersen from its competitors and also combated the "commodity" mentality.

Reviews and Compilations

Like the audit, this service is only provided by CPAs. While it may be true that the marginal value of one more review or compilation is not as high as the value of an audit, it still needs to be priced based on its value. Most customers need one of these services to comply with their bank covenants and maintain their lines of credit and other financing arrangements. These services also need to be priced at the margin. To most business people, the cost of a review or compilation is simply an additional interest premium for securing their loan. CPAs should never underestimate the value of this service, especially since they are the only professionals who can offer it.

Tax Services

Tax services are on the high end of the Value Curve. Given the average taxpayer's fear of the IRS (more Americans would choose to be mugged rather than face an IRS audit), tax services, from compliance to planning, offer Value Pricing opportunities. Now that contingency fees are being allowed in various states, you will begin to see innovative tax planning products that offer customers tax savings of gigantic proportions. The price for these services will be a percentage of the savings.

Some have argued that low-level tax compliance work will increasingly become a para-professional activity, while the professional will spend his or her time structuring and researching complex scenarios. This rings true, because it's very hard to compete with a $39 tax program or a web site that allows individuals to access forms and advice in preparing their taxes. This may affect a new customer's reference price, but your old customers are more likely to value your services enough to pay more. For many firms, the pricing of the tax services will represent a reference price for all other services. These services should not be discounted with the hope of receiving more lucrative work, for the same reasons discussed in the audit section earlier.

Never discount your tax services. Customers come to CPAs expecting to pay more. Otherwise they would have gone to a PA, an EA, or H&R Block. Do not offer discounts for filing early; do not tier your prices based on your internal work flow. All of this is completely *irrelevant* to the value of the service to the customer. When dealing with IRS issues such as collection problems, offers in compromise, and audits, price in accordance with your abilities and experience. Keep in mind the relationships that you have developed with various government officials that may enable you to perform services more efficiently for the customer. Also, with respect to estate taxation, remember that many people are spending other people's money on themselves or on others. Be on the lookout for these opportunities.

Some consultants distribute price sheets for a service, such as preparing tax returns. However, no one but the customer should decide the value of any service. Do not use price lists from a tax preparation program or from a standard list published by some other organization. These tools can be used as guidelines, but never delegate your pricing to some external force. You and your customers should decide on the value of any given service. That is what is meant by pricing on the margin.

There has been a lot of talk about radical tax reform in the Congress and at the grassroots level throughout the country. This talk was fueled by the Republican takeover of the Congress in 1994, and it has quelled quite a bit since then, due to good economic times. However, at the next downturn in the economy, this issue will come back on the national scene. Depending on the political makeup of the Congress and White House in the year 2001, major tax reform will certainly make its way into the national discussion. A lot of talking heads predict a national sales tax, a Value Added Tax, or a personal consumption tax, while others advocate a Flat Tax. The Flat Tax would do the most to transform the tax side of the CPA profession, as it would simplify the compliance required, though not completely eliminating it. A VAT would likely never pass in the United States (European tax systems hold lessons of failure, not success), and a national sales tax would also not pass, once the economic realities of the rate required for revenue neutrality were well understood. The Flat Tax appears to be the ultimate direction the Congress will take with respect to reform.

An issue lays buried beneath tax reform, however, and needs to be considered by professionals who do a lot of work in this area. This is the issue of estate and gift taxation. This tax generates less than 1 percent of all federal revenues and has been criticized by both sides of the political spectrum as costing more than it is worth. As a redistribution policy, it is an abject failure. This tax will probably come under serious assault in the next century and may just be wiped away with the stroke of a pen.

Management Advisory Services (MAS)

These services are usually at the top of the Value Curve and should be among the highest-priced services your firm offers. By pricing on the margin, you will be able to set the value in accordance with the particular circumstances of the moment, and the customer will often value the services even more highly than the standard hourly rate. By using the Retrospective Price clause you will be able to capture more of the con-sumer surplus.

Outside-In Pricing, whereby you ask the customers what the value of the service is worth to them, is also custom-made for MAS services. Many times, you may not know all that is involved with offering a particular MAS service (a computer installation with training of the accounting personnel, for instance), in which case you may want to set a minimum price and have the customer review the results and pay a premium based on satisfaction. By asking customers what they perceive the value to be, you are gaining their ego investment, giving them control over the decision, and involving them in determining the value after the engagement is over.

If you have entered into an FPA with a customer, and an MAS arises, issue a Change Order priced at the high end of the Value Curve. Since the basic services are already covered in the Fixed Price Agreement (FPA), an MAS service, most likely, is contributing to the profitability of the business or directly benefiting the owner(s).

Government Audits and Bankruptcy Work

Unfortunately, these are two areas where Value Pricing will take longer to become standard practice. Most government agencies require RFPs to include hourly budgets and rates. Bankruptcy work requires professionals to charge by the hour, and even round to the nearest tenth of an hour. Bankruptcy courts will look to the "lodestar" method to determine the reasonableness of a price. This method is described in Chapter 13. If these two services make up the majority of your practice, you are limited in your ability to move away from the Almighty Hour. Nonetheless, add-on work should be priced based on value. CPAs who specialize in these two areas always have opportunities arise in which the firm can command prices in accordance with value, not hours.

Litigation Support

Courts are still tied to hourly billing, but this area offers more opportunities for innovative pricing, such as contingency pricing and retrospective pricing. If you are ever questioned about an innovative pricing method by a court, point out that the American Bar Association itself is a proponent in the forefront of moving away from hourly billing. Cite the three books edited by Richard C. Reed (see the references section). Courts are going to have to accept the fact that a price is "reasonable" as long as it is agreed to by the parties voluntarily. This will be discussed more in Chapter 16.

New Customers

When making the transition from hourly billing to Value Pricing, starting with new customers is always easier, as they will be the most receptive to the approach. It is also an effective marketing differentiation which will attract customers who are, more and more, demanding fixed prices from their professionals.

The Juran Institute has found that less than 10 percent of customers defect because of price. Yet, most CPAs say they feel compelled to charge the same as, or even less than, their predecessor. This is a mistake. Consider the study performed by the Rockefeller Corporation, which discovered the following reasons for customer defections:

1%   The customer dies.

3%   The customer moves away.

5%   The customer has a friend who provides the same service.

9%   The customer is lost to a competitor.

14%   The customer is dissatisfied with the service provided.

68%   **The customer believes you do not care about them.**

In other words, two-thirds of customers defect because of the way they were *treated*. This study has been corroborated by another study conducted by August J. Aquila and Allan D. Koltin, published in the *Journal of Accountancy* in May 1992, titled "How to Lose Clients Without Really Trying." This article, which is excellent, earned them the 1992 Annual Literary Award for the best article of the year from the *Journal*. Here are the top seven reasons CPAs lose customers:

1. "My accountant just does not treat me right."
2. CPAs ignore clients.
3. CPAs fail to cooperate.
4. CPAs let partner contact lapse.
5. CPAs do not keep clients informed.
6. CPAs assume clients are technicians.
7. CPAs use clients as a training ground
   (Aquila and Koltin, 1992: 67–70)

Customers would not be in your office if they were satisfied with your predecessor. They defected over service issues—the way *they* were handled, not the way their *work* was handled—and not price. What the predecessor charged should be the minimum baseline for your price, and you should add a premium. The Value Proposition of every firm is Price, Service, and Quality. Since you cannot compete on quality, and price is not why new customers come to you, you can command premium prices only for quality service. Many CPAs disagree with me on this point. They have created their own self-fulfilling prophecy. By thinking that they gain new customers only by low-balling the price, they attract the undesirable customers who are price sensitive, not service sensitive. When these customers locate another professional who will do the work for less, they defect, even though good service was provided.

Quality service commands a premium price in other industries, and the empirical evidence is clear that most customers will pay more for better service. Witness Disney, FedEx, Marriott, and Cadillac. They do not compete on price; they compete on service.

Years ago a customer was referred to me by another CPA. In looking over the prior CPA's work, I found it to be in order and completed in a timely manner. When asked why she was leaving her CPA of more than 20 years, the new customer said four memorable words: *"He showed no compassion."* Earlier that year, her husband had passed away, and the prior CPA did not attend the funeral or send a sympathy card. The CPA lost this customer not because of deficient work, but because of the way he treated her. When I informed the woman that my price was *four* times that of her prior CPA, she did not blink, and she has been an excellent customer ever since.

When you are setting a price for new customers, start high. It is the *service* they are after, not the *price*. If they are interested only in price, it is better to find that out before they become customers.

Another variant in pricing is known as *phasing*. This is when a project (or a group of projects) is broken down into smaller segments that can be identified with a starting and completion point. For example, Phase I could cover those items that are needed immediately—accounting assistance, tax compliance issues, and a financial statement review. Phase II could deal with assistance on securing new financing, high-end tax planning, and other general business consulting. Phase III could deal with the unique services located at the top of the Value Curve.

This innovative pricing method is effective for several reasons: It allows the customer to pick and choose a level of commitment to the relationship; it reduces the customer's perceived risk by allowing the customer to "test drive" the firm to determine their satisfaction; it lowers the level of price resistance—sticker shock—for a new customer not familiar with the level of services offered by a CPA firm; and it proves to the customer that the firm is interested in doing more than just solving its basic accounting and tax needs.

Phased pricing has been adopted in legal firms, although with a slight variance in the method. Usually, a budget is negotiated for each phase. As the phases are completed, any excess price (or savings) is put into a suspense account. The firm can recoup the amount in the suspense account if it comes in under budget for the entire engagement. Even though this method has been used in conjunction with hourly billing, it does illustrate another way in which the risk is being shared between professional and customer.

The last point with respect to pricing for new customers involves using the retainer. Getting a retainer does more than reduce the risk of not getting paid; it demonstrates serious commitment on the part of the customer. No one is willing to pay for services, in advance, which that person does not value. Payment of a retainer also increases the ego investment of customers, which will enhance their commitment to the relationship. Another advantage of retainers is that they set a precedent that the firm expects to get paid, in a timely manner, for services provided.

The amount of the retainer is based on the perceived risk, commitment, and financial ability of the customer. A good rule of thumb is to set the retainer amount somewhere between 25 percent and 50 percent of the total FPA.

Veteran Customers

Your long-term customers will require a little more time and education to convert them to Value Pricing. You will have to outline the benefits of converting to this new method. One of the biggest benefits, and you should never forget to mention this, is that the risk is removed from them and placed on your firm. If you quote a price and the work takes longer than you thought, you absorb the cost of the overrun. When drafting an FPA for the first year, it is always easier to include more services and change the focus to the totality of your firm's offering. By including the Consulting Service you are dramatically changing the scope of the service, and if you are able to deliver more services, put them into the FPA and you should command a higher price from the customer.

One caveat with the strategy of adding as many services as you can applies to both new and old customers. Price services as they arise, using the Change Order, because, at the margin, you will command a higher price for them. A business owner is less price sensitive for help with his SBA loan one month before he attempts to secure it rather than 12 months in advance, when he is naturally more price sensitive. So when you are drafting an FPA, try to stick to the basic, compliance-oriented services, and let the value-added services be handled with Change Orders. You will command a higher price because you will possess more leverage.

Alumni Customers

This situation arises when your customer once worked for your firm, or one of your competitors, and is a CPA too (or an attorney). These folks know how the game is played and most likely will demand to know the amount of hours that will be spent providing the service. Here is a solution offered by a partner from a national firm: "You tell them the game has *changed* and we do not discuss hours anymore; we discuss value."

This tremendous answer cuts right to the heart of the issue: Does the customer care more about time spent or value derived? Most would answer, of course, value, and this is a good approach to take with your colleagues who may be, at some point, your customers.

Colleagues

Naturally, most colleagues will force you to discuss hours (unless they, too, have made the transition to Value Pricing). A good response is that the game has changed and that now you discuss value. Fellow professionals may be more receptive to the idea of paying for value than you may at first think. An interesting trend began in the mid-1980s. Public accountants in private industry began to outnumber those in public accounting. Over half of CPAs now work in private industry, and you are likely to find a CPA in the controller position in smaller size companies. In other words, it is more and more likely that the person who will exert tremendous influence on hiring your firm in the future will be a CPA.

Chapter 9 discussed the fact that we really live in a barter economy, and it is the relative price that is important, as opposed to the nominal price. One important relative price when dealing with CPAs who work in the customer's company is the price of performing the work internally. When pricing for various services, especially consulting engagements, always take into account how much work can be done internally vs. that which can be done by your firm.

Request for Proposal

> *Never forget that your weapon is made by the lowest bidder.*
>
> —Law #20 of Murphy's Laws of Combat

In their book, *The Strategy and Tactics of Pricing*, Thomas Nagle and Reed Holden explain the economic anomaly known as the winner's curse—that is, in a bidding situation with many bidders, the winning bidder is often a loser. Here's why:

> The more bidders there are, the more likely you will lose money on every job you win, even if on average you estimate costs correctly and both you and your competitors set bids that include a reasonable margin of profit. This is because the bids you win are not a random sample of the bids you make. You are much more likely to win jobs for which you have underestimated your costs and are unlikely to win those for which you have overestimated your cost. Consequently, the expected profitability of a job, conditional on the fact that you have won it, is much less than the expected profitability before winning. The difference between the conditional and unconditional probabilities increases with the number of competitors against whom you must bid (Nagle and Holden, 1995: 205).

In today's marketplace, competitive bidding is an alternative to negotiation for price buyers. Also, many companies use the RFP as an effective method to lower their professional services price, with no intention of switching providers. Be careful before committing firm resources to preparing RFPs. Make sure you understand the reason the company is asking for one, and try to develop an internal advocate who can help steer your RFP through the channel and keep you informed of the process.

In their book, *Co-opetition*, Adam Brandenburger and Barry Nalebuff, offer this sage advice with respect to RFPs:

> There seems to be a natural impulse to offer competition for free. After all, that is what business people are supposed to do, is not it? You want a bid? I'll give you a bid . . . .
>
> The right question to ask is: How important is it to the customer that you bid? If bidding is so important, then you should get compensated for playing the game. If it is not so important, then you are unlikely to get the business and even less likely to make money. You might want to reconsider bidding at all (Brandenburger and Nalebuff, 1996: 84).

What they are saying is that competition is valuable and not to be given away; i.e., "Get paid to play." An effective method of testing the customer's commitment is to engage in Outside-In Pricing. Ask him to offer you a price that he would be willing to pay to engage your services. Car dealers have used this technique for years. It prevents you from spending precious resources preparing proposals. Test the customer's commitment; find out how serious the customer is before you prepare a proposal. Ask for a guaranteed engagement letter for the project if you agree with the customer's price. Find out if you can propose on more of the company's business.

Another strategy with proposals follows the same principles as Value Pricing: *No surprises*. Your potential customer should know everything in your proposal—there should be no new knowledge. This means you have already determined your customer's expectations (and how to exceed them). Just by doing this, you will increase your chances of getting the business. If customers are worth bidding on, they are worth investing time up front to determine expectations, needs, and wants. In your pre-proposal meetings, if these issues are discussed, your proposal will stand out from the competition's and you should also command a higher price. Do not be shy about Value Pricing in a proposal situation. Differentiate your firm based on service. Why attract customers who do not value you anyway?

Once you submit a proposal, you lose all control (and leverage). All you can do then is call every week and ask, "Have you made a decision yet?" This is not a good position to be in. If you are going to surprise customers, do it by exceeding their expectations, perhaps by offering a service you know they want (or need) or by thinking of an innovative strategy or plan. Change the game; ignore the old rules.

Brandenburger and Nalebuff point out these eight hidden costs of bidding:

1. **There are better uses of your time.** Keeping your current customers happy is smarter than chasing after other people's customers. (The AICPA says that attracting a new customer is 11 times more costly than keeping an existing one. By investing in existing customer relationships, you are, in effect, increasing the effectiveness of your marketing and advertising 11 times).

2. **When you win the business, you lose money.** A customer you win on price alone is telling you he has no loyalty. If you think that getting the customer gives you an opportunity to make money later by raising price, think again. By coming to you, this customer has just revealed himself as someone who will switch suppliers to get a lower price. [Adverse Selection].

3. **The incumbent can retaliate.** If this is a good customer, then your win is someone else's loss. (If it is a bad customer, then you have already made a mistake.) The incumbent supplier is likely to respond. He can go after one of your customers. He may not get your customer, but he can surely force you to lower the price. If he succeeds in snagging your customer, then you and your rival have turned two high-margin accounts into two low-margin accounts. The end result: lose-lose.

4. **Your existing customers will want a better deal.** This is not a big problem, because a professional's customers can't compare service and price with others as easily as a job shop or other businesses.

5. **New customers will use the low price as a benchmark.** A bigger concern is that a professional would use the low price as a benchmark with other new customers.

6. **Competitors will also use the low price as a benchmark.** Even if you were willing to risk charging a higher price again in the future, your rivals might expect you to come in with a low price, and these

expectations become a self-fulfilling prophesy. [This illustrates the importance of not letting your competitors who do not price based on value determine your prices].

7. **It does not help to give your customer's competitors a better cost position.** Your future and that of your customer are naturally linked. If your future is tied to Coke, you do not want to help Pepsi get a lower price. Unless you have very good reason to believe that you can get Pepsi's business and keep Coke's, bidding for Pepsi's business is costly. You help your competitor's customer and thereby hurt your own.

8. **Do not destroy your competitors' glass houses.** The view that you win if competitors lose is simplistic and potentially dangerous. Remember to think co-opetition. If you lower your rival's profits, he then has less to lose and every reason to become more aggressive. He can go after your existing accounts with abandon. In contrast, the more money your rival is making, the more he has to lose from getting into a price war (ibid., 86–88).

Keep these hidden costs in mind when preparing a proposal. Make sure that customers are worth the trouble of bidding by testing their commitment, and do not waste your firm's precious time submitting bids that may be being used merely as leverage against a customer's existing professional.

Write-Up Work

Write-up work is another area that has been encroached on by businesses from outside the profession. Intuit, makers of Quickbooks, has a commanding 70 percent share of the North American small business accounting software market. What Intuit learned through market research was that 85 percent of companies in the United States were too small to employ an accountant. Most of the owners themselves, or members of their family, took care of the company's books, and they had no formal knowledge of debits and credits, let alone an audit trail. Intuit immediately spotted an opportunity, in that most of the makers of software for small businesses had overshot the market, with programs that offered more functionality than the average small business required.

In fact, Intuit developers had profound insight. The double-entry accounting method, so eloquently written about by Fra Luca Pacioli in 1494 (see Chapter 1), was devised in order to catch mistakes within the recorded entries. Computers typically don't make mistakes in addition and subtraction, and this fact allowed Intuit's software developers to simplify both its Quicken and Quickbooks products.

Write-up work is certainly another candidate for services in your firm's market niche. It still requires that you price it on value, and be sure to differentiate your firm from the software product. Emphasize the value of your being available to oversee the use of the software and your expertise and handling of the accounting records.

Write-up work is certainly on the low end of the Value Curve. Also, you will face competitive price pressure as well as the ever-present threat that the customer will bring the task in-house. However, you should still include the service as part of a comprehensive FPA, making sure you price it according to the totality of the firm's service offering.

Pricing Authority

Many professional firms now employ a marketing manager either full-time or part-time. In the past, this was unheard of—a nonprofessional selling professional services; today, it is relatively common, and the trend is increasing. It is worth taking some time to formulate your pricing strategy when you employ marketing and salespeople to sell your firm's services. How much authority should they have over pricing decisions? When is it appropriate for them to decide, unilaterally, to cut a price? Should there be minimum prices? These types of issues are very common in most other businesses and thus there is much experience to tap into when it comes to whether or not your pricing authority should be centralized or decentralized.

Normally, there are three types of pricing authority:

1. The sales force (or other decentralized unit) has full authority over all pricing decisions.
Advantages:

- The morale of the sales force in boosted since they have more authority and responsibility within the company.

- Because the sales force is closest to the marketplace and the customer, it has the information regarding a specific transaction and is best able to evaluate where on the demand curve the customer is positioned and the customer's willingness to pay. This allows the firm to capture the consumer surplus.
- The sales force can quickly react to marketplace changes and competitive threats.
- In negotiations with the customer, level of services and pricing are interrelated, and if the salesperson has no authority, the process can be hindered and unnecessarily stalled.
- Decentralization leads to the optimum price when the salesperson's commission is based on the contribution margin of the sale.

2. The sales force has limited authority. Down to a set minimum price level members of the sales force can make a decision. If the price is below that level they must obtain approval from superiors.

Advantages:

- The sales force is always tempted to cut the price to make the sale, even though a commission is based on the contribution margin. This can seriously hinder the firm's marketing strategy and position in the marketplace, as pricing affects both dramatically.
- By having pricing decisions centralized, the sales force is relieved of the psychological pressures of discussing price, which most sales people are afraid of "getting beat up" over.
- Centralization can also reduce the pressure from the buyer for price concessions. One of the axioms of purchasing agents is, "find out if the salesperson can cut the price. If he can, insist he does."
- Only top management is in the position to look at each market segment and decide on the optimal pricing strategy which capitalizes on their strengths while minimizing their weaknesses.

3. The sales force has no authority over pricing. Any changes from those prescribed by management must be approved.

Although each business must decide for itself how to split pricing authority, most marketing managers, who are experts in pricing literature, seem to agree that the centralization of pricing authority results in a higher probability of profit enhancing pricing.

In Chapter 7 it was mentioned that in the legal profession a new job of "estimator" may be created. However, it would be better if, at least initially, all pricing authority would rest with the partners, or at the least, with the person who has the best relationship with the customer. Professional services are valued largely because of the personal relationship, and a sales or marketing force cannot convey that sense of value, no matter how good they may otherwise be.

With respect to marketing managers, a disturbing trend is appearing, at least in CPA firms. Since there is so much pressure on them to pay off on the investment the firm is making in their position, they tend to undercut price with alacrity in too many situations, simply to bring in the business and look successful. Cutting price is a very effective way to increase demand; it is not an effective profit-maximizing strategy for a firm with a sophisticated view of its marketplace and niche. There are no easy answers when it comes to price, and each firm must develop its own strategy.

A group of partners and managers should establish the price on any new engagement, ideally with a full understanding of the customer and after meeting with them. Also, someone who is unfamiliar with the customer— but adept at pricing decisions and ascertaining value—should be present to ensure that the overall objectives of the firm are not being lost in the adrenaline rush that comes from the potential of bringing in new business.

There are problems with the strategy of "broad-based" niche marketing, in which prices are set even before any customers are brought on board. Unless there is an enormous amount of experience in the niche, these types of pricing decisions are usually formulated in a vacuum, which means that they have no relationship to the value any one customer may place on the firm's offering. It would be better to negotiate with each customer, for each service, and formulate an FPA in which the customer has a sense of control and ego investment in the process. Unless you are marketing undifferentiated services (such as simple tax compliance or simple wills and bankruptcies), reject the temptation to enter the marketplace with a predetermined pricing policy. Pricing is far too important to be formulated without any input from the customer. And it is with the customer—ultimately—that the final pricing authority lies.

Financial Services

Financial services and commissions have entered the CPA profession. The major consolidators—from American Express to Century Business Services—are buying up CPA firms in the hope of tapping into the most trusted and respected business advisor relationship. For American Express, it's an alternative distribution channel marketing strategy; for the CPA profession, it is an enormous opportunity. And, most important of all, the customer is demanding it.

Financial services have become a growth industry for the profession because of the regulatory and legislative changes, customer demands, and profit potential. According to *Millionaire Next Door*, the number of estates valued at more than one million dollars was 40,921 in 1996 and is expected to be 100,650 by 2005, while the estimated number of millionaires will be 5,626,409, or 5,239 per 100,000 households in that same year (Stanley and Danko, 1996: 213, 225). As the baby boom generation passes its 2 trillion dollars of wealth to its kids, the nature and scope of the profession will be permanently altered.

As Chris Frederiksen pointed out at a 1999 conference: "CPAs probably control half the wealth of the nation and yet are involved in less than one tenth of 1 percent of the transactions." This strikes at the heart of the independence and objectivity on which the profession has built its illustrious reputation. But the notions of independence and objectivity may just be obsolete for all but those involved in financial statement auditing. The fact of the matter is that customers don't want the CPA to be independent and objective. They want you to help them achieve their goals. They trust their CPA more than a financial advisor or a stockbroker. The successful firm, Charles Schwab, started with the strategy of noncommissioned brokers. Then, in the 1980s, the company's market research showed that customers did want advice relating to investments and managing financial affairs. This required sending investors into the world of commissioned salespeople, what Charles Schwab himself termed "the lion's den." In response, the company created Schwab Institutional, a network of independent fee-based financial advisors to whom Schwab could refer its customers. Today, more than $100 billion in invested Schwab accounts is managed by these advisors (Berry, 1999: 146).

Many practitioners posit the theory that this trend will not work for the profession because customers are not really interested in "one-stop shopping." They point to the disaster of Sears' financial supermarket as an example of why it won't work. This example is not what it seems, however. When Sears entered into the financial services market in the 1980s—with Allstate, Dean Witter, and the Discover Card—it wasn't long before the strategy backfired, and the company was forced to retreat. Former Sears CEO Arthur C. Martinez diagnosed the real problem:

> What was wrong was that too much of the strategic focus, management energy, and financial capital [had gone] to building the financial supermarket side of the business and no attention, or let's say insufficient attention, was paid to the retail side, which was the mother lode of the whole thing. If you didn't have customers coming into your store, happy with their relationship with the store, they weren't necessarily going to be interested in anything else you had to offer. Strategically, the idea [of the financial supermarket] was sound. The problem was, while they were building another floor on the house, the foundation was rotting (O'Shea and Madigan, 1998: 121–122).

Moving into the financial services market will dramatically affect a firm's pricing strategies. One trend that has been taking place throughout the country is that of life insurance salespeople selling policies to estates, earning the commission, and from that paying the CPA or attorney for the estate planning and other services. Something is terribly wrong when a salesman can earn enough to pay the person with the expertise for his or her work. Obviously, this imbalance will be brought to parity as more and more CPAs offer insurance services themselves.

There are enormous profits to be made from selling products on a commission, especially if one breaks it down into earnings per hour. How many hours does it take to sell an estate's life insurance vs. doing its tax compliance and strategy? If partners bring the same paradigm of hourly rates into this new arena, they are likely to undervalue their traditional work in order to get the commission. This would be a serious mistake.

There is no doubt that some CPA services will become "loss leaders" in order to attract the customer's portfolio, pension plan, etc. It may make sense to give away, or significantly reduce, the price of tax compliance services in order to get this type of work; this trend is already taking place. But as the level of service moves up the Value Curve—where the customer is relatively price insensitive—the firm should not discount its price just to secure a life insurance sale. This is why it is so important to understand that price is based on value, not on internal cost, and certainly not on time.

Minimum and Set-Up Pricing

One way to ensure that your firm maintains a consistent pricing message within its marketplace is to establish a minimum price, as well as a set-up price, for all new customers. By establishing a minimum price, the firm is sending a message to all involved, that they cannot be all things to all people. One of the first things any new marketing manager should ascertain is who the firm should serve. A minimum price ensures that the firm won't spend its limited resources on customers that don't value its offering. A good minimum price is 1 percent of a firm's (or office's) gross revenue; no customer should be accepted whose price does not rise to that level. This pricing policy is dynamic, it grows with your firm.

Also, a set-up price is, in effect, one method of implementing a two-part tariff, as discussed in Chapter 9. Start by charging new customers a set-up price, ranging, for example, from $500 to $1,000 simply for setting up the customer file, doing due diligence research, contacting the predecessor CPA (or attorney), and performing everything else that is entailed in taking on a new customer. This is a very effective strategy for tapping into any consumer surplus that may exist. It also develops customer buy-in and ego investment at the beginning of the engagement, thereby committing the customer to your firm. If you are too shy to ask for a retainer, the set-up price is an effective alternative.

Menu Pricing

Menu pricing has a long and successful history among marketers. This is the bundling of a certain group of products or services into one price. Think of a restaurant pricing a full meal vs. a la carte; or American Express offering different levels of service to its Green, Gold, and Platinum Cardmembers; or an auto manufacturer offering a myriad of options on a car. Menu pricing enables a business to differentiate its products in the minds of its buyers, a classic segmentation strategy. It also may encourage buyers to trade up to a higher-priced product. Kent B. Monroe explains this in *Pricing: Making Profitable Decisions*:

> Bundling is ubiquitous and thus seemingly escapes notice. However, because it is so commonplace it has not received recognition as an important marketing strategy. Yet if properly developed and implemented, a price bundling strategy can enhance a customer's perceptions of value, provide competitive advantage, lead to cost economies, and effect a profitable pricing strategy. If bundling is improperly done, it can lead to lost sales, reduced profits, and a deterioration of customer satisfaction.
>
> Essentially, bundling is a segmentation strategy based on the theory that different segments value different combinations of products or services differently. Unless the firm's managers understand customer segmentation, it is likely that a successful strategy will not be developed. Some customers find a one-stop purchasing source desirable. Full-service banks attempt to capture such customers by offering full financial services at one institution. However, other customers want a simple checking and savings service only. If the bank forced all customers to pay for full financial services which they neither need nor want, or priced each service separately, neither customer segment would be satisfied. In either situation, the bank would be treating very different customers in a similar manner (Monroe, 1990: 319).

The movie industry once practiced the strategy known as *block booking*. Individual films were not rented to theaters; theaters were required to rent a block of films. Many thought this was a way for the distributors to force theaters to take the good along with the bad films. Economist George Stigler in 1963 proposed another reason this strategy was rational. He used the example of *Gone with the Wind* and *Getting Gertie's Garter*, two movies with widely different popularity. Stigler proposed what two theaters, A and B, would pay for the films individually:

	Gone with the Wind	*Getting Gertie's Garter*
Theater A	$8,000	$2,500
Theater B	$7,000	$3,000

Both theater owners are willing to pay substantially more for *Gone with the Wind*. The bundling strategy is effective if the distributor can reverse the relative value of the two theaters. *Gone with the Wind* is more valuable to Theater A than to Theater B, but the reverse is true for *Getting Gertie's Garter*. To rent both films separately at fixed prices, the distributor could charge no more than $7,000 for *Gone with the Wind* and $2,500 for *Getting Gertie's Garter*, for a total of $9,500 for the pair. But Theater A values the pair at $10,500 and Theater B at $10,000. Thus, by selling both films in a bundle at $10,000, the distributor is able to obtain $500 more for the pair than if they sold the films individually. This is segmented pricing because each theater pays the difference between the price of the films when sold separately ($9,500) and the price when sold together ($10,000). Theater A pays the extra $500 for *Gone with the Wind* while Theater B pays it for *Getting Gertie's Garter* (Nagle, July 1983: 17).

How has the strategy been employed in professional service firms? One firm in Australia offers its customers three levels of services, each presented in menu form: Compliance Level, Management Accounting Level, and Business Advisory Level. A partner in the firm has developed, with the assistance of his Professional Development Advisor from Results Accountants' Systems, the following explanation of each level, along with other characteristics of a Total Quality Service firm, to form a menu pricing structure:

The COMPLIANCE SERVICE incorporates . . .

Interim Financial Statements   You will receive a set of financial accounts during the year, which gives important information about how your business is operating during the year. This will give you the chance to make changes during the rest of the year if necessary.

Year-End Tax Planning Review   We agree, no one likes paying taxes. So that your share is fair and equitable, we will do everything we can within the guidelines. So that you avoid the need for last-minute tax strategies, you will have your options reviewed in the last quarter of the financial year.

Taxation Audit Protection   You will not incur any professional costs from us if you are selected for taxation audit. And we will cover up to $3,000 of specialist legal advice as part of your service. You will, of course be liable for any tax or penalties that arise from an audit.

An Analysis of Where Your Money Came From and Where It Went   You will receive an analysis that shows just where money came from during the year and where it went to. And we do this in a graphical way so that it is easy for you to see how the government still has their hand out for their share when you may not have any money in the bank. (But we will be working together to ensure this is never the case)

Trend Analysis   You will receive an analysis of the most important trends in the progress of your business. We do this in a graphical way so that the trends become clear to you.

An Annual Cash Flow Projection and Profit Plan   This assures that your business performs to the expectation that you commit to at your strategic meeting at the beginning of the year. We will review this together when we review your interim financial accounts. And we adjust for variances to get a realistic view for the rest of the year.

Guaranteed Turnaround Time for your Work of Less than 20 Working Days   We guarantee your work will be completed within 20 working days of you providing all materials to us. This will enable you to make pro-active decisions, rather than reacting to historical data. If we fail to deliver on our promise we will pay you $100 for every day the work is not completed in the timeframe. This is our guarantee to you.

Guaranteed Completion of Taxation Returns   All of your statutory requirements will be completed by 30th November of the new financial year. If all the materials required have been supplied and we fail to deliver on our promise we will pay you $100 per day for every day the work is not completed in the timeframe. This is our guarantee to you. And no, you won't be penalized for early lodgment. You don't have to pay earlier for early lodgment.

Guaranteed Response Time to Return Your Telephone Calls   If for some reason your account manager is not able to take your call and no-one else is able to immediately assist you, your call will be returned before the end of the next working day.

A Fixed Investment   The value of this service is established with you in advance and you can select a payment plan, which suits your budget. This way there are no surprises for you.

Our Work Is Guaranteed   You rightly deserve quality work completed in a timely manner. If you are not delighted with the work we do for you, we respect your right to withhold your fee.

The MANAGEMENT ACCOUNTING SERVICE incorporates . . .

Quarterly Financial Statements   You will receive a set of financial accounts during the year, which gives important information about how your business is operating during the year. This will give you the chance to make changes during the rest of the year if necessary.

Year End Tax Planning Review   We agree, no-one likes paying taxes. So that your share is fair and equitable, we will do everything within the guidelines so that your share is fair and equitable. So that you avoid the need for last minute tax strategies, you will have your options reviewed in the last quarter of the financial year.

Unlimited Access to Advice on Ad Hoc Matters   You can phone your account manager at any time for advice on ad hoc matters in the knowledge that we will not be charging you for that advice. This is subject to the understanding that if an occasion of service exceeds 15 minutes, you will be charged, but only after we have consulted with you and only if you feel that you got value from the consultation.

Taxation Audit Protection   You will not incur any professional costs from us if you are selected for taxation audit. And we will cover up to $3,000 of specialist legal advice as part of your service. You will, of course be liable for any tax or penalties, that arise from an audit.

An Analysis of Where Your Money Came From and Where It Went   You will receive an analysis that shows just where money came from during the year and where it went to. And we do this in a graphical way so that it is easy for you to see how the government still has their hand out for their share when you may not have any money in the bank. (But we will be working together to ensure this is never the case)

Trend Analysis　You will receive an analysis of the most important trends in the progress of your business. We do this in a graphical way so that the trends become clear to you.

A Quarterly Cash Flow Projection and Profit Plan　This assures that your business performs to the expectation that you commit to at your strategic meeting at the beginning of the year. We will review this together when we review your quarterly financial accounts. And we adjust for variances to get a realistic view for the rest of the year.

Your Business Compared to That of Your Peers　We have access to key financial performance indicators of businesses within your industry. Your business will be compared to these, so that you are aware of your progression toward business excellence.

Net Worth Change　Are you in business to improve your net worth? If not, we suggest that you should be. And to help you stay committed to this path, your asset base will be broken up into each economic sector and examined for economic return. Your results will be graphically represented, so that you can see for yourself your increasing net worth. And exactly where it is coming from.

Guaranteed Turnaround Time for Your Work of Less than 15 Working Days　We guarantee your work will be completed within 15 working days of you providing all materials to us. This will enable you to make pro-active decisions, rather than reacting to historical data. If we fail to deliver on our promise we will pay you $100 for every day the work is not completed in the timeframe. This is our guarantee to you.

Guaranteed Completion of Taxation Returns　All of your statutory requirements will be completed by 31st October of the new financial year. If all the materials required have been supplied and we fail to deliver on our promise we will pay you $100 per day for every day the work is not completed in the timeframe. This is our guarantee to you. And no, you won't be penalized for early lodgment. You don't have to pay earlier for early lodgment.

Guaranteed Response Time to Return Your Telephone Calls　If for some reason your account manager is not able to take your call and no-one else is able to immediately assist you, your call will be returned before the end of the next working day.

A Fixed Investment   The value of this service is established with you in advance and you can select a payment plan, which suits your budget. This way there are no surprises for you.

Our Work Is Guaranteed   You rightly deserve quality work completed in a timely manner. If you are not delighted with the work we do for you, we respect your right to withhold your fee.

The BUSINESS ADVISORY SERVICE incorporates . . .

Monthly Financial Statements   You will receive a set of financial accounts during the year, which gives important information about how your business is operating during the year. This will give you the chance to make changes during the rest of the year if necessary.

Year End Tax Planning Review   We agree, no-one likes paying taxes. So that your share is fair and equitable, we will do everything within the guidelines so that your share is fair and equitable. So that you avoid the need for last minute tax strategies, you will have your options reviewed in the last quarter of the financial year.

Unlimited Access to Advice on Ad Hoc Matters   You can phone or visit your account manager at any time for advice on ad hoc matters in the knowledge that we will not be charging you for that advice. This is subject to the understanding that if an occasion of service exceeds 15 minutes, you will be charged, but only after we have consulted with you and only if you feel that you got value from the consultation.

Taxation Audit Protection   You will not incur any professional costs from us if you are selected for taxation audit. And we will cover up to $3,000 of specialist legal advice as part of your service. You will, of course be liable for any tax or penalties, that arise from an audit.

An Analysis of Where Your Money Came From and Where It Went   You will receive an analysis that shows just where money came from during the year and where it went to. And we do this in a graphical way so that it is easy for you to see how the government still has their hand out for their share when you may not have any money in the bank. (But we will be working together to ensure this is never the case)

Trend Analysis   You will receive an analysis of the most important trends in the progress of your business. We do this in a graphical way so that the trends become clear to you.

A 12 Month Cash Flow Projection and Profit Plan   This assures that your business performs to the expectation that you commit to at your strategic meeting at the beginning of the year. We will review this together when we review your monthly financial accounts. And we adjust for variances to get a realistic view for the rest of the year.

Your Business Compared to That of Your Peers   We have access to key financial performance indicators of businesses within your industry. Your business will be compared to these, so that you are aware of your progression toward business excellence.

Net Worth Change   Are you in business to improve your net worth? If not, we suggest that you should be. And to help you stay committed to this path, your asset base will be broken up into each economic sector and examined for economic return. Your results will be graphically represented, so that you can see for yourself your increasing net worth. And exactly where it is coming from.

Your Key Performance Indicator Reviewed Monthly   And what is a KPI? This is a measurement of the performance of those activities within your business that you absolutely MUST get right. How do you know which activities you must get right. Your business's governing economic purpose will be identified and from this we will extract those activities which are most critical to its success. Let them know that you will be working with them pro-actively each month to review the results. It's not "coaching" — this comes with the BD work. But it will help add value.

Guaranteed Turnaround Time for your Work of Less than 10 Working Days   We guarantee your work will be completed within

10 working days of you providing all materials to us. This will enable you to make pro-active decisions, rather than reacting to historical data. If we fail to deliver on our promise we will pay you $100 for every day the work is not completed in the timeframe. This is our guarantee to you.

Guaranteed Completion of Taxation Returns   All of your statutory requirements will be completed by 31st October of the new financial year. If all the materials required have been supplied and we fail to deliver on our promise we will pay you $100 per day for every day the work is not completed in the timeframe. This is our guarantee to you. And no, you won't be penalized for early lodgment. You don't have to pay earlier for early lodgment.

Guaranteed Response Time to Return Your Telephone Calls   If for some reason your account manager is not able to take your call and no-one else is able to immediately assist you, your call will be returned before the end of the next working day.

A Fixed Investment   The value of this service is established with you in advance and you can select a payment plan, which suits your budget. This way there are no surprises for you.

Our Work Is Guaranteed   You rightly deserve quality work completed in a timely manner. If you are not delighted with the work we do for you, we respect your right to withhold your fee.

This type of pricing is not without its disadvantages, however. One issue is that the customers may not perceive the options as tailored to their specific situations, and thus they may feel as if they are being sold an off-the-shelf bundle of goods. They may not want or need many of the items included. Another problem with this type of pricing is that firms offer a fixed price, set in advance—with no customer involvement—for each level of service. This is a serious mistake. Pricing should never take place in a vacuum, and because the customer is the final arbiter of value, one should always negotiate a price with the input of the customer. Finally, this type of pricing may give the marketing manager and the partners a false sense of security. They will think that they have covered anything that a business owner may want or need, but this is rarely the case. Packaging services into groups is an excellent strategy, but not at the expense of creatively customizing services in order to meet any one customer's specific circumstances.

Notwithstanding the problems with this method, it carries many advantages. A thoughtfully crafted menu pricing strategy does allow your firm to respond to (or forestall) certain competitive threats. It can enhance your revenues while minimizing your revenue loss due to price fluctuations. This method can also help you manage the cost of delivering services to a particular niche as well as capitalize on marginal price changes for any one customer. One last important advantage is that customers seem to approve of the policy.

Electronic Commerce

Like the personal computer, the Internet has changed the world. It has torn down geographical boundaries and has given the average individual more information than government leaders or industrialists ever dreamed imaginable at the start of the Industrial Revolution. When the Internet first arrived on the scene, many dismissed it as a fad—the Citizen Band radio for computer geeks. They couldn't have been more wrong. What separates the Internet from, say, television, is that one can make money with it, because it enhances human capital. Rather than turning people into mindless "mouse potatoes," the Internet can be used to get what you want, when you want it, exactly the way you want it. It is the difference between taking a train—and being held at the whim of fixed schedules and destinations—and taking a car, going at your own pace, stopping when you want and leaving when you wish.

The amazing power of this tool was destined to alter—forever—the face of commerce. Estimates on the size of e-commerce vary, as it is difficult to measure this new phenomena. One survey conducted by ActiveMedia, using data collected in early 1998 from web site executives and business managers worldwide, showed that one million dollars in sales per month was not uncommon among leading sites, such as Dell Computer, Cisco, and Boeing. An Ernst & Young study for the National Retail Federation found 32 percent of consumers with Internet access had purchased goods online. The percent of Internet users making purchases more than doubled in a year. Cyberdialogue found that 48 percent of online buyers were satisfied and 48 percent were very satisfied with the experience, and 19 percent indicated they were shopping in stores less (Gilder, May 1998: 5).

Also on the rise are Internet purchases by businesses, as a survey by Thomas Register and VISA U.S.A. discovered. Forty percent of 2,000 respondents used the Internet daily to make purchases, 10 percent use the Internet to make more than half of their purchases, and 21 percent plan to do so by the end of 1998. A similar survey by AccuStaff found 54 percent of companies have a home page, and an additional 40 percent intend to have one within the next 12 months. Of those companies with web sites, 65 percent report sales made from them (ibid., 5). According to the Ernst & Young 6th Annual Report on Technology in Banking and Financial Services, 89 percent of U.S. financial firms expect to have Internet transactions in 1999 (Gilder, July 1997: 1). Certainly the Internet has already eclipsed the U.S. Postal Service as a carrier of mail. By one estimate, one trillion e-mail messages are sent compared with 180 billion postal deliveries. It is estimated that e-commerce could grow to $100 billion by the year 2000, while other estimates are even higher. What is interesting about the Internet is not the predictions of its future, but the implications the technology will have on the future.

Nothing but Net

Scott McNealy of Sun Microsystems started saying in 1996, "The network is the computer." The personal computer was optimized for the desktop. All of the complexity sat in the PC through its processor and operating system software. But today, with the 200-fold rise in Internet traffic, most users spend more time accessing remote memories than they do their own desktop memory. The day may come when, as long predicted by technology expert George Gilder, television dies. Television, after all, forces the viewer to adhere to a broadcaster's schedule while the Internet delivers— through fiber optics or satellites—the user's first choice, when and where the user wants it. You don't need 500 television channels. You need only one, as long as you can get your first choice. That is the promise of the Internet acting as your computer.

Think for a moment of the implications this will have on the entertainment industry, to pick just one example. As George Gilder explains:

> The key thing computer networking does to any business is
> change vertical systems into horizontal systems. It eliminates
> middlemen—middle executives—of all descriptions. And the

heart of Hollywood today is intermediation. About 70 percent of the cost of making a movie is in areas such as distribution and advertising, and about 30 percent goes to the people involved in making the movie.

Most of that 70 percent will be collapsed by a truly pervasive fiber-optic network system. It will collapse when you can make it available to the entire world, and you don't need to attract miscellaneous audience to theaters in Des Moines, San Jose, Seattle, and Pittsfield [MA] at once. The 70 percent cost of the film drops to 5 percent, or even less for some.

Meanwhile, the remaining 30 percent of the cost of a film is getting these people whose star properties come from their lowest-common-denominator appeal and from their monopoly position of being able to finance those 70 percent costs. Those costs can be drastically reduced (Gregorsky, 1998: 80).

While the Internet will shift more power to the customer and make it harder for the seller to capitalize on asymmetrical information, there are some compelling advantages to e-commerce, from the vendors perspective, according to John Hagel III and Arthur G. Armstrong in *Net Gain: Expanding Markets through Virtual Communities*:

- **Reduced search costs**   Both vendors and likely customers will be able to locate one another more easily.
- **Increased propensity for customers to buy**   Similar to the introduction of the Automatic Teller Machines in the 1980s, once customers get familiar with using the Internet to transact business, the probability of other purchases made online will increase.
- **Enhanced ability to target**   Not only will customers be able to find exactly what they want, vendors will also be able to target specific communities, based upon membership profiles, to locate their specific niche.
- **Greater ability to tailor and add value to existing products and services**   Known as one-to-one marketing, firms will be able to customize products and services, even to a mass market. Also, because of the interactive feedback dynamic of the Internet, vendors will

be able to learn more about each customer with every purchase, and will be better equipped to market and sell additional products and services to them.

- **Lower capital and investment in bricks and mortar** Just like Amazon.com, which replaced inventory with information, the Internet allows communities to exist without expensive buildings in fixed locations that people must wait in traffic to get to. This creates a significant advantage for banks, retail outlets, and even professional service firms.
- **Broader geographic reach** The Internet tears down geographical boundaries effectively, opening the entire world to both vendor and customer.
- **Disintermediation potential** Vendors will be in a better position to deal directly with their customers, as Gilder pointed out in the entertainment industry example above. This will enable one link—the middleman—to be removed from the value chain, lowering overall price to the customer (Hagel and Armstrong, 1997: 10–12).

All of these forces, combined, will shift the demand curve to the right for any one particular vendor. The lower costs associated with transactions via the Internet will put downward pressure on prices in some markets. In fact, the notion of a fixed price may well be obsolete in the virtual community. This will take place largely as the result of customers being better informed; having more information means having more power. Lowering the amount of asymmetrical information that exists will put customers—and businesses, for that matter—in a better position to bargain and get exactly what they want, at the price they want it. While one could look at this and say that the consumer surplus will, more and more, be kept by the customer, that may be a premature conclusion. It is also very possible that the vendors will be able to tap into the consumer surplus more readily because they too will have more information on the customer's perceived value at their disposal.

The Internet is the perfect medium in which to price on the margin. Sites such as Priceline.com allow customers to set their own price for airline and hotel reservations. Mortgages, cars, and even energy are now sold in the same manner over the Internet. Does this negate the theory of Value Pricing? Not at all. Airlines, for instance, will give discounts only to leisure travelers, with advance purchase and other restrictions, or based upon load capacities. Airlines will still discriminate against the business traveler, but they now will be better able to offer empty, last-minute seats to those customers seeking a deal.

This is not to say that the Internet doesn't create pricing challenges. It does. Customers will naturally gravitate to the lowest price, at first. But customer service and loyalty will still remain very important, in the long run, to any successful Internet business. The Internet is a dynamic medium and will allow customer loyalty, finally, to be a two-way street, rather than the one-way street most businesses have viewed it in the past. Now that customers will have a number of options available at their fingertips— shelf space is not a restriction in a virtual world—why should they deal with you? Answering that question involves more than offering the cheapest price, especially for professional service providers. After all, would you choose your heart operation from a doctor who gave you the lowest bid? The answer lies in Total Quality Service, which is still critical over the Internet, especially when you consider how fast word-of-mouth can spread online.

The Internet will allow businesses to experiment with pricing to select groups of customers, and thus pricing is likely to become much more volatile in this environment. It will also allow vendors to customize packages and menu pricing to the various needs of specific market segments.

One innovative web site is CPAAuction.com. The creator of this site believes that the audit is a commodity. Customers at his web site register for a fee of $25 for 12 months and submit their financial statements. Then they are sent out for bids among member CPA firms. If after registering, the business selects a CPA firm from the auction, or decides to stay with their present firm for a lower audit fee, or receives a bid from a CPA firm which is lower than their last year audit fee, they will pay an additional $500 to CPA Auction. If they do none of the above, they are under no obligation to pay.

This is interesting, and it may become the wave of the future, and it may be used for audits, the CPA's one true monopoly. The problem with this form of blind bidding is that no relationship with the customer is developed to assess their wants and needs adequately. Also, it will simply attract customers to your firm who value the audit the least and will be the first to move on when they find a cheaper price—which they always will. It also doesn't allow the audit to be priced actuarially because it is, in essence, an insurance policy, and it further perpetuates the notion among customers that all financial statement audits (and CPAs) are the same.

Nevertheless, the free market is sovereign and experiments such as this will take place. For some smaller firms, or start-up firms, this may be one avenue of growth. However, it is recommended that any firm engaging in this type of pricing policy be cognizant of the message it is sending into the marketplace and the type of customer it is likely to attract. If you are considering becoming involved in this type of pricing, be sure this fits in with your overall marketing strategy.

Summary and Conclusions

This chapter discussed various pricing strategies that can be used when pricing particular services for a customer. When it comes to new customers vs. long-term customers, firms must understand the importance of their long-term customers and how much more profitable these are than the new ones. You have no business getting new customers if you are not pleasing your existing ones. The goal should be obtaining *better* business, not just *more* business.

Examine some closed files in your office (a checklist is included in "Useful Checklists" at the end of the book and on the disc.) They contain a wealth of information—who performed the work, how much was spent, what technology was used, how much was charged, and ultimately, collected. Try to determine if any consumer surplus existed that could have been tapped into. This is a good exercise to perform with your fellow partners, managers, and staff to develop a Value Pricing culture in your firm.

13 ALTERNATIVE METHODS OF PRICING BY ENGAGEMENT

The fixed price should be used as often as possible. Other pricing methods need to be considered, however. One reason is that the transition to Value Pricing may be gradual and you may wish to use other pricing methods along with Value Pricing until you build your confidence and negotiation skills. Also, Value Pricing may be used in combination with other pricing methods, such as retrospective price or a contingent price.

The following are the prevalent pricing methods in the accounting and legal professions, with the exception of fixed price and hourly billing, which have been covered in detail in earlier chapters. Advantages and disadvantages are cited, along with suggestions on when to use them.

At the end of the chapter is a list of pricing methods appropriate for specific engagements, such as estate planning, payroll services, and tax planning.

Contingent Pricing

Contingent prices depend upon the results achieved for the customer and require a clear agreement on what the desired results should be. The AICPA's Code of Professional Conduct (AICPA, Professional Standards, vol. 2, ET sec. 302) defines a contingent fee as follows: "A fee established for the performance of any service pursuant to an arrangement in which no fee will be charged unless a specified finding or result is attained, or in which the amount of the fee is otherwise dependent upon the finding or result of such service."

Bans on CPA advertising and the acceptance of commissions and contingent fees date back to 1918. With the passage of the wartime excess profits tax, many unqualified tax practitioners were attracted to the profession and proclaimed to be "tax experts," charging a contingency for any tax savings they were able to provide. This got the attention of the Treasury Department, which insisted that the American Institute of Accountants (AIA) pass rules prohibiting contingent fees and "unseemly" advertising, and in 1919 the AIA did just that.

Here is an explanation of the situation from *A History of Accountancy in the United States*:

> In 1919, the institute's council responded, banning contingent fees after a heated debate. The rule read as follows: "No member shall render professional services, the anticipated fee for which shall be contingent upon his findings and results thereof. (This rule shall be construed as inhibiting only services in which the accountant's findings or expert opinion might be influenced by consideration of personal financial interest)." The sentence in parentheses was deleted in 1920 because some practitioners contended that it permitted tax work by accountants on a contingency fee. This new rule proved ineffective and was widely ignored. In 1923, the AIA passed a yet more stringent rule, banning contingent fees absolutely: "Members and associates should neither render nor offer to render services for which the fees are contingent." Practitioners could accept no contingent fees for any type of service.
>
> Even institute members rebelled against the ban. Robert H. Montgomery, a past president of the American Association of Public Accountants and one of the most influential members of the AIA, and Walter Staub mentioned the rule in their 1923 edition of *Auditing Principles* but concluded it was too strict to be enforceable. The authors suggested that tax practitioners might ignore the rule and accept work on a contingent fee basis. Normally, influential members of an organization are expected to comply with its norms; when they do not it becomes clear that the organization does not have the authority to enforce its sanctions. The American Society of Certified Public Accountants condemned the ban on contingent fees; these restrictions provided support for the society's claims that the institute sought to protect the elite in the profession. The institute's efforts to restrict advertising simply added more fuel to the fire (Previts and Merino, 1998: 247).

Today, despite the resistance of various state societies, and even the AICPA at one point, the marketplace has asserted its sovereignty and deregulation of the profession—as in so many industries since the late 1970s—has begun. Many believe this will be the death knell for the profession; others believe it is a tremendous opportunity for those firms that take the lead and march the profession towards its inevitable destiny.

Advantages

- Price is dependent on results achieved, not on time spent, allowing firms to capitalize on internal efficiencies.
- It can be used with other pricing methods to ensure that the firm receives some minimum price for its efforts.
- The professional can reap "supernormal" profits because of the additional risk assumed.
- The customer's expectations are determined prior to the engagement, thereby clarifying the firm's value-added services.
- The customers who can't afford to pay have access to professional services.

Disadvantages

- Resources devoted to the engagement may exceed the original estimates with no commensurate increase in price.
- The firm assumes the risk of the engagement and the potential loss of not achieving the desired outcome.
- Uneven cash flow may result.
- It cannot be used in conjunction with attest services where independence is a requirement.

When to Use

- The engagement has a high probability of success.
- A firm has developed expertise in handling similar contingent-priced engagements.
- A customer may be otherwise unable to afford the firm's services unless the desired outcome is achieved.
- Regulatory agencies allow for a contingent price to be charged.

Recommended Engagements

- Mergers and acquisitions
- Negotiating the buying or selling of a business
- Representation before governmental taxing authorities, or obtaining private letter rulings
- Engagements that influence the drafting or promulgation of a regulation or statute
- Innovative tax strategies that provide substantial tax savings to the customer
- Personal financial planning where a percentage of the total portfolio is the contingent price
- Other engagements that lend themselves to a specific and desirable outcome

Blended Hourly Rates

Blended hourly rates are used when the firm knows the mix of personnel needed to complete the engagement but may not know exactly how long the project will take. Thus, one hourly rate is billed for all hours worked on a particular engagement, regardless of who does the work. For example, if a particular engagement calls for a partner at $200 per hour, a senior associate at $150 per hour and a staff person at $100 per hour, and the firm is not sure how long the project will take, a blended rate may be computed for the entire project. Suppose the partner will spend 25 percent of the total time, the senior associate 35 percent, and the staff person 40 percent; the blended rate is computed as follows:

$$\begin{array}{ll} \$200 \times 25\% = & \$50.00 \\ \$150 \times 35\% = & 52.50 \\ \$100 \times 40\% = & \underline{40.00} \\ \text{Blended rate} & \underline{\underline{\$142.50}} \end{array}$$

The firm may quote a rate of $145 per hour in this example. Every hour worked on the project, no matter who performs it, is priced at that rate. If the firm is able to manage the engagement more efficiently, perhaps by delegating more of the work to the staff person, the realization rate will increase.

Advantages

- Generally, the advantages are the same as those of the hourly rate.
- Negotiating a single rate with the customer is easier when numerous professionals are involved.
- The firm has the potential to realize more profit if work is performed more efficiently than estimated.

Disadvantages

- All of the disadvantages of the hourly rate method apply.

When to Use

- The customer absolutely demands it.
- The firm declines to assume any risk from the pricing of the engagement.
- A third party demands hourly billing—e.g., government agencies and courts, which recognize only hourly billing.

Recommended Engagements

- One-time consultations when no other benchmark of value can be agreed upon.
- Engagements in which the uncertainties are so prevalent that no estimate can be made as to the effort required.

Fixed Price Plus Hourly Rates

With this hybrid method, the portions of the engagement that can be defined are priced on a fixed-price basis and those aspects that cannot be defined, due to variables or uncertainties, are priced on an hourly basis. For instance, in an estate-planning engagement, during the initial phase when the strategy is being formulated and preliminary information is being gathered, an hourly rate may apply. Then, once the plan has been agreed upon, a fixed price may be negotiated for implementation.

Advantages

- The professional and the customer share the engagement risk.
- The customer is aware of the fixed-price portion in advance.
- The advantages of the fixed price and the hourly rate methods are combined.

Disadvantages

- The firm assumes some risk by using the fixed price method for a portion of the engagement.
- The disadvantages of the fixed price and the hourly rate methods apply.

When to Use

- Engagements that have many unknown variables at the outset and when the firm is not comfortable quoting a fixed price for the entire project.
- The customer demands it.

Recommended Engagements

- Complex estate-planning
- Litigation services
- Compliance services (audits, reviews, compilations, and tax) when any add-on services would be performed on an hourly rate basis
- Complex IRS audits, offers in compromise, and private letter rulings

Hourly Rates Plus a Contingency

This method is a combination of the hourly rate and a contingency based upon a determinable outcome. It is a way for the professional to share the risk of the downside of a transaction, such as a merger or acquisition, while also sharing in the upside potential. Because the professional will receive at least the hourly rate agreed upon, that portion of the risk is borne by the customer. However, if the transaction is a success, the professional will also share in the rewards. Usually, this method requires the firm to discount its "standard" hourly rate in order to share in the upside potential.

Advantages

- The professional and the customer share in the risks and the rewards.
- The hourly rate may cover the firm's internal cost of servicing the engagement.
- The customer will not pay the "standard" hourly rate if the project is unsuccessful and will share the benefits proportionately if it is.
- The customer may be able to acquire professional services not otherwise affordable.
- The advantages of both the hourly rate and the contingent price apply.

Disadvantages

- The professional must make an accurate assessment of the probability of a successful engagement, since he is assuming more of a risk by discounting the "standard" rate.
- Disagreement can result if the contingent portion of the price is not clearly agreed to, or understood, by the customer.
- The disadvantages of the hourly rate and contingent methods apply.

When to Use

- Situations are at the top of the Value Curve involving large dollar amounts, a high probability of a successful (and therefore value-added) outcome, and a willingness to share in the risks with the customer. If the successful outcome is absolutely guaranteed, it may be wise to forego the hourly rate and simply use a contingent price based on the outcome.
- The customer has an excellent relationship with the firm.
- The regulatory agencies allow for a contingent price to be charged.

Recommended Engagements

- Unique services (those custom-designed to a particular customer)

- Mergers and acquisitions
- Estate-planning
- Innovative tax strategies and governmental audits
- Business buy/sell
- Financing packages (SBA loans, lines of credit, etc.)
- Divorce proceedings
- Litigation support

Percentage Pricing

Usually, percentage prices are based on schedules related to the amount involved in the matter being handled. These amounts may be predetermined or ultimately determined by a future outcome. Examples would include a percentage of the estate being probated or a percentage of the dollar amount of a real estate transaction or a bond issue. The percentage rate may be constant or graduated. Traditionally, legal services have been more suited to this type of pricing than accounting services.

Advantages

- Provides ease in delineating to the customer the terms of the engagement and the price to be charged.
- The firm's liability exposure should be covered adequately because the price is determined by the dollar amount involved.
- The price is not dependent upon the time spent.
- If the percentages and the amount of the transaction are known beforehand, the advantages of the fixed price apply.
- If the percentages and the amount of the transaction are unknown beforehand, the advantages of the contingent price apply.

Disadvantages

- Too high a percentage may not be competitive in the marketplace.
- Too low a percentage may not cover the firm's internal costs.
- If complications arise during the engagement, the risk is borne by the firm, unless a Change Order has been agreed to by the customer and is provided for in the engagement agreement.

- If the percentage and the amount of the transaction are known, the disadvantages of the fixed price apply.
- If the percentage and the amount of the transaction are unknown, the disadvantages of the contingent price apply.

When to Use

- A large dollar amount is involved and the customer and professional are willing to share in the risks and the rewards of outcome.

Recommended Engagements

- Real estate transactions
- Business sales and purchases
- Personal financial planning, where a percentage of the portfolio managed is charged
- Sales of life insurance and investment products (becoming increasingly popular among CPAs moving into these lines of businesses)
- Tax strategies, governmental audits
- Financing packages

Retrospective Pricing

This method is appropriate for engagements that have several possible outcomes. Nevertheless, the factors that ultimately determine the value of the project should be included in the Fixed Price Agreement or Change Order. This method can be combined with a minimum or maximum fixed price. The price, ultimately, is determined by the *customer* (not the professional). This method is sometimes referred to as a "TIP" clause.

Advantages

- Since the price is set at the end of the engagement, all of the uncertainties and unknowns no longer exist. This allows the customer and professional to agree upon the actual value of the services provided.
- The price is based upon the value of the service, not the time spent performing it.

- Because the customer sets the price, disputes and slow payments are eliminated.
- It allows the firm to capture a portion of the consumer surplus.

Disadvantages

- The customer doesn't know what the price will be beforehand.
- The professional's perception of value may differ from the customer's.
- If no progress payments are received from the customer, the firm will suffer cash flow consequences.

When to Use

- A trusting, long-term relationship exists between the professional and the customer, with each being aware of the value-added nature of the relationship.
- The professional believes that a better-than-expected benefit will accrue to the customer.
- A professional has rendered a high value-added service, but may not have adequately discussed price beforehand.
- The professional has performed outstanding work, above and beyond the customer's expectations.
- Engagements are at the top end of the Value Curve.
- Contingent prices are not allowed and price can be based on customer satisfaction rather than any specific outcome.

Recommended Engagements

- Business sales and purchases
- Financing packages
- Litigation, arbitration, and mediation services
- Divorce planning and mediation
- Tax strategies, governmental audits and hearings
- Any project involving the professional in negotiations involving large dollar amounts or significant consequences to the customer
- One-time engagements in which the firm can easily perform the service and the value perceived by the customer is large

Availability-Only Retainer

Sometimes referred to as a "pure retainer" or "right-to-call retainer," this is a payment to the professional for no specific services (or limited services, as specified) performed, in return for the professional's commitment to be available when requested, and to refrain from servicing other parties that may pose a conflict to the customer (e.g., a competitor or adverse party). This type of arrangement is rare in an accounting firm.

Advantages

- The professional may not have to perform any services.
- The customer is assured of access (or representation) by the professional.
- The customer is assured that the professional will not perform work or represent any party who is adverse to the customer.
- The customer may perceive that the professional association is prestigious.

Disadvantages

- The professional will be unable to accept work from similar customers in the market.
- The customer may determine that the amount paid does not justify the value received from the retainer.
- The professional's loss of additional work may exceed the amount of the retainer.

When to Use

- The benefits to both parties exceed the costs.
- The monetary amount involved justifies being restricted from obtaining additional work.

Recommended Engagements

- When the professional's expertise or high visibility in the marketplace can lend prestige to the customer (e.g., an expert witness)

- Executive search for a customer
- Acquiring or selling a business on behalf of a customer

Retainer as a Deposit Against Future Services

Although not technically a pricing method, the retainer as a deposit against future services is a way for the firm to ensure payment from the customer. Use this method whenever possible because it greatly enhances cash flow. This method can be combined with any of the pricing methods discussed and is very effective for new customers whose credibility has not yet been established.

Advantages

- The customer makes an "ego investment" and commits up front to the relationship.
- Accounts receivable collection problems are minimized and cash flow is maximized.
- The firm is assured of payment.

Disadvantages

- The client must pay up front before receiving any benefit from the services to be rendered.
- It the retainer balance at the end of the engagement is insufficient to cover the price charged, a potential collection problem arises.
- Since the customer is paying before receiving any services, expectations *will* rise and if the firm does not deliver Total Quality Service, the customer may be dissatisfied and defect.

When to Use

- The integrity of the customers or their willingness or ability to pay the prices charged by the firm is in question.
- You want to set a precedent with new customers that the firm expects to be paid (even if just partially) up front.

Recommended Engagements

- Tax collection representations, especially delinquent customers
- Tax audits
- Insolvent customers

Unit Pricing

This is where a fixed price is charged for a specific service, without regard to the time spent. This is sometimes referred to as task-based billing. For example, an accounting firm may price tax returns by the form (though this policy does not allow the firm to capture the consumer surplus that may exist for any one customer).

Advantages

- Time recordkeeping is simplified.
- Potential for pricing premiums exists if time for performing the task can be minimized.
- Customer and professional can determine the price up-front.

Disadvantages

- This may cause confusion if the customer believes the firm is pricing by the hour.
- This requires adequate representation of the unit price for each service.
- The firm is not allowed to capture the consumer surplus.

When to Use

- The professional has accurate knowledge of the internal cost of providing the service.
- The customer demands this type of pricing method.

Recommended Engagements

- Tax compliance work (*charge per schedule*)

- Bookkeeping and write-up work
- Budgeting and cash flow projections
- Payroll services

Lodestar Pricing

Richard C. Reed explains "lodestar" in *Billing Innovations*:

> The lodestar method of setting fees originated in the federal case of *Lindy Brothers Builders, Inc. v. American Radiator & Standard Sanitary Corp.*, 487 F.2d 161 (3d Cir. 1973) and has been adopted in some states. The method involves multiplying the hours spent by a reasonable billing rate per hour to determine the "lodestar." Then that amount is multiplied by a factor, e.g., 1.4, 1.7, 3.0, or 0.8, for considerations other than time spent.
>
> Court decisions have restricted the factors that can be considered as a multiplier, contending that those factors are subsumed in the hourly billing rate. For example, "expertise" originally was a factor in determining the amount of the multiplier, but now is generally considered to be reflected in the hourly billing rate. Uncertainty of payment remains a factor for the multiplier. (Reed, 1996: 24)

Advantages

- The hourly rate may be increased or decreased based on criteria other than time spent.
- This method has the same advantages as the hourly rate method.

Disadvantages

- These are the same as those of the hourly rate method.
- The courts tend to disallow a portion of the hours spent.
- The court is second-guessing what was required from the professional.

- The lodestar formula might not reflect the value of the services provided.

When to Use

- The court system requires it.

Guaranteed Pricing

The guaranteed price is secured by a 100 percent money back Service Guarantee clause in the Fixed Price Agreement that states: "If you are not completely satisfied with the services performed by ABC, CPAs, we will, at the option of [customer's name], either refund the price or accept a portion of said price that reflects [customer's name] level of satisfaction. We will assume you are satisfied upon final payment received under the terms of this Agreement."

Advantages

- It communicates a commitment to excellence and Total Quality Service.
- Every member of the firm is cognizant of the importance of exceeding the customer's expectations.
- Most likely, the competition is not offering this type of guarantee, conferring to the firm an enormous competitive advantage.
- Price resistance and buyer's remorse are overcome.
- The firm will do an adequate job of pre-qualifying customers, since a high level of trust is required in order to provide a guarantee.
- All things being equal, a service that is guaranteed is more valuable than one that is not, and thus a premium can be charged.
- It gives the customer an incentive to complain and gives the firm a second chance to resolve issues and earn continued trust and loyalty.
- It identifies customers who are out to take advantage of the firm and allows for them to be dropped from the customer base.
- By offering an overt guarantee (i.e., by publicizing it in the firm's marketing and advertising material), your firm will enhance its com-

petitive position in the market and increase the value perceived by the customer.

Disadvantages

- Firms are set up for failure if they cannot deliver Total Quality Service that exceeds customer expectations.
- Refunds (partial or full) will be required when the customer has a legitimate complaint about the firm's service.

When to Use

- Customers are new.
- Customers are long-time customers.
- This method, set forth in the Request for Proposals, is a way to distinguish your firm from the competition.

Outside-In Pricing

One of the most innovative pricing methods, outside-in pricing, starts from *outside* the firm and is based on the premise that the ultimate arbiter of value is the person paying—the customer. Price negotiations are started by asking the customer what they believe the service is worth.

Advantages

- It allows the professional and the customer to discover their perception of value.
- It has the potential of identifying the firm's "first-class passengers," that is, those who are *willing* and *able* to pay more than the market price.
- It involves the customers in pricing the firm's services, gaining their "ego investment."
- It allows the firm to build customer relationship and goodwill based upon a mutually advantageous partnership.

- It transfers some of the customer's consumer surplus to the firm without diminishing the value received by the customer.

Disadvantages

- Customers may quote a price that is unreasonably low and may be reluctant to change their minds. (In that case, withdraw from the engagement.)
- Customers and professionals are put in a negotiating position, which many professionals find distasteful. However, many customers negotiate on a daily basis in running their businesses and are completely comfortable negotiating price with a trusted and respected professional.

When to Use

- The *value* (not the price) of the service has been discussed but no work has yet been performed.
- The firm is working on a marginal engagement for an existing customer who has an excellent relationship with the firm.
- The professional knows that the value of the service exceeds the price that would be charged based upon the time spent

Possible Pricing Methods to Use for Specific Engagements

The following chart lists several possible pricing combinations. Any number of combinations of pricing methods may be used, depending on the nature of the engagement, the relationship with the customer, the dollar amount involved, the risks being assumed by the parties, and a myriad of other factors. Remember, in almost every engagement, the Outside-In Price (whereby the customer proclaims the value of the service) is possible as a starting point to negotiating a Value Price. Also, a 100% Money Back Service Guarantee clause can be used with any of the pricing methods mentioned. Finally, these engagements may present themselves in the standard Fixed Price Agreement or in a Change Order.

Engagement	Suggested Pricing Method(s)
Arbitration/Mediation Support	Fixed Price Plus a Contingency; Hourly Rate Plus a Contingency; Retrospective Price
Bookkeeping and Write-Up Work	Fixed Price; Unit; Outside-In Price
Budgets and Cash-Flow Projections	Fixed Price; Unit; Outside-In Price
Buy/Sell Businesses	Contingent Price; Hourly Rate Plus a Contingency; Fixed Price Plus a Contingency; Percentage; Retrospective Price
Buy/Sell Business (on behalf of customer)	Availability-Only Retainer; Contingent Price; Fixed Price Plus a Contingency; Percentage
Divorce Planning/Engagements	Hourly Rate Plus a Contingency; Fixed Price Plus a Contingency; Retrospective Price
Estate Planning (simple)	Fixed Price; Contingent Price
Estate Planning (complex)	Fixed Price Plus Hourly Rate; Hourly Rate Plus a Contingency; Fixed Price Plus a Contingency
Executive Search	Availability-Only Retainer; Percentage
Experiential Services	Fixed Price Plus a Contingency; Hourly Rate Plus a Contingency; Retrospective Price; Outside-In Price
Financial Statement Audits, Reviews, Compilations	Fixed Price

Engagement	Suggested Pricing Method(s)
Financial Statement Audits, Reviews, Compilations (and Add-On Services)	Fixed Price; Fixed Price Plus Hourly; Fixed Price and Change Orders
Financing Packages	Hourly Rate Plus a Contingency; Fixed Price Plus a Contingency; Percentage; Retrospective Price
Governmental Tax Audits (simple)	Fixed Price; Contingent Price
Governmental Tax Audits (complex)	Fixed Price Plus Hourly Rate; Percentage; Retrospective Price
Insolvent Customer	Retainer as a Deposit Against Future Services
Investment Product Sales	Percentage
Litigation Support	Fixed Price Plus Hourly; Fixed Price Plus a Contingency; Hourly Rate Plus a Contingency; Retrospective Price; Lodestar (when required)
Meetings and Telephone Calls	Fixed Price, included as an Annual Consulting Service; any resulting engagements should be priced using a Change Order
Mergers & Acquisitions	Contingent Price; Fixed Price Plus a Contingency; Hourly Rate Plus a Contingency; Percentage
Offers in Compromise, Private Letter Rulings	Fixed Price Plus Hourly; Percentage; Retrospective Price
One-Time Consultations; Second Opinions	Fixed Price; Hourly Rate; Blended Hourly Rate

Engagement	Suggested Pricing Method(s)
Payroll Services	Unit; Fixed Price
Personal Financial Planning	Contingent Price; Percentage
Real Estate Transactions	Percentage; Fixed Price Plus a Contingency; Retrospective Price
Request For Proposals (RFPs)	100% Money Back Service Guarantee Clause
Special Expertise	Availability-Only Retainer
Tax Collections	Retainer as a Deposit Against Future Services; Fixed Price; Fixed Price Plus Hourly; Contingent Price; Retrospective Price
Tax Compliance (simple)	Fixed Price; Unit
Tax Planning & Strategies	Contingent Price; Hourly Rate Plus a Contingency; Fixed Price Plus a Contingency; Percentage; Retrospective Price
Unique Services (customer-tailored)	Fixed Price Plus a Contingency; Hourly Rate Plus a Contingency; Outside-In Price; Retrospective Price

14 TOTAL QUALITY SERVICE

We try to remember that medicine is for the patient. We try to never forget that medicine is for the people. It is not for the profits. The profits follow, and if we have remembered that, they have never failed to appear. The better we have remembered it, the larger they have been.

—George W. Merck, president of Merck & Co., 1932–1957

Comedian Steven Wright once wryly remarked that he stayed in a hotel that was so old, the wake-up call was a letter slid under his door. This joke depicts the state of professional service businesses today. The customer service revolution has been slow in coming to the accounting and law professions, but it has definitely arrived and it is time for the professions to take notice of the economics of customer loyalty, and the service principles needed to obtain that loyalty.

The world today is a service economy. In fact, the traditional distinction between "manufacturing industries" and "service industries" is obsolete. All businesses are in the service business—the only difference is the relative degree of tangible and intangible product delivered to the customer. The act of manufacturing a car, computer, television, or toaster is a way of serving others just as much as drafting a will, giving a haircut, or providing medical care.

In reality, over half of the dollars spent in any developed economy buy nothing tangible. Healthcare accounts for more than 10 percent of the GNP in advanced economies, and so do entertainment and travel (the world's largest industry). General Motors' largest supplier is not a steel or glass factory, but a healthcare provider.

Why is good, quality service so rare in a service economy? Everyone has favorite restaurants, hairstylists, tailors, and stores. The main reason people continue to patronize a particular establishment is that the business continually provide outstanding service. Many of the most cherished service stories come from cottage-type industries. But then customers will patronize a grocery or department store and have to wait ten minutes for the privilege of handing over their money or being treated rudely by a surly clerk.

Chapter 3 discussed why you are in business and the Spirit of Service, and noted the FedEx mission statement: People. Service. Profits. This chapter will discuss some of the more prevalent customer service philosophies and principles that are vital to creating a culture embodying the Spirit of Service. Much of the customer service revolution taking place today is really an attempt to turn back the clock, to the days during the Great Depression, when businesses knew the value of each customer and how important their loyalty was. To say that one "can't turn back the clock" is to be a prisoner of the moment. The things of highest value are not affected by the passage of time; otherwise the very concept of truth becomes impossible.

Total Quality Service (TQS) is an essential prerequisite to Value Pricing. After all, the reason for innovative and customized pricing is to enhance customer relationships and engender loyalty. Because service companies really sell a promise, the customer's confidence and trust in the professional is the most precious asset a firm has. Due to the intangible nature of professional services, the customer constantly looks for items of tangibility to assess the skills and competence of a firm. Trust is an essential ingredient in this process because it reduces the risk and vulnerability of the customer.

Professionals, especially CPAs, have very high trust among their customers, something the profession is very proud of and works diligently to maintain. Unfortunately, that work tends to focus on the technical aspects of the job rather than on the interpersonal skills required to provide outstanding service to customers.

Just as the firm cannot specifically measure the Spirit of Service within its culture, trust is difficult to measure with customers. Trust is not a matter of legality; it is a matter of the heart. Countless surveys of customers of CPAs, for instance, report they are very satisfied with the service they are receiving, because they believe their CPA is "doing a good job." However, very few could articulate exactly what they meant by "doing a good job." This is difficult for most professionals to deal with because it appears to be based on emotions and feelings, rather than on logic and calculation.

At least information is available on how customers tend to select their CPAs and why they remain loyal to them. (Chapter 12 explores why customers tend to leave CPA firms.) Selection and loyalty have little to do with characteristics that can be measured quantitatively, such as the following:

- Interpersonal skills
- Aggressiveness
- Interest in the customer
- Ability to explain procedures in terms the customer can understand
- Willingness to give advice
- Perceived honesty
  (Winston, 1995: 170)

Service quality is certainly less consistent than product quality, making services a high-risk purchase. Also, services are usually not as enjoyable as purchasing products. All this needs to be taken into account when developing relationships with customers. Pondering the characteristics mentioned in the survey above, one is left with the conclusion that obtaining and keeping customers is more a matter of seduction than competence. This is not to say that technical quality is not important, but that it is no longer enough to keep customers loyal.

The Value Proposition

All businesses, no matter what they do, provide a Value Proposition to their customers, consisting of the following three components:

- Quality
- Price
- Service

Think of businesses that compete almost entirely on quality. Certainly professional firms come to mind, but so do Intel, Ford (Quality is Job #1), and perhaps most predominantly, Mercedes-Benz. During the late 1980s, in fact, Mercedes became quite arrogant about its automobiles and their position in the marketplace. After all, Daimler Benz invented the auto industry, and everyone knew the German engineering was the finest in the world. Then Lexus arrived and the Mercedes share of the German market sank from 11.6 percent in 1985 to 6.4 percent in 1992, while the number of cars Mercedes sold in the United States dropped from about 100,000 in 1986 to 59,000 in 1991.

What happened? Why didn't the customer realize that Mercedes made the finest quality cars in the world? Wasn't quality alone enough to ensure Mercedes a share of the market? The answer, of course, is no. Customers tend to ask, "What have you done for me lately?" Lexus came on the market and provided a better value for the dollar and didn't rely on what it had accomplished in the past (because they didn't have a past). Note that Lexus owners are not necessarily price sensitive, but they are value conscious, and it appeared Lexus offered superior value.

Think about the number one complaint in the restaurant industry: poor service. Not lousy food (quality), but lousy service. Quality among professionals is similar, in that it meets certain minimum standards (which tend to be very high). Therefore, you cannot compete on quality alone, because in the customer's eyes all professionals are equally qualified. Even if you are in a niche, unless you have absolutely no competitors, anywhere, then rest assured the customer views your quality as no different than your competitor in the same niche.

Nothing is fascinating about competing based upon price, unless you want to be a low-cost provider like Wal-Mart, Costco, or Southwest Airlines. No doubt some professionals have selected this strategy—Jacoby & Meyers and H&R Block come to mind—and it is viable, as the success of the companies mentioned testify. Especially when quality is considered to be constant among professionals, price can no doubt become a key indicator of buying preference.

In fact, the very lack of perceived quality differences among professionals from the customer's viewpoint, leads managers and partners to utilize price as their main marketing tool. They frequently cut price because it can be implemented quickly, targeted to a specific customer and is cheap to perform. But as Leonard Berry points in *Discovering the Soul of Service*:

> One of the biggest mistakes managers make is assuming that value and price mean the same thing to customers. They do not. Price is part of value but not its equivalent. To customers, value is the benefits received for the burdens experienced; it is what customers receive in exchange for what they must endure to receive it. Burdens have both a monetary component (price) and a nonmonetary component (for example,

unknowledgeable service providers, inconvenient service locations or hours of operation, busy telephone lines) (Berry,
1999: 12).

Cutting price to attract new business sends the message to the marketplace that your firm is willing to compete on price alone. If you are
interested in pricing at above-market levels, than this is not a prudent
strategy. In the days of e-commerce, some professional, somewhere, is
always willing to perform the work you do for less money, and the price-
conscious buyer will find them. Don't fall into the trap of believing that all
customers care about is the price; it is emphatic they do not. They care
about the perceived benefits, relative to the price, and service quality is
certainly among the attributes they look at to gauge the reasonableness of
any price.

Now think of businesses that compete based upon service excellence:
American Express, Cadillac, Disney, FedEx, Lexus, Marriott, Nordstrom,
and Xerox. All of these companies have one thing in common: quality
service. FedEx has a commanding share of the overnight delivery market
because it provides unsurpassed customer service. The empirical evidence
is in, and it shows that customers are more than willing to pay premium
prices for outstanding service.

The beauty of competing based upon service is that it is invisible to your
competition. A competitor can match your technical quality. If the competitor doesn't possess it in-house, it can be outsourced. The competitor
can also match, and cut, your price. But your service quality cannot be seen
at all. Your relationship and interpersonal skills are something the competitor cannot monitor. All of the service leaders mentioned above understand this and use it to their advantage. Donald E. Petersen, former chairman of Ford Motor Co., initiated the Ford Taurus and Total Quality
Management (TQM) improvements which brought the company back
from the edge of a precipice. He began to realize the importance of being
focused on customer service and stated, "If we aren't customer-driven, our
cars won't be either."

Even as customers have become more sophisticated and better informed, service value is still largely a visceral reaction; it is hard to
measure, but you know it when you experience it. A professional's value is
based on a myriad of factors, the most important of which are the relationship with the customer and the customer's perception of the level of
interest and concern for his or her well-being. Department store owners or

auto dealers, whose product offerings are considered fairly generic or easily substitutable, have a tougher time winning customers than professionals do. Professionals have a monopoly on themselves. Professionals need to understand this concept and to Value Price based upon service excellence accordingly.

The Moment of Truth

We talk a lot about making the best first impressions. Now let's run ahead and think about making the best last impression. The last impression people have of us will stay with them until we have a chance to change it—if we ever have another chance!

—Ron Willingham

The moment of truth is a phrase that has its origins in *the hour of truth*, a term used in bullfighting to signal the third and final hour, the killing of the bull. In a business context, the moment of truth is far more prosaic, but to the life of an organization, it is potentially just as fatal as to the bull.

As president of Scandinavian Airlines, Jan Carlzon led the money-losing airline into the transformation to one of the leading customer service organizations, and hence, one of the most profitable airlines in Europe. He did it by focusing the entire organization on the moment of truth. In his book, *Moments of Truth*, Carlzon explains his philosophy:

> Each of our 10 million customers came in contact with approximately five SAS employees, and this contact lasted an average of 15 seconds each time. Thus, SAS is "created" 50 million times a year, 15 seconds at a time. These 50 million "moments of truth" are the moments that ultimately determine whether SAS will succeed or fail as a company. They are the moments when we must prove to our customers that SAS is their best alternative (Carlzon, 1987: 3).

Most business people have heard about the Moment of Truth (MOT) business philosophy, but there remain some misconceptions about the MOT. Some define it as any time the company is "called on the carpet" to answer a complaint or settle a dispute. But others see the MOT as much broader than a recovery system for customer complaints. According to Karl Albrecht's definition, the Moment of Truth is:

> Any episode in which the customer comes into contact with the organization and gets an impression of its service (Albrecht, 1992: 116).

Therefore, from the customer's perspective, a MOT might be a phone call, an office visit, receipt of a bill from the firm, a chance meeting on the street or at a social event, and even receipt of a letter from the IRS (who will the customer think of first?). By itself, each MOT is pretty minor. However, over time, the accumulated effects of thousands of MOTs are like placing grains of sand on a scale, one side being mediocrity and the other outstanding service. Over time, the scale will definitely tip in one direction or the other.

There are generally only three possible outcomes for each MOT:

- Neutral experience
- Positive experience (moments of magic)
- Negative experience (moments of misery)

The neutral experience is the most rare; it's not often a customer comes into contact with a company and is left completely indifferent about its service experience. Many companies, from Disney to Saturn, have reengineered the way they do business based upon the MOT philosophy. Disney, for example, learned that in its EPCOT park at Walt Disney World, children would complain about the lack of characters roaming the park as they do in the Magic Kingdom. Since then, Disney has turned the characters loose in EPCOT, creating millions of moments of magic for its guests. Saturn took a look at the process of purchasing a car (usually the first) from the customer's perspective, and they were not happy with what they found—confrontational, pushy salesman, surly service managers, and incomprehensible finance and insurance people. Saturn changed each MOT with the customer and ended up implementing a very pleasant sales experience for what should be an exciting purchase for any customer.

A positive experience with a company can result in 100 percent faithfulness to them. When a CPA's customer was confined to a wheelchair and could not mail his tax return information , FedEx was called and asked if they could go to the man's apartment and pick up the information and package it for the CPA. The reply was "no problem." Not only did they do that, but when the driver arrived at the customer's apartment, he retrieved the documents, phoned the CPA, read off the documents, and asked if there was anything else needed. This was all done for the regular delivery price. Can you imagine the U.S. Postal Service offering that level of service? It would take an act of Congress, and it still wouldn't be done right.

These examples illustrate the power of using the MOT philosophy to structure your business, always thinking from the customer's perspective and making it a delight for them to do business with your firm. By focusing on the MOT, the attention of the firm changes from the *activity* to the *outcome* of the service experience. The professional is focusing more intently on the outcome of the encounter with the customer than on the technical aspects of the project. While attention is paid to the technical aspect of what is being done, the customer encounter isn't being ignored in the process. It is not so much what the customers get; it's how they are treated when they get it that counts.

Even when customers experience moments of misery, there is an underlying opportunity to turn the experience into a moment of magic. One innovative CPA firm files a Power of Attorney for all of its customers, every year, to ensure that they receive any correspondence from the IRS. Usually, the CPA firm will open the letter before the customer and thus can begin to settle whatever the issue may be. If the customer receives a phone call from the firm indicating that the problem has been solved, or is being handled, imagine how good the customer must feel having such a proactive CPA looking out for them.

The MOT is also why it is so important to deliver work face-to-face to customers and even take the time to explain it to them. This may be an impossible task to do with all customers, but it certainly can be done with the top 20 percent of your customers. Face-to-face encounters are perhaps the most underused marketing tool in any firm's strategy, and delivering work in person not only gives the customer something other than the bill to gauge value, it can also lead to additional work.

Each MOT is an opportunity to unleash the firm's creativity in making the customer feel appreciated and special. Cherish each and every one of them, never take them for granted, and insist that your firm's personnel commit all the energy and resources required in order to gain the right to future MOTs with the customer. Nordstrom's policy is TLC—Think Like a Customer. No MOT, no matter how small, is ever insignificant.

The Importance of Customer Loyalty

How much are you willing to spend to acquire a new customer? You should be willing to spend at least that much to retain one. The obsession with customer acquisition rather than customer retention is a holdover from the professional's fat and lazy days, when the supply of customers was plentiful and competition was slim. Those are days are gone. In today's world, the big money is made not in winning new customers but in retaining existing ones.

Too often people think of success in business in terms of financial statistics and ratios. Yet these are nothing more than the results of customer behavior. Reward the customer, encourage him to come back, provide him with more value than he pays in cash, and you'll retain him. Realistically, all management in any business can do is manage the internal resources—land, labor, and capital. As one lady remarked to a rude clerk, "I believe you have things backward. You are overhead. I am profit" (LeBoeuf, 1989: 26).

Unfortunately, customer loyalty and its economic effects were largely ignored until the late 1980s, and were ignored by the professions even later than that. Pick up any business book today and one of the first things you'll read is that customer loyalty is dead. According to studies done by Bain & Co. the average U.S. corporation loses 50 percent of its customers in five years, half of its employees in four, and half of its investors in less than one. In the last 20 years, banks have gone from holding 40 percent of customer's assets to 20 percent.

Brand loyalty is also said to be dead, especially with the rise of generic products. And now with the Internet, the dynamics of loyalty are undergoing another radical change.

Is customer loyalty actually dead? Are people really less loyal today than in the past? There may be some truth to it, given the fact that the children of the baby boomers are starting to take over their parents' businesses. These young people don't follow the traditions of their parents, and they are not at all tolerant of poor or slow service. They use e-mail, not snail-mail. They demand instantaneous results and put far less emphasis on efforts. And, as professionals are discovering, much to their chagrin, one of the first acts they perform upon taking the helm is to change bankers, lawyers, and CPAs.

However, loyalty is not dead. Most people would choose loyalty over the alternative if for no other reason than that it lowers search and transaction costs. People tend to be loyal to their spouses, families, neighborhoods, and the non-profit agencies where they volunteer considerable time and effort. What is dead in the business world today—or at least largely ignored until recently—is a *reason* to be loyal. One has to earn loyalty—you don't get it by just showing up and doing the job (no matter how well you may perform). The frequent flyer programs that the airlines adopted in 1981, followed by reward points from hotels and rental car agencies, have proven quite successful in earning a customer's continued loyalty. It is time for professional firms to recognize the importance of customer loyalty—and the dramatic impact it can have on their profitability—with the goal of retaining their best appreciating assets: their customers.

The Economic Effect of Customer Loyalty

Perhaps another reason the economics of customer loyalty have been ignored is that traditional accounting methods fail to capture the information necessary to measure its effect. Generally Accepted Accounting Principles are woefully inadequate for this task because they fail to distinguish between sales to old and new customers; they don't allow acquisition costs to be amortized over the customer's life—and thus hide the value of any one customer's loyalty in aggregates—and they completely ignore human capital on the balance sheet (which is a measure of relationships).

For these reasons many businesses are starting to perform customer retention accounting, with the insurance companies leading the way. According to Frederick F. Reichheld, in *Loyalty Effect*, loyalty-based models explain the success or failure of a particular business better than market share, economies of scale, or cost position. Bain & Co. has conducted studies showing that by raising customer retention rates a mere 5 percentage points, a business could increase the value of an average customer by 25 to 100 percent.

Firms in the top quartile of marketing success usually generate anywhere from 25 to 40 percent of their new business from sales of additional services to existing customers. If you are a smaller firm, or a sole practitioner, you can generate anywhere from 50 to 80 percent of growth from existing customers.

According to Reichheld, existing customers are more profitable for the following reasons:

- Acquisition Cost—Acquiring a customer, according to the AICPA, can cost 11 times more than retaining one, lowering the return on new customers from the beginning of the relationship.
- Base Profit—The longer you retain the customer, the more base profit, the better return on your acquisition investment.
- Per-Customer Revenue Growth—Accelerates over time, as veteran customers utilize more of your services than do new customers (they are familiar with your firm's capabilities and trust you).
- Operating Costs—Over time, customers become more efficient dealing with your firm; you've both climbed down the learning curve; less research is required on your part, the customer is more familiar with your staff, etc.
- Referrals—Long-term customers are much more likely to refer additional business to your firm, and those referrals are usually of a better quality; veteran customers can communicate a more accurate picture of your firm (who knows better then they do?).
- Price Premium—Veteran customers are less price sensitive; they value not only your services but also the relationship, because they have an ego investment in it.
(Reichheld, 1996: 42–50)

There are primarily three ways to maximize the net present value of your firm's customer base: 1) Cut costs without reducing your firm's value proposition; 2) Improve value at a greater rate than you increase your costs; and 3) Adjust your pricing to capture the consumer surplus. One example of the first strategy is the virtual office, which can lower a professional's overhead without reducing the value the professional offers. The second strategy is employed by entering into new markets or niches or by offering existing customers a wider array of services. And, of course, the third strategy is what this book is concerned with—pricing your services on value, not hours.

Given all of this empirical evidence that customer retention is much more profitable than customer acquisition, it is interesting to ponder why the professions have ignored this trend. As Theodore Levitt explained in a 1983 *Harvard Business Review* article:

> The sale. . . merely consummates the courtship, at which point the marriage begins. How good the marriage is depends on how well the seller manages the relationship. The quality

> of the marriage determines whether there will be continued
> or expanded business, or troubles and divorce. The era of the
> one-night stand is gone. Marriage is both necessary and more
> convenient (Hart and Bogan, 1992: 182).

The marriage analogy isn't perfect. The onus is not shared equally between the partners; it falls disproportionately on the firm to maintain continuous customer delight.

Examples of the loyalty effect are widespread. Companies began to recognize the power of retention in the late 1980s. McDonald's, for instance, builds relationships with kids—by providing birthday parties, toys, and playgrounds—because children influence a parent's choice of where to eat.

Certainly hotels and car rental companies have learned the loyalty lesson. Rapid checkouts and concierge floors are examples of these companies providing their "A" customers with a higher level of service, while extracting a premium price. Also, these strategies have the added bonus of holding out carrots to the "B" and "C" customers with the message: Patronize us more, and you too can share in these perks.

Perhaps the most successful of the loyalty programs is the frequent flyer program, started by American Airlines in May 1981. American Airlines essentially combined three things to create this tremendous value: plastic cards embossed with the member's frequent flyer account number, a record of the member's travel history (which American was able to capture through its successful SABRE reservation system), and empty seats on airplanes. One measure of the program's success is delay tolerance: prior to 1981, the typical traveler would only wait one-half hour before trying to switch carriers owing to a delay; today, after nearly 20 years of frequent flyer programs, that tolerance has increased to over three and one-half hours. Frequent flyer programs generate more than two billion dollars of revenue for the airline industry, as they receive .01 cent per mile from alliance programs with credit cards, hotels, and rental cars (half of all the miles rewarded are on the ground).

From a pricing perspective, the frequent flyer programs are pure marketing genius. If you're a frequent flyer with United Airlines and pay $2,000 for a ticket to the east coast, you perceive it as less than the price because you accrue miles towards free flights. However, if you take a competitor carrier and pay the same $2,000, you receive no benefit in terms of miles, and thus you pay full fare. This strategy enables the airlines to avoid serious price wars, because they are charging their competitor's customers higher prices while charging their loyal customers less (from the customer's viewpoint).

Many law firms have started a "frequent litigation" program, offering discounts for utilizing the firm's services more. Professional service firms should consider rewarding existing customers, perhaps through a discount off of a Change Order, for marginal services provided to existing FPA customers (usually, among the most loyal in the firm). This discount can be thought of as retention marketing, which usually generates higher returns than acquisition marketing and doesn't suffer from the problem expressed in department store magnate John Wannamaker's famous quip: "I am certain that half of what I spend on advertising is money wasted. But I don't know which half." Anytime you invest in a current relationship, you are bound to reap rewards that are greater than those you will get by chasing after new business.

Professionals have the advantage of creating what is known as possessive loyalty—that is, when the customer uses a possessive pronoun to describe his attorney or accountant (e.g., my CPA). Possessive loyalty exhibits confidence, trust, and perhaps even dependency on the professional. This is a form of loyalty any other business would love to engender.

With the focus during the 1980s on the Total Quality Management movement and the Zero Defections movement, TQS changes the focus. Zero defects and zero defections are not mutually exclusive goals. Certainly the former can be managed through TQM, technical training, proper supervision, etc. But the latter can only be brought about by possessing the Spirit of Service within your firm's culture. Because even if you were to achieve zero defects in your firm—where absolutely everything you do is perfect—you would not be immune from customer defections. TQS puts the emphasis where it should be: Customer perception of value and customer loyalty.

Customers will continue to patronize businesses where they are invited and remain where they are appreciated. Your firm will get the behavior it rewards. Customer loyalty is worth rewarding. Professional services are based on personal relationships. People don't hire firms, they hire individuals within those firms. A Nordstrom employee sums up the attitude best: "We are trained to make the customer, not the sale. We are trained to make customers."

Firing Customers

Some people are puzzled about how to reconcile TQS with firing customers. It is a good idea to fire customers who do not value your firm's services. However, as was pointed out in the Preface, your customers are not going to improve until you do. This is why TQS is necessary in order to provide service excellence.

Once you have traveled down that road, firing customers becomes essential to your firm's success. This is driven, in part, by the continuing specialization of the marketplace; firms can no longer be everything to everyone. The era of the general practitioner is over. Another driving force behind firing customers is the lack of capacity. In the past, professional firms always could rely on easy access to a qualified labor pool. Those days are gone. The percentage of the population aged 25 to 34 has been declining since 1985, and it will continue to drop into the next century, from 23 percent of the population to 17 percent. David Maister sums up the predicament well:

> Educated people with a few years of business experience are in increasing demand by businesses of all types, and will have many more options in building their careers than their baby-boom elders. To place the potential impact of this in perspective, consider the following statistic: the "oil shock" of the early 1970s was caused by only a 5 percent shrinkage in worldwide supply. Professional firms are facing a 25 percent shrinkage in their nonpartner labor force. There is going to be a huge people shortage and its effects will be major (O'Shea and Madigan, 1998: 300).

This labor shortage is forcing firms to focus in specialized areas and on certain customer segments. Firms are learning the Pareto Principle: less is more. Cutting the 80 percent of customers who don't value your firm enables you to focus on the 20 percent who do. Many professionals protest that cutting up to 80 percent of their customer base would be suicidal, making the firm too dependent on a small group of customers, and, anyway, even those customers in the 80 percent category contribute to the firm's overhead.

There are many retorts to this argument, one of the best being you are already dependent on a small number of customers anyway. By not concentrating on them adequately, you put them at a higher risk of defection. Remember the corollary to Gresham's Law: Bad customers drive out good customers. Through rewarding customer loyalty and providing TQS, your goal is zero defections. You can't focus on 100 percent of your customer base, giving them the attention and services they require; but you can focus on 20 percent of your customers. By trimming your customer base, you are removing complexity from your firm and thereby operating more efficiently

Do not immediately fire 80 percent of your customer base; you need to do this incrementally. First run a Pareto analysis of your customers and divide your customers accordingly. You will discover another corollary to the Pareto Law: the 50/5 principle, meaning 5 percent of your customers generate 50 percent of your revenue and profits. Start by getting rid of the low-end customers.

CPA firms employ many tactics to fire customers. Some write letters explaining that their market focus has changed, and they are of the opinion they can no longer adequately serve the needs of the customer, and perhaps refer them to pre-selected competitors. Other firms will send out letters raising the upcoming year's prices, anywhere from a factor of two to four. These firms have discovered an interesting phenomena when they raise prices: over half of the customers chose to stay. This shows the amount of consumer surplus that exists in the relationship. You have to deploy the strategy that is right for your firm and your customers.

Another way to ensure you are following the Pareto Principle is to take on only those customers that understand and are willing to pay for your firm's Value Proposition. Be up front with prospective customers and tell them you are interested in developing long-term relationships, and you want to be the sole source for their company's needs. This will weed out the price buyers from truly valuable customers. And remember the loyalty effect: you are much better off keeping existing customers than chasing after new ones. It is acceptable not to do business, but it is unacceptable to do bad business. Growing simply for the sake of growth is bad business. Not only does it force your firm to scramble and hire undesirable people, but it takes your attention away from your most profitable customers.

It would also be helpful to take into account David Maister's personality grading system, as pointed out in his book *True Professionalism*. Essentially, this means grading customers not on the traditional measures of revenue such as speed of payment and referral quality, but on whether or not you like the business they are in and you like them personally. This may seem naive to some, but in fact you will be a more successful professional if you work with people you truly care about rather than just chasing the Almighty Dollar.

One innovative CPA firm implemented its firing strategy in a unique way. As a holiday bonus one year, each staff member was allowed to select two customers to fire. Not only did this boost the morale in the office, but it also increased cross-selling efforts to existing customers and put more money on the firm's bottom line. Terminating personal relationships is never easy, especially when they are with customers who have been with you since you started. But in order to move forward you must leave some things behind. You can't fight the Pareto Principle. It is much easier to harness its power and focus on those few customers who value your firm the most.

Summary and Conclusions

The paradigm shift that needs to take place in the professions today is a shift not only in how professionals view the world, but also the way they live in it. The TQS train has already left the station, and you have two choices: Be on it, or be under it.

The enlightened firms that have adopted TQS will continue to grow, improve, and prosper in the coming millennium. If you were to examine all of the great sources of wealth creation throughout the history of the world, from the titans of the Industrial Revolution at the turn of the century to Bill Gates today, you would notice this profoundly important truth: In every era, the businesses that succeeded and achieved excellence took a clear stand for the customer. Being a professional is more than doing outstanding technical work. The central purpose of professionals is to serve.

It is impossible to maintain Value Pricing, over the long run, without offering TQS. Immerse your firm in the philosophies and practices of TQS. Benchmark other businesses—not just other professional service firms—in order to learn what they are doing to offer better, more consistent service. Don't believe you can't learn from FedEx or Disney just because being a "professional" is different from these businesses. All businesses exist solely to serve others. TQS offers a vision, a new way of thinking and operating, emphasizing customer value and a sense of service to others first.

15 THE CPA AS CONSULTANT

Andersen Consulting's battle with Andersen Worldwide has become the soap opera of the business world. What has evolved might be called "The War of the Butterflies and the Bean Counters." These companies hire MBA graduates in remarkable numbers. But who wants to commit to a career at a company going through such public and painful troubles? Won't clients, too, think twice before seeking advice from an institution that is itself confused and conflicted?

—James O'Shea and Charles Madigan, *Dangerous Company*

Making the transition from traditional CPA to business consultant is something that many practitioners will be struggling with in the new millennium. More and more, customers are demanding expanded services from their CPAs in addition to the customary accounting and tax services; they want advice on how to run their businesses better—not just their accounting systems—and what the competition is doing. In other words, they want their CPA to stop playing financial historian and instead help them prepare for the future. One customer indicated that the financial statement compilation provided to him on an annual basis to run his business and make decisions is tantamount to using his smoke alarm to time his cookies. It's a valid point.

Chapter 2 discussed the CPA Vision Project and how important it will be for CPAs to make the transition from historians to "certified professional advisors," otherwise known as consultants. Many fine books cover this topic. This chapter focuses on a different perspective of the accounting profession making its transition—the customer's perspective. Although the market is demanding more and more consulting services from accountants, the profession has tended to focus on its own needs rather than those of the customer.

In recent years, a backlash has begun against the management consulting industry. Books such as *Dangerous Company*, *The Witch Doctors*, and *Fad Surfing in the Boardroom* have sounded the clarion against this infantile—and often self-contradictory—profession. Much of the criticism is starting to resonate with customers. Just as in every other industry, the customer is becoming more sophisticated with respect to hiring these "management gurus." To say the least, there is mendacity in the consulting profession, and CPAs need to be aware of how they should counteract these charges and not fall prey to the disadvantages that plague this industry.

The Kennedy Research Group, which closely tracks the management consulting industry, estimates that the global consulting market is 62 billion dollars. It also projects an average growth rate of 16.1 percent a year through the year 2000, thus growing to approximately 100 billion dollars (O'Shea and Madigan, 1998: ix). One can always judge the sense of humor the makers of predictions have by the number of decimal places in their projections. In any event, there are myriad reasons for this incredible growth, including the following:

- The global economy is healthy and companies flush with cash seem eager to purchase advice to grow even bigger with more efficiency.
- Management consulting companies have not been shy about marketing their services.
- The reluctance to bring in outsiders for help, once quite strong, has diminished.
- Technology is changing so rapidly it is almost impossible to stay abreast and consulting firms that have built a reputation as technology leaders have gained an edge
- With the death of communism around the world, and the rise of free markets and privatization, consulting companies have helped to smooth the transition from planned economies to market economies, bringing in much needed human and intellectual capital.
- Deregulation has taken away the privileged status of once-safe industries and opened the door to heavy levels of competition, forcing companies to search for how to do more with less.
- A certain amount of the alacrity to hire consultants is due to internal management figuring if a bold new initiative fails, they can always blame the outside consultants.

In the past two decades, many accounting firms have seen the percentage of revenue earned from consulting increase at a faster pace than any other category of service offering. Offering consulting services not only help firms retain customer loyalty, earn a larger percentage of the customer's budget, and capture some of the consumer surplus, but they also help ensure that the customers remain a viable enterprise themselves. As pointed out by Richard A. Payne, President of Results Accountants' Systems, according to results from several hundred Client Advisory Boards from around the world, three recurring themes come from customers of CPA firms:

- We don't *want* an accountant, but we *need* one.

- We are generally happy with our accountant, but we're sure there are other things the firm could be doing for us.

- If our accountant could show us a better way to run our business, we would be willing to pay for that advice. We are not concerned about fee levels, but we are concerned about service levels (specifically, the timely response to our requests for assistance, and proactivity in relation to matters we should be aware of, but aren't) and the tangible value we derive (cash flow, profit, and value improvement).
  (Payne, October 1998: 10)

This is proof that customers are yearning for their CPAs to take a more proactive role in their business, and price is not an issue. If one listens closely enough, the market will tell you the price it is willing to pay. Perhaps the biggest strength the profession has as it makes this transition is its position as the most trusted and respected of all business advisors. This is an asset the typical management consultant longs for, even among the major consulting firms. Capitalizing on this strength will make the transition a lot less tumultuous.

Consulting requires a dramatic change in mindset. Accountants have always been regarded as experts, whether in GAAP or tax law. Ask a CPA a question, and he will give you an accurate response. This type of knowledge is crucial to the practice of traditional accounting but can become a hindrance in consulting. As William Reeb points out in his book, *Start Consulting*, "In the business advisory role *coming up with the solutions is often not nearly as important as asking the client the right questions*" [Emphasis in original] (Reeb, 1998: 71).

To become consultants, CPAs have to adopt this approach, and the customer's thinking must change as well. The old stereotype of the meek and diffident accountant with the green eyeshade has to make way for the comprehensive business advisor. In several airports around the country an ad appeared that read something to the effect of "Who counts beans for Starbucks?" The ad was for Deloitte & Touche and it perpetuated the stereotype of accountants as bean counters, albeit in a humorous way. It is doubtful that the ad inspired anyone to place a call to the firm to count his beans. It's that type of marketing that does the profession no favors and earns CPAs the reputation deserved, as put forth in the following passage from Reid Buckley's book, *Sex, Power, and Pericles* (Reid is William F. Buckley, Jr.'s younger brother and presently runs the Buckley School of Public Speaking in Camden, South Carolina):

> Straight logical progression is the ticket when what one wants is the facts and nothing but the facts, ma'am. This is what you desire when you ask your accountant or CFO for the financial status of your company. Is it operating at a profit or a loss? Period. The good Lord spare anyone a CPA who draws up an emotional or mystical/religious presentation of his company's financial shape, or who indulges in poetic flights of the imagination when what a person needs to know is how much boodle he must part with to meet his payroll taxes.
>
> The accountant may validly analyze the numbers advanced in support of vision, but his report on past performance is never predictive, and his opinion on the validity of the vision itself is worthless. Past performance may be a commentary on current performance, never a harbinger of future performance. It can't be.
>
> Yesterday's profit and loss statement is as useful in foretelling what tomorrow may bring as poking about in the entrails of birds or dipping tea leaves (Buckley, 1996: 38–39).

Unfortunately, this stereotype has persisted despite all of the advertising and promotion to the contrary by the profession in the past two decades. In a recent AICPA survey after an image campaign, only 47 percent felt "CPAs can help individuals and businesses plan for the future," while only 44 percent agreed that "CPAs see more than the numbers, they see opportunities" (Reeb, 1998: 233).

According to Reeb, "We have done a horrible job letting our clients know what we are capable of doing. Clearly, not only do we not understand our market, but our market doesn't understand us either" (ibid., 233–234).

Fortunately, customers are beginning, even if slowly, to regard their CPA as a sort of financial psychiatrist. When they ask for business advice, they are not necessarily looking for a "right" or "wrong" answer but rather the perspective of the CPA. This makes the typical CPA uncomfortable, because too many variables could sway the decision one way or the other. Not only are CPAs afraid of being wrong, with the accompanying fear of failure, but they are also afraid of rejection. CPAs are afraid that if they speak their piece, the customer may get upset and defect or lose confidence in the CPA as a trusted business advisor. But customers don't expect your suggestions to be perfect. Do not let the best become the enemy of the good.

As a group, CPAs have incredible knowledge and wisdom, not to mention practical business experience, but they are also so caught up in the fear of being sued, in GAAP rules and pronouncements, and in tax laws and regulations, that they sometimes lose sight of why the customer is paying them in the first place. Customers expect CPAs to add to their intellectual capital, and as the Results survey above shows, they are willing to pay dearly for it.

However, a perusal of any CPE catalog from any state society reveals that most of the courses relate to technical topics, such as taxes, accounting, and auditing. Very little effort is put into the more consultative aspects of the business. The August 1997 issue of the *Journal of Accountancy* has an interesting graphical representation of the composition of revenue of the nine largest firms. Andersen Worldwide derives 65 percent of its revenues from management consulting services, approximately 19 percent from accounting and auditing, and the remaining 16 percent from tax. If one were to examine those ratios 20 years ago, probably they would have been approximately the opposite, meaning that more than 50 percent of revenues came from auditing, 35 percent from tax, and the rest came from consulting. Is it any wonder that for the past decade or so, Andersen has been the largest accounting firm in the world?

In 1989 Arthur Andersen's auditing division embarked on a project called "Vision 2000," setting up a task force composed of 75 partners and 25 young visionaries. The company consulted customers such as Jack Welch, CEO of General Electric, and Charles Handy, a well known international management consultant. The results of this task force are described in *The Witch Doctors*:

> The dreamer-accountants decided that the company's aim should be to change from auditing the books of its clients to auditing their businesses. To meet this more consultative role, the accountants came up with an equation and a slogan. The equation was $K = (P+I)S$, where K is knowledge; P, our people; I, information; and S, the power of sharing. The slogan was "Andersen, The World's Greatest Place to Do Great Work." Although this must surely count among the shabbiest battle cries in history, Andersen's accountants swear that the process has helped redirect their company (Micklethwait and Wooldridge, 1996: 151-52).

Today, Andersen Consulting spends 6 percent of its gross revenue on training and the average employee spends 135 hours each year in a classroom, compared to the average company's 1.4 percent of payroll spent on educating the work force.

Timothy J. Beauchemin was a consultant to CPAs and a Contributing Editor to the *CPA Profitability Monthly* newsletter, published by Harcourt Professional Publishing (and now merged with *Partner-to-Partner Advisory*). He passed away in February 1997, causing a tremendous loss to the profession, as he was truly a seminal thinker in many areas. In the December 1995 issue of the newsletter he wrote a fascinating article, "Thinking About the Future," wherein he stated that the only long-term growth opportunity for accountants would be in consulting. He then offered this profound question as a test of a true consultant:

> Unfortunately, consulting is something that most firms are not that good at. To see whether this comment describes your firm, answer this simple question: If your biggest client fell dead today, could you go in tomorrow and run the client's business well enough to grow it at a 15 percent compounded annual growth rate? If, like most firms, you couldn't, you should not be giving business advice other than on accounting or tax issues. The bad news is that most CPAs are doing an adequate job in the tax and accounting area, but if you can consistently grow companies in a particular industry, and

everyone in that industry knows it, you will find people begging for your services. Few CPA "business consultants" meet this 15 percent growth criteria. The ones that can do extremely well.

The way to become a true business consultant is to develop a "positive frame." You have to talk about what to do, rather than what *not* to do. CPAs typically have a "negative frame" [Emphasis in original] (Beauchemin, December 1995: 10– 11).

That's a high standard to meet, but certainly a worthwhile goal to strive for, not with all customers, but definitely with the top four or five, who probably make up a large percentage of the gross revenue. If the firm does not meet Beauchemin's test, then its prices are considered merely over-head, albeit necessary, by the customer. If it does qualify, the firm is suddenly in the profit column of the customer's income statement and therefore is able to add more value and command higher prices for all of its services.

Customer Fears in Hiring a Consultant

Howard Shenson conducted a survey of 600 companies which had used, or were planning to use, consultants, and asked them their major fears. As pointed out in *High Income Consulting*, by Tom Lambert, "the following fears are presented in order of importance, with the first being regarded as most important by most respondents":

- Consultant incompetence
- Lack of management control
- Continued dependency
- Excessive fees
- Lack of time
- Need for a consultant seen as an admission of management failure
- Fear of disclosing sensitive data
- Improper diagnosis or needs analysis
- Pushing a product
  (Lambert, 1997: 213–16)

This is by no means a comprehensive list, but it is representative of the fears most customers have in hiring consultants. A closer examination of these fears will show CPAs how they can assuage them for their customers.

Consultant incompetence   Usually, a business hires a consultant because they don't have the internal expertise, so it is no wonder that they doubt their ability to judge the competence of a specialist This concern is aggravated by consulting firms that send fresh-out-of-school kids in their twenties to tell management how to run their businesses. As A. Michael Noll, a professor at the Annenberg School for Communications at the University of Southern California and former Bell Labs employee, said: "How do you know if they are the world's best? What businesses have they managed? Look at the people they send, all under thirty and fresh out of business school, where they are mouthing whatever crazy ideas their professors threw at them in class" (O'Shea and Madigan, 1998: 9).

In fact, youth is being used in various (and quite humorous) advertising campaigns. In her book, *Fad Surfing in the Boardroom*, Eileen Shapiro defines child labor as: That mass of freshly minted BAs and MBAs who have no operating experience and who are therefore assembled by consulting firms into the teams to turn around client companies or otherwise instruct and enlighten senior people within client companies" (Shapiro, 1995: 214).

The issue is deeper than young kids with MBAs trying to tell senior management how to run their businesses. The issue goes right to the heart of consulting in general, and that is that there are no easy answers, no one-size-fits-all solutions to the messy world of human interactions known as business. Most of the knowledge customers have of their businesses has been developed over many decades and generations, and it is the ultimate form of hubris for anyone—a consultant or CPA—to come in and think he could operate the place any better.

The majority of the most important knowledge in any field of endeavor, be it sports, entertainment, or business, is tacit knowledge. This form of knowledge is extremely difficult to articulate and relatively expensive to transfer, traveling often only through apprenticeship and trial-and-error. Your local coffee house knowing exactly how you like your morning ritual, a barber understanding exactly how his customer likes his haircut, the local hotel understanding how the college football schedule influences the demand for rooms—all point to the fluctuating value of location, location, location.

The chemist and philosopher Michael Polanyi explains tacit knowledge in his 1958 book, *Personal Knowledge*:

> Maxims are rules, the correct application of which is part of the art which they govern. The true maxims of golfing or of poetry increase our insight into golfing or poetry and may even give valuable guidance to golfers and poets; but these maxims would instantly condemn themselves to absurdity if they tried to replace the golfer's skill or the poet's art. Maxims cannot be understood, still less applied by anyone not already possessing a good practical knowledge of the art. They derive their interest from our appreciation of the art and cannot themselves either replace or establish that appreciation (Postrel, 1998: 90).

The fear of incompetence, therefore, is highly justified. A consultant must know the art in question before he can understand it, much less render any advice about it. This is why it is so important to approach each consulting engagement as a learning experience and not to assume you are the expert. Perhaps the greatest management consultant who has ever lived, Peter Drucker, summed it up best: "My greatest strength as a consultant is to be ignorant and ask a few questions."

Lack of management control   You have read horror stories of consultants who run amok among various businesses, seemingly oblivious to the wealth of tacit knowledge that exists among the firm's personnel. Policies and procedures that were implemented produced dismal failures. In the past, management gave their consultants great autonomy. The consultants weren't necessarily accountable to anyone but to whom they issued their final report before moving on to the next victim.

This has changed. Management has asserted their autonomy and let it be known that the consultant works for (and with) the firm and will be held accountable for the results—good or bad—their advice produces. Management, and consultants, have gotten much better about defining the scope of the project, agreeing on benchmarks of performance, and knowing which party will be responsible for various stages in the project. Part of this was brought about because of the perverse incentives inherent in hourly billing, but more importantly because customers want to feel in control of their purchase decisions.

Reeb has this practical approach to letting management control the scope and involvement of the engagement:

> We start by discussing the cash, capacity, and capability technique. It always seems to comfort clients when they understand that—*we offer various degrees of involvement* [and] *they control our degree of involvement* [Emphasis in original] (Reeb, 1998: 163).

This is why it is vital to get the customer's ego investment at the beginning of the relationship and to let the customer design and scope out the project. Using Reeb's technique will not only lead to a more harmonious relationship but also will give the consulting project a higher probability of success because the customer had a strong role in developing and implementing it based upon the customer's own assessment and resources.

Continued dependency　No doubt some consultants will construct a device that no one else can comprehend, with the goal of trying to create lifetime employment. Consultants are, in effect, change agents. And in the past, they have paid very little attention to the consequences of their prescriptions. But any good consultant should be able to communicate the advantages and disadvantages of an innovation before introducing it to customers. Unfortunately, this is seldom done, or if it is done, the disadvantages are often trivialized or, worse yet, ignored altogether.

According to Everett Rogers, in *Diffusion of Innovations*, "seven roles can be identified for the change agent in the process of introducing an innovation in a client system":

1. **To develop a need for change**　The change agent helps identify needs, points out alternatives to existing problems, and they may also create needs.

2. **To establish an information-exchange relationship**　The change agent must enhance his relationship with the customer by being perceived as credible, competent, trustworthy, and empathizing with the customer's needs and problems. Customers must accept the change agent before they will accept any innovations or solutions they propose.

3. **To diagnose problems**　The consultant must determine why existing alternatives are not meeting the customer's needs.

4. **To create an intent in the client to change** Once the consultant has ascertained the various actions required in order for the customer to achieve their goals, they must seek to motivate the customer's interest in their proposed innovation.

5. **To translate an intent to action** This is where inter-personal network influences can help the consultant effectuate change. Altering the opinion of a group's leaders, for instance, is one effective strategy.

6. **To stabilize adoption and prevent discontinuance** Consulting programs have a habit of dying, out of apathy or simple disinterest. The consultant must help the customer "stay the course" until the results of the innovation can be assessed based on a fair trial.

7. **To achieve a terminal relationship** This is perhaps the biggest challenge of all for most consultants—getting the customer to the point of coping with the problem, or solving it completely, whereby they no longer need the consultant (Rogers, 1995: 337).

The last role is the most difficult, but it refers to the termination of one specific engagement rather than to the termination of the relationship. There will always be other issues and problems to tackle, but the mark of a good consultant is his or her ability to effectuate the needed changes inside the customer's organizations until the organization is self-sufficient.

Excessive fees This fear is well justified, given the perverse and much abused incentives of hourly billing. From lawyers to consultants, nothing causes customers as much angst and anxiety as getting billed for every minute, especially when they don't know the price before the engagement starts. By using Fixed Price Agreements, Change Orders, and the other methods explored in this book, you will be able to sell based on value—rather than on hours—and you will see this fear rapidly diminish.

Lack of time As the consulting business has been in a boom cycle these last couple of decades, many have entered the profession without adequate resources, taking on jobs that cannot be completed. Combine that with undercutting price in order to secure the job (because small firms have low overhead) and you have a prescription for disaster in the eyes of the customer.

CPAs can easily overcome this fear by assuring their customers that they have adequate staff and training to complete the job, by pricing based on value, and by relying on the internal expertise of the customer. Reeb points out:

> The tradition of the CPA performing all of the work has evolved from years of practical real world experience. Why? Because CPA firms first focused on large SEC-regulated companies. As time passed, that support has filtered down into smaller and smaller companies. Now CPAs provide services from the Fortune 100 companies to the start-up mom-and-pop shops. However, many CPAs attempt to use the same methodology for delivering services to all sizes of businesses. The problem is... *the one-approach-fits-all method just doesn't work* [Emphasis in original] (Reeb, 1998: 111).

Sufficient knowledge of the engagement, and proper supervision, are among the cornerstones of the profession's code of conduct, so this fear should not be a major roadblock for customers of CPA firms.

Need for a consultant is seen as an admission of failure   This point of view is bound to be held by at least some in the organization, and while they may not be the decision-makers with respect to hiring the consultant, they can certainly block programs of change and lower the probability of a successful engagement. So much of what a consultant does is facilitate change. It is important to be aware of those within the management structure who may sabotage your efforts. Also, with the necessity to specialize in today's rapidly changing environment, most management teams understand that they simply can't keep up with everything, and thus it always helps to reiterate to the customer that your firm is a specialist in this area and can assist them rapidly and add value to their business.

Fear of disclosing sensitive data   This is one area CPAs don't have a problem with in comparison to the average consultant. Businesses trust their CPAs with all sorts of sensitive information, so this is not a major concern. CPAs should, of course, always follow the professional rules of client confidentiality.

Improper diagnosis or needs analysis   The management consultant industry is bedeviled by fads and new programs they pass off as the cure-all to all ills, which is why they've earned the reputation of being modern day witch doctors. Programs such as TQM and reengineering have had their share of failure, and yet some consultants insist on pushing a one-size-fits-all solution to any problem. Diagnosing the situation of the customer, through a proper needs analysis, is an important step to any consulting engagement. Imagine a doctor who prescribed medication or treatment without first diagnosing the patient—a sure invitation to malpractice.

However, there is an important caveat to this step in the process. Unlike traditional CPA services, in which the diagnosis is usually done early on and is not a significant part of the engagement, consultants are paid to diagnose problems, and thus CPAs need to avoid what Reeb calls "premature speculation." Resist the temptation to jump right into the conclusion, even if it is readily apparent to you, because the problem you've identified may only be the tip of the iceberg and not the real concern of the customer.

Consulting engagements should be unbundled, according to Reeb, and "a clear distinction made between the costs for *advice, direction and vision, and human resources required to complete the work*" [Emphasis in original] (ibid., 111). This method also makes it easier to Value Price the engagement, as each step required will have specific benchmarks and any results can be determined in these stages.

Pushing a product   With CPAs entering into relationships with various software companies—even becoming Value-Added Resellers—and now selling financial products, this fear has the potential to take on more significance. Nobody likes to have a product pushed at them without a clear understanding that it is the best choice among the available alternatives. If you happen to sell a particular product, this fear can be overcome by staying true to your product's niche market and not trying to force it onto a customer whose situation doesn't fit the problem or solution your product was meant to solve.

The idea that just because you sell a particular product you won't take into account the special needs of the customer is anarchistic thinking. Just as automobile salesmen sell particular makes, the free market has a way of allocating customers and vendors based upon mutual advantage and desire. If your firm has developed, for example, a proprietary software program for the medical profession, chances are you won't be able to sell it to all interested parties. As long as you are honest about the product's capacity—and limitations—selling a product does not, per se, block you from being an effective consultant.

Words to Avoid

Consultants have the reputation, whether justified or not, of offering up solutions to all problems, and at times their marketing and advertising can promise more than they are realistically able to deliver. It reminds one of what Warren Burger, then Supreme Court Chief Justice said on the introduction of lawyer ads: "Some of the advertising would make a used-car dealer blush." And *Consultant News* pointed out, "We've never seen a winning proposal that says "maybe we can solve your problem. How much is too much?" (O'Shea and Madigan, 1998: 100).

The courts have begun to answer that question. In *UOP v. Andersen Consulting, Consultant News*, in its review of the case, concluded that the company had presented a "Litany of Language to Avoid in Proposals. Here's some of what could get you into trouble:. . . We continually deliver success. . . We are able to respond to customer needs up to 50 percent faster. . . We know how to manage risk. . . We are prepared to assume responsibility for the price and quality of the solution. . . We can create an environment in which all team members work cooperatively. . . We deliver on scope, schedule, quality, and cost commitments. . . Our project manager will have ultimate responsibility for ensuring successful development. . . Our philosophy is to get the job done, not excusing the responsibilities" (ibid., 99-100).

The Consultant Customer's Bill of Rights

In their book *Dangerous Company*, James O'Shea and Charles Madigan end with a list of questions that potential employers of consultants should ask themselves and advice to heed before they hire anyone. It is thought-provoking and it may become necessary for CPAs to be able to answer these questions in the coming transition from compliance to consulting. In a sense, it is a Customer's Bill of Rights.

1) Why are you doing this? What do you want to achieve? The more clearly the goal is defined, the greater the chance of reaching it. If you don't know what you want to do, don't make the call.

2) That being achieved, Do you need outsiders to help reach this goal? Don't forget to assess the brilliance within your own company before you go trying to buy some from outside. Maybe you don't need an

army of consultants. Maybe you just need your very own MBA, whom you can easily steal from a consulting company.

3) If you hire a consulting company, which characters will they send? Be ruthless in this part of the process. If you know the reputations of the partners, or if they display a special, tested expertise, demand that they pay good and frequent attention to your needs. Make it a part of the contract. If they are promising the best, make certain that is what shows up. Do not be meek about sending away people who make you uncomfortable.

4) What will it cost? (And how long will it take?) Avoid open-ended arrangements and vague promises. Demand specificity in contracts, including the dark parts about what happens if the consulting engagement doesn't work. Be tight with your money. Base payments on performance and on your satisfaction. If the task involves high risk, make certain the consulting company is sharing in the risk, not just in the rewards, of the relationship.

5) Never give up control. The best consulting engagements do not take over operations, they complement them. Make certain your own managers retain control over everything, share in decision-making, and understand that for the duration of the contract, they are responsible and in charge.

6) Don't be unhappy for even a day. Ignored consultants can shower down all kinds of havoc on a company. If you sense something is going wrong, confront it immediately and demand repairs. Consultants do not answer to boards of directors, but you do. At these prices, happiness should be assumed.

7) Beware of glib talkers with books. The fact that someone can stack up case after case in which a practice seemed to work is no guarantee that it will work for you. Insist on tailor-made consulting engagements that recognize the unique nature of your business. If you are buying into the book pitch, ask how much time the actual author will be on-site working through his philosophies, then listen closely to the response. Don't be afraid to trim elegant proposals right down to their essence.

8) Value your employees. One of the most common complaints about consultants is that they talk down to the locals or ignore their ideas. Long after the consultants leave, your staff will be on board. How they

feel about the outsiders has a lot to do with whether the engagement will work. The best consulting companies know this and will go to great lengths to avoid morale problems. You are buying intelligence, not arrogance.

9) Measure the process. Make certain you have your own internal measure of how a procedure is progressing. Consulting companies do, and they generally try to make this a part of the process. But there is a big conflict of interest in this area and their inclination is to make you happy and stay fully engaged. Find someone you trust who knows what a devil's advocate is and let him or her monitor the consulting process. Listen frequently to the advocate's report.

10) If it's not broke, don't try to fix it. It is in the consulting company's interest to find trouble where you see calm waters. The consultants' goal will be to sell much broader involvement than you might want or need. They can't help it. It is part of their nature. But it doesn't have to be part of yours.

Perhaps the best advice is the oldest. Niccolo Machiavelli had this to say about seeking advice: "Here is an infallible rule: a prince who is not himself wise cannot be wisely advised. . . Good advice depends on the shrewdness of the prince who seeks it, and not the shrewdness of the prince on good advice" (ibid., 302–303).

Summary and Conclusions

In order to ascend the Value Curve, CPAs will have to enter the consulting arena. Like the financial services market, this profession does not have the best of reputations. CPAs will elevate the level of professionalism and competence in this profession, as long as they always consider the customer's best interest to be paramount.

Most of the fears of customers who engage consultants can be allayed by implementing Total Quality Service, Value Pricing, Fixed Price Agreements, Change Orders, and the Service Guarantee, discussed throughout this book.

Entering consulting is an enormous opportunity for the profession, one to look forward to with anticipation and alacrity. It is part of the transformation from compliance worker to Certified Professional Advisor.

16 ETHICS, HOURLY BILLING, AND VALUE PRICING

Market competition leads a self-interested person to wake up in the morning, look outside at the earth and produce from its raw materials, not what he wants, but what others want. Not in the quantities he prefers, but in the quantities his neighbors prefer. Not at the price he dreams of charging, but at a price reflecting how much his neighbors value what he has done.

—Friedrich A. Hayek

Capitalism offers nothing but frustrations and rebuffs to those who wish—because of claimed superiority of intelligence, birth, credentials, or ideals—to get without giving, to take without risking, to profit without sacrifice, to be exalted without humbling themselves to understand others and meet their needs.

—George Gilder

Throughout history, the issue of the morality of profits has been debated endlessly, as it should be. Richard John Neuhaus, in his book *Doing Well and Doing Good: The Challenge to the Christian Capitalist*, discusses the ancient debate of a "just" price:

> The idea that there is a right amount or a "just" amount always runs up against the question, Compared to what? The conventional answer is that one pays what the market demands, or what the market will bear. From Athens to Elizabethan England to the Great Terror of the French Revolution, societies have experimented with "sumptuary laws" setting limits on people's income and expenditures. The experiments have never worked out very well, the obvious reason being that it is almost impossible to agree on standards. Few egalitarians, even among the well-to-do, propose a top in-

come limit that is less than what they themselves receive (Neuhaus, 1992: 193).

If a price is going to be judged based on whether or not it is "just," the first question to ponder is, Who will decide what is "just"? One of the proclivities of professionals is to believe that solutions to these sorts of issues are best solved outside the parameters of the marketplace. For instance, they will turn to governing bodies, such as the American Bar Association or the AICPA, or they will turn to the various government organizations that control the licensure of the profession. This is a serious mistake. The free market already provides an answer to the question of a "just" price—*whatever someone is willing to pay*. That may sound heretical, but it's not. An old legal maxim says: *Emptor emit quam minimo potest, venditor vendit quam maximo potest*. (The buyer buys for as little as possible; the seller sells for as much as possible). The customer is sovereign and in the long-run will make the best choices on how to spend his money to maximize utility.

To believe the market is imperfect in this area is to underestimate your own sovereignty as a customer and put your faith in some third party— usually the government or the courts—to determine what is "fair." No third party has access to all of the relevant information that is contained in a price. This is precisely why wage and price controls have failed *everywhere* they have been tried. If it is immoral for a person—or a firm—to charge premium prices to customers, does it follow that it is immoral for buyers to seek out low prices? Moreover, why is an oil company condemned for earning windfall profits when market conditions change, while an individual homeowner who realizes a tidy profit off of a hot real estate market is applauded? Why are individuals and companies held to different standards?

The solution to the problem of a "just" price lies in the conflict of interest that is inherent between buyers and sellers—the seller is seeking the highest price and the buyer is seeking the lowest. The 8 trillion dollar plus economy is evidence that most price issues are resolved, without the aid of a third party, between the buyer and seller.

Perhaps it is not so much *price* that bothers people as it is *profits*. Profits have a bad reputation because most people simply do not know where they come from. As discussed in Chapter 7, profits come from *risk*. Recently, the state of Florida entered into a settlement with various major tobacco companies whereby the state will receive a multi-billion-dollar settlement.

The attorneys who litigated the case for the state agreed to accept a 25 percent contingency, and they assumed all of the risks of taking the engagement. Some of them even mortgaged their homes to finance the investigative research and other expenses that were necessary. The attorneys' share of the settlement worked out to be something on the order of thousands of dollars per hour. A judge has ruled that the fee is unconscionable. However, the attorneys assumed all of the *risk*, and since that is where profits come from, they are entitled to the agreed-upon percentage. The state also has no business claiming, *in retrospect*, that the fee is unreasonable. All parties entered into the contract, and except in cases of fraud or coercion, they should be required to abide by their commitment.

Are such supernormal profits moral? In his seminal book, *Wealth and Poverty*, George Gilder, a senior fellow at the Discovery Institute in Seattle, Washington, had this reply to economist John Kenneth Galbraith's long-standing criticism of business firms seeking large profits:

> Galbraith maintains that businesses, far from giving without predetermined returns, actually seek to control their markets, often with aid of government, to "administer" prices and quantities of production and exclude all rivals. This revelation is sometimes offered in the spirit of a child discovering that his parents indulge in sexual intercourse. But we must grant that the child is right. For all their ideological commitment to free enterprise, businesses are primarily devoted to successful enterprise, pursue it any way they can, and are delighted to benefit when government blocks the competition. In precisely the same way that many "liberal" economists can profess egalitarian socialism while waxing rich on the capitalist system, corporations can feed off of government while celebrating free markets (Gilder, 1993: 47–48).

Profits are a sign that a useful social purpose is being filled and needs are being met. No profit could exist without people voluntarily entering into a transaction where each receives more than they give up. Otherwise, everyone could simply exchange five-dollar bills. What could be more equal? This isn't done because while it may be equal, it would also be completely pointless. For an exchange to make any sense, each party must receive a *gain* from the exchange. That being said, here is how economists define various profits that are earned in the marketplace:

Normal Profits—The return to the owner of a firm that operates in a perfectly competitive market, in long-run equilibrium. In a perfectly competitive market, when a firm maximizes profits, each factor of production will receive a per unit payment exactly equal to what it produces at the margin. The market price, or the cost of a factor, is equal to the value of its marginal product. . . . When firms are earning normal profits, net *economic* return is zero, since revenues exactly equal costs, where costs include the cost of capital, which is the market rental rate of capital.

Supernormal Profits—Profits in excess of normal profits. [These] occur when revenues exceed costs, again including the cost of capital. [They] are often identified with monopoly profits.

Rents—When an agent owns a good that has a special characteristic which, through no effort of the agent, is valuable. Professional athletes or musicians are often given as examples of recipients of rents.

Profits from Immoral Activities—[Profits from] extortion, theft, blackmail, etc.

Windfall Profits—When the event causing the profits is a complete surprise to the profit maker. An example is the OPEC oil embargo of 1974 and its effect on oil companies.

(Cowan and Rizzo, 1995: 3–6)

All businesses strive to earn supernormal or windfall profits. Nothing is unusual about this universal desire, and the fact that professionals or industries organize licensing boards and cartels should convince you that these types of profits are actively sought after. When people charge that a corporation is making too much money, the first thing to ask is this: "If you believe that is so, why don't you purchase its stock?"

Profits come from *risk*, and that includes, as economist Joseph A. Schumpeter so poetically phrased it, the entrepreneurial innovations that make up the "perennial gale of creative destruction." Entire industries have been eliminated due to this characteristic of free markets. Horse-drawn buggy manufacturers didn't invent the automobile and slide rule manufacturers did not make the calculator. Both of these innovations rose up and decimated existing stocks of infrastructure.

In a free market, the income that is earned, the prices that are set, and the profits that are made, are all the result of volitional acts—*capitalist acts between consenting adults*, as one commentator put it. Nobody has written more eloquently on wealth and poverty, capitalism, and the spirit of enterprise than George Gilder. Here is what he wrote in *Forbes ASAP*, December 2, 1996:

> Barbarian intellectuals in the United States complain of widening gaps between rich and poor. What in fact is happening is a rising trajectory of lifetime incomes. In an economy dominated by a few large companies, entry-level work may be well paid, but lifetime incomes and productivity are capped. In an entrepreneurial economy, where large corporations downsize and new companies proliferate, individuals can more readily fulfill their potentials. Thus their ultimate incomes are higher.
>
> In the past, capital equipment was costly and production complex and dominated by large firms. Bill Gates might have spent his life working his way up the chain of command at IBM or General Electric, thus avoiding an immense contribution to income inequality in America. Instead, he began a new company at a poverty-level entry income with capital goods costing a few thousand dollars.
>
> The income floor, after all, will always be zero, while the ceiling in a free economy is effectively infinite. As more people fulfill their potential, the ostensible "gap" increases. But it is not chiefly a horizontal gap between individuals. It is a gap between people's earnings in entry jobs and their peak earnings later in life. It is morally desirable that this gap increase.
>
> The key to the moral superiority of capitalism is that people get rich by imaginatively serving the needs of others. The key to the productive superiority of capitalism is that the people who have proven their ability to create wealth gain the right to reinvest it.
>
> Demonstrably a brilliant investor and creator of wealth, Bill Gates gains the burden and opportunity to reinvest it.

> Socialist economies fail because they tax away and institutionalize the fruits of invention and creativity (Gilder, 1996: 280–82).

This view of capitalism being a moral system is certainly not one that is propagated in the mainstream. Most popular culture and institutions, from movies and television shows to research organizations, villainize business people and business firms, endlessly portraying them as power-hungry, stop-at-nothing-to-get-ahead, ruthless members of society. This view is pernicious, not to mention completely out of touch with how the world works. A business, in its essence, is a moral institution, as it requires moral conduct to succeed in the long run. Michael Novak in *Business as a Calling: Work and the Examined Life* lists seven moral requirements for business success, which he labels "Internal Responsibilities":

1. **To satisfy customers with goods and services of real value.** Like other acts of freedom, launching a new business is in the beginning an act of faith; one has to trust one's instincts and one's vision and hope that these are well enough grounded to build success. It is the customers who, in the end, decide.

2. **To make a reasonable return on the funds entrusted to the business corporation by its investors.** [Is it moral to lose other people's money?]

3. **To create new wealth.** This is no small responsibility. If the business corporation does not meet it, who else in society will?

4. **To create new jobs.** You cannot create employees without creating employers.

5. **To defeat envy through generating upward mobility and putting empirical ground under the conviction that hard work and talent are fairly rewarded.** The founders of the American republic recognized that most other republics in history had failed and that the reason they failed was envy: the envy of one faction for another, one family for another, one clan for another, or of the poor toward the rich. . . . The best way to do this is to generate economic growth through as many diverse industries and

economic initiatives as possible, so that every family has the realistic possibility of seeing its economic condition improve within the next three or four years. Poor families do not ask for paradise, but they do want to see tangible signs of improvement over time. When such horizons are open, people do not compare their condition with that of their neighbors; rather, they compare their own position today with where they hope to be in three or four years. They give no ground to envy. . . . Only then can people see that hard work, goodwill, ingenuity, and talent pay off. When people lose their faith in this possibility, cynicism soon follows.

6. **To promote invention, ingenuity, and in general, "progress in the arts and useful sciences" (Article I, Section 8, U.S. Constitution).** The great social matrix of such invention, discovery and ingenuity is the business corporation.

7. **To diversify the interests of the republic.** The interests of road builders are not those of canal builders, or of builders of railroads, or of airlines companies. The sheer dynamism of economic invention makes far less probable the coalescing of a simple majority, which could act as a tyrant to minorities. The economic interests of some citizens are, in an important sense, at cross-purposes with the economic interests of others, and this is crucial to preventing the tyranny of a majority (Novak, 1996: 138–45).

Fra Luca Pacioli, in *Particularis de Computis et Scripturis*, his treatise on double-entry bookkeeping, emphasized religious and moral teachings. Chapter 2, "Inventory", states the following:

Begin with the assumption that a businessman has a goal when he goes into business. That goal he pursues enthusiastically. That goal, the goal of every businessman who intends to be successful, is to make a lawful and reasonable profit.

Therefore, businessman should begin their business records with the date AD, marking every transaction so that they always remember to be ethical and, at work, always act mindful of His Holy name.

Among Christian businessmen, it is also common to mark the initial account books with the sign of the cross (Pacioli, 1494: 4, 12).

When Pope John Paul II introduced an encyclical titled *Centesimus Annus* on May 1, 1991, he said: "Economic freedom is an aspect of human freedom, which cannot be separated from its other aspects and which must contribute to the full realization of people in order to construct an authentic human community" (Neuhaus, 1992: 184). Encyclicals are not addressed solely to the Catholic faithful but "to all people of goodwill." They are the Church's "social doctrine." This particular encyclical is remarkable, for the Pope is basically saying that the new capitalism is a moral system, and that prosperity is dependent upon economic freedom. Here are some of the more interesting passages, as they relate to economic freedom and the role of profits in society (references are to the paragraph number of the encyclical):

> Man, who was created for freedom, bears within himself the wound of original sin. Man tends toward good, but he is also capable of evil. He can transcend his immediate interest and still remain bound to it. The social order will be the more stable the more it takes this fact into account and does not place in opposition personal interest and the interests of society as a whole, but rather seeks to bring them into fruitful harmony (¶ 25).
>
> At one time, the *natural fruitfulness of the earth* was the primary factor of wealth. In our time, *the role of human work* is increasingly the productive factor both of nonmaterial and material wealth. Also, more than ever is *work with others* and *work for others*; it is a matter of doing something for someone else (¶ 31).
>
> In our time, another form of ownership is becoming no less important than land: *the possession of know-how, technology, and skill.* The wealth of the industrialized nations is based much more on this kind of ownership than on natural resources. A person produces something so that others may use it after they have paid a just price, mutually agreed upon through free bargaining. It is precisely the ability to foresee both the needs of others and the combination of productive

factors most adapted to satisfying those needs that constitutes another important source of wealth in modern society. In this way, the role of disciplined and creative *human work* and *initiative and entrepreneurial ability* become increasingly decisive (¶ 32).

The Church acknowledges the legitimate *role of profit* as an indication that a business is functioning well. When a firm makes a profit, this means that productive factors have been properly employed and corresponding human needs have been satisfied. But profitability is not the only indicator of a firm's condition. It is possible for the financial accounts to be in order, and yet for the people—who are the firm's most valuable asset—to be humiliated and their dignity offended. This is morally inadmissible [and] will eventually have negative repercussions on the firm's economic efficiency. The purpose of a business firm is to be a *community of persons* endeavoring to satisfy basic needs at the service of the whole of society (¶35).

Hourly Billing—The Perfect Crime?

While keeping in mind the above precepts of how a free market economy works in the real world, and why it is a moral system, let's examine the ethical issues attorneys are dealing with as they make the transition from hourly billing to Value Pricing. CPAs and other professionals can learn from the experience of attorneys what problems they will likely encounter.

Lawyers have a much bigger public relations problem than do CPAs. A review of rankings of respected occupations shows CPAs right up there with members of the clergy and doctors. Attorneys have not earned the same reputation. The percentage of Americans who gave lawyers high ratings for honest and ethical standards fell from 27 percent in 1985 to 17 percent in 1994. According to the ABA, "One major contributing factor to the discouraging public opinion of the legal profession appears to be the billing practices of some of its members" (Ross, 1996: 5).

Legal auditors and ethics professionals have devoted substantial amounts of time and energy trying to diffuse these types of problems. In fact, every state except Massachusetts and California has adopted some form of mandatory reporting requirement whereby an attorney has an express legal duty to report to supervising attorneys or the appropriate bar authority another attorney who is engaging in unethical billing practices. As Professor William G. Ross points out, in his book *The Honest Hour*, Rule 8.3(a) of the Model Rules of Professional Conduct provides that:

> A lawyer having knowledge that another lawyer has committed a violation of the Rules of Professional Conduct that raises a substantial question as to that lawyer's honesty, trustworthiness or fitness as a lawyer in other respects, shall inform the appropriate professional authority (ibid., 199).

This is precisely how the Webster Hubbell case was prosecuted the first time. His fellow partners reported his unethical billing practices.

One legal auditor, James P. Schratz, cites that in his experience "30 to 50 percent of entries are questionable in 80 percent of the bills that he audits" (ibid., 30).

Ross states the following in his book:

> Most dishonest billing is the perfect crime. Because there is no practical manner of verifying the accuracy of most time records, every attorney who has billed time knows that hourly billing creates tempting opportunities for fraud (ibid., 23).

In fact, an entire legal auditing industry has been created at an average billing rate of $175 per hour. Under pressure from these auditors, most law firms will very quickly reduce their bills by 25 percent.

Legal Auditors on Value Pricing

Some of the most vitriolic denunciations of Value Pricing come from legal auditors. They also reject the fact that the hourly billing method is disappearing. Ross ends his book *The Honest Hour* by saying, "Despite its potential for abuse, time remains the best means of billing clients. Hourly billing therefore ought to be reformed rather than abandoned" (ibid., 263).

But if the hourly billing method is as good as the legal auditors purport it to be, then why did *their* industry arise in the first place? What makes legal auditors believe that they are the ultimate judge and jury with respect to the fairness of a transaction? Are they simply trying to maintain a billing system that provides for their job security and standard of living? Legal auditors owe their existence to mistrust and asymmetrical information between the lawyer and the customer. Remove these factors and legal auditors will become superfluous.

Ethical problems arise in hourly billing due to the misalignment of interests created by the system. Attorneys may not have malevolent motives when engaging in padding their hours; Ross says that "much overbilling is the result of attorneys' failure to understand the real goals and needs of their clients" (ibid., 53). The problem is that professionals are padding their time sheets because they know that the value of the service they provided is worth more than the time spent. If that is the case, then the solution is not to try to cope with the ethical issues of hourly billing but to scrap hourly billing entirely and reach a price agreement with the customer before the service is provided. Unfortunately for attorneys, the ABA and the courts have opted for the strategy of trying to impose standards for time-based billing. Here is a partial listing of the issues on which they are spending an inordinate amount of brainpower to solve:

- Double billing—billing two customers for different work performed at the same time.
- Recycled work—billing customers by the hour for work that was created at another time for another customer.
- Overstaffing of lawyers—assigning too many lawyers to a case or project to fulfill billable hour quotas.
- Excessive research.
- Attorneys performing clerical and administrative tasks and billing at their hourly rates.
- Charging for travel time.
- Attorney conferences—chitchat on the customer's dime or valuable timesaving devices?
- Charging for small units of time—rounding up to the quarter hour or charging for every minute?
- Overhead expenses—charging (and possibly marking up) general overhead expenses such as copies, faxes, phone calls, secretary time, and overtime.

Although this list is not comprehensive, it represents the major ethical issues of hourly billing. Each one is worth examining in greater detail.

Double Billing and Recycled Work

The ABA Committee on Ethics and Professional Responsibility issued its Formal Opinion 93-379, in December 1993, declaring double billing unethical, stating "the lawyer who has agreed to bill on the basis of hours expended does not fulfill her ethical duty if she bills the client for more time than she actually spent on the client's behalf" (*Alternative Billing: The Sequel*, San Francisco, Tab 7, page 8).

Here is what they said regarding a hypothetical example of an attorney flying on behalf of one client while preparing a brief on the plane for another client, and an attorney charging for a recycled work product:

> A lawyer who flies for six hours for one client while working for five hours on behalf of another, has not earned eleven billable hours. A lawyer who is able to reuse old work product has not re-earned the hours previously billed and compensated when the work product was first generated.

Thus, the ABA Committee concluded:

> Rather than looking to profit from the fortuity of coincidental scheduling, the desire to get work done rather than watch a movie, or the luck of being asked the identical question twice, the lawyer who has agreed to bill solely on the basis of time spent is obliged to pass the benefits of these economies on to the client. The practice of billing several clients for the same time or work product, since it results in the earning of an unreasonable fee, therefore is contrary to the mandate of the Model Rules (ibid., 8–9).

Ross elaborates on this opinion:

> The Opinion states that when an attorney has agreed to charge clients on an hourly basis "and it turns out that the lawyer is particularly efficient in accomplishing a given result, it nonetheless will not be permissible to charge the client for more hours than were actually expended on the matter. When that basis for billing the client has been agreed to, the economies associated with the result must inure to the benefit

of the client, not give rise to an opportunity to bill a client phantom hours" (Ross, 1996: 80).

The ABA Opinion suggests that the lawyer is reaping a windfall from "the luck of being asked the identical question twice," just as the attorney who is able to bill two clients for work performed at the same time is receiving an unfair advantage.

The ABA's condemnation of hourly billing for recycled work is consistent with judicial decisions that have reduced fees when attorneys have billed for work that was developed in previous cases. As one court has explained, "accumulated expertise may be a factor justifying a higher hourly rate, but it is clearly improper to make multiple charges for work that has only been done once" (ibid., 84).

What is curious is that the ABA could ignore the economic value derived by the customer. The hourly billing method is impeding attorneys from reaping the rewards they deserve for the value they provide. After all, the hourly billing method was adopted because studies found the attorneys who used it were making more money than those who were not. And now, the exact opposite seems to be taking place. Rather than suggesting attorneys now adopt other pricing methods, the ABA is wasting time pondering the picayune issue of attorneys sitting on airplanes not watching movies.

Overstaffing of Lawyers

Legal auditor James P. Quinn contends that overstaffing is "the one factor that has contributed more than any other to excessive legal costs" (ibid., 99). It has also been the topic of scorn from judges in various cases. But what causes overstaffing? It is the perverse incentive built into hourly billing, which rewards *efforts* over *results*. If everyone in a firm has to meet an hourly quota, then you can bet that bodies will be thrown at work out of proportion to what is necessary. This is perhaps why customers of major law firms have protested and refuse to pay for any associate not employed by the law firm for at least three years. The customer is simply tired of paying for the on-the-job training of inexperienced associates and is demanding that a case be staffed in accordance with his needs, not the billable hour goals of the firm. And rightfully so.

Excessive Research

Excessive research is another deleterious effect of hourly billing. Because firms have no incentive to be efficient, they tend to recreate the wheel on each new engagement in order to bill as many hours as possible. This is the equivalent of Ford redesigning each car before assembling it, thereby ensuring the maximum labor input to meet the hourly goals. This is absurd. Duplication of effort takes place in all professional firms, and it is a consequence of the hourly billing system. Ross cites the policy of Wells Fargo Bank, which "requires its outside counsel to obtain prior approval for any legal research in excess of three hours" (ibid., 120). Since competition has become so intense, these hourly costs are finally being eliminated. Professionals may not like it, but they need to accept it because the market rules.

Surgeons Piercing Ears

Judge Joseph F. Weis, Jr. wrote in a statutory fee decision in 1983, "A Michelangelo should not charge Sistine Chapel rates for painting a farmer's barn" (ibid., 137). Courts have recognized that sometimes it is necessary for attorneys to perform clerical tasks, and that in these instances the attorney should bill them out at reduced rates. Once again, this is a result of the Almighty Hour mentality, where work gets hoarded by whoever is on the case (to meet billable hour quotas) rather than being delegated to the level where it can be performed in a most cost efficient way.

Travel Time

Courts have tended to allow attorneys only a portion of their travel time, and bankruptcy courts have stated that travel time is considered part of the attorney's overhead and thus built in to their hourly rates. Ross points out the following case:

> Rejecting an attorney's argument that he ought to receive full compensation for travel to the local courthouse because he was thinking about the hearing while he was traveling, one court declared that "this is a slippery slope argument. If a court allows compensation for this, then ultimately shower time will be compensable." [Ross adds] Even shower time,

however, should be compensable if an attorney is thinking
about a client's problems (ibid., 153).

Would a customer share Ross' opinion? No customer of sound mind
would contemplate paying for shower time. This is a clear example of the
preposterous line of reasoning that develops when you believe that all
value is the result of time. No other business even considers this line of
thought, but professionals are mired in it.

Attorney Conferences

Ross conducted his own surveys in 1991, 1994, and 1995, and "inside
counsel ranked conferences as one of the most unproductive activities of
outside counsel" (ibid., 157). The social network in any firm represents an
enormous asset, and it probably is underused in pursuit of the Almighty
Hour. Why should you seek out those in your own firm to see if they have
dealt with a similar issue, if you know a project will provide a few days of
billable hours and the customer will pay for it? Take away the Almighty
Hour as the source of price, and professionals will engage in conferences
only when the benefits outweigh the costs.

Rounding Up Time Charges

Is it ethical for a professional to round up to the nearest tenth of an hour? A
quarter hour? Bankruptcy courts have mandated six-minute billing incre-
ments. Ross takes this issue to its extreme by proposing the following
recommendation:

> The use of smaller billing increments would seem likely to
> encourage ethical behavior by dampening the temptation of
> attorneys to use liberal rounding techniques. Accordingly,
> clients would be wise to insist that their attorneys bill in
> increments of six minutes or less.
>
> Indeed, it might therefore make sense for attorneys to
> begin billing time in one-minute increments in order to as-
> sure maximum accuracy in billing. The use of such small
> increments would not be burdensome to attorneys because,
> as we have seen, most tasks are performed in aggregates of

> many minutes or hours, and it takes the same amount of time
> to record each task, regardless of the duration of the task or
> the minimum billing increment. Literal accuracy, of course,
> would not be demanded of tasks that took more than a few
> minutes. For example, an attorney who spent 177 minutes on
> a project might be excused for estimating her time at three
> hours and billing 180 minutes (ibid., 168).

How many practicing attorneys would agree with Ross that accounting
for *every minute* would not be a burdensome task? But that's not even the
right question. The right question is this: Is there a direct relationship
between a minute and the value of a service? The answer is an unequivocal
no. To go to the absurd extreme of tracking every minute shows that the
focus of the Almighty Hour is wrong; attorneys are focusing all their
efforts on trying to solve these problems rather than on pursuing the
opportunities that exist with Value Pricing.

Overhead Expenses

The ABA Opinion condemns marking up overhead expenses, and states:
"In the absence of an agreement to the contrary, it is impermissible for a
lawyer to create an additional source of profit for the law firm beyond that
which is contained in the provision of professional services themselves"
(ibid., 173). Again, this issue is best settled between the customer and the
professional, discussed up front and understood by each party. Firms
would do well not to consider overhead expenses as profit centers because
that distracts the customer (and the professional) from focusing on the true
source of value—the service rendered rather than the number of faxes,
copies, and phone calls made. By charging for such items you are putting
the focus on things customers do not value and distracting them from the
things they do value. This is the wrong approach. You should avoid any
charge that is part of your fixed overhead (direct expenses are, of course, an
exception). After all, the only true profit center is a customer's check that
does not bounce.

Lawyers will freely admit that hourly billing creates a conflict of
interest between the attorney and the customer, yet some of them desper-
ately cling to the method as if it were sacrosanct. The hopeful sign is that
attorneys are leaving the hourly billing method in droves. Customers are
demanding to know the price of legal and accounting services in advance,

as shown in this testimonial from Ronald A. Williams, Vice President and Assistant General Counsel for Wal-Mart Stores, Inc.:

Wal-Mart Flat Fee Program

In regard to premises liability, product liability, truck liability, and pharmaceutical liability litigation, Wal-Mart has entered into flat fee agreements in 35 areas of the country. This program has been in existence for the past 6 years and Wal-Mart has had great success with it.

Under the Wal-Mart arrangement the company and the law firm agree that a set amount will be paid on each lawsuit that is sent to the law firm. It is also agreed that all of the lawsuits received in the area the law firm covers will be sent to that law firm. Under this arrangement this flat fee amount includes all attorneys fees and inside expenses such as copying, telephone charges, fax charges, computer research charges, delivery charges, mailing charges, and auto mileage charges. There is also agreement among the parties that if the matter is tendered to another entity and it takes over the defense of the case within 60 days there will be no flat fee due in the matter. On the other hand, the parties recognize that the arrangement should incorporate a "squeal factor" in which the law firm can request that on a very special case the flat fee not apply. This would be a particular case which is out of the ordinary and would not be considered to be the normal "run of the mill" case. However, such a case must be extraordinary since the whole intent of the arrangement is that in some cases the firm would do very well in regard to the number of hours spent on the case and in other cases they would not do as well since there would be considerable matter of work to be done, including a trial.

The philosophy of such an arrangement is that this is a long term partnership between the law firm and Wal-Mart and over the period of this long term relationship all of these matters will average out and the law firm will make a profit from the cases in view of the fact that a good number of them will settle or be dismissed without a trial. The distinct advantage to Wal-Mart in these cases is that bills do not have to be reviewed nor does there have to be any discussion between Wal-Mart and the attorney concerning the amount of time spent on a certain matter. Furthermore, Wal-Mart knows exactly how much each case will cost and can budget for those costs (*Alternative Billing*: Tab 6: 5–6).

This is precisely the solution to the ethical dilemmas that are confounding the ABA, courts, and lawyers. Notice that this is a *customer-imposed change*. Wal-Mart will not deal with firms unless they countenance this type of partnership. How long will it take for other major corporations to adopt the same practices? How long will it take them to adopt these same arrangements with their CPAs? It's already happening, despite what the legal auditors say about the immortality of hourly billing. When you and the customer see things differently, you will only succeed when you begin to view the world the same way they do.

There are signs that the legal profession is beginning to get the message. The Committee of the American Bar Association (ABA) Section of Business Law issued a report in November 1988, titled "Business and Ethics Implications of Alternative Billing Practices: Report on Alternative Billing Arrangements," which proposed the following modifications to Model Rule 1.5 (see a discussion of this rule in Chapter 10):

> The Committee believes that the following items might well be added to Rule 1.5 (a) as factors to be used in testing fee "reasonableness":
>
> 1. The size and complexity of the transaction or matter for which the lawyer is retained; and
> 2. The client's sophistication and extent of experience in business matters.
>
> The Committee also continues to support the proposition that reasonableness should be presumed "if the client and the lawyer reach an agreement with respect to a billing arrangement after disclosure and understanding" and fees are charged in accordance with that agreement (*The Business Lawyer*; Vol. 54, November 1998: 204).

Fairness and Pricing

The notion of a "fair" or "just" price has bedeviled philosophers, religious leaders, rulers of nations, and businessman for centuries. During the Dark Ages merchants could be put to death for exceeding the communal concept of a "just" price. In 301 A.D., Diocletian, the Roman Emperor, issued an edict fixing prices for nearly 800 items and punishing violators with death. Of course, whenever you fix a price below its market level, you will get shortages, which is precisely what happened.

In ancient China, India, and Rome, and almost everywhere throughout the Middle Ages, all interest charges were called "usury" and were prohibited entirely, making economic progress through lending and risk-taking all but impossible. Even today, "price gougers" are subject to societal condemnation, regulatory harassment, and editorial vitriol. Oil companies are frequently a prime target of public outrage, especially when prices at the pump vary from one location to another. Pharmaceutical companies are held in contempt when they charge $1 per pill, even if the dosage reduces the cost of medical intervention by other means.

On the other hand, popular movie stars, directors, and entertainment companies (such as TV networks and Disney) can earn above-normal profits without so much as a whisper of public protest. Premium ice creams and chocolates, which are very expensive and yield enormous profits, also escape criticism. Why the different standards? Is the consumer a hypocrite or just emotionally responding to the issue of fairness?

Traditional economic theory has long ignored subjective issues such as fairness, tending instead to rely on the rational man economic model (as discussed in Chapter 5). But there is no doubt that in the real world, the perception of fairness can, and does, influence the purchasing behavior of consumers. This is an interesting economic anomaly, because rational theory would predict that a consumer would purchase a commodity as long as the price was below his or her reservation price. It is simply not rational to refuse to purchase a product or service because you perceive the terms of the transaction to be unfair.

In his book *Passions Within Reason: The Strategic Role of the Emotions*, economist Robert H. Frank posits a "fairness model" to explain this anomaly:

> People will sometimes reject transactions in which the other
> party gets the lion's share of the surplus, even though the

price at which the product sells may compare favorably with their own reservation price (Frank, 1988: 167).

Consider the following illustration:

> You are lying on the beach on a hot day. All you have to drink is ice water. For the last hour, you have been thinking about how much you would enjoy a nice cold bottle of your favorite beer. A companion gets up to make a phone call and offers to bring back a beer. He says that the beer might be expensive and asks the maximum price you are willing to pay. If the price is higher, he will not buy it. What price do you tell him if (1) the only nearby place where beer is sold is a fancy resort hotel, or (2) the only nearby place is a small, run-down grocery store? (Nagle and Holden, 1995: 309).

The median price stated from the fancy hotel was $2.65 and from the grocery store $1.50. Note that the consumer would be drinking the beer on the beach and not entering the hotel or store where the beer was purchased, and thus—under the theory of rationality—should be willing to pay the same amount no matter where the beer is ultimately purchased. But most people who participated in this survey expressed the feeling they would rather go thirsty than be "ripped off" by the grocery store.

Frank's "fairness model" is certainly influencing the behavior of these consumers. It may be argued that this experiment is not valid because the participants were asked to imagine sitting on a beach in the hot sun, rather than actually doing so. Therefore they are stating how they think they would react under those circumstances but this is different from their "revealed preference."

The example, however, does give insight into the process of negotiating with the customer, a process in which perceptions of fairness are very important to both sides. It is vitally important to understand each customer's perception of fairness and what the customer expects from a professional. Violating those perceptions will lead to irreparable damage to the relationship, even if the perceptions are not rational. Sometimes you can overcome irrational perceptions of fairness by educating the customer; other times you cannot. You must decide whether you can abide by the customer's perceptions of fairness in the transaction, and the more you learn about what those perceptions are, the better you will be able to perform in accordance with them.

The Market as an Arbiter of Value

Put a group of professionals in a room, and eventually the discussion will turn to quality as well as to ethical issues. A focus group for the California Society of CPAs discussed the Business Services Network (BSN), which is a resource for its members to access various consultants and business services, via the Internet. The BSN will be financed by the advertisers who list their services and products—various consultants who work with CPAs, attorneys, banks, and Microsoft.

This led to a discussion on the topic of quality control. How would the Society ensure that the advertisers were competent, ethical professionals? Many participants feared that the BSN would become a venue where anyone could pay and thus get posted on the network without any assurance of quality. Many suggestions were proffered to guarantee quality. But is the Society competent enough to ensure quality? Or will the market weed out the incompetent providers long before the Society even figures out who is incompetent? CPAs may get burned by an unethical service provider listed on the BSN, but that is the risk of the free market. If someone is posted on the BSN, it is the customer's responsibility to check references and if a customer ends up being taken advantage of, the customer will post that information on the BSN to help new customers make a more informed decision. Does some omnipotent body exist that decides if it is permissible for a given manufacturer to sell an item, such as a laptop computer? This is not necessary because the market will ruthlessly take out charlatans and quacks. The market is what ensures the quality of the computer manufacturer.

Professionals naturally look to third parties to solve problems, be it ethical issues or quality issues. Anyone who understands free markets knows that these problems take care of themselves. People are mistaken who believe that the government is effective at ensuring quality. Organizations such as the Contractors Licensing Board are virtually useless in insuring the quality of contractors. The best protection is competition and tort law, not a government agency. All the government agency will do is protect the contractor from the consumer, which is what government licensing is all about. Ask yourself which group of products and services have gotten better in recent decades: automobiles, electronics, computers, and transportation, or public schools, police protection, Social Security, and Amtrak. The best insurance possible against consumers being taken advantage of is to give consumers competition and leave them free to choose among a host of providers.

Summary and Conclusions

The members of the American Bar Association should not be disparaged for taking up these issues. The problem is that they are applying the labor theory of value to legal services and ignoring the subjective theory of value.

Professionals who are convinced that all value is determined by hours spent face a dilemma. One wonders if two professionals, leaving a movie together, are timid about expressing their opinions on the movie. According to the labor theory of value, the movie should be equally valuable to both, as it took the same amount of production time. Obviously, this is faulty reasoning. Yet hourly billing is a direct extension of this labor theory of value.

The value of any professional service—or any other product or service offered in the marketplace—is that which is agreed upon by the parties to the transaction. If both parties do not feel like they are benefiting from the exchange, it will not take place.

The New York State Bar Association had this to say with respect to alternative pricing methods:

> Indeed, subject to the economic realities of the situation and an attorney's professional obligations, virtually any billing method that attorney and client can both agree upon and abide by will result, almost by definition, in a fair fee (*Alternative Billing*, 1997: 55).

The concepts discussed in this book—ascertaining customer expectations, discussing price up front, entering into Fixed Price Agreements, and involving customers in the design and terms of your services—are the rational alternative to the ethical quandaries discussed in this chapter. Value Pricing requires character, integrity, and honest dealings, which are less likely to be cultivated with the use of hourly billing, since in Value Pricing the interests of the professional and the customer will be aligned.

17 VALUE PRICING AND SELF-ESTEEM

*The greatest danger is not that our aim is too high and we miss it
but that our aim is too low and we reach it.*

—Michelangelo

CPAs tend to suffer from write-downs and low pricing. One reason is low self-esteem, which directly affects the pricing of a professional's services.

Allan S. Boress, editor of the *CPA Profitability Monthly Newsletter*, offers some explanations of why CPAs capitulate so easily:

- The CPA does not have enough quality clients.
- The client doesn't really want to work with a CPA but has to deal with such issues as tax compliance.
- The client sees little value in what the CPA does.
- The client beats up the CPA because it is a negotiation tactic.
- Fee arrangements are not discussed up front.
  (Boress, 1996: 5–6)

Confident Pricing and Self-Esteem

These are all good explanations; however they do not really get at the root of why CPAs have not been confident enough to engage wholeheartedly in Value Pricing. The deeper reasons lie in the issue of self-esteem. In the August 1996 issue of the *CPA Profitability Monthly Newsletter*, Timothy J. Beauchemin wrote an article titled "No More Begging for Work: Self Esteem Is the Key to a Better Practice." This provided the definitive answer as to why CPAs are so conservative when it comes to pricing. Here is a portion of what Beauchemin wrote:

> I see too much of what I call "begging" in our industry—
> begging for work (especially by under pricing) and then

begging to get paid. I have never really understood why this is, particularly when you consider the training, hard work, and risk that accountants go through. The only explanation I can see is that accountants tend to have rather low self images, unfairly and unreasonably low, but low just the same (Beauchemin, 1996: 4).

Low self-esteem does go right to the heart of why CPAs question the value of the service they provide. Many participants in one of my seminars have commented that they would "feel guilty" about charging a substantial multiple of their hourly rate. They say this as if they are taking advantage of the customer. This attitude is shocking. Why would they attend a course titled *The Shift from Hourly Billing to Value Pricing* if they did not want to increase their net incomes?

Do you truly believe that the benchmark of your value is the hours you spend? What about the years of experience that stand behind that 15-minute tax-planning brainstorm that saves your customer thousands of dollars in taxes? Is the value really one-quarter your hourly rate? CPAs are so imprisoned by the hourly billing method that it has affected their own concept of self-worth and has lowered their self-esteem. Do you think other businesses "feel guilty" about pricing based upon value? Do the airline executives feel guilty about charging the first-class passenger four to ten times the cost of coach, even though it doesn't cost that much more to fly them? Do General Motors executives feel guilty about charging a higher price for a Cadillac than for an Oldsmobile, even though they are churned out of the same factory with minimal cost difference?

The lesson is vital, and it is this: **Before you can charge a premium price, you first have to believe, internally, that you are worth it. If you do not think you are worth multiples of your hourly rate, your customers never will believe it either.**

A good example of pricing comes from a customer who owns an industrial coating shop and is very adroit at pricing. He has done all the time and motion studies, cost analyses, and labor overhead allocations on his automated line for purposes of bidding. Yet, every time he bids a job, he considers a myriad of factors, and the price is usually much higher than the "standard cost-accounting rates." He explained his method of pricing by telling of an early business experience. Before he owned his business, he worked as a carpenter, building decks, fences, etc. As he was working on a deck for a particular customer whom he really did not like, he hit his hand with a hammer, causing it to swell immediately. Just then, the homeowner emerged and asked him how much the deck was going to cost. At that point, he was so frustrated—and in dire pain—he did not care whether or not he lost the job, so he quoted a price three times what he thought the "time and material" cost would be. The homeowner did not blink. He said he learned a valuable lesson that day, and it was this: Pricing = Guts.

Have you ever dealt with a professional, such as a doctor or a consultant, who came highly recommended? When you learned of the price, did you try to negotiate it downward? Most highly recommended professionals will not budge on their pricing, because they know they deserve it and are worth it. They are secure and confident in their worth, and they price above the market as a result. Obviously, not everyone can do this. But the ones who do all possess a common characteristic: *high self-esteem.*

The ultimate treatise on self-esteem is the book *The Six Pillars of Self-Esteem*, by Nathaniel Branden. Branden defines self-esteem as:

1. Confidence in our ability to think, confidence in our ability to cope with the basic challenges of life; and
2. Confidence in our right to be successful and happy, the feeling of being worthy, deserving, entitled to assert our needs and wants, achieve our values, and enjoy the fruits of our efforts.

   (Branden, 1994: 4)

This directly relates to the guilty feelings of CPAs with respect to Value Pricing.

Branden further points out: "[Self-esteem] is directly affected by how we act. Causation flows in both directions. There is a continuous feedback loop between our actions in the world and our self-esteem. The level of our self-esteem influences how we act, and how we act influences the level of our self-esteem" (ibid., 4). And please do not think your level of self-esteem is set, once and for all, in childhood. It is not. You can increase it, and you can decrease it as well; Branden's book covers this subject well and is recommended reading for anyone interested in this vital subject.

Pause for a moment and think about how you act with your customers. When they object to your price, what is your first reaction? In the majority of cases, the first thing a CPA will do is to cut the price, in hopes of pleasing the customer. Why? Not only are professionals loss adverse, but they are not convinced they are worth what they are quoting. So rather than educating the customer as to the value they are providing, professionals capitulate and cut their price, which cuts the value of the service. Quoting a premium price, and sticking to it, takes a positive self-image and sense of self-worth. As Beauchemin pointed out in his article, most accountants do not possess either. This is attributable to several factors:

- CPAs tend to come from middle-class and blue-collar families.
- The profession is relatively easy to enter compared with law or medicine.
- The profession does not require an Ivy League school to get certified.
- The profession is fairly open in employment, with grades, rather than connections, being the primary determinant for getting hired.
- The profession offers a good salary, even during apprenticeship. (Beauchemin, 1996: 4)

Like most professionals, CPAs take all customer complaints and defections personally. After all, what CPAs sell is *themselves*, so it is only natural for them to take negative feedback from customers personally. You should not detach yourself from your professional pride and sense of identity; rather, you should understand your own role in determining your attitude and sense of self-worth. All actions start as thoughts in your mind. As Boress points out: "You will never be paid more than what you think you are worth" (Boress, 1995: 27).

In his article, Beauchemin told of the changes he and his partner implemented to get over their "inferiority complex." They enhanced their office, bought a Mercedes, increased their prices to near the top of the market, and told prospects "If you want the best, you have to pay for it" (Beauchemin, 1996: 4). Probably the biggest change they made was to grade their existing clients *A, B, C, D,* and *F,* firing all of the *F* clients, including one that was a large portion of their revenue. The *F* clients were referred to their competition. They also referred to the competition clients who did not pay, clients who were rude to the staff, and clients who were not managing their businesses in an ethical manner. Finally, he recommends the following:

> Take any of your weak staff members who just are not cutting it, and send them to your competition. Two things will soon happen. First, the environment in your office will be so

positive that the work will move quicker and the growth will come sooner as others are attracted to your wonderfully powerful firm karma. Second, your competition will soon be having severe operational problems—making you look even better! I've done all this. I know it works (Beauchemin, 1996: 5).

By taking such bold—some might even say drastic—actions, your self-esteem is bound to increase. By surrounding yourself only with *A* customers and excellent staff members, you will begin to feel better about yourself and your firm.

Branden says *"Self-esteem is the reputation we acquire with ourselves"* (Branden, 1994: 69). That is profound. Professionals are deeply concerned, and rightfully so, with their reputations: They care what their customers think of them, of their firm, of their integrity. But what about their reputations with themselves? Most professionals were never taught even to ask the question. According to Branden:

> If low self-esteem correlates with resistance to change and clinging to the known and familiar then never in the history of the world has low self-esteem been as economically disadvantageous as it is today. If high self-esteem correlates with comfort in managing change and in letting go of yesterday's attachments, then high self-esteem confers a competitive edge (ibid., 242).

Intellectual Capital

In today's world, intellectual capital is the source of all wealth; even the Pope recognizes this fact in his encyclical. When the source of wealth shifts from matter to mind, then the mind becomes more important. And if the mind is important, then self-esteem is critical and will have a substantial impact on what price you can command in the marketplace. When entertainment moguls Steven Spielberg, David Geffen, and Jeffrey Katzenberg formed DreamWorks SKG, they were willing to sell a one-third stake in their brand new company for 900 million dollars. It doesn't take a CPA to calculate that these three valued their new venture at 2.7 billion dollars. That's not bad for a start-up with rented offices, copy machine leases, and virtually no tangible capital. Do you think they used cost-plus accounting in setting their value?

CPAs often voice objections to Value Pricing such as, "It will not work in my market; it is too competitive." Or, "I practice in a small town, and my customers talk with one another. I can't engage in price discrimination without losing their trust and confidence in me." These objections, and others, are known as the *fallacy of the exception*. Even after presenting empirical evidence that practically all businesses price discriminate, some CPAs remain unconvinced that it would work for them. Yet when Vidal Sassoon entered the business in the United States, he charged $50 for a haircut. My father's union buddies, the competition, were of the opinion that *nobody* would pay that much for a haircut. They couldn't have been more wrong. The argument of two customers talking with one another about a firm's price carries more weight, but not much more. This is really the exception, not the rule, even in a small town. And if you do not have the imagination and creativity to justify different prices, then you probably do not have what it takes to price discriminate in the first place. If you are truly concerned that two customers are completely identical, then simply charge them the same price. But do not let that type of exception tie your hands behind your back and prevent you from pursuing the opportunities inherent in price discrimination with other customers.

Viewing the Success of Others

People with high self-esteem are not threatened by the success of others. On the contrary, they are truly happy for another's success and will go out of their way to learn from them. The man who is not afraid of competition doesn't have any. An example of this is Rush Limbaugh and his Excellence In Broadcasting Radio Network. For years, the left (Rush's opposition, so to speak), has been searching for its own "Rush" who could make an impact on the airwaves similar to Rush's (over 22 million listeners in any week tune in to him). Mario Cuomo tried it. Jerry Brown tried it. Others tried it. Each time, Rush would proclaim, "Come on in, the water is warm." He was so confident of his own abilities that he did not see these potential competitors as a serious threat. He turned out to be right. Cuomo and Brown both are off the air. CPAs should have the same attitude about American Express, and others entering their markets.

One CPA who uses Value Pricing should not view others who do as competition. If all CPAs learned Value Pricing, it would raise the prices for all services across the profession. It is not a zero-sum game. Consider a customer who is used to paying a substantial premium for his accounting and tax services. If this customer moves and becomes *your* customer, will you not benefit from the high price he's used to paying (assuming you provide the same Total Quality Service)?

Summary and Conclusions

Customers prefer to associate with successful professionals. Customers want their professionals to be successful because *they* want to be successful. Do not feel guilty or ashamed of your success. Do not be afraid to show opulence in front of your customers.

Harry Beckwith tells a wonderful story about Picasso in his book *Selling the Invisible*.

> A woman was strolling along a street in Paris when she spotted Picasso sketching at a sidewalk cafe. Not so thrilled that she could not be slightly presumptuous, the woman asked Picasso if he might sketch her, and charge accordingly.
>
> Picasso obliged. In just minutes, there she was: an original Picasso.
>
> "And what do I owe you?" she asked.
>
> "Five thousand francs," he answered.
>
> "But it only took you three minutes," she politely reminded him.
>
> "No," Picasso said. "It took me all my life."
> (Beckwith, 1997: 137–38)

Charge by the years, not by the hour.

18 ANTITRUST LAW

Monopoly had become as popular a subject in economics as sin has been in religion. There is a characteristic difference: Economists are paid better to attack monopoly that the clergy are to wrestle with sin. It is to be observed that the economists who defend monopoly in antitrust cases are better paid than the government's economists: Do sinners always earn more than the virtuous who combat them? Probably yes; one must be compensated for bearing the opprobrium of sinning.

—George J. Stigler, Memoirs of an Unregulated Economist

After the Civil War, and with the development of better transportation systems that integrated a host of local markets into a national market, business corporations grew to unprecedented size in order to take advantage of economies of scale. As this process unfolded, many small and undercapitalized businesses went bankrupt or were purchased by larger concerns. The public was suspicious of this concentration of economic power, and politicians responded in 1890 by passing the first antitrust law, The Sherman Antitrust Act. The act was thought the perfect remedy to stop any business from monopolizing its market and to restore efficient competition to the economy.

Over the years, antitrust policy as evolved through further legislative acts and amendments, regulatory guidelines and judicial interpretation. The goal of this chapter is to make you aware of the implications of the antitrust laws on various pricing decisions. As professionals consult with customers on pricing, they need to be aware of the major antitrust laws and acts that proscribe certain pricing tactics. Although services are not subject to certain provisions of these laws—for instance, price discrimination—many other business are affected, and the laws need to be taken into account when formulating pricing strategy.

This chapter is not intended to be a comprehensive examination of the legal and strategic ramifications of antitrust law, but rather to be an introduction to the cornerstones of antitrust policy: The Sherman Antitrust

Act, 1890; the Federal Trade Commission Act (FTC Act), 1914; the Clayton Act, 1914; and the Robinson–Patman Act, 1936. Discussion will cover the justifications for them and the criticisms leveled against them in recent years.

The Sherman Antitrust Act, 1890

Section I

Every contract, combination in the form of trust or otherwise, or conspiracy, in restraint of trade or commerce among the several States, or with foreign nations, is hereby declared to be illegal.

Section II

Every person who shall monopolize, or attempt to monopolize, or combine or conspire with any other person or persons, to monopolize any part of the trade or commerce among the several States, or with foreign nations, shall be deemed guilty.

The first legal action involving this act to reach the Supreme Court was the E.C. Knight case, decided in 1895. For the Justice Department, the case turned out to be a mild disaster. While the court admitted that the acquisition of the E.C. Knight Company and three other independent sugar refineries owned by the American Sugar Refining Company did tend to create a monopoly in sugar manufacturing, it held that the "sugar trust" was not in violation of the Sherman Act.

In 1904, the federal government won its first case in *United States v. Northern Securities*, preventing a merger allegedly designed to reduce price competition between two railroads. Energized by its victory in this case, the Justice Department initiated a number of legal actions against large corporate holdings, none of which were as important as the one filed in a St. Louis Federal Court on November 15, 1906 against the Standard Oil Company of New Jersey.

The modern petroleum industry began in 1846 when Dr. Abraham Gesner, a Canadian geologist, discovered that oil could be distilled from coal, and kerosene could be drawn off and used as an illuminant. By 1880, John D. Rockefeller was the king of the industry, with his Standard Oil

Company holding the dominant market share. How did he achieve such a dominant market position? "Between 1870 and 1885, the price of refined kerosene dropped from 26 cents to 8 cents per gallon. In the same period, the Standard Oil Company reduced average costs per gallon from almost 3 cents in 1870 to 0.452 cents in 1885" (Armentano, 1990: 60).

Legend has it that this was predatory pricing: the act of deliberately underselling competitors in certain markets in order to drive them out of business. Once they are gone, the monopolist raises the price in the absence of competition. History books have immortalized this view of Standard Oil and predatory pricing has been a major concern of government antitrust lawyers, politicians, and the general public. However, like most conventional wisdom, this theory is more conventional than wisdom, as explained by Dominick T. Armentano in his indictment of antitrust laws, *Antitrust and Monopoly: Anatomy of a Policy Failure*:

> Unfortunately for lovers of legends, this one has been laid theoretically and empirically prostrate. In a now classic article, John S. McGee theorized that Standard Oil did not employ predatory practices because it would have been economically foolish to have done so. In the first place, McGee argued, such practices are very costly for the large firm; it always stands relatively more to lose since it, by definition, does the most business. Second, the uncertainty of the length of the forthcoming battle, and thus its indeterminate expense, must surely make firms wary of initiating a price war. Third, competitors can simply close down and wait for the price to return to profitable levels; or new owners might purchase bankrupt facilities and ready them to compete with the predator. Fourth, such wars inevitably spread to surrounding markets, endangering the predator's profits in his "safe" areas. And last, predatory practices already assume a "war chest" of monopoly profits to see the firm through the costly battles; firms apparently cannot initiate predatory practices unless they already possess monopoly power. But if this is true, firms cannot gain initial monopoly positions through predatory practices.
>
> Thus. . . Standard's position in oil refining grew rapidly because of the natural decline of small competitors; the increasing capital and innovation requirements of large-scale

oil technology; the economic advantages achieved through intelligent entrepreneurship; the ownership of tank cars and pipelines; vertical integration into barrels, cans, glues, exporting; and the consequent lower transportation costs provided by the railroads. It did not grow from any general reliance on alleged predatory practices (ibid., 63–64).

Even though the government won its case against Standard Oil, and other tobacco trusts, supporters of antitrust were still not satisfied with the narrow interpretations by the court, and Congress began work on two additional legislative initiatives designed to prevent further anti-competitive business practices.

The Federal Trade Commission Act (FTC Act), 1914

The Federal Trade Commission was established in order to enforce the provisions of the Sherman Antitrust Act in a more rapid manner than could be achieved by judicial law. Section 5 of the FTC Act reads: "The Commission is hereby empowered and directed to prevent persons, partnerships, or corporations. . . from using unfair methods of competition in commerce." The FTC could ban a business practice merely because of the suspicion that it promoted unfair competition, without the permission of a court.

Also, the FTC has the authority to subject pricing practices to administrative review, not in order to punish past wrongdoing, but to make new law. The FTC is empowered to order a business to cease and desist from any practice it deems unfair, even if that practice would not necessarily be deemed unfair or anti-competitive in a court of law.

The Clayton Act, 1914

The Clayton Act was passed to correct various defects and omissions of the Sherman Act. Specifically, it prohibits anticompetitive mergers, tying arrangements, exclusive dealing agreements, interlocking directorates, and the acquisition of stock in competitor companies. Also, Section 2(a), as amended by the Robinson–Patman Act, prohibits predatory price discrimination:

That is shall be unlawful for any person engaged in commerce, in the course of such commerce, either directly or indirectly, to discriminate in price between different purchasers of commodities of like grade and quality, where either or any of the purchases involved in such discrimination are in commerce, where such commodities are sold for use, consumption, or resale within the United States or any Territory thereof or the District of Columbia or any insular possession or other place under the jurisdiction of the United States, and where the effect of such discrimination may be substantially to lessen competition or tend to create a monopoly in any line of commerce, or to injure, destroy, or prevent competition with any person who either grants or knowingly receives the benefit of such discrimination, or with customers of either of them: *Provided*, That nothing herein contained shall prevent differentials which make only due allowance for differences in the cost of manufacture, sale, or delivery resulting from the differing methods or quantities in which such commodities are to such purchasers sold or delivered: *Provided*, however, That the Federal Trade Commission may, after due investigation and hearing to all interested parties, fix and establish quantity limits, and revise the same as it finds necessary, as to particular commodities or classes of commodities, where it finds that available purchasers in greater quantities are so few as to render differentials on account thereof unjustly discriminatory or promotive of monopoly in any line of commerce; and the foregoing shall then not be construed to permit differentials based on differences in quantities greater than those so fixed and established: *And provided further*, That nothing herein contained shall prevent persons engaged in selling goods, wares, or merchandise in commerce from selecting their own customers in bona fide transactions and not in restraint of trade: *And provided further*, That nothing herein contained shall prevent price changes from time to time where in response to changing conditions affecting the market for or the marketability of the goods concerned, such as but not limited to actual or imminent deterioration of perishable goods, obsolescence of seasonal goods, distress sales under court process, or sales in good faith in discontinuance of business in the goods concerned (ibid., 281–282).

The Robinson–Patman Act of 1936

After the passage of the Clayton Act in 1914, chain stores grew rapidly and increased their buying power, and this type of price discrimination was thought to threaten the survival of independent wholesalers and retailers. Therefore, in 1936, Congress passed the Robinson–Patman Act in order to strengthen the Clayton Act. This was in the middle of the New Deal and protecting small businesses was viewed as a legitimate goal of antitrust policy. Small business interest groups, in fact, were the impetus behind the passage of the Act, which was actually drafted by the U.S. Wholesale Grocers' Association. The Act contained the following major provisions:

> Deleted the exemption, which existed in the original Clayton Act, that allowed firms to price discriminate among buyers who purchased different quantities of a good.
>
> Forbade price rebates to selected buyers in the form of fees for brokerage, handling, processing, or any other services when those same fees were not offered to all buyers equally.
>
> Made it illegal for buyers (that is, the large chains) to solicit lower prices from manufacturers if those prices would be discriminatory under the amended Clayton Act (Nagle and Holden, 1995: 365).

These Acts are the major foundation of antitrust policy today. They have been amended many times by later legislative acts and special exemptions have been granted to various interest groups, such as labor unions, insurance companies, and farm cooperatives.

Price Discrimination as Prohibited by the Acts

Since so much of this book has dealt with price discrimination, it is worth exploring the judicial interpretations of this ubiquitous practice and to ensure, if you are advising a customer on pricing strategy, that you don't run afoul of these laws.

The term *commodities of like grade and quality*, as used in the Clayton Act, has been interpreted narrowly by the courts to mean tangible goods; the Act does not apply to discrimination in services. Price discrimination among final consumers is prohibited under the Civil Rights Act if the basis for such discrimination is the race, religion, or sex of the purchaser. Further, any tangible difference in the materials, workmanship, or design is recognized as a difference in grade or quality, and thus a manufacturer can sell a deluxe model (think of Oldsmobile vs. Cadillac), or a customized model, at a premium price that more than reflects the cost of production, without violating the law.

One of the landmark legal cases in the price discrimination area is *The Borden Company v. Federal Trade Commission, 339 F. 2d 133*. In April of 1958 the Federal Trade Commission issued a complaint against the Borden Company, accusing it of selling goods of like grade and quality to different buyers at different prices with the effect of reducing competition. The goods in question were Borden's private label evaporated milk and "identical" milk that it made and sold under private label. The price difference between the two milks was substantial, and the FTC charged that this difference violated the Robinson–Patman Act. On November 28, 1962, the FTC ordered the Borden company to cease price discriminating on goods of like grade and quality sold to different buyers at different prices.

On December 4, 1964, a Circuit Court of Appeals dismissed the FTC's cease-and-desist order against Borden. As Armentano documents in *Antitrust and Monopoly*:

> Circuit Judge Joseph C. Hutcheson, Jr., reviewing the undisputed facts in the case, argued that the first issue was "whether or not the Commission applied the correct legal test in deciding that the commodities sold at different prices were of like grade and quality."
>
> Judge Hutcheson indicated that the record clearly showed that Borden's own brand of evaporated milk did command a premium price in the market, and that the Borden product was recognized as a premium product by both consumers and dealers who sold evaporated milk. To support these conclusions, the court quoted testimony of grocers that had stated that consumers asked for the Borden brand by name, and could not be convinced to accept some other brand. Significant price differentials had to exist, apparently, before dealers would even stock and sell other brands. That dealers continued to purchase both products and the different prices indicated, to the court, that one was a "premium line" and one was not.

But was the "demonstrated consumer preference" for the Borden brand to receive legal recognition? The Circuit Court thought it should. Contrary to what the FTC declared, there was no clear Congressional intent on the matter of "private brands" and price discrimination. In fact, if the intent of the Robinson–Patman and the rest of the antitrust statutes generally was to avoid price rigidity and price uniformity, then "commercial factors" had to be considered in pricing.

[Armentano then quotes from the Court's opinion]:

An established brand name may have a large following among purchasers. This fact can be of great economic significance in a competitive market. We do not believe it was the intention of Congress that such clearly demonstrable consumer preference should simply be ignored in determining when products may be priced differently. As a practical matter, such preferences may be far more significant in determining the market value of a product than are its physical characteristics (Armentano, 1990: 189).

The Court ruled in favor of Borden and set aside the FTC order. Subsequently, the Supreme Court reversed the Circuit Court of Appeals decision on the issue of "like grade and quality," and remanded the Borden case back to the Appeals Court. Also, the Supreme Court hypothesized that if a manufacturer sold its branded, higher priced milk to a retailer, but refused to sell the private-label brand to him:

the retailer who was permitted to buy and sell only the more expensive brand would have no chance to see to those who always buy the cheaper product or to convince others, by experience or otherwise, of the fact which he and all other dealers already know—that the cheaper product is actually identical with that carrying the more expensive label (ibid., 190).

Justice Stewart and Harland dissented from the majority, and Stewart wrote, rather disgustedly:

In the guise of protecting producers and purchasers from discriminatory price competition, the Court ignores legitimate market preferences and endows the Federal Trade Commission with authority to disrupt price relationships between products whose identity has been measured in the laboratory but rejected in the marketplace. I do not believe that such power was conferred upon the Commission by Congress (ibid., 191).

The Circuit Court again considered, and again dismissed, the FTC cease-and-desist order, ruling that "the record does not contain substantial injury to competition at the seller's level." Recall the discussion, from Chapter 5, of the price difference between Lancome and Loreal cosmetics. The brand is far more important to customers than the actual ingredients of the make-up, and thus a higher price is charged for Lancome than for Loreal.

Another key phrase in the Clayton Act quoted above is *in commerce*, which has been interpreted to mean an injured party has to be a business whose ability to compete has been hampered by a discriminatory price. Consumers can always be charged different prices since they are not using the products in commerce. A wholesaler, however, may be found in violation for charging different retailers different prices, since the retailers are engaged in commerce.

The term *substantially to lessen competition* has two interpretations:

> Price discrimination will be found to violate the law if it harms competition at either of two levels. *Primary-level* competition is between the firm that price discriminates and its own competitors. *Secondary-level* competition is between two firms that are customers of the firm that price discriminates (or are customers of a middleman who is, in turn, a customer of the price discriminating firm). The courts do not want to discourage price-cutting at the primary level, even when it is discriminatory, unless competition is clearly harmed (Nagle and Holden, 1995: 376).

There are three specific affirmative legal defenses a company can invoke to protect itself from prosecution for illegal price discrimination: meeting competition, changing market conditions, or cost justification.

Criticisms of Antitrust Policy

Antitrust policy has come under intense scrutiny in recent decades, especially by the economics profession. As the Nobel Prize winning economist Gary S. Becker points out in his book, *The Economics of Life*:

> During the 1980s both the government and private antitrust cases have declined dramatically, while malpractice, product liability, and other business litigation has boomed. Specialists in antitrust law have shifted to other business areas as the once-prosperous antitrust field has fallen on difficult times.
>
> The immediate cause of the decline has been the growing influence of economic analysis of competition and business practices on the thinking of judges and government officials. That analysis shows that competition usually promotes efficiency and the well-being of consumers and that anticompetitive behavior arises mainly from unwise public policies and a natural tendency for rival producers to collude on prices and production.
>
> Conspiracies in restraint of trade tend to break down eventually without an active antitrust policy. Companies that are part of a conspiracy cheat on their output quotas, and high prices attract new companies into their industry. The experience of OPEC illustrates the spontaneous breakdown of an open conspiracy outside antitrust laws. However, antitrust policy can certainly discourage business conspiracies by imposing large fines and other punishments.
>
> Competition will weed out inefficient behavior without government intervention. Antitrust action should only challenge behavior that obviously encourages collusion, such as agreements among rival producers to divide a market into exclusive territories.
>
> Since domestic producers try to use their political clout to reduce foreign competition through tariffs or import quotas, an open trade policy is as valuable as antitrust laws in the fight against collusion and anticompetitive behavior (Becker and Becker, 1997: 162–63).

Another Nobel Prize winning economist, George J. Stigler, began his career as a proponent of vigorous antitrust laws and enforcement. After studying the issue most of his professional life, however, he came to doubt the efficacy of antitrust policy. Here is how he summed up his opposition to the Robinson–Patman Act in 1969, before the Subcommittee on Small Business and the Robinson–Patman Act of the House Select Committee on Small Business:

> The Robinson–Patman Act is opposed by virtually all economists. I hope the Sub-committee will reflect upon the fact that if all the prominent economists in favor of the Robinson–Patman Act were put in a Volkswagen, there would still be room for a portly chauffeur (Stigler, 1985: 127–28).

Perhaps the best indictment of antitrust policy is Dominick T. Armentano's *Antitrust and Monopoly*. His work is a major exploration of the economic theories underlying antitrust law, and how those theories are flawed, as well as the major court cases and regulatory actions in the antitrust area. He concludes that both "antitrust theory and history are an elaborate mythology with no solid foundation in either logic or fact." Here is a partial summary of his more scathing conclusions:

> In many of the classic antitrust cases, both public and private, the indicted defendant firms had lowered their prices, expanded their outputs, engaged in rapid technological change, and generally behaved in ways consistent with an efficient and rivalrous market process. Indeed, it was precisely this rivalrous behavior that may have precipitated the antitrust legal action. There is now wider recognition among antitrust specialists that competition is a process—not an equilibrium condition—and that antitrust (especially in the private cases) has been employed often as a legal club to thwart competitive behavior and protect existing market structure.
>
> Government, and not the market, is the source of monopoly power. Government licensing, certificates of public convenience, franchises, tariffs, and other legally restrictive devices can and do create monopoly, and monopoly power, for specific business organizations protected from open competi-

tion. Thus, ironically or intentionally, the bulk of the abusive monopoly in the business system has always been beyond the scope of antitrust law and antitrust policy.

Various scholars have demonstrated that these particular "antitrust" statutes were often supported and employed by established business interests in an attempt to restrain and restrict the competitive process. Unable to compete effectively with more efficient business organizations, certain special interests sought political and legislative restrictions in an attempt to secure or enhance existing market positions.

In many and important and embarrassing ways, the Borden controversy is a fitting climax—a climax of absurdity—with respect to price discrimination under the antitrust laws. It is the theoretical dead-end to which a mechanistic, demand-ignoring, "costs (should) determine prices" theorem can be pushed. The products under discussion were clearly distinguished in the mind, and in the market behavior of the consumers; the products did not really compete directly with each other; the products had different brand names, sold in different ways and at different prices, to different buyers. Yet they were declared by an "expert" regulatory commission and by the highest court in the land to be "equal" and of like grade and quality. Declaring it, apparently, would make it so.

What was the Borden Company to do under the circumstances? Were they to adulterate the production of private-brand evaporated milk in order to make it chemically "unequal"? Or were they to raise the price of the private-label milk to the Borden brand "equivalent"? The latter proposal would surely end the alleged "discrimination," although it could bring a huge loss in the sales to Borden on their private-label accounts. Of course they could lower the price of the Borden brand to the private label rates; but this action could bring the Justice Department down upon Borden for attempting to eliminate competition from the market. One would also have to assume, since Borden had not voluntarily adopted this policy, that such a reduction in price would lower, rather than increase, Borden's profits. In summation, therefore, Borden was illegally discriminating in price, and no change in its prices could have, it appears, been wholly consistent with the antitrust laws. Any change Borden might have made, other than giving up its private-label business altogether (a refusal to deal?), might have tended to "injure" someone in violation of the law (Armentano, 1990: 2, 3, 6, 191–192).

In studying the history of antitrust cases and policy, one is left with the conclusion that almost any type of pricing behavior by a company is in violation of the law. If a company raises its prices above its competitors, it must be a monopoly. If a company lowers its prices below that of its competitors, it is obviously engaging in predatory behavior. If a company maintains its prices for any period of time, it must be colluding with its competitors to fix prices.

Summary and Conclusions

Antitrust has a rich and fascinating history, rooted firmly in economic theory, as well as emotional appeal among the public, politicians, and the media. The Robber Barons have an infamous reputation among American culture, even though many would argue that it is a misapplied name for entrepreneurs who brought needed goods and services—at constantly lower prices—to the masses.

In any event, professionals need to be cognizant of the law and its implications for devising pricing strategies and tactics. And although the laws don't apply to services, if your customer is in manufacturing, or deals with distributors, then appropriate legal advice needs to be obtained to ensure that you are complying with all applicable federal and state antitrust laws.

19 ADVANCED PRICE THEORY

*Pricing is the moment of truth—all of marketing
comes to focus in the pricing decision.*

Raymond Corey, *Industrial Marketing: Cases and Concepts*, 1962

This chapter provides additional theories and concepts regarding advanced price theory. These can be used not only in the pricing of professional services, but also when professionals consult with their customers on pricing strategies and tactics. Although the information in this chapter is not necessary in order to implement Value Pricing inside your professional firm, if you are interested in price theory, the material will help you advance to the next level. Therefore, the contents are more broad and apply to a wider range of pricing scenarios than those encountered in a professional service firm.

The Three Functions of Price

Before the microeconomic ramifications of price are explored, it is essential to understand the macroeconomic function that prices perform. In any economy—from a planned, centralized structure, to a free market—prices perform three critical functions:

1) Prices transmit information;
2) Prices provide an incentive to adopt methods of production that are least costly and therefore use available resources for the most highly valued purposes; and
3) Prices determine who gets how much of the product—the distribution of income.

(Friedman and Friedman, 1990: 14)

In a sense, prices are a form of economic speech, and as such, should be protected with the same force and vigor with which the First Amendment protects free political and religious speech. In fact, Milton and Rose Friedman proposed such a constitutional amendment, in their book, *Free to Choose*: "Congress shall make no laws abridging the freedom of sellers of goods or labor to price their products or services" (ibid., 1990: 305).

When a government tries to suppress the freedom of prices to perform their functions, disaster usually develops. Whether it is the inability of the former communist countries to feed themselves—through the forced collectivization of agriculture—or wage and price controls—leading to chronic shortages of goods and services—trying to control prices by any mechanism other than the voluntary transactions between consenting adults is an abject failure. Corruption, black markets, violence, and endemic crime are usually the results of suppressing economic freedom.

There is little understanding, even among professionals, of the role prices play in any economy, be it communist or capitalist. The major theme running through this book is that ultimately it is the consumer who determines the value of anything in this world. In *Planned Chaos*, the great economist Ludwig von Mises writes:

> In the market economy the consumers are supreme. Their buying and their abstention from buying ultimately determine what the entrepreneurs produce and in what quantity and quality. It determines directly the prices of the consumer's goods and indirectly the prices of all producers' goods, e.g., labor and material factors of production. It determines the emergence of profits and losses and the formation of the rate of interest. It determines every individual's income. The focal point of the market economy is the market, i.e., the process of the formation of commodity prices, wage rates, and interest rates and their derivatives, profits, and losses. It makes all men in their capacity as producers responsible to the consumers. This dependence is direct with entrepreneurs, capitalists, farmers and professional men, and indirect with people working for salaries and wages. The market adjusts the efforts of all those engaged in supplying the needs of the consumers to the wishes of those for whom they produce, the consumers. It subjects production to consumption.
>
> It is the consumers who make poor people rich and rich people poor. It is the consumers who fix the wages of a movie star and an opera singer at a higher level than those of a welder or an accountant (Mises, 1947: 25–26).

To the often-made charge that a free market ends in complete chaos, with no central direction or unifying goals, Mises directs this stinging missive:

> No "automatic" and "anonymous" force actuate the "mechanism" of the market. The only factors directing the market and determining prices are purposive acts of men. There is no automatism; there are men consciously aiming at ends chosen and deliberately resorting to definite means for the attainment of these ends. There are no mysterious mechanical forces; there is only the will of every individual to satisfy his demand for various goods. There is no anonymity; there are you and I and Bill and Joe and all the rest. And each of us is engaged both in production and consumption. Each contributes his share to the determination of prices.
>
> The dilemma is not between automatic forces and planned action. It is between the democratic process of the market in which every individual has his share and the exclusive rule of a dictatorial body. Whatever people do in the market economy, is the execution of their own plans. In this sense every human action means planning. What those calling themselves planners advocate is not the substitution of planned action for letting things go. It is the substitution of the planner's own plan for the plan of his fellowmen. The planner is a potential dictator who wants to deprive all other people of the power to plan and act according to their own plans. He aims at one thing only: the exclusive absolute preeminence of his own plan.
>
> There is no such thing as an "excessive" advocacy of economic freedom. Men must choose between the market economy and socialism. The state can preserve the market economy in protecting life, health and private property against violent or fraudulent aggression; or it can itself control the conduct of all production activities. Some agency must determine what should be produced. If it is not the consumers by means of demand and supply on the market, it must be the government by compulsion (ibid., 29, 34).

It is hard to argue with Mises' logic, especially given the abject failure of planned economies throughout the world. Using this background of the macroeconomic importance of price, the discussion can move on to the microeconomics of pricing and how this integrates with the marketing function in business firms.

Pricing and Marketing

Pricing is an art. But art is not above scientific analysis or critical judgment. No matter how creative and beautiful an engineer designs a bridge, it still must be structurally sound. And while economic theory, especially "price theory," has great insight into the role prices play in an economy, it doesn't offer much guidance as to how those prices are set, at the margin, in the day-to-day running of a business enterprise.

Pricing is also a multidisciplinary and multifunctional subject, with conflicts between economists, accountants, financial management, marketing management, legal advisors, and government regulators. Pricing is seldom taught, in any great detail or systematic way, in the business schools, even among MBA and graduate students. Surveys conducted in the 1950s indicated that prices were set rather mechanistically, based upon cost-plus methods or simply imitating competitors.

With the arrival of a global economy, by the 1980s, this attitude began to change. "A 1984 survey revealed that top marketing executives considered pricing the most critical issue with which they had to contend" (Nagle and Holden, 1995: 14). In today's business environment, all but the most naive companies set their prices based on cost-plus formulas, or the me-too pricing of their competitors. If the business world has paid little attention to pricing, then professionals have been downright negligent in heeding this all-important marketing function.

Cost-Plus Pricing's Epitaph

In the past, cost-plus pricing has been the most popular way to set prices. The method appears to have achieved this status because it is financially prudent and is seen to be "fair." You mark up your costs by a reasonable return and you achieve a reasonable profit. This is simple, in theory, but in practice it is a prescription for mediocre financial results. As Thomas Nagle and Reed Holden point out in their excellent book, *The Strategy and Tactics of Pricing*:

The problem with cost-driven pricing is fundamental. In most industries it is impossible to determine a product's unit cost before determining its price. Why? Because unit costs change with volume. This cost change occurs because a significant portion of costs are "fixed' and must somehow be "allocated' to determine the full unit cost. Unfortunately, since these allocations depend on volume, which changes with changes in price, unit cost is a moving target (ibid: 3).

If one follows the internal logic of cost-plus pricing versus Value Pricing, it would look like this (adapted from ibid., 5):

Cost-Plus Pricing

Product → Cost → Price → Value → Customers

Value Pricing

Customers → Value → Price → Cost → Product

Notice how Value Pricing completely reverses the order of the strategic decisions necessary in offering products and services to the marketplace. The traditional cost-plus theory (and the theory which guides most professional firm's pricing policies) starts with a product and asks, "How much does it cost us to produce this product?" The answer dictates the price, which, it is hoped, is less than the perceived value to the ultimate customer. Alternatively, Value Pricing turns this process inside out, asking "How much does the customer value this offering?" Only then is the price determined, and that price also dictates the costs that will be incurred in producing the final product. The target price is not an estimate of internal costs to the firm but an external value to the customer. As Nagle and Holden point out:

> Strategic pricers do not ask, "What prices do we need to cover our costs and earn a profit?" Rather, they ask, "What costs can we afford to incur, given the prices achievable in the market, and still earn a profit?" Strategic pricers do not ask, "What price is this customer willing to pay?" but "What is our product worth to this customer and how can we better

communicate that value, thus justifying the price?" When value doesn't justify price to some customers, strategic pricers don't surreptitiously discount. Instead, they consider how they can segment the market with different products or distribution channels to serve these customers without undermining the perceived value to other customers. And strategic pricers never ask, "What prices do we need to meet our sales or market-share objectives?" Instead, they ask, "What level of sales or market share can we most profitably achieve?" (ibid., 2).

This is precisely how Lee Iacocca derived his success with the Ford Mustang in 1964. Iacocca didn't start with a group of costs in order to compete against the successful General Motors Corvette; he began, instead, by learning about what the customers wanted, and how much they would be willing to pay for it. This response determined what the car would have to sell for, which in turn dictated the amount of internal costs that could be justified to produce it. In April 1964, Ford introduced the Mustang at a base price of $2,368 and more were sold in the first year than any other car Ford had ever built, with net profits after the first two years of $1.1 billion, in 1964 dollars, "which was far more than any of Ford's competitors made selling their "good" sports cars, priced to cover costs and achieve a target rate of return" (ibid., 6–7).

This is not to say that internal costs are unimportant, or irrelevant, to the pricing decision. But the effective pricer will invest only in those costs that can be recouped through the value offered in the market, not the other way around. Costs do not dictate quantities produced, but rather the price acceptable to the market will dictate which markets can be adequately served, and what quantities they demand. Consider the airlines. When the cost of jet fuel rises, airlines are not naive enough to try to pass on the entire cost increase to their customers while at the same time maintaining their existing flight schedules. Instead they will do something such as reduce or eliminate discount fares or reduce the number of flights.

More significantly, not all costs are relevant for every pricing decision. One of the disservices that cost accountants foisted upon service industries was the idea of fixed vs. variable costs. Since these costs need to be fully allocated over a given quantity of units, this procedure often results in a completely arbitrary allocation. One of the concepts that activity-based costing, and marketing managers, use is that of the avoidable cost—that is, those costs that either have not yet been incurred or that can be reversed. The opposite of avoidable costs are sunk costs, those costs which are irreversible. Only avoidable costs are relevant for pricing decisions.

Avoidable costs deal mostly with the future costs, not the historical costs, of making a sale. In 1999, gas prices in Northern California jumped to close to $2 per gallon, causing much public outcry and consternation, not to mention political posturing among politicians. If you were to inquire of people how much it costs an oil company to sell a gallon of gas, they would most likely respond with the cost of the oil, plus refining it and distributing it to the stations. But oil company executives understand that these historical costs are irrelevant and it is the replacement cost that is important in determining the sales price. Conventional accounting ignores this reality. Even last-in, first-out (LIFO) doesn't capture the true essence of the pricing dilemma. Actually, one needs to calculate the next-in, first-out (NIFO) cost in order to determine the sales price at the pump. Since each gallon sold of the old gasoline has to be replaced with a new gallon, it is the replacement cost that is important, not the historical cost.

The other difference between basing pricing on avoidable costs rather than on traditional cost-plus methods is deciding when certain costs are to be considered. At some point—especially in the long run—every cost is incremental and therefore avoidable. The importance of this concept is that it is customers, not costs, that determine what a product or service can sell for, and this drives which costs can be profitably incurred, given the expected revenue.

The Limitations of Economic Demand Theory

In Chapter 5, the law of demand and demand elasticity was discussed. It was stated that before buyers were considered to be on the demand curve, they had to be both willing and able to purchase the product. These are not the only assumptions made in that particular model. The model also assumes rational behavior among buyers, and to the economist that means perfect information about prices, being able to process that information perfectly, prices that do not affect subjective wants or satisfaction, and perfect information about tastes and preferences.

These are big assumptions, and may not actually be realistic in the marketplace, where information is often imperfect or not readily available, though the Internet is changing this dramatically. (See the discussion of electronic commerce in Chapter 12). Given this level of imperfection among buyers, perception becomes very important. If customers do not possess perfect information with respect to a product or service, they tend to resort to reference prices. This could be what they have paid in the past, the perceived average market cost, or a perceived "fair" price. This is why buyer's experience "sticker shock" when they haven't purchased a car in four to six years, even though the price of cars may not have increased as much as food or other consumer products. It also explains why seniors react more negatively to prices; they have reference prices from an earlier time that are much lower. Usually, buyers don't have any one specific acceptable price, but rather a range of prices they might be willing to pay for an item.

This leads to an interesting phenomenon. Not only will customers refrain from buying if the price is far above their reference price, they will also refrain from buying if that price is too far below their acceptable range. This latter phenomenon is not considered in the traditional law of demand. Customers' responses to prices are based on more than simple rational calculation, as assumed in traditional economic demand models. Yet most pricing experts agree that the mental behavior governing a customer's response to price is too little understood. In a purely rational sense, a difference of $400 between two products is the same no matter what the product price is. However, that same $400 is perceived to be a much larger difference for a $1,000 purchase than it is for a $20,000 purchase. In one study, 68 percent of the respondents said they were willing to drive to another store to save $5 on a calculator selling for $15; but if the same calculator costs $125, only 29 percent of the respondents were willing to do so (Nagle and Holden, 1995: 300).

The tendency of buyers to engage in this type of calculation is known the *Weber-Fechner Law*, which states that *buyers perceive price differences in proportional terms, not absolute terms*. This refers to the percentage change in price, and not to the absolute level, and indicates that there is an upper and lower threshold of price in the mind of each customer. If the price falls outside of that band, the customer will ignore the offering.

The notion of perceived value is difficult for even a customer to determine, let alone a firm trying to market to that customer. Part of the marketing department's job is to raise the price customers are willing to pay for their offering. The calculation of perceived value looks something like this:

$$\text{Perceived value} \quad = \quad \frac{\text{perceived benefits}}{\text{perceived price}}$$

Perceived price = perceived total cost to the buyer: purchase price + start-up costs (acquisition costs, transportation, installation, order handling) + postpurchase costs (repairs and maintenance and risk of failure or poor performance)

Perceived benefits = some combination of physical attributes, service attributes, and technical support available in relation to the particular use of the product, as well as the purchase price and other indicators of perceived quality (Monroe, 1990: 88).

All of these perceptions are relatively difficult to quantify and this complicates the marketer's job even further. Even how the product is going to be used affects the customer's perception of its value. "In one study, it was determined that buyers were willing to pay significantly more for a pair of pants to be worn to a symphony or cocktail party than if the pants were to be worn at a football game or rock concert" (ibid., 62). In fact, perception plays such an important role in the minds of customers, it might be deemed the sixth "P" of marketing. The topic of perceptions and psychology and their effect on pricing will be covered later in this chapter.

Three Generic Pricing Strategies

As was discussed in the chapter on Total Quality Service, the Value Proposition of any firm is Price, Quality, and Service. Price can be an effective way to compete for some companies. Think of Wal-Mart, Southwest Airlines, Costco, Dell Computers, or Timex watches. All of these companies have used price as an effective competitive differentiation and have relentlessly driven out needless costs from their operations. On the opposite side of the spectrum there is Nordstrom, Cadillac, Mercedes, FedEx, and Disney, all of which command premium prices because they offer premium service. In the middle might be companies such as Buick and Casio watches, in which price plays a more neutral role.

Any business has to decide between three generic pricing strategies: skim pricing, penetration pricing, and neutral pricing. Selecting one of these strategies is a major marketing decision, not to be taken lightly, and must be adopted by the leaders of the organization, as it will transmit a definitive message to the marketplace regarding the firm's offering.

Skim Pricing

In any market, a certain segment of buyers is relatively price insensitive because these buyers value the offering so highly. Think of early adopters in the technology industry who rush to purchase the latest and greatest gadgets or newest high speed computers and printers. Skim pricing is a conscious decision to sell to this segment at prices above market-level, thereby earning more profit than could be made selling at a lower price to an albeit wider market. The firm isn't so much interested in market share as it is in extracting the perceived value from this smaller segment of the market. Polaroid, for example, knew that a certain group of customers valued highly the ability to see their pictures immediately (real estate agents, insurance claims adjusters, grandparents with discretionary income) and thus engaged in skim pricing from this segment of the market, even if this strategy severely limited its penetration into the wider market. Apple Computer maintained the same strategy by forbidding cloning and keeping its gross profit margins higher than the industry average from devoted Macintosh users.

While many business consultants argue that market share determines profitability, this is patently false if one examines the empirical evidence in the marketplace. Sears certainly has a larger share of the retail market than does Nordstrom, but it would be nonsensical to argue that Nordstrom isn't profitable or as successful as Sears.

Penetration Pricing

Penetration pricing is when the firm decides to set the price below the product's value to the customer, thereby ensuring a larger customer base. It is the trade-off of higher sales volume vs. higher margins and can be a very effective strategy, especially for new entrants into a particular market.

Penetration prices are not necessarily cheap, but they are low relative to the perceived value. For instance, Lexus used a penetration pricing strategy in order to compete successfully with Mercedes, Audi, BMW, and Porsche in the early 1990s. The Lexus wasn't necessarily cheap, but it was less expensive than its competitors and thus was perceived to offer a higher value. MCI and Sprint used penetration pricing against AT&T after the telecommunications market was deregulated, to great success.

Neutral Pricing

In effect, this strategy minimizes the role of pricing in the marketing mix by not using price to gain or to restrict market share. A company may select this strategy when it knows its product, promotion, or distribution offers other powerful advantages to the customer. The neutral price doesn't mean a price in between that of competitors, but it means neutral in relationship to value. Toshiba laptop computers, for example, are consistently priced above market level, but because they offer such excellent value, the market still perceives the price as neutral.

Another reason to adopt a neutral price is to maintain the coherence of a product line. General Motors, for instance, prices the Chevrolet Camaro at a level that makes it affordable to a wider market, even though there is a certain segment of that market willing to pay more for its sporty appearance and performance. Because GM already had a skimmed price product in its lineup (the Corvette), it didn't want to be redundant by offering another one.

Market Segmentation

One of the mistakes made by many companies, especially professional service firms, is their tendency to think of the "market" rather than the individuals who make up the market. As such, they develop pricing strategies based upon averages, even though this is woefully inadequate and seriously flawed and leads to extreme pricing errors. After all, there is no such thing as an "average" customer. This is why it is so important to segment a company's customers into different markets and price according to the value offered in each segment, which is called *market segmentation*.

In Chapter 5 we studied how various businesses employ market segmentation in order to capture the consumer surplus. Cosmetic companies and airlines all engage in market segmentation in order to charge different prices to different customers. Book publishers offer hard covers and soft covers. This is an extremely important pricing tactic, especially when you are trying to serve multiple segments within a given market. Following is a list of some of the many ways to segment a market among buyers and charge different prices to different customers.

Segmenting by buyer identification   Senior discounts, children's prices, college students, and coupon clippers are all examples of ways to identify different buyers.

Segmenting by purchase location   Dentists, opticians and other professionals sometimes maintain separate offices, in different parts of the same city, or in different cities, that charge different prices based upon the economic and demographic make-up of each. With the increasing use of the Internet to make purchases, being able to segment by location will become more and more difficult.

Segmenting by time of purchase   Theaters offering midday matinees, restaurants having cheaper prices for lunch rather than dinner, and cellular and utility companies price based upon peak and off-peak times.

Segmenting by purchase quantity   Quantity discounts are usually based on volume, order size, step discounts or two-part prices. Customers who buy in large volumes tend to be more price sensitive and less costly to service, and they have more incentive to shop for a cheaper price. Thus, they are offered volume discounts. When offering discounts to business buyers, one must be careful not to violate the antitrust laws against price discrimination, as discussed in Chapter 18.

Two-part pricing involves two separate charges to consume a single product. Amusement parks might charge an entrance fee and then price tickets for certain attractions extra. Rental car companies use a flat price plus a price per mile, health care and country clubs charge both membership fees and monthly dues, while night clubs charge a cover at the door as well as for drinks and food.

Segmenting by product design   Different versions in a product or service offering are a very effective way to segment a market. Premium gasoline, for instance, only costs the oil companies approximately $0.04 more in refining, but sells at the pump anywhere from $0.10 to $0.15 more.

Segmenting by product bundling   Restaurants bundle food on the dinner menu as opposed to ala carte, usually at cheaper prices. Symphonies, theaters, and sports teams bundle a package of events into season tickets (See the discussion of menu pricing, and how this type of bundling applies to the professional service firm, in Chapter 12).

Segmenting by tie-ins and meterings Before the Clayton Antitrust Act of 1914, tie-in sales were common. American Can, for instance, leased its canning machines with the requirement that they be used to close only American's cans. Since the passage of the Clayton Act, the courts have refused to accept tying agreements, except for service contracts where it is essential to maintain the performance and/or the reputation of a new product. While using the tying method with a contract may be illegal, opportunities still exist to use this tactic without contract. For example, razor blade manufacturers design unique razors that require customers to purchase their blades for refill.

Segmented pricing is among the most effective pricing tactics that a business can employ, and it also among the most difficult. It takes enormous creativity, market and customer research in order to be effective. With the increasing propensity for customers to utilize the Internet to make their purchases, market segmentation will take on a new dynamic. While it will become easier to segment potential customers based upon their profiles and buying habits, it will also require experimentation with different pricing policies. Nevertheless, customer segmentation is a part of any effective marketing strategy, and its potential to add to profitability should never be ignored.

Search, Experience, and Credence Attributes

From a marketing perspective, products and services can be separated into three classes: search products, experience products, and credence products. Search products or services have attributes customers can readily evaluate before they purchase. A hotel room price, an airline schedule, television reception, or the quality of a home entertainment system can all be evaluated before a purchase is made. Well informed buyers will be aware of the substitutes that exist for these types of products and thus are more likely to be price sensitive than other buyers. This, in turn, will induce sellers to copy the most popular features and benefits of these types of products. Price elasticity is high with respect to products with many substitutes, and since most buyers will be aware of their alternatives, prices will be held within a competitive band.

Experience products or services can be evaluated only after purchase. Dinner in a new restaurant, a concert or theater performance, a new movie, or a hairstyle all must first be experienced before judgment can be passed on their relative value. These types of products and services tend to be more differentiated than search products or services and buyers tend to be less price elastic, especially for the first purchase. However, since they will form an opinion after the experience, if it is not favorable, no amount of differentiation will bring them back.

Credence products or services have attributes that buyers cannot confidently evaluate, even after one or more purchases. Thus, buyers tend to rely on the reputation of the brand name, testimonial from someone they know (or respect), service quality, and price. Credence products include healthcare; legal services; and accounting, tax, and consulting services. Credence products and services are more likely than the others to be customized, making them difficult to compare to other offerings. Since there are fewer substitutes to a customized product or service, and there is more risk in purchasing these types of products and services, price elasticity tends to be relatively low—that is, the majority of customers purchasing credence products and services are relatively price insensitive.

One of the lessons of categorizing products and services in this fashion applies to menu pricing, or bundling various offerings. In order for price bundling to be effective, at least one of the bundled offerings should be a search product because buyers of that product will tend to be more price sensitive and then can be induced to move up—in price—to the more valuable credence offerings.

Price Sensitivity

The three categories discussed above help marketing managers determine a customer's price sensitivity to products and services, as well as the customer's perceptions of value. Other methods also help to determine the price sensitivity of the customer. One might get the impression, given the sophistication of economic research techniques and marketing studies (especially with modern-day computers), that measuring price sensitivity among customers would be more of a science than an art. That impression, however, would be incorrect. Here is how Nagle and Holden explain this misconception:

> The implication that somehow soft managerial judgments
> about buyers are actually more fundamental to successful

pricing than are numerical estimates based on hard data may come as somewhat of a surprise. Managerial judgments are necessarily imprecise, while in contrast, an empirical estimate of price sensitivity is a definite, concise number that management can use for profit projections and planning. However, the fact that empirical estimates of price sensitivity are concise does not imply that they are accurate. The history of marketing research reveals that estimates of price sensitivity are frequently far off the mark. . . . Accuracy is a virtue in formulating pricing strategy; conciseness is only a convenience.

If one were forced to choose between estimating price sensitivity by informed judgment or by concise empirical estimation, judgment would be the better choice. No estimation technique can capture the full richness of the factors that enter a purchase decision. In fact, measurements of price sensitivity are concise precisely because they exclude all the factors that are not conveniently measurable.

Managers deceive themselves into thinking that an estimate of price sensitivity based on hard date is as precise as it is concise (Nagle and Holden, 1995: 349–350).

The above is certainly true with respect to the purchase of credence products and services, perhaps less true with search products and services. Many factors influence a customer's price sensitivity, and managers need to understand these factors long before setting a price to various market segments.

Nagle and Holden identify the following ten factors affecting price sensitivity:

1. Perceived substitutes effect

This effect states that buyers are more price sensitive the higher the product's price relative to its perceived substitutes. New customers to a market may be unaware of substitutes and thus may pay higher prices than more experienced buyers. Restaurants in resort areas face less pressure to compete based upon price (which locals may describe as "tourist traps"). Branding can also overcome, to a certain extent, the substitute effect. Woolite, for example, has maintained a relatively expensive price because it positions itself as an alternative to dry cleaning. Customers have a reference price when there are many substitutes, and as long as the offering is within that range it will be considered acceptable.

2. Unique value effect

Buyers are less price sensitive the more they value the unique attributes of the offering. This is precisely why marketers expend so much energy and creativity trying to differentiate their offering from that of their competitors. Heinz ketchup, for example, developed a secret formula for making its product thicker and was able to increase its market share from 27 to 48 percent while maintaining a 15 percent wholesale price premium. The Volvo automobile has a reputation as the safest car, an attribute many find desirable and are willing to pay a premium to acquire (not just in price but lower fuel economy and performance).

Auction houses rely on the unique value effect in order to command the prices they do among their bidders. Rare artifacts from the John F. Kennedy estate are known as "positional" or "expressive" goods, since the people who purchase them are trying to position themselves in society, or express who or what they are (art collectors, for example).

3. Switching cost effect

Buyers will be less price sensitive the higher the costs (monetary and nonmonetary) of switching vendors. Airlines that have a fleet of Boeing airplanes may be reluctant to switch to Airbus because of the enormous investment they have in their pilots, flight crews, and the mechanics of operating a certain plane. Many people are unwilling to give up certain software products due to the learning and familiarity they have with their existing product. Personal relationships are most susceptible to this type of perceived cost, due to the emotional investment the customer has made in the relationship. Childcare providers, doctors, lawyers, and accountants all can benefit from this effect, especially if they provide Total Quality Service.

4. Difficult comparison effect

Customers are less price sensitive with a known or reputable supplier when they have difficulty in comparing alternatives. People eat at McDonald's, continue to use AT&T, lodge at Marriott, and shop at J.C. Penney because they are familiar with these offerings and perceive them to be less risky than unknown alternatives. Stockbrokers price based on different criteria (shares of stock traded or value of shares traded), making it difficult for the customer to compare one with the other. IBM was perhaps the best example of this effect, with the famous saying, "No one ever got fired for choosing IBM."

5. Price quality effect

Buyers are less sensitive to a product's price to the extent that a higher price signals better quality. These products can include image products, exclusive products, and products without any other cues as to their relative quality. Rolls Royce is an example of an image product because it would be hard to argue it offers more superior value to, say, a Lexus or Mercedes. A Rolex watch is another example. Certainly one does not buy it for accurate timekeeping. These type of prestige products are an important form of marketing. Witness designer clothing and accessories, American Express' Gold and Platinum Cards—which command enormous premiums over alternative cards—and first-class travel, which many people use not because of more leg room but because of the reduced probability of sitting next to loud children or talkative sightseers when they are trying to get work done.

Some products might even be judged solely on price. A synthetic car wax failed in the market at a price of $0.69 until the price was raised to $1.69 Many consumers still have a common visceral reaction that high price equates to high value (and quality). Marketers have discovered that utilizing a high price for new products is quite effective for signaling quality to the marketplace. Other marketing research has shown that while discounting familiar brands can increase sales, the same strategy for unknown brands can actually reduce sales.

6. Expenditure effect

Buyers are more price sensitive when the expenditure is larger, either in dollar terms or as a percentage of household income. A one-office accounting firm may not pay much attention to the price of paper clips, but an international firm that buys in large quantities will. Business purchases will look at the total amount of the purchase, while households will compare the expenditure to total income. Many people won't expend much energy shopping for the lowest price of gum, but they will put more effort into searching for an automobile or a home. Higher income customers often will pay higher prices because they do not have the time to shop as thoroughly as low income individuals.

7. End-benefit effect

This effect is especially important when selling to other businesses. What is the end-benefit they are seeking? Is it cost-minimization, maximum output, or quality improvement? This is often gauged by the share of the total cost. For instance, when steel suppliers sell to auto manufacturers, the price of the steel is a large component of the cost of the car; when steel is sold to a luggage manufacturer, the steel cost is relatively minimal compared to the other material used. High-end auto wax, marketed to luxury car owners at $40 and up is not a significant cost to operating a $50,000 automobile. "AOG," in the airline industry, stands for Airplane On Ground, and usually an AOG is awaiting some small replacement part. How price sensitive is the airline with respect to a $100 electrical switch that could get the plane back in the air and saves countless thousands of dollars?

The end-benefit effect also is psychological. Think of going out for a romantic anniversary dinner and paying with a two-for-one coupon. Most people view price shopping as tacky when the purchase involves something emotional. Wedding florists, caterers, and bands certainly understand this principle. The larger the end-benefit, the less price sensitive the buyer will be. Think of the Michelin tire ads, showing a picture of a baby in diapers next to its radial tire, proclaiming: "Michelin. Because so much is riding on your tires."

8. Shared-cost effect

Chapter 4 looked at the fact that when you spend someone else's money on yourself, you are not prone to be price conscious. This is why airlines, hotels, and rental car companies can all price discriminate against the business traveler, because most of them are not paying their own way. This is also explains some of the success of the frequent flyer and other reward programs. Many business travelers value these rewards and won't accept alternative offerings, especially since they are reimbursed anyway. Also, publications, educational seminars, and other business expenses are tax deductible and this reduces the buyer's price sensitivity relating to various business expenses.

9. Fairness effect

Notions of fairness can certainly effect the customer, even when they are not economically (or mathematically) rational. If a gas station sells gas for $1.30 per gallon, and gives a $0.10 discount if the buyer pay with cash and another gas station offers the same gallon at $1.20, but they charge a $0.10 surcharge if the customer pays with a credit card, which station will sell more gas to credit card users? The economic cost is the exact same, but most people will psychologically prefer to deal with the first station and not the second because there appears to be something inherently unfair about being assessed a surcharge.

In the past, rental car companies charged their customers if they brought back the car with less than a full tank of gas, and the price was usually two to three times the market rate. Many business travelers, who value their time more than vacationers, viewed this as being completely unfair, so they took the time to fill the tank before returning the car. Finally, the rental car companies figured out that fairness was an issue, and now they price their "gas options" at less than the prevailing market price, inducing a large percentage of the business travelers to opt to pay them for the gas. This has turned into a nice profitable service for the rental car companies, now that it is perceived as being fair.

Perceptions of fairness are differentiated based upon whether the product or service is a necessity or a luxury. This is why the pharmaceutical industry can receive such public condemnation when it prices new wonder drugs at a premium, even if these drugs prevent other, more costly, medical interventions. It is also why people will boycott stores that hike up the price of needed food, water, and building materials after a natural disaster. Companies that price based on capacity or season are careful to maintain relatively high regular prices so that they can be seen as giving discounts to most customers, which is perceived as being "more fair" than charging a premium above a lower "regular" price. Insurance companies emphasize peace of mind and security, rather than preventing a loss, which most customers resent having to pay for.

10. Inventory effect

The ability of buyers to carry an inventory will also affect their price sensitivity. Amateur cooks with large pantries will stock up on a good deal but a single person living in a small apartment will not. The perishability of the item in question is another factor to consider.

Analyzing price sensitivity is certainly an important task for any business that wants to maximize the value it receives from its offering. Taking into account the ten factors above that affect price sensitivity is a good start. Nagle and Holden offer the following set of questions that should be asked about each of the above factors in preparing a managerial analysis of price sensitivity (ibid., 95–99):

1. Perceived substitutes effect

What alternatives are buyers (or segments of buyers) typically aware of when making a purchase?

To what extent are buyers aware of the prices of those substitutes?

To what extent can buyers' price expectations be influenced by the positioning of one brand relative to particular alternatives, or by the alternatives offered them?

2. Unique value effect

Does the product have any unique (tangible or intangible) attributes that differentiate it from competing products?

What attributes do customers believe are important when choosing a supplier?

How much do buyers value unique, differentiating attributes?

How can one increase the perceived importance of differentiating attributes and/or reduce the importance of those offered by the competition?

3. Switching cost effect

To what extent have buyers already made investments (both monetary and psychological) in dealing with one supplier that they would need to incur again if they switched suppliers?

For how long are buyers locked in by those expenditures?

4. Difficult comparison effect

How difficult is it for buyers to compare the offers of different suppliers? (Be sure to account for the Internet in your answer).

Can the attributes of a product be determined by observation, or must the product be purchased and consumed to learn what it offers?

What portion of the market has positive past experience with your products? With the brands of the competition?

Is the product highly complex, requiring costly specialists to evaluate its differentiating attributes?

Are the prices of different suppliers easily comparable, or are they stated for different sizes and combinations that make comparisons difficult?

5. Price-quality effect

Is a prestige image an important attribute of the product?

Is the product enhanced in value when its price excludes some consumers?

Is the product of unknown quality and are there few reliable cues for ascertaining quality before purchase?

6. Expenditure effect

How significant are buyers' expenditures for the product in absolute dollar terms (for business buyers) and as a portion of income (for end consumers)?

7. End-benefit effect

What end-benefits do buyers seek from the product?

How price sensitive are buyers to the cost of the end-benefit?

What portion of the end-benefit does the price of the product account for?

To what extent can the product be repositioned in customers' minds as related to an end-benefit for which the buyer is less cost sensitive or which has a larger total cost?

8. Shared-cost effect

Does the buyer pay the full cost of the product?

If not, what portion of the cost does the buyer pay?

9. Fairness effect

How does the product's current price compare with prices people have paid in the past for products in this category?

What do buyers expect to pay for similar products in similar purchase contexts?

Is the product seen as necessary to maintain a previously enjoyed standard of living, or is it purchased to gain something more out of life?

10. Inventory effect

Do buyers hold inventories of the product?

Do they expect the current price to be temporary?

Pricing and the Competition

Pricing does not take place in a vacuum. It is more akin to a game of chess, where one player will make a move, alter the dynamics of the game, and the opponent will try to counteract that move. Frequently managers will complain about pricing problems and pressures, but these are rarely mere pricing problems. They usually deal with communication, branding, image, product, distribution, segmentation, and other ill-conceived, or often ignored, functions of a cohesive marketing strategy.

Managers will also let capacity utilization play a devastating psychological game with their pricing, especially when they are underutilized. The logic will always be better some job (at a low cost) than no job at all. This could have very serious long-run consequences, such as sending a message to the market that you will capitulate on your pricing policies.

Also, almost all companies claim to want to sell a differentiated product or service to the market, but often the sales force is not given the proper training or the proper incentives. Pricing on value takes time and energy, and many salespeople will resort to their comfort zone and cut price in order to make the sales quotas. Price is perhaps the quickest way to influence sales volume, and it is certainly easier than branding, image, distribution, packaging, marketing and product changes, not to mention cheaper.

It must be constantly remembered that pricing can only capture value—it does not create it. Value is created based on a company's competitive advantages. If a company is not attaining its desired price from the market, usually more is wrong than simple cutthroat competition.

A business should be cognizant of its competitors pricing strategies; customers certainly will be, especially through the Internet. But don't fall into the often repeated error of thinking that your competitors set the upper boundary of your price. Your customers set the boundaries of your price, both the lower and the upper end. If you listen closely enough, your customers will always communicate to you—both in words, and more importantly, in actions—what price they are willing and able to pay.

Summary and Conclusions

Pricing cannot be reduced to neat mathematical formulas and checklists. To be successful, pricing must be adapted to both the internal and external environments of the business. Pricing is a strategic marketing decision and deserves just as much attention as packaging, distribution, advertising, and promotion. Pricing decisions need to be made with a full understanding of the long-term ramifications of those decisions. Lowering price to make the next sale should never be permitted, unless it is part of a coherent marketing strategy. The four cardinal rules of strategic marketing are: Know your costs; know your demand; know your competition and your market; and most, importantly, know your objectives.

Anything less will subject you to the vagaries and whims of your competition and sales force. Following the strategies outlined in this chapter will help you achieve your pricing goals, and hence your profitability goals.

20 CONCLUSION

*There is nothing more difficult to take in hand, more perilous
to conduct, or more uncertain in its success than to take the lead in
the introduction of a new order of things.*

—Niccolo Machiavelli,
Florentine statesman
and philosopher

Things do not change; we change.

—Henry David Thoreau

Rigidity is what most organizations manifest when faced with either superior competition or outdated processes. They blindly cling to "that is the way we have always done it" in defiance of the evidence that this way is no longer relevant to success. Charles F. Kettering, the automotive inventor and pioneer, said it best: "If you have always done it that way it is probably wrong." Edward de Bono explains the phenomenon of change, and how it almost always is imposed from the outside, in his book *Sur/petition: Creating Value Monopolies When Everyone Else Is Merely Competing:*

> The value of being familiar with a field is that both the explicit and hidden patterns are available and applicable, and they cover most situations. It is also possible, however, to become trapped within these familiar patterns. That is where a certain kind of creative innocence comes in. A person who does not have these established patterns can see something in a fresh way.
>
> That is also why industries that have traditionally been inward looking (particularly the auto industry and retailing) are slow to change. A person within the field can never have the freshness of innocence, so creativity has to be obtained in a different way—through the deliberate escape from fixed patterns (de Bono, 1993: 51–52).

This is the history of business. New ideas, inventions, and experiments from the tinkerer in the garage change the world, while rendering obsolete the existing modes of production, infrastructure, and status quo. The automobile replaced the horse and buggy, the calculator replaced the slide rule, the personal computer replaced the typewriter.

The legal and accounting professions, however, have been slow to adopt and even resistant to adopt the changes taking place in the marketplace today. Never before has this mentality been such a hindrance to success in today's rapidly changing marketplace. *How many CPAs does it take to change a light bulb? Ten. One to change it and nine to talk about how great the old one was.*

Innovation and creativity always come as a surprise from outside the traditional paradigms of the experts. Otherwise, you could plan on it and incorporate it into your existing strategies and processes and the economy could be run simply by governmental bureaucrats and computers. Here are some all-time best blunders on the part of the "experts":

> In 1886, the Gottlieb Daimler Company [Mercedes Benz today] predicted the ultimate size of the world's automobile market to be an eventual total of one million, rationalizing that there could be no more than one million trained chauffeurs in the world.

> "Flight by machines heavier than air is impractical and insignificant, if not utterly impossible." (Simon Newcomb, an astronomer of some note, 1902)

> "The horse is here to stay, but the automobile is only a novelty—a fad." (The president of the Michigan Savings Bank to Henry Ford's lawyer in 1903).

> "It is an idle dream to imagine that . . . automobiles will take the place of railways in the long distance movement of . . . passengers." (American Road Congress, 1913)

> "There is no likelihood man can ever tap the power of the atom." (Robert Millikan, Nobel Prize winner in physics, 1920)

> "The problem with television is that people must sit and keep their eyes glued to the screen. The average American family doesn't have time for it" (The New York Times, 1939).

"I think there is a world market for about five computers."
(Thomas J. Watson, chairman of IBM, 1943)

Engage in this thought experiment: The following go to the government industrial planning board with ideas on launching a new product (or service):

1. A failed haberdasher
2. A Harvard sophomore dropout
3. A junior college dropout
4. General Motors executives

Which one is the government most likely to invest in? If you answered General Motors, move to the head of the class. Government will always focus on the status quo because that is where the votes are. The employees of General Motors can easily understand that their new project was funded by a certain political party, and therefore they will vote accordingly. However, the government doesn't have much to gain by investing in the other three individuals. But who are they? The failed haberdasher is Sam Walton, founder of Wal-Mart. The Harvard sophomore dropout is Bill Gates, founder of Microsoft. The six-month junior college dropout is Rush Limbaugh, founder of the Excellence In Broadcasting (EIB) Network. All of these entrepreneurs were scoffed at by the existing establishment. Rush Limbaugh was incessantly told that his format for a call-in talk radio show would never work.

Risk Taking

Entrepreneurs are society's perennial risk takers, and they almost always disrupt the status quo. According to Steven E. Landsburg:

> Entrepreneurial initiatives are intensely personal. In the 1950s Joseph Wilson (later head of Xerox) had a vision of the copying machine as a tool that would transform American business. At the time, few shared his vision. Most visions fail. Should such visions be pursued? From a social point of view, risk-averse individuals underinvest in risky projects. The existence of corporations helps to solve this problem, since the

shareholders, with diversified portfolios, will encourage appropriate risk-taking. However, intensely personal visions cannot always be effectively pursued by large corporations. In such cases only the prospect of great personal fortune will induce individuals to take great risks. A society that attempted to limit the amassing of great wealth might be a society without copying machines (Landsburg, 1996: 652–53).

The future brings risk, and if your future includes implementing Value Pricing, then it will bring even more risk. But risk is also where profits come from. The more risks you take, the higher your rewards will be. In his comprehensive study of risk, *Against the Gods: The Remarkable Story of Risk*, Peter Bernstein points out:

The word "risk" is derived from the early Italian *risicare*, which means "to dare." In this sense, risk is a choice rather than a fate. The actions we dare to take, which depend on how free we are to make choices, are what the story of risk is all about. And that story helps define what it means to be a human being (Bernstein, 1996: 8, 105).

Paradigm Shift

The word paradigm comes from the Greek word *pattern*. A paradigm is nothing more than a mental model of the way the world works. But as the Jewish folk saying says, "We do not see things as they are. We see them as *we* are." In his book, *Paradigms: The Business of Discovering the Future*, Joel Arthur Barker makes the following points with respect to paradigms:

1. Our perceptions of the world are strongly influenced by paradigms.
2. Because we become so good at using our present paradigms, we resist changing them.
3. It is the outsider who usually creates the new paradigm.
4. Practitioners of the old paradigm who choose to change to the new paradigm early, must do so as an act of faith rather than as the result of factual proof, because there will never be enough proof to be convincing in the early stages.

5. Those who change to a successful new paradigm gain a new way of seeing the world and new approaches for solving problems as a result of the shift to the new rules.

6. A new paradigm puts everyone back to zero, so practitioners of the old paradigm, who may have had great advantage, lose much or all of their leverage.

(Barker, 1993: 198–99)

Changing your paradigms is the equivalent of climbing out of your comfort zones. That is not something routinely done without considerable anxiety. People don't *have* mental models. People *are* their mental models. The models are part of who you are, your experiences, and how you see the world.

An analogy from football is offered by Robert J. Kriegel and Louis Patler in *If It Ain't Broke...Break It!*

> A vivid example of the pitfalls of sticking to the conventional game plan in times of change occurred in football just after the turn of this century. In 1905, football was a low-scoring game of running and kicking. Guys in leather helmets and a smattering of padding plodded down the field toward the goal line. The offense consisted of formations like the "flying wedge," in which seven players ran together into the middle of the opposition in the hope of gaining three or four yards at a time. It was a tough, gritty game.
>
> Then, in 1906, the forward pass was legalized, making it possible to gain 40 yards with a flick of a wrist. During the first season, however, most teams stayed almost entirely within their conventional, tried and true running game.
>
> Recognizing that they were entering a new era in which the old strategy of "three yards and a cloud of dust" would fast become obsolete, St. Louis University's coaches adapted quickly, switching to an offense that used the forward pass extensively. That season *they outscored their opponents 402 to 11!* [Emphasis in original] (Kriegel and Patler, 1991:4)

Whenever the concepts discussed in this book are introduced to a firm, certain individuals always act like an organism's immune system and try to kill off anything that is foreign. That is fine, as it prevents organizations from wasting time and resources pursuing panaceas that probably would never work anyway.

However, this book has presented a compelling case for why hourly billing is an antiquated paradigm. All businesses struggle with pricing, one of the most complex, unsolvable enigmas of running an organization. No book, seminar, or consultant can remove the tension that Value Pricing will no doubt cause you.

Not a Fad

The most frequent comment on my course is something to the effect of: "Timely concepts." However, the concepts discussed in this book are not "timely." They are *timeless*. Most of them come from the great economists of the seventeenth and eighteenth century, who can hardly be characterized as "fad thinkers" or "management gurus."

In his book *Billing Innovations*, Richard Reed cites a survey conducted in 1993 by Altman Weil Pensa on alternative billing (Value Pricing):

> Of the respondents, 43.4 percent stated they were developing billing and pricing alternatives in response to client requests or demands; 29.5 percent indicated that they were actively developing alternative billing and pricing policies; 22.5 percent said they were not pursuing alternative billing strategies.
>
> The survey indicated that the most commonly used alternative to hourly billing was the fixed or flat fee for defined services. The practice area where alternative pricing strategies was most frequently used was in litigation, notwithstanding the sentiments of litigators expressed in 1987 that hourly billing was the only way to bill. The survey also reflected that other predominant practice areas where alternative billing strategies had been employed included corporate, real estate, estate planning, banking, employment, and personal injury (in that order). The attitude about alternative billing showed that 51.2 percent felt it "somewhat necessary," 24.8 percent "not critical," 20.9 percent "critical to survival/success," and 0.8 percent "unacceptable" (Reed, 1996: 97).

Reed continues to cite other surveys, such as *The National Law Journal's Annual Billing Survey* for 1993, which showed more than "one-third of the respondent firms used methods other than the straight hourly fee" (ibid., 97). The Mead Data Central survey found that "43 percent of the firms anticipated a decreased use of *standard* hourly billing." Further, "48 percent of America's largest law firms have made operational changes as a result of a shift in their billing methods. Large firms (those with 30 or more lawyers) are the firms most likely to have made these changes" (ibid., 99).

To counter the charge from professionals that firms that have switched to Value Pricing have been burned, the Mead Data Central survey offers this analysis:

> Firms that made operational changes in response to changes in billing practices are just as likely to say that profits increased as a result of changes in billing practices (45%) as they are to say their profits remained the same (44%). Fewer than on in ten (9%) large firms reported that profits decreased due to changes in billing practices. Computerization is the action most commonly taken to maintain or increase firm profitability. Half (54%) of large firms reported increased profitability due to changes in operations and technology. Even though relatively few firms derive a majority of their income from alternative billing methods, those that rely most on those methods appear more likely than other firms to report increases in profitability.
>
> The Mead Data Central study acknowledges that the business of law is changing. Law firms are beginning to respond to the demands of the market (ibid., 99).

For remaining skeptics, the 1993 Altman Weil Pensa survey mentioned above was updated in 1995, with 129 respondents from law firms ranging in size. Reed reports what this recent survey discovered:

- Litigation remains the practice area in which alternative methods are most frequently used.
- 64.3 percent of the respondents use alternative methods for both litigation and nonlitigation matters.
- 36.2 percent of the respondents believe that alternative billing is critical to survival/success, compared to 20.9 percent in 1993.

- In 1995, 79.5 percent of the respondents expect the use of alternative billing strategies will increase.
  (ibid., 100–101)

The shift from hourly billing has now affected the majority of lawyers, and CPAs are next. Just as CPAs followed the attorneys into hourly billing, they will follow them right back out of it. According to Everett M. Rogers, in the *Diffusion of Innovations*, when 13 percent of a population accept a new idea it's only a matter of time before at least 84 percent accept the idea, with *time* being the unknown (it's rare that any idea gets universal, 100 percent acceptance). This is the phenomena of critical mass, which is at the heart of any new innovation diffusion process. Once critical mass is reached, it is often impossible to halt the further diffusion of a new innovation. *The Adoption Model* illustrates how innovators and early adopters are leaders. The majority of the population waits for these leaders to undertake the process of change before joining in.

- **Innovators** are venturesome and willing to try new ideas at some risk. They are the first 2 1/2 percent to adopt innovation.
- **Early Adopters** are guided by respect from others. They are opinion leaders in their community and adopt new ideas early but carefully. They are the next 13 1/2 percent to adopt innovation.
- **Early Majority** are deliberate. They adopt new ideas before the average person but are rarely leaders. They are the next 34 percent to adopt innovation.
- **Late Majority** are skeptical. They adopt innovation only after a majority of people have tried it. They are the next 34 percent to adopt innovation.
- **Laggards** are bound by tradition, suspicious of changes, mix with other tradition-bound people, and adopt innovation only because it has now taken on a measure of tradition itself. They are the last 16 percent to adopt innovation, and often only make change when there are no alternatives (AICPA, 1998: 26).

A Testable Hypothesis

Some innovations are adopted more quickly than others. It all depends upon the perception of individuals as to whether or not a certain innovation is viewed as superior to the alternatives. According to Everett Rogers in *Diffusion of Innovations*, an innovation has the following five characteristics:

1. **Relative advantage**, as perceived by individuals
2. **Compatibility**—consistency with the existing values, past experiences, and needs of potential adopters
3. **Complexity**—the degree to which an innovation is perceived as difficult to understand and use. New ideas that are simpler to understand are adopted more rapidly than innovations that require the adopter to develop new skills and understandings.
4. **Trialability**—the degree to which an innovation may be experimented with on a limited basis, which are generally more quickly adopted than innovations that are not divisible.
5. **Observability**—the degree to which the results of an innovation are visible to others. The easier it is for individuals to see the results of an innovation, the more likely they are to adopt it (Rogers, 1995: 15–16).

Value Pricing scores well in all five of these characteristics, especially in trialability. It is a testable hypothesis; it is subject to being falsified by your experience in adopting it. Once you have gone through the FPA and Change Order process, you will then be able to observe objectively whether or not Value Pricing is an innovation you want your firm to adopt.

The Past Doesn't Equal the Future

When the American Bar Association published its first book on alternatives to hourly billing, they concluded that in all likelihood, hourly billing would always exist as a benchmark to value. Reed had this to say on the transformation in thought that he has witnessed in the legal profession:

> Although in preparing the two earlier books the Task Force on Alternative Billing Methods never contended that hourly billing would completely disappear, it is probable that straight hourly billing (billing by hours spent without limit and without regard for the benefits conferred) will virtually disappear in the years ahead.

Without a doubt, quality and value will be the keys to excellence and success in the years to come. Lawyer-client relationships based on mutual trust and satisfaction are prerequisites. The time has come to say goodbye to time as the *sole* criterion for measuring the value of legal services [Emphasis in original] (ibid., xiv).

No doubt all professionals are experiencing tumultuous change. James R. Kurtz, Publisher of *Outlook* magazine, wrote in the Fall 1996 issue about the dramatic changes taking place in the accounting profession:

The CPA profession is unquestionably midstream in unprecedented change. I can say that with the authority of someone who has been a student of the profession for 25 years.

Change is constant, but what we are now experiencing is distinct in three major ways:

1. The change is much **more comprehensive**. Many disciplines throughout Western culture are undergoing major paradigm shifts. Major transformational challenges in the environment, education, economics, religion, science, and health impact the larger social context in which they reside. Therefore, we must be much more aware of the larger context in order to become aware of changes affecting us.

2. The change is **discontinuous**; therefore, it is harder to predict based on past experience. Most of our training is based on past experience. In fact, the process of learning may be described as transforming experience into knowledge. The proper response to discontinuous change is continual learning.

3. Multitudes of paradigm shifts are **still in progress**, so it's anyone's guess what the new rules of success will be, and how each one will affect the others. There are no formulae, checklists, or advice to be relied upon in adapting to change this time. We are more dependent upon our *own thinking* than ever before.

Margaret J. Wheatley describes major change in *Leadership and the New Science*. She writes, "The new science cogently explains that there is no objective reality 'out there' waiting to reveal its secrets . . . there is only what we create through our engagement with others and events."

Creating through engagement with others and events is the heart of CPA services. The technical knowledge of the profession is not useful until it is applied to real problems or opportunities for clients or employers. Awash in the turbulence of the new changes, they are more in need of innovative services by CPAs than ever before.

Absorbing new principles or views of the world will undoubtedly take some time and will make for lots of doubt about their validity during the next decade. My point here is not to announce a brand new solution, but to point a beacon of light at a very important source of new thinking which is likely to have profound effects on our lives and the CPA profession.

The primary dilemma for individuals and organizations during this period is that the old paradigms have not entirely lost relevance to successful behavior, nor have the emerging new paradigms been completely framed. One has to be aware of the existing rules *and* the possibilities of new rules emerging on a constant basis.

Think about it, because we *are* becoming something distinctly different! [Emphasis in original] (Kurtz, 1996: 5)

The old paradigm of hourly billing is losing relevance to successful behavior. Old strategies rarely produce new results. There is enough empirical evidence from both inside and outside of the profession to convince an observer of this fact. On the other hand, Value Pricing—the new paradigm—has not been completely framed. Accept the challenge to help establish a new pricing tradition for the professions, one based on value, and free yourself from the tyranny of time.

According to the German philosopher Arthur Schopenhauer, all truth goes through three steps:

First, it is ridiculed.

Second, it is violently opposed.

Third, it is accepted as self-evident.

The purpose of this book is to encourage you to stretch beyond the traditional dimensions and move to the third level of truth by accepting these ideas as self-evident. Pricing for value will enable you to be paid what you are worth; stop sacrificing profits on the altar of the Almighty Hour.

I am always interested in your successes (and failures) with respect to implementing these concepts. Please feel free to contact me to share your thoughts or discuss a particular issue.

Ronald J. Baker, CPA
Baker & Barnett, CPAs
770 Tamalpais Drive, Suite 221
Corte Madera, CA 94925
(415) 927-7114
(415) 927-7154 fax
E-mail: BANDBCPAS@aol.com

The Things That Haven't Been Done Before

—Edgar Guest

The things that haven't been done before,
Those are the things to try;
Columbus dreamed of an unknown shore
At the rim of the far-flung sky,
And his heart was bold and his faith was strong
As he ventured in dangers new,
And he paid no heed to the jeering throng
Or the fears of the doubting crew.
The many will follow the beaten track
With guideposts on the way.
They live and have lived for ages back
With a chart for every day.
Someone has told them it is safe to go
On the road he has traveled o'er,
And all that they ever strive to know
Are the things that were known before.
A few strike out, without map or chart,
Where never a man has been,
From the beaten paths they draw apart
To see what no man has seen.
There are deeds they hunger alone to do;
Though battered and bruised and sore,
They blaze the path for the many, who
Do nothing not done before.
The things that haven't been done before
Are the tasks worthwhile today;
Are you one of the flock that follows, or
Are you one that shall lead the way?
Are you one of the timid souls that quail
At the jeers of a doubting crew,
Or dare you, whether you win or fail,
Strike out for a goal that is new?

APPENDIX

FREQUENTLY ASKED QUESTIONS, AND ANSWERS

Here are some of the most frequently asked questions about Value Pricing.

Q: Isn't price discrimination in violation of the antitrust laws and therefore illegal?

A: The antitrust laws do not apply to services, so price discrimination is not illegal. Further, the laws against price discrimination don't apply to sales of goods and services to the final user. Price discrimination is so ubiquitous that outlawing it would be impossible. It is simply capitalist acts between consenting adults. Price is a form of free speech in a market economy and should be respected as such. However, you should become educated with respect to the antitrust laws and how they may affect your customer's pricing decisions, especially if you are engaging in any consulting activities related to this topic.

Q: Price discrimination just won't work in my small town, because my customers tend to know one another.

A: I don't think this is as big a problem as it first appears. First, no two customers have the same needs and wants—let alone the same package of services provided by their professional. Second, customers readily understand charging different prices to different people, based upon a myriad of factors. They probably do this in their own businesses. Third, if you enter into an FPA with a customer, that document has been drafted with their involvement and ego investment, and is specifically tailored to them, making comparisons difficult. Finally, if this is truly a concern, and you have two customers who you know communicate about what they pay their professional, then you will need to be able to justify the price differential. However, don't let the tail wag the dog. This is the exception, not the rule, and you shouldn't let it prevent you in engaging in pricing based upon value. Remember Peter Drucker's sage advice: Don't solve problems, pursue opportunities.

Q: How will I know if I am making money on any one customer if I don't keep time sheets?

A: The real answer to this is that the time it takes you to perform a service is absolutely irrelevant to its value to the customer. Services have such a high gross profit that, if you priced based upon value, you would make a profit. The notion of cost accounting doesn't work well in service industries, where there are virtually no variable costs. Most of your costs are fixed—at least in the short run—and this is why most service industries have stopped trying to apply traditional cost accounting techniques to their businesses. Activity Based Costing is starting to yield more accurate information for service industries, based upon yield and load factors, as in the airline industry. The only reason professionals pay such fastidious attention to time is because it is intimately linked to their pricing. If you price based upon value, hours become superfluous.

Q: If I have two similar jobs in my practice and one is taking much longer than the other, how would I know to price them differently if I didn't record time?

A: Again, this is Marx's labor theory of value raising its ugly head. The time it takes you to perform a job is irrelevant to its price. If each job is priced based upon the value to that customer, and one job is taking more effort than the other, perhaps the firm is not as efficient as it should be. Maybe opportunities for Change Orders have been missed. Rarely are two jobs exactly alike. This is exactly the trap of hourly billing, and why we need to move away from it. Even thinking about this issue distracts you from focusing on the value delivered to the customer, which is going to be greater than your internal costs.

Q: You say customers don't pay for efforts, just results. How can you reconcile that view with a doctor who gets paid whether his or her treatment is successful or not (whether the patient lives or dies)? Or an attorney who loses a lawsuit? Aren't efforts, too, rewarded in a free market?

A: Absolutely, efforts are rewarded in a free market. But some are rewarded more than others. And it is the ones—in the long run—that produce the best results that are rewarded the most. How else could one explain the difference in pay between Michael Jordan and the average NBA player?

Would you pay for a car that "tried" to work? Lawyers who work on a contingency basis already share the risk of losing the lawsuit. Customers are demanding risk-sharing with their professionals, a trend that will continue.

The medical example is an excellent one, and it really points out the theory of price leverage. When you are ill—especially if you are critically ill— you will value a doctor's intervention, even if there is a low probability of its success. You are, in essence, taking a chance on the treatment. A service that is desired is more valuable than one that has been delivered. And people desire medical care, even if the treatment is not successful. The argument has been made that this is akin to taking advantage of people in an emergency. But how else should medical care be delivered? If people don't pay for it individually, they will pay for it through higher taxes. Then the government will ration the care, not based on price, but on other criteria. There is no such thing as free care. Witness the abject failure of socialized medicine.

Q: How can Value Pricing possibly apply to all firms, in all markets?

A: There is more than one way to implement Value Pricing. You will have to apply it to the specifics of your location, your customers, and your firm. But on a broad level, these concepts work. Value Pricing is based upon empirical evidence of how the real world works, and it is understood by most business people. Most marketing professionals understand these concepts and it is second nature to them. It is time other professionals caught up.

Q: I wholeheartedly believe in these concepts. How can I get my partners to buy in to this? Some of them are just adamant about the importance of keeping time and pricing based upon it.

A: There are no easy answers to this dilemma. Some people will always resist change or the adoption of a new idea. It is simple human nature. You will need to convince them with empirical evidence. Confronted with facts (and success), most professionals are rational enough to change their minds. But make no mistake, changing a firm's pricing policies requires leadership. And as Margaret Thatcher is fond of saying, consensus is the absence of leadership. The managing partner is going to have to take a strong stand on implementing Value Pricing and stick to it. Start Value Pricing on new customers, gain some successes—which will build confidence—and then, gradually, switch your entire firm over to this form of pricing.

Q: How do you see the wave of consolidations that are taking place in the profession? What do you think of the profession's entry into financial services, and how will this affect pricing in the future?

A: It is too early to tell what the ultimate impact on pricing will be with companies such as American Express Tax and Business Services, Century Business Services, and HRB Business Services buying up accounting firms. The same situation exists for the law profession now that Arthur Andersen is the world's largest law firm.

The major impetus behind the consolidations is a mature industry, but other forces are at work. The trend of changing from a CPA firm to a full-service financial organization—offering one-stop shopping—is certainly a factor. Also, many partners near retirement are selling to these consolidators because their staff won't buy the firm and sustain them in retirement.

The interesting dynamic with the consolidators is the fact they will be national firms—which gives them a certain economies of scale—and marketing organizations. Marketers understand the importance of price. Some "loss leaders" may be given away—simple tax returns, for instance—in order to obtain the customer's investment portfolio business. It's too early to tell whether or not the consolidations will spell the death of hourly billing. One thing is certain: when AmEx is conducting marketing during the Superbowl, the competitive playing field is bound to change.

Q: Why is there so much resistance to ending hourly billing and implementing Value Pricing?

A: This is due partly to the habit, long entrenched, of billing by the hour. It is due partly to the risk-adverse nature of professionals, especially CPAs, and to professionals' desire to be objective about their pricing. You don't get much more objective than counting minutes and hours, even though the standard rate is completely arbitrary. Lack of understanding the role that pricing plays in marketing is also a reason, made more severe by the paucity of literature on the subject within the professions in the past. Further, viewing customers as price sensitive, and cutting prices to obtain and retain customers, is always easier then innovation, offering Total Quality Service, building relationships, and discussing value. This becomes a self-fulfilling prophecy within firms. You cut price to obtain the customer, and end up attracting the very customers who are price sensitive and will leave when they find a cheaper price, despite the level of service. Finally, pricing has always been an uncomfortable topic to deal with for the professional. In fact, in the 1950s and 1960s, lawyers were taught not to discuss price, to the serious discomfort of their customers. Yet the evidence is overwhelming that the customer wants the professional to discuss this sensitive topic.

USEFUL CHECKLISTS

DISCOVERING AND FOLLOWING THROUGH ON CUSTOMER EXPECTATIONS

Treat customers *individually,* not *equally.*

Focus on what the customer is *buying*, not what your firm is attempting to *sell.*

Determine whether the customer is buying good feelings or solutions to problems.

Provide *both* good feelings and solutions to problems.

Determine what the customer values most.

Focus on *results*, not efforts.

Emphasize the *benefits* of your services, not their *features.*

Don't focus on *what* you do (or *how* you do it), but on how the customer will benefit.

If the customer's expectations are unreasonable, educate the customer on a more realistic expectation or withdraw from the engagement.

Communicate the expectations you discover to each firm member who serves the customer.

Work to exceed the customer's expectations.

Ask each customer regularly for feedback, using open-ended questions, such as:

- How are we doing?
- How could we do better?
- How do you feel about our level of service?

Have staff members ask the above questions of their counterparts at the customer's business and monitor the feedback.

CHECKLIST FOR EXAMINING CLOSED FILES

Customer Name:

Year (or period):

Partner-In-Charge:

Description of services rendered:

Was there a Fixed Price Agreement?   ❏ Yes   ❏ No

Was there an engagement letter?   ❏ Yes   ❏ No

Pricing method which was used?

_____

_____

Were the desired results obtained for the customer?   ❏ Yes   ❏ No

Explain the value received by the customer:

_____

_____

How could we have done a better job for the customer?

_____

_____

What could the firm have done differently in servicing this customer?

_____

_____

Should any processes, procedures or systems be
implemented as a result of this engagement?   ❏ Yes   ❏ No

Are there any generic forms, letters, memos or other
written communications that may be utilized on similar
engagements?   ❏ Yes   ❏ No

Will the firm repeat this engagement for this customer?   ❏ Yes   ❏ No

Was this engagement profitable for the firm?   ❏ Yes   ❏ No

Has customer satisfaction been obtained for this
engagement?   ❏ Yes   ❏ No

If Yes, how (formal survey, oral communication, etc.)?

_____

Is it documented in the file and in the customer profile
in the firm's database?   ❏ Yes   ❏ No

If No, why not?

_____

_____

Were any opportunities for cross-selling services
discovered?   ❏ Yes   ❏ No

If Yes, describe the additional services provided:

_____

_____

Would you use the same pricing method if you had to
do over again?   ❏ Yes   ❏ No

What technology, if any, was used on the engagement?

_____

_____

Could this engagement have been provided by any
other member of the firm more efficiently?   ❏ Yes   ❏ No

If Yes, by whom?

_____

_____

Why?

_____

_____

CONSIDERATIONS BEFORE ACCEPTING A NEW CUSTOMER

Make sure the customer is *able* to pay your price.

- Check references (banker, attorney, insurance agent, etc.).
- Contact the predecessor CPA and learn as much as you can about why the customer defected (or why the professional withdrew from the engagement).
- Review a Dunn & Bradstreet (or other agency) report on the customer's business and ascertain if it is consistent with the financial information you've received.

Make sure the customer is *willing* to pay your price.

- Discover exactly what this customer expects from your firm.
- Get a retainer up front, before you begin any services.

Remember: *Never discount your price to obtain a customer.*

ITEMS TO CONSIDER BEFORE CONDUCTING A FIXED PRICE AGREEMENT (FPA) MEETING WITH A CUSTOMER

____ Review the *demographic* characteristics (age, sex, income, neighborhood, etc.) of the customer and try to determine the customer's *ability* to pay you.

- Age
- Sex
- Income
- Neighborhood
- Other_____

____ Review the *psychographic* characteristics of the customer and try to determine what the customer is *willing* to pay you:

- Is the customer risk (or loss) adverse?
- Does the customer demand a high level of detail or just a summary of your work and the big picture consequences?
- What are the major concerns and problems in the customer's life at the moment?
- What are the customer's expectations of your firm? How can you exceed them?

____ Determine who is paying for the customer's professional services and how price sensitive is the customer (see Chapter 4).

____ Determine where the services are located on the Value Curve (Chapter 2).

____ Determine where the customer is on your firm's demand curve.

QUESTIONS TO ASK YOURSELF BEFORE YOU SET A PRICE

These are factors to be considered in determining the reasonableness of a price:

1. How much time and labor will be required?

   _____

   _____

   What novelty and difficulty will be involved?

   _____

   _____

   What skills will be needed to perform the services?

   _____

   _____

2. What is the likelihood, if apparent to the client, that acceptance of the assignment will preclude other employment?

   _____

   _____

3. What is the customary price for similar services in the locality?

   _____

   _____

4. What amount is involved for the results obtained?

   _____

   _____

5. What time limits are imposed by the client or circumstances?

   _____

   _____

6. What are the nature and length of the professional relationship with

the client?

_____

_____

7. What is the experience, reputation, and ability of the lawyers or CPAs performing the services?

_____

_____

8. Is the price fixed or contingent?

_____

9. What special expertise or knowledge do you have about the engagement?

_____

_____

10. What special resources are available to you, such as software, or access to similar engagements completed for other clients?

_____

_____

11. What special contacts do you have that may facilitate a transaction?

_____

_____

12. Does opportunity exist to achieve unique results? Why?

_____

_____

13. What is your firm's risk assumption or credit liability?

_____

_____

14. What extra effort will you expend, based on deadlines or any form of

accommodation for the client?

_____

_____

15. What is the potential profit or loss to the client?

_____

_____

16. Is the "nobody else can do it" factor present?

_____

_____

17. What is the degree of the convenience the transaction involves?

_____

_____

18. What is your comfort level?

_____

_____

Adapted from *Innovative Billing and Collection Methods That Work*, by Charles and Joseph Larson, and from The American Bar Association's Model Rules of Professional Conduct.

Here are more questions to consider, preferably with the team that services the customer:

- **Who on the organizational chart am I dealing with?**

_____

_____

The higher up on the chart, the less price sensitive the person will be. A CEO is not going to take the time to interview multiple service providers and will be more interested in benefits than in price.

- **Who referred the customer to me?**

_____

_____

If it was a "warm" referral source, your firm is, most likely, already sold to the customer and you should be able to command a higher price.

- **What is the nature of the relationship with the referral source?**

_____

_____

(Same reasoning as the preceding point.)

- **What is the time line on the decision to select a CPA?**

_____

_____

The shorter the time line, the greater the probability you will get the business.

- **What are the impending deadlines driving the decision to engage a CPA?**

_____

_____

The shorter the time line, the higher price you can command for quick delivery time.

- **Who is paying for the service?**

_____

_____

Recall the four ways one can spend money. If the customer is in Category III, you should be able to charge a premium because they will be less price sensitive.

- **Are there any competitors in the arena with you? Who?**

This may provide you with an opportunity to first achieve parity with any potential competitor and then to focus on your firm's strengths. Never denigrate a competitor! You don't build your firm's value by knocking down your competitors. First achieve parity with them, and then focus on your strengths.

- **Do you have any price information from those competitors (bids, RFPs, etc.)?**

This is another way of gauging price sensitivity. Don't feel the need to be the low price bidder. Focus on service as part of your firm's Value Proposition—Price, Quality, and Service. Any professional can match (or beat) your price and quality. But they can't even observe your service—the relationship you have with the customer. And premium service commands premium prices.

- **How profitable is the organization? How long has it been in business?**

The longer in business and more profitable they are, the less price sensitive they are.

- **Who was the prior CPA and why is the customer changing? [Adverse Selection]**

Pre-qualify the customer. Your goal is not just *more* business, but *better* business. Only work for customers who understand and are willing to pay for the value you can provide.

- **If it is a new business, who is the banker, the attorney, etc.?**

_____

_____

Again, this is part of your pre-qualifying process.

- **How sophisticated is the customer with respect to my services?**

_____

_____

The less sophisticated, the more you must educate the customer as to the value of your services.

- **What is the relative price the customer would pay for the service?**

_____

_____

Relative price is the price the customer would pay for doing the project internally or outsourcing it, or the cost of not doing it at all. Think of it as the opportunity cost of hiring your firm.

- **Is the service you are providing a need or a want?**

_____

_____

A need is an essential service—a tax return or a compilation for a bank loan. A want can almost always command a higher price.

- **Does this customer add to the firm's skills, or am I simply using existing skills?**

_____

_____

Developing new skills in new markets with new customers adds to the stock of human capital in your firm.

- **Does this customer open up a new niche or market segment for the firm?**

  _____

  _____

(Same advantages as preceding point.)

- **Do I like this customer? Is the customer in a business I am interested in?**

  _____

  _____

This is the personality test. In the long run, your firm should only work with people you enjoy, in industries that interest you.

QUESTIONS YOU SHOULD ASK THE CUSTOMER DURING THE FPA MEETING

- What do you expect from us?
- What is your current pain?
- What keeps you awake at night?
- How do you see us helping you address these challenges and opportunities?
- What growth plans do you have?
- If price were not an issue, what role would you want your CPA to play in your business?
- Do you expect capital needs? New financing?
- Do you anticipate any mergers, purchases, divestitures, recapitalizations, or reorganizations in the near future?
- We know you are investing in Total Quality Service, as are we. What are the service standards you would like for us to provide you?
- How important is our satisfaction guarantee to you?
- How important is rapid response on accounting and tax questions? What do you consider rapid response?
- Why are you changing professionals? What did you not like about your former firm that you do not want us to repeat?*
- How did you enjoy working with your former firm?**
- Do you envision any other changes in your needs?
- Are you concerned about any of your asset, liability, or income statement accounts to which we should pay particularly close attention?
- What is your budget for this type of service?

---

* Do not denigrate the predecessor CPA (or attorney). First, this insults the customer and reminds the customer of a poor decision. Second, it diminishes respect and confidence in the profession as a whole and lowers the public's perception of our professionalism.

** Even though the customer is changing firms, it is almost certain that the customer liked certain characteristics of the predecessor. Find out what those were and exceed them. For instance, if they said the prior CPA always returned phone calls within one day, return phone calls within four hours.

- If we were to attend certain of your internal management meetings as observers, would you be comfortable with that?
- How do you suggest we best learn about your business so we can relate your operations to the financial information and so we can be more proactive in helping you maximize your business success?
- May our associates tour your facilities?
- What trade journals do you read? What seminars and trade shows do you regularly attend? Would it be possible for us to attend these with you?

HANDLING PRICE OBJECTIONS

Use the following method for handling objections:

1. **Listen carefully; hear the customer out.** Avoid the temptation to talk or try to solve the objection right then and there.
2. **Confirm your understanding of the objection.** Repeat it back to the customer to ensure you understand exactly what the objection is.
3. **Acknowledge the customer's point of view.** Practice empathy; don't try to impose your view on the customer, but help the customer become convinced of your view.
4. **Answer the objection.** Ultimately, you must answer the customer's objection if the FPA is to be authorized. You may postpone the price objection to the end of the meeting if you are still trying to build your firm's value, but in the end, price must be dealt with.
5. **Confirm that your answer satisfied the concern.**
6. **Attempt to get authorization for the FPA.** If the customer still objects, continue with the meeting until you reach an agreement as to your value.

OVERCOMING OBJECTIONS TO PRICE

Here are some specific methods for overcoming objections to price:

1. Postpone the price objection.

Here are two responses that postpone the price objection until you have had a chance to build your firm's value:

- I can appreciate that you would be interested in the price, and I assure you we will discuss it completely, but before we even consider the price, I want to be sure that our service can satisfy your needs. Will that be all right?
- Mr. Smith, your concern for price is quite understandable. The actual amount paid for the service, however, will depend upon the nature of the services you ultimately select. Let's consider the price for the services after we establish the specific services you will require. Is that fair?

2. Use the lowest common denominator.

Break down the price into the lowest common denominator, usually monthly. That is a much more manageable number to deal with than the total FPA price.

3. Use comparison.

An effective comparison to make is that of your customer's pricing policies with your own, using a statement such as the following:

> Mr. Becker, your own company makes a high-grade product that commands an exceptionally high price, and deservedly so. Your tool-and-die products warrant their outstanding reputation because of the top-quality materials used to make them. Our high-level of service and attention to helping you create more value in your business are naturally suited for you. Sure, you can buy less expensive financial help than ours, but you would not be satisfied with their performance.

Testimonials from other customers can also help prove your case.

4. To get volume up, sell down.

Always present your most expensive price first, and then move down.

5. Use the "bracket up for money" strategy.

Present pricing as follows for the customer:

> Most customers who desire this level of service are prepared
> to invest $12,000. A fortunate few can invest between $15,000
> and $20,000. And then there are those on a limited or fixed
> budget who can't go higher than $10,000. May I ask which of
> these categories your company fits into most comfortably?

Begin your pricing at a level that is approximately 20% above your price
($12,000). Then, continue by quoting 50% to 100% above your price
($15,000-$20,000). Finally, give your actual price ($10,000). Psychologi-
cally, you are tapping into the instinct of the customer that says: **Expensive
= Good**. Most likely, the customer won't want to be in the bottom category,
and will opt for the middle amount.

6. Focus on the difference.

Perhaps you're trying to price the FPA at $20,000, but the customer wants
$15,000. Focus on the $5,000 difference, which is the smaller, more
manageable amount.

7. Focus on other terms of the FPA.

If price is an objection, work on the other terms of the FPA first. Perhaps
you can change the payment terms; perhaps you can cut some services.
    Learn to accept price objections for what they are—opportunities in
disguise. They are a sign of an interested customer, and with practice and
skill, you will be able to overcome them without cutting your price.

CHECKLIST FOR EXPLAINING EACH SECTION OF THE FPA

Date of the FPA:

- Usually this is the last quarter of the calendar or fiscal year for the next year's services.

Professional services provided:

- Describe each service and the corresponding responsibilities of each party in fulfilling that service.
- Consider using the Annual Consulting Service, and detail exactly what the firm will provide for this service.

Unanticipated services:

- Include a clause explaining the firm's policy for services not included in the FPA (usually, this is done by using a Change Order).
- Consider offering long-term customers a discount (10 to 20%, perhaps) on any Change Orders that arise during the year (a "frequent flyer" program).
- Offer the "frequent flyer" discount on an agreed-upon price. Do not lock yourself into any type of standard hourly rate.

Service guarantee:

- Offer a 100% Money Back Service Guarantee in order to command a premium price and overcome price resistance and buyer's remorse.

Quality review:

- If any of the services will be reviewed in-house, you may detail that program and indicate that this review is included in the price of the service.

Payment terms:

- Detail the exact payment terms in order to overcome payment resistance.

Revision clause (optional):

- Consider using the revision clause as a way to ensure constant communication and customer satisfaction with the entire FPA.
- This clause is helpful for new customers not yet familiar with your firm.
- This reduces the risk of both parties, as the Agreement can be revised in light of mutual experience.
- Price resistance and buyer's remorse are reduced by this clause.
- This clause is not needed with long-term customers.

Termination clause:

- Always leave the customer a way out of the FPA.
- Termination should be required in writing with advance notice (usually 10 to 30 days).
- Be sure that the customer understands that full payment will be required for all services rendered prior to termination. Any amount due is payable immediately upon termination, and any refund due the customer will be paid at termination.

SUGGESTED READING

*How many a man has dated a new era
in his life from the reading of a book.*

–Henry David Thoreau

I am regularly asked which books I recommend as "essential reading" out of all the ones I cite. This is always a difficult task, as my first inclination is to answer, "Read them all." However, some are certainly better than others. Therefore, I have put together the following list, by category, which I believe are some of the best books (and publications) by the leading authors on the particular subject matter.

Economics, Marketing, and Price Theory

Far from being the "dismal science," economics is actually the study of human behavior. Many economists have contributed to my knowledge of this fascinating discipline. The ones I recommend the most are the following:

Friedman, Milton, and Rose Friedman. *Free to Choose: A Personal Statement*. New York: Harcourt Brace, 1990. This is one of Friedman's classics, in the tradition of his *Capitalism and Freedom*. He is one economist who can make the complex understandable and deserves to be read as widely as possible.

Friedman, David D. *Price Theory: An Intermediate Text*. Cincinnati: South-Western Publishing Co., 1992, and *Hidden Order: The Economics of Everyday Life*. New York: HarperBusiness, 1996. David Friedman is Milton Friedman's son and a distinguished economist in his own right. The first book listed is his intermediate textbook for economic students while the second one is for the general audience. Both are excellent and highly entertaining.

Gilder, George. *Recapturing the Spirit of Enterprise*. San Francisco, California: ICS Press, 1992, and *Wealth and Poverty: A New Edition of the Classic*. San Francisco: ICS Press, 1993. In my opinion, Gilder is the best author on economics, sociology, technology, and anthropology that you will find anywhere. His work has inspired me and changed my vision of the way the world works. These two books are his classics, but he has written others. If you read only two books from this list, read anything by Gilder—twice. Gilder is a senior fellow at Seattle's Discovery Institute. Visit their Web site at www.discovery.org. From there you can link to The Official George Gilder Web site.

Landsburg, Steven E. *The Armchair Economist: Economics & Everyday Life*. New York: The Free Press, 1993; *Price Theory and Applications, Third Edition*. St. Paul, MN: West Publishing Company, 1996, and *Fair Play: What Your Child Can Teach You About Economics, Values, and the Meaning of Life*. New York: The Free Press, 1997. In the tradition of David Friedman, Landsburg is another dynamic economist who is an entertaining read. He will challenge, and no doubt persuade, you on many points with his cogent analysis of contemporary issues. Even his textbook is excellent, although very complicated. His new work, *Fair Play*, relates today's complex economic and social problems down to the child's sandbox on the playground.

Stanley, Thomas J., and William D. Danko. *The Millionaire Next Door: The Surprising Secrets of America's Wealthy*. Atlanta, Georgia: Longstreet Press, Inc., 1996. This book will shatter every myth perpetuated about the wealthy in America and how they live, work, and behave. It is well-researched and a must read for CPAs and attorneys alike.

Young, S. David. *The Rule of Experts: Occupational Licensing in America*. Washington, D.C.: The CATO Institute, 1987. This absolutely demolishes the argument in favor of any occupational licensure, using economic theory and empirical evidence. This is one of those issues on which a majority of economists agree, and yet they are ignored when it comes to the debate.

Hourly Billing (and Its Alternatives)

There is a paucity of books dealing with the shift from hourly billing to Value Pricing. Nonetheless, a few do exist.

Aquila, August J. *Breaking The Paradigm: New Approaches to Pricing Accounting Services*. New York: American Institute of Certified Public Accountants, Inc., 1995. Aquila is vice-president of acquisitions for American Express Tax and Business Services. This book was among the first in the accounting profession to challenge the conventional wisdom of hourly billing. To order, contact: American Institute of Certified Public Accountants, Order Department, (800) 862-4272; (800) 362-5066 (fax).

Aquila is always insightful and his writings can be found monthly (as Contributing Editor) in *CPA Profitability Monthly*, and (as Editor) in *Partner-to-Partner Advisory*, both published by Harcourt Brace Professional Publishing. These two newsletters, in my opinion, are the best publications dealing with the topics of marketing, Value Pricing, customer service, and management that can be found specifically for the accounting profession. To order, call: 1-800-831-7799.

Cross, Robert G. *Revenue Management*. New York: Bantam, 1997. This book sheds light on why airline pricing is complex and sophisticated. Written by an attorney, it is one of the best books on the real-world application of price discrimination.

Larson, Charles B., and Joseph W. *Innovative Billing and Collection Methods That Work*. Burr Ridge, Illinois: Irwin Professional Publishing, 1994. This book is also among the first works to challenge not only the billing methods of CPAs but also their collection methods. Although light on theory, it does offer some illuminating discussion of pricing according to value. Contact Western CPE, The University of Montana, Missoula, MT 59812, 1-800-243-7395.

Reed, Richard C., Ed. *Beyond the Billable Hour: An Anthology of Alternative Billing Methods*. Chicago: American Bar Association, 1989, and *Win-Win Billing Strategies: Alternatives That Satisfy Your Clients and You*. Chicago: American Bar Association, 1992. These two works are the result of a task force put together by the American Bar Association to study alternatives to the hourly billing method in the mid 1980s. The first one offers an excellent historical look at hourly billing and why the law profession was so quick to adopt it as the primary method for pricing its services. The second work gives many examples of how lawyers have implemented Value Pricing. If you are an attorney, read both books. If you are a CPA, the second one is adequate.

Reed, Richard C. *Billing Innovations: New Win-Win Ways to End Hourly Billing*. Chicago: American Bar Association, 1996. This book was authored by Reed, the leader in the move away from hourly billing in the legal profession. It's very interesting to read all three books in their chronological order, especially for attorneys, as this documents the thought process that Reed went through regarding the shift from hourly billing to Value Pricing. I also recommend this third work for CPAs, although it is written primarily for lawyers. Contact: Publication Orders, American Bar Association, P.O. Box 10892, Chicago, IL 60610-0892. Or call (312) 988-5522 (Customer Service); (312) 988-5568 (fax); e-mail orders: abasvcctr@abanet.org; web site: www.abanet.org/lpm/catalog.

Ross, William G. *The Honest Hour: The Ethics of Time-Based Billing by Attorneys*. Durham, North Carolina: Carolina Academic Press, 1996. This book, by Cumberland School of Law of Samford University (Birmingham, Alabama) professor William Ross is the most comprehensive volume that I have discovered on the history of hourly billing and the ethical dilemmas of hourly billing and Value Pricing.

Management Consultants and Consulting

Though the field lacks serious, disciplined thinkers (unlike the economics profession), some consultants do offer intelligent guidance to the businesses of today.

Drucker, Peter F. *Adventures of a Bystander*. New Jersey: Transaction Publishers, 1994, and *Managing in a Time of Great Change*. New York: Truman Talley Books/Dutton, 1995. Drucker is the one truly serious thinker that the management consultant industry can point to with justifiable pride. No doubt you should read as many of this prolific writer's works as possible, but I found these two enlightening. His autobiography was the genesis for my thinking on the question, Do you learn more from success or failure? Drucker's main competitive advantage among the management gurus is that he can write intelligently and not bore his reader, a trait lacking in the overwhelming majority of business authors.

Maister, David H. *Managing the Professional Service Firm.* New York: The Free Press, 1993, and *True Professionalism: The Courage to Care About Your People, Your Clients, and Your Career.* New York: The Free Press, 1997. Maister is another of those rare thinkers and consultants to professional service firms worldwide who can write with insight and truly make you think about what it means to be a professional.

Micklethwait, John, and Adrian Wooldridge. *The Witch Doctors: What Management Gurus Are Saying and Why It Matters.* New York: Random House, 1996. This piercing work gave voice to the backlash against the $11.4 billion profession known as "management consultancy." Although the authors concede far too much power to the consultants in altering the course of life, referring to them as "the unacknowledged legislators of mankind," their four defects of the "witch doctors" of our age are right on target. The profession has yet to refute successfully the charges against it, so eloquently laid out in this book. For all those who have suffered through many a poorly written business book, Micklethwait and Wooldridge offer a refreshing alternative.

Reichheld, Frederick F., and Thomas Teal. *The Loyalty Effect: The Hidden Force Behind Growth, Profits, and Lasting Value.* Boston: Harvard Business School Press, 1996. This is a seminal work on the economics of customer loyalty. Sure to be a classic, this book focuses on the need for business to concentrate more on customer *retention* than *acquisition.* The book is rooted in economic theory and offers many examples of firms today that understand the bottom-line impact of customer loyalty. Reichheld is with Bain & Company, the pioneer in customer loyalty economics.

Profits and Morality

At last, this issue is being given the attention it deserves from theologians, politicians, economists, sociologists, the media, and the general public.

Gilder, George, "The Soul of Silicon." This was a speech Gilder delivered to the Vatican in May 1997. It is one of the most profound works I have ever read on why profits are moral. This is Gilder at his best. You can locate this speech at the Discovery Institute (Seattle, WA) Web site, at www.discovery.org.

Neuhaus, Richard John. *Doing Well and Doing Good: The Challenge to the Christian Capitalist*. New York: Doubleday, 1992. This is an excellent exposition, from a theological perspective, on the morality of making money.

Novak, Michael. *The Catholic Ethic and the Spirit of Capitalism*. New York: The Free Press, 1993, and *Business as a Calling: Work and the Examined Life*. New York: The Free Press, 1996. These seminal works, from another theologian, are well written and are essential reading on current thought among religions regarding the morality of capitalism and business.

Paul II, Pope John. *Centesimus Annus* ("The Hundredth Year"). This is Pope John Paul II's ninth encyclical, and it states positively that capitalism is superior to socialism in solving society's most pressing problems.

Psychology

Branden, Nathaniel. *The Six Pillars of Self-Esteem*. New York: Bantam, 1994. This is the ultimate treatise on self-esteem. The chapter on self-esteem and work is especially relevant to Value Pricing concepts.

Cialdini, Robert B. *Influence: The New Psychology of Modern Persuasion*. New York: Quill, 1993. Containing many examples from marketing and advertising, this absolutely fascinating discussion of human behavior is entertaining and informative.

Selling

Beckwith, Harry. *Selling the Invisible*. New York: Warner Books, 1997. This work contains many good marketing ideas for professional service firms, which sell the "invisible."

Boress, Allan S. *The "I Hate Selling" Book: Business-Building Advice for Consultants, Attorneys, Accountants, Engineers, Architects and Other Professionals.* New York: AMACOM, 1995. Most professionals loathe the thought of selling. This book gives practical guidance on how to increase selling success. Boress is a leading consultant to the CPA profession and editor of the *CPA Profitability Monthly.*

Bosworth, Michael T. *Solution Selling: A System for Difficult to Sell Products.* Chicago: Irwin Professional Publishing, 1994. *Solution Selling* emphasizes the customer in the sales process and offers many useful strategies for discovering and emphasizing value-added services.

Hopkins, Tom. *How to Master the Art of Selling.* New York: Warner Books, 1980. This is an all-time sales classic.

Rackham, Neil. *SPIN Selling.* New York: McGraw-Hill Book Company, 1988. This is, literally, the best-validated sales method available today, developed from research studies of 35,000 sales calls, used by the top sales forces across the world. Rackham presents SPIN selling as a testable hypothesis.

Total Quality Service

Albrecht, Karl. *The Only Thing That Matters: Bringing the Power of the Customer into the Center of Your Business.* New York: HarperBusiness, 1992. This book, the bible of the Total Quality Service movement, written by one of its founding fathers, helps the reader to understand the customer service revolution taking place worldwide.

Aquila, August J., and Allan D. Koltin. "How to Lose Clients Without Really Trying." *Journal of Accountancy*, May 1992. This is a masterful article, which won the authors the 1992 Annual Literary award for the best article of the year.

Marcus, Stanley. *Minding the Store.* New York: Dutton, 1993, and *Quest for the Best.* New York: Dutton, 1993. From the son of one of the founders of Neiman–Marcus comes this interesting autobiography on the customer service ethic that made Neiman–Marcus the premiere retailer in the United States.

For ordering various books above, contact:

Publication Orders
American Bar Association
P.O. Box 10892
Chicago, IL 60610–0892
(800) 285–2221
(312) 988–5522 (Customer Service)
(312) 988–5568 (fax)
E-mail orders: abasvcctr@abanet.org
Web Site: www.abanet.org/lpm/catalog

Laissez Faire Books
938 Howard Street, #202
San Francisco, CA 94103
(800) 326–0996
(415) 541–9780
E-mail orders: www.LFB.org

American Institute of Certified Public Accountants
Order Department
(800) 862–4272
(800) 362–5066 (fax)

Also, I recommend that you subscribe to the *Partner-to-Partner Advisory*, a Harcourt professional publication edited by August Aquila. This newsletter is loaded with ideas and advice on how to get the most out of your practice, written by some of the country's leading CPA consultants.

To order, call: (800) 831–7799 or visit web site: www.hbpp.com

REFERENCES

Albrecht, Karl. *The Northbound Train: Finding the Purpose, Setting the Direction, Shaping the Destiny of Your Organization.* New York: AMACOM, 1994.

————. *The Only Thing That Matters: Bringing the Power of the Customer into the Center of Your Business.* New York: HarperBusiness, 1992.

American Bar Association, Economics of Tort and Insurance Law Practice Committee of the Tort & Insurance Practice Section, *Alternative Billing: The Sequel.* San Francisco: Fairmont Hotel, March 13, 1997 Seminar and Material.

American Institute of Certified Public Accountants. *CPA Vision Project: 2011 and Beyond.* New York: AICPA, 1998.

Aquila, August J. *Breaking The Paradigm: New Approaches to Pricing Accounting Services.* New York: American Institute of Certified Public Accountants, Inc., 1995.

Aquila, August J., and Allan D. Koltin. "How to Lose Clients Without Really Trying." *Journal of Accountancy*, May 1992.

Armentano, Dominick T. *Antitrust and Monopoly: Anatomy of a Policy Failure*, Second Edition. New York: Holmes & Meier, 1990.

Armey, Dick. *The Freedom Revolution: The New Republican House Majority Leader Tells Why Big Government Failed, Why Freedom Works, and How We Will Rebuild America.* Washington, D.C.: Regnery Publishing, Inc., 1995.

Baker, Ronald J. "Alternatives to the Federal Income Tax." California CPA Education Foundation CPE Seminar, 1999.

————. "How to Build A Successful Practice with Total Quality Service." California CPA Education Foundation CPE Seminar, 1999.

Barker, Joel Arthur. *Paradigms: The Business of Discovering the Future.* New York: HarperBusiness, 1993.

Beauchemin, Timothy J. *Five Star Client Service System.* Audio Cassette program, Houston, TX: Enterprise 2000, Inc., 1990.

————. "Thinking About the Future." *CPA Profitability Monthly*, Volume 1995, Issue 12, December 1995.

———— . "No More Begging for Work: Self Esteem Is the Key to a Better Practice." *CPA Profitability Monthly*, Volume 1996, Issue 8, August 1996.

Becker, Gary S. and Guity Nashat Becker. *The Economics of Life: From Baseball to Affirmative Action to Immigration, How Real-World Issues Affect Our Everday Life.* New York: McGraw Hill, 1997.

Beckwith, Harry. *Selling the Invisible:* New York: Warner Books, 1997.

Bernstein, Peter L. *Against the Gods: The Remarkable Story of Risk.* New York: John Wiley & Sons, Inc., 1996.

Berry, Leonard L. Discovering the Soul of Service: The Nine Drivers of Sustainable Business Success. New York: The Free Press, 1999.

Boress, Allan S. *Building Entrepreneurial People.* New York: Harcourt Brace Professional Publishing, 1995.

———— . *The "I Hate Selling" Book*: *Business-Building Advice for Consultants, Attorneys, Accountants, Engineers, Architects and Other Professionals.* New York: AMACOM, 1994.

———— . "Choosing Your Clients." *CPA Profitability Monthly*, Volume 1996, Issue 8, August 1996.

Bosworth, Michael T. *Solution Selling: Creating Buyers in Difficult Selling Markets.* Chicago: Irwin Professional Publishing, 1995.

Branden, Nathaniel. *The Six Pillars of Self-Esteem.* New York: Bantam, 1994.

Brandenburger, Adam M., and Barry J. Nalebuff. *Co-opetition: The Game Theory That's Changing the Game of Business*. New York: Currency Doubleday, 1996.

Buchholz, Todd G. *New Ideas From Dead Economists: An Introduction to Modern Economic Thought*. New York: Plume, 1989.

Buckley, Reid. *Sex, Power, and Pericles: Principles of Advanced Public Speaking*. Camden, SC: Peor Es Nada Press, 1996.

The Business Lawyer. "Business and Ethics Implications of Alternative Billing Practices: Report on Alternative Billing Arrangements." The Business Lawyer; Vol. 54, November 1998.

Carlzon, Jan. *Moments of Truth: New Strategies for Today's Customer-Driven Economy*. New York: Harper & Row, Publishers, Inc., 1987.

Cialdini, Robert B. *Influence: The New Psychology of Modern Persuasion*. New York: Quill, 1993.

Cowan, Robin, and Mario J. Rizzo, Ed. *Profits & Morality*. Chicago: The University of Chicago Press, 1995.

Cross, Robert G. *Revenue Management*. New York: Bantam, 1997.

Davis, Kevin. *Getting into Your Customer's Head: Secrets of Selling Your Competitors Don't Know*. New York: Times Books, 1996.

de Bono, Edward. *Sur/Petition: Creating Value Monopolies When Everyone Else Is Merely Competing*. New York: HarperBusiness, 1993.

deKieffer, Esq., Donald E. *How Lawyers Screw Their Clients: And What You Can Do About It*. New York: Barricade Books Inc., 1995.

Drucker, Peter F. *Adventures of a Bystander*. New Jersey: Transaction Publishers, 1994.

————. *Managing in a Time of Great Change*. New York: Truman Talley Books/Dutton, 1995.

Frank, Robert H. *Passions Within Reason: The Strategic Role of the Emotions*. New York: W.W. Norton & Company, 1988.

Friedman, David D. *Hidden Order: The Economics of Everyday Life*. New York: HarperBusiness, 1996.

Friedman, Milton, and Simon Kuznets. *Income from Independent Professional Practice*. New York: National Bureau of Economic Research, 1945.

Friedman, Milton, and Rose Friedman. *Free to Choose: A Personal Statement*. New York: Harcourt Brace, 1990.

Gilder, George. "Gilder Technology Report," Volume II, Number 7, July 1997.

_____. "Gilder Technology Report," Volume III, Number 5, May 1998.

———— . *Recapturing the Spirit of Enterprise*. San Francisco: ICS Press, 1992.

———— . *Wealth and Poverty: A New Edition of the Classic*. San Francisco: ICS Press, 1993.

————. "Civilization Can't Afford to Forget." *Forbes ASAP*, December 2, 1996.

Gregorsky, Frank, Editor. *Speaking of George Gilder*. Seattle, Washington: Discovery Institute, 1998.

Grenier, Ray, and George Metes. *Going Virtual: Moving Your Organization into the 21st Century*. New Jersey: Prentice Hall P T R, 1995.

Hagel III, John and Arthur G. Armstrong. *Net Gain: Expanding Markets Through Virtual Communities*. Boston Massachusetts: Harvard Business School Press, 1997.

Hart, Christopher, W.L., and Christopher E. Bogan. *The Baldrige: What It Is, How It's Won, How to Use It to Improve Quality in Your Company*. New York: McGraw-Hill, Inc. 1992.

Hayek, Friedrich A. "The Use of Knowledge in Society," *American Economic Review* 35 (September 1945): 519–530.

Hiebeler, Robert, Thomas B. Kelly and Charles Ketteman. *Best Practices: Building Your Business with Customer-Focused Solutions.* New York: Simon & Schuster, 1998.

Hill, Napoleon. *Think and Grow Rich.* New York: Fawcett Columbine, 1987.

Hopkins, Tom. *How to Master the Art of Selling.* New York: Warner Books, 1980.

Kehrer, Daniel. *Doing Business Boldly.* New York: Times Books, 1989.

Kessler, Sheila. *Measuring And Managing Customer Satisfaction: Going for the Gold.* Milwaukee: ASQC Quality Press, 1996.

Koch, Richard. *The 80/20 Principle: The Secret of Achieving More With Less.* New York: Currency Doubleday, 1998.

Kriegel, Robert J., and David Brandt. *Sacred Cows Make the Best Burgers: Developing Change Ready People and Organizations.* New York: Warner Books, 1996.

Kriegel, Robert J., and Louis Patler. *If It Ain't Broke . . . Break It! And Other Unconventional Wisdom for a Changing Business World.* New York: Warner Books, 1992.

Kurtz, James R. "We Are Becoming Something Distinctly Different." *Outlook*, Fall 1996.

Lacey, Robert. *Sotheby's: Bidding for Class.* New York: Little. Brown and Company, 1998.

Lambert, Tom. *High Income Consulting: How to Build and Market Your Professional Practice*, Second Edition. London: Nicholas Brealey Publishing, 1997.

Landsburg, Steven E. *The Armchair Economist: Economics and Everyday Life.* New York: The Free Press, 1993.

————. *Price Theory and Applications, Third Edition*. St. Paul, MN: West Publising Company, 1996.

Larson, Charles B., and Joseph W. Larson. *Innovative Billing and Collection Methods That Work*. Burr Ridge, IL: Irwin Professional Publishing, 1994.

LeBoeuf, Michael. *How to Win Customers and Keep Them for Life*. New York: Berkeley Books, 1989.

Levine, Robert. *A Geography of Time: The Temporal Misadventures of a Social Psychologist, or How Every Culture Keeps Time Just a Little Bit Differently*. New York: BasicBooks, 1997.

Levitt, Theodore. *Thinking About Management*. New York: The Free Press, 1991.

Maister, David H. *True Professionalism: The Courage to Care About Your People, Your Clients, and Your Career*. New York: The Free Press, 1997.

Mandel, Michael. *The High-Risk Society*. New York: Random House, 1996.

Marcus, Stanley. *Minding the Store*. New York: Dutton, 1993.

————. *Quest for the Best*. New York: Dutton, 1993.

Marx, Karl. *Wage-Labour and Capital and Value, Price and Profit*. New York: International Publishers, 1995 edition.

Micklethwait, John, and Adrian Wooldridge. *The Witch Doctors: What Management Gurus Are Saying and Why It Matters*. New York: Random House, 1996.

Mises, Ludwig von. *Planned Chaos*. New York: The Foundation for Economic Education, Inc., 1977.

Monroe, Kent B. *Pricing: Making Profitable Decisions*, Second Edition. New York: McGraw Hill, 1990.

Morgan, J. Harris. *How To Draft Bills Clients Rush to Pay*. Chicago: American Bar Association, 1995.

Nagle, Thomas T. "Economic Foundations for Pricing." Chicago, Illinois: University of Chicago Graduate School of Business: July 1983, Report No. 83-106.

Nagle, Thomas T., and Reed K. Holden. *The Strategy and Tactics of Pricing: A Guide to Profitable Decision Making*, Second Edition. New Jersey: Prentice Hall, 1995.

Neuhaus, Richard John. *Doing Well and Doing Good: The Challenge to the Christian Capitalist*. New York: Doubleday, 1992.

Novak, Michael. *Business as a Calling: Work and the Examined Life*. New York: The Free Press, 1996.

O'Shea, James, and Charles Madigan. *Dangerous Company: Management Consultants and the Businesses They Save and Ruin*. New York: Penguin Books, 1998.

Pacioli, Fra Luca. *Particularis de Computis et Scripturis, 1494, A Contemporary Interpretation by Jeremy Cripps*. Seattle, Washington: Pacioli Society, Seattle University, 1995.

Payne, Richard A. "The Emerging Competitive Landscape Occupied by the Accounting Profession: Challenges, Opportunities, and Imperatives." Pleasanton, California: Results Accountants' Systems, October 1998. Ras-net.com.

Peppers, Don, and Martha Rogers. *The One to One Enterprise: Tools for Competing in the Interactive Age*. New York: Doubleday, 1997.

Peters, Tom. *The Circle of Innovation: You Can't Shrink Your Way To Greatness*. New York: Random House, 1998.

————. *The Pursuit of Wow!: Every Person's Guide To Topsy-Turvy Times*. New York: Random House, 1995.

————. *The Tom Peters Seminar: Crazy Times Call for Crazy Organizations.* New York: Vintage Books, 1994.

Postrel, Virginia. *The Future and Its Enemies: The Growing Conflict Over Creativity, Enterprise, and Progress.* New York: The Free Press, 1998.

Previts, Gary John and Barbara Dubis Merino. *A History of Accountancy in the United States: The Cultural Significance of Accounting.* Columbus, Ohio: Ohio State University Press, 1998.

Putnam, Anthony O. *Marketing Your Services: A Step-by-Step Guide for Small Businesses and Professionals.* New Yourk: John Wiley & Sons, Inc., 1990.

Rackham, Neil. *SPIN Selling.* New York: McGraw-Hill Book Company, 1988.

Reeb, CPA, William L. *Start Consulting: How to Walk the Talk.* New York: American Institute of Certified Public Accountants, 1998.

Reed, Richard C., Ed. *Beyond The Billable Hour.* Chicago: American Bar Association, 1989.

———— . *Win-Win Billing Strategies: Alternatives That Satisfy Your Clients and You.* Chicago: American Bar Association, 1992.

————. *Billing Innovations: New Win-Win Ways to End Hourly Billing.* Chicago: American Bar Association, 1996.

Reichheld, Frederick F. and Thomas Teal. *The Loyalty Effect: The Hidden Force Behind Growth, Profits, and Lasting Value.* Boston: Harvard Business School Press, 1996.

Rogers, Everett M. *Diffusion of Innovations.* New York: Free Press, 1995.

Rosenbluth, Hal F. *The Customer Comes Second and Other Secrets.* New York: William Morrow, 1992.

Ross, William G. *The Honest Hour: The Ethics of Time-Based Billing by Attorneys.* Durham, NC: Carolina Academic Press, 1996.

Shapiro, Eileen C., *Fad Surfing in the Boardroom: Managing in the Age of Instant Answers*. New York: Addison-Wesley Publishing Company, Inc., 1995.

Skousen, Mark, and Kenna C. Taylor. *Puzzles and Paradoxes in Economics*. Brookfield, VT: Edward Elgar Publishing Company, 1997.

Stanley, Ph.D., Thomas J. and William D. Danko, Ph.D. *The Millionaire Next Door: The Surprising Secrets of America's Wealthy*. Atlanta, Georgia: Longstreet Press, 1996.

Stewart, Thomas A. *Intellectual Capital: The New Wealth of Organizations*. New York: Currency/Doubleday, 1997.

Stigler, George J. *Memoirs of an Unregulated Economist*. New York: Basic Books, Inc., Publishers, 1985.

Will, George F. *Suddenly: The American Idea Abroad and at Home 1986–1990*. New York: The Free Press, 1992.

Winston, William J., Editor. *Marketing for CPAs, Accountants, and Tax Professionals*. New York: The Haworth Press, 1995.

Woods, Earl, and Pete McDaniel. *Training a Tiger: A Father's Guide to Raising a Winner in Both Golf and Life*. New York: Harper & Row, Publishers, 1987.

Wriston, Walter. *Risk and Other Four-Letter Words*. New York: Harper & Row, Publishers, 1987.

2000

The Professional's Guide To

VALUE PRICING

CPE PROGRAM

Harcourt
Professional Publishing

San Diego New York Chicago London

CPE Requirements.
Please read this.

CPE requirements and course acceptability vary from state to state. Your state board is the final authority for the number of credit hours allowed for a particular program, as well as the classification of courses, under its specific licensing requirement. Contact your state board of accountancy for information concerning your state's requirements for the acceptability of this course, the number of CPE credit hours you must earn, and the acceptable fields of study. This course is not currently registered under the Florida QA Service.

INTRODUCTION

Thank you for choosing this self-study CPE course from Harcourt Professional Publishing. Our goal is to provide you with the clearest, most concise, and most up-to-date information to help further your professional development, as well as the most convenient method to help you satisfy your continuing professional education requirements.

This course is intended to be used in conjunction with *The Professional's Guide to Value Pricing*. This course has the following characteristics:

Prerequisites: Basic knowledge of management

Recommended CPE Credit: 4 hours

Level of Knowledge: Intermediate—Builds on a basic level of understanding in order to relate fundamental principles or skills to practical situations and extend them to a broader range of applications. This level is for participants with some exposure to the subject.

Field of Study: Management

The Professional's Guide to Value Pricing Self-Study CPE Program is designed to provide 4 hours of CPE credit, which may be obtained by submitting the exam for grading and earning a passing score.

In accordance with the standards of the National Registry of CPE Sponsors, each credit hour awarded for this program is based on 100 minutes of average completion time. Credit hours are recommended in accordance with the Statement on Standards for Formal Continuing Professional Education (CPE) Programs, published by the AICPA. CPE requirements vary from state to state. Your state board is the final authority for the number of credit hours allowed for a particular program, as well as the classification of courses, under its specific licensing requirement. Contact your State Board of Accountancy for information concerning your state's requirements on the number of CPE credit hours you must earn and the acceptable fields of study.

To receive credit, complete the course according to the instructions, take the test, and submit the completed answer sheet.

This exam costs $64.00. Payment options are shown on the answer sheet.

Please allow 2–3 weeks (from the date of our receipt of the exam) for grading. A passing score is 70 percent or above. Participants who pass the test will receive a Certificate of Completion to acknowledge their achievement. The Self-Study CPE Program offered in conjunction with *The Professional's Guide to Value Pricing* will expire on December 31, 2000. Participants may submit completed tests for the program until that date.

Instructions for Taking This Course

This course consists of chapter learning objectives, reading assignments, and an examination. Complete each step listed below:

1. Review the chapter learning objectives.
2. Read the assigned material in *The Professional's Guide to Value Pricing*
3. After completing all assigned chapters, take the examination, writing each answer on the appropriate line on the answer sheet.
4. When you have completed the examination, remove the answer sheet, place it in a stamped envelope, and send it to:

> *The Professional's Guide to Value Pricing* CPE Coordinator
> Harcourt Professional Publishing
> 525 B Street, Suite 1900
> San Diego, CA 92101

Be sure to indicate your method of payment on the answer sheet.

> **Note:** You may make copies of the answer sheet to allow additional people to take the test. Each additional test costs $64.00.

SELF-STUDY CONTINUING PROFESSIONAL EDUCATION
THE PROFESSIONAL'S GUIDE TO VALUE PRICING

History of the Accounting Profession

Complete this section to:

- Gain a basic understanding of the antecedents of Generally Accepted Accounting Principles (GAAP) and the growth in demand for public accountants.
- Learn the major developments affecting the practice of accounting from World War II to the present.

Read Chapter 1, "A Brief History of the Accounting Profession."

The Accounting Profession in the New Millennium

Complete this section to:

- Understand why the accounting profession is in the mature stage of the Product Life Cycle and what effect this will have on its future.
- Learn the theory of the Value Curve and the implications it has for your firm's ability to engage in Value Pricing.
- Understand why CPAs must change from thinking like accountants to thinking like financial consultants.

Read Chapter 2, "The Accounting Profession in the New Millennium."

Why Are People in Business?

Complete this section to:

- Learn that profits are a lagging indicator of customer behavior, and understand why a business must focus on the customer in order to earn a profit.

- Understand why companies that offer Total Quality Service outperform those that do not, and how Total Quality Service is rooted in pre–World War II business ideas and common sense.
- Discover more about the "P" in CPA and The Spirit of Service.
- Gain a better understanding of the historical meaning of the word *client* and why the word *customer* better describes the relationship between a professional and the person he or she serves.

Read Chapter 3, "Why Are People in Business?"

What and How People Buy

Complete this section to:

- Learn what customers are really buying when they spend their money.
- Gain an understanding of the dynamics of customer expectations and how they are measured.
- Understand why professionals must focus on *who* benefits from what they do, not *what* they do or *how* they do it or *who* they are.
- Learn the four ways, in any economy, that people can spend money and the implications this has on a professional firm's ability to Value Price.

Read Chapter 4, "What and How People Buy."

Economics and Price Discrimination

Complete this section to:

- Learn the value of studying economics and why economics is grounded in the theory of rationality.
- Understand the theory of price discrimination, its four requirements, and the three degrees of price discrimination.
- Discover why all customers are not equal, and explore some real-world examples of how different industries capture the consumer surplus.

Read Chapter 5, "Why Is Movie Theater Popcorn So Expensive?"

Hourly Billing

Complete this section to:

- Learn where hourly billing began and what its original purpose was.
- Understand how hourly billing transformed from a cost-accounting tool to a pricing method.

Read Chapter 6, "The Genesis of Hourly Billing."

Harmful Effects of Hourly Billing

Complete this section to:

- Explore the limited advantages of hourly billing as a pricing method.
- Learn where all profits come from and the importance of risk-taking in any economy.
- Learn the many disadvantages of hourly billing as a pricing method and how it hinders the professional's ability to earn more than the hourly rate.

Read Chapter 7, "The Deleterious Effects of Hourly Billing."

Write-Downs and Price Psychology

Complete this section to:

- Learn why CPAs write down and write off more than they write up.
- Learn the two reasons why customers will not pay professionals.
- Explore whether we learn more from success or from failure in a business environment.
- Study why some professionals are able to engage in Value Pricing with success.
- Learn the three components of the Value Proposition.
- Learn the theory of price psychology and the implications it has for Value Pricing.

Read Chapter 8, "Write-Downs and Price Psychology."

The Advantages of Value Pricing and Using the Fixed Price Agreement and Change Orders

Complete this section to:

- Learn why the word *price* is better than the words *fee* and *billing*.

- Learn the true definition, from an economic perspective, of Value Pricing, and gain an understanding of pricing on the margin.

- Discover the difference between an absolute price and a relative price and how this affects the ability to Value Price.

- Learn the purpose of the Fixed Price Agreement Meeting and how to conduct it.

- Learn the many advantages of entering into a Fixed Price Agreement with the customer.

- Learn the importance of implementing a service guarantee in your firm in order to Value Price.

- Read a sample Fixed Price Agreement and learn how to tailor it to your firm.

- Learn effective questions to ask yourself and the customer in order to Value Price.

- Discover how to negotiate price and how to deal with objections.

- Learn how to implement and use Change Orders.

- Explore ways to maximize the consumer surplus with alternative pricing strategies.

- Learn how to solicit feedback from customers in order to ascertain satisfaction.

- Learn why customers defect.

- Learn how to make the transition from hourly billing to Value Pricing with new and veteran customers.

   Read Chapter 9, "The Advantages of Value Pricing"; Chapter 10, "Preparing for the Fixed Price Agreement Meeting"; and Chapter 11, "The Fixed Price Agreement and Change Orders."

Total Quality Service

Complete this section to:

- Gain a basic understanding of some of the more prevalent service philosophies and principles that are vital to creating a Total Quality Service (TQS) culture.
- Learn the "Moment of Truth" (MOT) philosophy and how you can use MOTs to transform your firm to a service-oriented business.
- Discover the vital importance of earning the loyalty of your most valued customers and the wisdom of firing your less-desirable clients.

Read Chapter 14, "Total Quality Service."

Consulting

Complete this section to:

- Learn the evolution and importance of consulting services to the accounting profession.
- Acquire a list of the major fears customers face when hiring a consultant—and how to assuage these fears.
- Discover the seven roles of change agents in the process of introducing an innovation in a client system.
- Become aware of the Consultant Customer's Bill of Rights.

Read Chapter 15, "The CPA as Consultant."

Ethics

Complete this section to:

- Explore how the free market sets "just" prices, and the different types of profits that firms can earn.
- Learn the seven moral requirements for business success.
- Learn the ethical issues that the law profession is dealing with as it makes its transition from hourly billing to Value Pricing.

- Learn why the free market is the best arbiter of value.

Read Chapter 16, "Ethics, Hourly Billing, and Value Pricing."

Self-Esteem

Complete this section to:

- Learn what professionals must first do in order to engage in Value Pricing.
- Discover the importance of self-esteem and why CPAs, as a profession, tend to have low self-esteem.

Read Chapter 17, "Self-Esteem and Value Pricing."

Antitrust Law

Complete this section to:

- Gain a basic understanding of the cornerstones of antitrust policy, including the Sherman Antitrust Act, the FTC Act, the Clayton Act, and the Robinson-Patman Act.
- Learn how to avoid running afoul of these laws, something that is particularly important if you have customers in manufacturing or who deal with distributors. Although services are not subject to certain provisions of the laws, professionals who consult with customers on pricing and other business tactics need to take these laws into account on a regular basis.

Read Chapter 18, "Antitrust Law."

Advanced Price Theory

Complete this section to:

- Use advanced pricing techniques, not only in pricing your services, but also in consulting with your customers on their pricing strategies.

- Learn the Weber-Fechner Law, which states that *buyers perceive price differences in proportionate terms, not absolute terms.* This indicates there is an upper and a lower threshold of price in the mind of each customer. If the price falls out of that range, the customer will ignore the offering.
- Discover some of the ways to segment your market among buyers, and thus charge different prices to different customers.
- Learn the three classes of products and services: search, experience, and credence.
- Learn the ten factors that influence a customer's price sensitivity. Baker offers several questions for each factor to help you prepare an analysis of your customer's price sensitivity in that area.

Read Chapter 19, "Advanced Price Theory."

Conclusion

Complete this section to:

- Discover why experts rarely innovate and why most dynamic change comes from outside the status quo.
- Learn the importance of risk-taking.
- Learn why Value Pricing is not just another management "fad."

Read Chapter 20, "Conclusion."

EXAMINATION FOR CPE CREDIT

1. *Multiple choice:* Which of the following is *not* a stage of the Product Life Cycle?

   a. Introduction

   b. Growth

   c. Adolescence

   d. Decline

2. *Multiple choice:* Baker feels strongly that CPA firm "clients" should instead be called:

   a. Customers.

   b. Patrons.

   c. Marks.

   d. All of the above.

3. *True or false:* Prior to every engagement, it is essential to ask the customer "What are your expectations?"

4. *Multiple choice:* Customers should be treated:

   a. Equally.

   b. Shoddily.

   c. Individually.

   d. Worse than clients.

5. *Multiple choice:* To be included on a demand curve, customers must be:

   a. Willing and able to buy the product.

   b. Unwilling but able to buy the product.

   c. Willing but unable to buy the product.

   d. All of the above

6. *Multiple choice:* If you cannot identify what your customers are willing and able to pay for a given service, you are leaving what percentage of your gross revenue on the table?

   a. 10 percent

   b. Between 5 percent and 25 percent

   c. 32 percent

   d. Between 20 percent and 50 percent

7. *Multiple choice:* Who created the *Labor Theory of Value*?

   a. Albert Einstein

   b. Karl Marx

   c. Thomas Edison

   d. Ben Franklin

   e. None of the above

8. *Multiple choice:* In the professions, the practice of hourly billing dates back to the:

   a. 1800s.

   b. 1920s.

   c. 1940s.

   d. 1950s.

9. *Multiple choice:* Which of the following is *not* an advantage of hourly billing?

   a. Transfers risk to the CPA

   b. Is relatively easy and efficient

   c. Documents effort in case of litigation

   d. Is a cost-accounting tool

10. *True or false:* When you and your customer see things differently, Baker advises that *you* change.

11. *True or false:* Hourly billing measures the wrong things.

12. *Multiple choice:* The advantages of Value Pricing include the following:

   a. Clarifying the customer's expectations

   b. Pre-qualifying the customer

   c. Providing the opportunity to cross-sell

   d. None of the above

   e. All of the above

13. *True or false:* Quoting fixed prices projects inexperience.

14. *Multiple choice:* When a customer complains, a firm gains:

   a. Useless information.

   b. A chance to correct the problem.

   c. An opportunity to increase customer loyalty.

   d. Items b and c.

   e. None of the above.

15. *True or false:* The golden rule with respect to resolving a customer complaint is not *who is right* but, rather, *what is right.*

16. *Multiple choice:* Marriott Hotels discovered that, if guests had no problems during their stay, their return rate was 89 percent. However, if guests did have problems during their stay and these problems were resolved to their satisfaction, their return rate became:

   a. 69 percent.

   b. 74 percent.

   c. 91 percent.

   d. 94 percent.

17. *Multiple choice:* If you use Value Pricing, you can increase your prices every:

   a. Month.

   b. Year.

   c. Five years.

   d. Decade.

18. *Multiple choice:* When meeting with a customer to discuss a Fixed Price Agreement (FPA), you should plan to hold the meeting at:

    a. The customer's office.

    b. Your office.

    c. Your conference room.

    d. A neutral territory.

19. *Multiple choice:* A well-written FPA will include sections on providing the following:

    a. Professional services

    b. A guarantee

    c. Quality review

    c. All of the above

20. *Multiple choice:* Which of the following is an innovative pricing method recommended by Baker?

    a. Outside-in

    b. Inside-out

    c. Over-and-beyond

    d. Items b and c

21. *Multiple choice:* According to a study performed by the Rockefeller Corporation, by a very large margin the most likely reason for customer defection occurs when the customer:

    a. Moves away.

    b. Is wooed away by a competitor.

    c. Believes you do not care about them.

    d. Dies.

22. *Multiple choice:* When you are setting a price for a new customer, start:

    a. High.

    b. Low (to win them over).

c. About the same as his/her previous CPA.

d. None of the above.

23. *Multiple choice:* Which of the following is *not* a component of the Value Proposition that all businesses provide to their customers?

    a. Quality

    b. Price

    c. Profits

    d. Service

24. *True or false:* According to the AICPA, acquiring a customer can cost 11 times more than retaining one.

25. *Multiple choice:* Andersen Worldwide derives what percentage of its revenues from management consulting services?

    a. 3 percent

    b. 15 percent

    c. 45 percent

    d. 65 percent

26. *True or false:* Profits are a sign that a useful social purpose is being filled and that needs are being met.

27. *Multiple choice:* Michael Novak's moral requirements for business success include the creation of:

    a. Wealth.

    b. Jobs.

    c. Office buildings.

    d. All of the above

    e. Items a and b.

28. *Multiple choice:* CPAs can learn from the insurance business policy of *adverse selection*, which means:

    a. Set your rates as high as possible.

    b. Do not accept all who wish to purchase your services.

c. Select your target prospects via their financial statistics.

d. Choose only those new customers who wish to buy more than one policy.

29. *Multiple choice:* According to Larson and Larson in *Innovative Billing and Collection Methods That Work,* factors that result in favorable CPA firm profit include:

a. Good clients.

b. Effective engagement planning.

c. Superior communication.

d. All of the above.

e. Items a and b.

30. *Multiple choice:* One primary reason the prices for services have a much wider range than prices for products is that (service) price information is generally:

a. A secret.

b. Readily available.

c. Scarce.

d. Of little consequence.

31. *Multiple choice:* What do the top rainmakers view as the best indicator of marketing success?

a. Mailer response rates of 20 percent or more

b. Increased revenue

c. Expanded client list

d. Profitability of new business generated

32. *Multiple choice:* Tim Beauchemin identified two characteristics of price psychology as price leverage and pricing _____:

a. Advantage.

b. Emotions.

c. Decisions.

d. Relationships.

33. *Multiple choice:* According to Baker, customers will experience three primary pricing emotions at various times through the purchasing cycle. Which of the following is *not* a primary pricing emotion?

    a. Price resistance

    b. Payment resistance

    c. Price anxiety

    d. Payment anxiety

34. *Multiple choice:* Many people automatically equate high price with high _____:

    a. Quality.

    b. Value.

    c. Items a & b

    d. None of the above

35. *Multiple choice:* Before you can charge a premium price, you first have to:

    a. Take an additional 20 hours of CPE.

    b. Believe, internally, that you are worth it.

    c. Upgrade your office environment.

    d. Stop taking additional 1040 clients.

36. *True or false:* Perceived value = $\dfrac{\text{Perceived benefits}}{\text{Perceived price}}$

37. *True or false:* Credence products have attributes that clients can confidently evaluate.

38. *Multiple choice:* Pricing is most akin to a game of:

    a. Chess.

    b. Craps.

    c. Tennis.

    d. Solitaire.

39. *Multiple choice:* The cardinal rules of strategic marketing include knowing your:

    a. Costs.

    b. Demand.

    c. Competition and market.

    d. Objectives.

    e. All of the above.

40. *True or false:* Old strategies rarely produce new results.

2000 Professional's Guide to Value Pricing CPE Program

Please record your CPE answers in the space provided on the left and return this page for scoring. Simply place the completed answer sheet in a stamped envelope and mail it to:

The Professional's Guide to Value Pricing CPE Coordinator
Harcourt Professional Publishing
525 B Street, Suite 1900
San Diego, California, 92101-4495

METHOD OF PAYMENT

☐ **Payment enclosed ($64.00).**
(Make checks payable to Harcourt, Inc.)

Please add appropriate sales tax.
Be sure to sign your order below.

Charge my:
☐ MasterCard ☐ Visa ☐ American Express

Account number _____

Expiration date _____
Please sign below for all credit card orders.

☐ **Bill me.** *Be sure to sign your order below.*

Signature _____

NAME _____

FIRM NAME _____

ADDRESS _____

PHONE ( ) _____

CPA LICENSE # _____

ISBN: 0-15-607070-7

TO ORDER: Call Toll-Free 1-800-831-7799

See the reverse side of this page for the CPE evaluation.

CPE ANSWERS

1. _____
2. _____
3. _____
4. _____
5. _____
6. _____
7. _____
8. _____
9. _____
10. _____
11. _____
12. _____
13. _____
14. _____
15. _____
16. _____
17. _____
18. _____
19. _____
20. _____

21. _____
22. _____
23. _____
24. _____
25. _____
26. _____
27. _____
28. _____
29. _____
30. _____
31. _____
32. _____
33. _____
34. _____
35. _____
36. _____
37. _____
38. _____
39. _____
40. _____

2000 The Professional's Guide to Value Pricing CPE Evaluation

1. Were you informed in advance of the:
   a. Objectives of the course? Y N
   b. Experience level needed to complete the course? Y N
   c. Program content? Y N
   d. Nature and extent of preparation necessary? Y N
   e. Teaching method? Y N
   f. Number of CPE credit hours? Y N

2. Do you agree with the publisher's assessment of:
   a. Objectives of the course? Y N
   b. Experience level needed to complete the course? Y N
   c. Program content? Y N
   d. Nature and extent of advance preparation necessary? Y N
   e. Teaching method? Y N
   f. Number of CPE credit hours? Y N

3. Was the material relevant? Y N

4. Was the presentation of the material effective? Y N

5. Did the program increase your professional competence? Y N

6. Was the program content timely and effective? Y N

Please make any other comments that you feel would improve this course. We appreciate the time you take to complete this questionnaire. Be assured that all of your comments will be considered carefully.

INDEX

W

READ THE TERMS AND CONDITIONS OF THIS LICENSE AGREEMENT CAREFULLY BEFORE INSTALLING THE SOFTWARE (THE "PROGRAM") TO ACCOMPANY THE 2000 VALUE PRICING (THE "BOOK"). THE PROGRAM IS COPYRIGHTED AND LICENSED (NOT SOLD). BY INSTALLING THE PROGRAM, YOU ARE ACCEPTING AND AGREEING TO THE TERMS OF THIS LICENSE AGREEMENT. IF YOU ARE NOT WILLING TO BE BOUND BY THE TERMS OF THIS LICENSE AGREEMENT, YOU SHOULD PROMPTLY RETURN THE PACKAGE IN RESELLABLE CONDITION AND YOU WILL RECEIVE A REFUND OF YOUR MONEY. THIS LICENSE AGREEMENT REPRESENTS THE ENTIRE AGREEMENT CONCERNING THE PROGRAM BETWEEN YOU AND HARCOURT BRACE & COMPANY (REFERRED TO AS "LICENSOR"), AND IT SUPERSEDES ANY PRIOR PROPOSAL, REPRESENTATION, OR UNDERSTANDING BETWEEN THE PARTIES.

1. License Grant. Licensor hereby grants to you, and you accept, a nonexclusive license to use the Program CD-ROM and the computer programs contained therein in machine-readable, object code form only (collectively referred to as the "Software"), and the accompanying User Documentation, only as authorized in this License Agreement. The Software may be used only on a single computer owned, leased, or otherwise controlled by you; or in the event of the inoperability of that computer, on a backup computer selected by you. Neither concurrent use on two or more computers nor use in a local area network or other network is permitted without separate authorization and the possible payment of other license fees. You agree that you will not assign, sublease, transfer, pledge, lease, rent, or share your rights under the License Agreement. You agree that you may not reverse engineer, decompile dissemble, or otherwise adapt, modify, or translate the Software.

Upon loading the Software into your computer, you may retain the Program CD-ROM for backup purposes. In addition, you may make one copy of the Software on a set of diskettes (or other storage medium) for the purpose of backup in the event the Program Diskettes are damaged or destroyed. You may make one copy of any additional User Documentation (such as the README.TXT file or the "About the Computer Disc" section of the Book) for backup purposes. Any such copies of the Software or the User Documentation shall include Licensor's copyright and other proprietary notices. Except as authorized under this paragraph, no copies of the program or any portions thereof may be made by you or any person under your authority or control.

2. Licensor's Rights. You acknowledge and agree that the Software and the User Documentation are proprietary products of Licensor protected under U.S. copyright law. You further acknowledge and agree that all right, title, and interest in and to the Program, including associated intellectual property rights, are and shall remain with Licensor. This License Agreement does not convey to you an interest in or to the Program, including associated intellectual property rights, are and shall remain with Licensor. This License Agreement does not convey to you an interest in or to the Program, but only a limited right of use revocable in accordance with the terms of the License Agreement.

3. License Fees. The license fees paid by you are paid in consideration of the licenses granted under this License Agreement.

4. Term. This License Agreement is effective upon your installing this software and shall continue until terminated. You may terminate this License Agreement at any time by returning the Program and all copies thereof and extracts therefrom to Licensor. Licensor may terminate this License Agreement upon the breach by you of any term hereof. Upon such termination by Licensor, you agree to return to Licensor the Program and all copies and portions thereof.

5. Limited Warranty. Licensor warrants, for our benefit alone, for a period of 90 days from the date of commencement of this License Agreement (referred to as the "Warranty Period") that the Program CD-ROM in which the Software is contained is free from defects in material and workmanship. If during the Warranty Period, a defect appears in the Program diskettes, you may return the Program to Licensor for either replacement or, at Licensor's option, refund of amounts paid by you under this License Agreement. You agree that the foregoing constitutes your sole and exclusive remedy for breach by Licensor of any warranties made under this Agreement. EXCEPT FOR THE WARRANTIES SET FORTH ABOVE, THE PROGRAM, AND THE SOFTWARE CONTAINED THEREIN, ARE LICENSED "AS IS," AND LICENSOR DISCLAIMS ANY AND ALL OTHER WARRANTIES, WHETHER EXPRESS OR IMPLIED, INCLUDING, WITHOUT LIMITATION, ANY IMPLIED WARRANTIES OF MERCHANTABILITY OR FITNESS FOR A PARTICULAR PURPOSE.

6. Limitation of Liability. Licensor's cumulative liability to you or any other party for any loss or damages resulting from any claims, demands, or actions arising out of or relating to this Agreement shall not exceed the license free paid to Licensor for the use of the Program. IN NO EVENT SHALL LICENSOR BE LIABLE FOR ANY INDIRECT, INCIDENTAL, CONSEQUENTIAL, SPECIAL, OR EXEMPLARY DAMAGES (INCLUDING, BUT NOT LIMITED TO, LOSS OF DATA, BUSINESS INTERRUPTION, OR LOST PROFITS) EVEN IF LICENSOR HAS BEEN ADVISED OF THE POSSIBILITY OF SUCH DAMAGES.

7. Miscellaneous. This License Agreement shall be construed and governed in accordance with the laws of the State of California. Should any term of this License Agreement be declared void or unenforceable by any court of competent jurisdiction, such declaration shall have no effect on the remaining terms hereof. The failure of either party to enforce any rights granted hereunder or to take action against the other party in the event of any breach hereunder shall not be deemed a waiver by that party as to subsequent enforcement of rights or subsequent actions in the event of future breaches.